Contents

D0796027

Contents

Correspondence Workbook

Correspondence, whether it is by letter, fax, or email, is a key aspect of the world of commerce and business. It reflects on the competence and professionalism of the person who has written it and the company he or she works for. Clear, effective correspondence is an important part of running an efficient business, and can promote good relations. Unclear or confusing correspondence can cause many problems, and can lead to misunderstandings, delays, lost business, and poor relations between individuals, departments, and companies. Therefore, writing skills – *what* is written and *how* it is expressed – should be as much a part of a business education as accountancy or economics.

The Oxford Handbook of Commercial Correspondence is intended for people who need to write commercial correspondence in English as part of their work, and for students of business and commerce who plan to make a career in the business world. It aims to provide practical help in writing commercial correspondence of all kinds, including letters, faxes, emails, reports, memos, social correspondence, and application letters and cvs. It explains how to write clearly and effectively, and demonstrates how it is possible to be polite without seeming timid, direct yet not rude, concise rather than abrupt, and firm but not inflexible.

Users of earlier editions of this book will notice that, while it retains the core elements of previous editions, this third edition has been revised and updated to reflect changes and developments in commercial correspondence, in particular the wider use of email in the business world.

The book deals with the structure, presentation, content, and style of all kinds of correspondence. It covers various types of transaction including enquiries, quotations, orders, payments, credit, complaints, and adjustments, and provides background information and examples of commercial correspondence from the main types of commercial organization, for example banks, insurance companies, agencies, and companies involved in transportation, including shipping.

For the purposes of this book, we have chosen the blocked style of correspondence with no punctuation and have used some representative styles of presentation and layout. You may find other ways of doing things which are perfectly acceptable, and individual companies may have their own preferred style for correspondence. The most important thing is to be clear and consistent in whatever you choose to do.

Unit 1 introduces the three main kinds of commercial correspondence – letters, faxes, and emails. The characteristic features of each are illustrated with examples, and guidance is given on when each kind should be used. Unit 2, again fully illustrated with examples, deals with the important areas of content and style. Each unit thereafter follows the same pattern:
— An introduction to the topics covered in the unit, and an explanation of key terminology and the functions of the organizations likely to be involved.
— An analysis of the objectives to aim for when you are writing, with, where appropriate, lists of alternative phrases, sentences, or paragraphs which you can substitute in different situations.
— Example correspondence and transactions, together with comprehension questions focusing on content, vocabulary, style, and the roles of the correspondents.
— At the end of the unit, a summary of key information in 'Points to remember' to refresh your memory.

At the back of the book you will find:
— An answer key to the comprehension questions.
— A new glossary of useful business and commercial vocabulary to help you consolidate and build your knowledge.
— A revised and extended index to help you access information throughout the book quickly and easily.

The accompanying Workbook provides supplementary practice material.

The correspondence and documents used reflect authentic transactions and supply information about commercial practice in the UK. The Handbook also helps you to gain a better understanding of the sometimes confusing roles of different commercial organizations, e.g. merchant banks and commercial banks, Lloyd's and other insurance companies, The Baltic Exchange and the Shipping Conference.

The Oxford Handbook of Commercial Correspondence has been designed to provide a comprehensive guide and reference to the essential writing skills needed in the commercial world. Above all, we hope that this book will enable you to improve your writing skills so that you can approach any business writing task with increased confidence.

1

Letters

LAYOUT 1 ▶

The letter opposite is from a private individual in Denmark to a company in the UK. It shows the basic features of a simple business letter.

Sender's address

In correspondence that does not have a LETTERHEAD, the sender's address is placed in the top right-hand corner of the page. It is also acceptable, but less common, to place it in the top left-hand corner. Punctuation is rarely used in addresses these days.

The BLOCKED STYLE is the most widely used, i.e. each line starts directly below the one above.

In contrast with practice in some other countries, in the UK it is not usual to write the sender's name before his or her address.

Date

The date is written directly below the sender's address, separated from it by a space. In the case of correspondence with a letterhead ▶see page 12, it is usually written on the right-hand side of the page.

The month in the date should not be written in figures as this can be confusing; for example *11.3.03* means *11 March 2003* in British English, where the sequence is day–month–year, but *3 November 2003* in American English, where the sequence is month–day–year.

It is acceptable to write the date with or without the abbreviations *-th* and *-nd*, e.g. *24th October* or *24 October*, and to transpose the date and the month, e.g. *October 24* or *24 October*. These are matters of personal preference, but whatever you choose you should be consistent throughout your correspondence.

Inside address

The INSIDE ADDRESS is written below the sender's address and on the left-hand side of the page.

Surname known

If you know the name of the person you are writing to, write it as the first line of the address. Include either the person's initial/s or his or her first given name, e.g. *Mr J.E. Smith* or *Mr John Smith*, NOT *Mr Smith*.

COURTESY TITLES used in addresses are as follows:
— *Mr* (pronounced /ˈmɪstə/) is the usual courtesy title for a man. The unabbreviated form *Mister* should not be used.
— *Mrs* (pronounced /ˈmɪsɪz/, no unabbreviated form) is used for a married woman.
— *Miss* (pronounced /ˈmɪs/, not an abbreviation) is used for an unmarried woman.
— *Ms* (pronounced /mɪz/ or /məs/, no unabbreviated form) is used for both married and unmarried women. It is advisable to use this form of address when you are unsure whether the woman you are writing to is married or not, or do not know which title she prefers.
— *Messrs* (pronounced /ˈmesəz/, abbreviation for French '*Messieurs*', which is never used) is used occasionally for two or more men, e.g. *Messrs P. Jones and B.L. Parker*, but more commonly forms part of the name of a company, e.g. *Messrs Collier, Clark & Co.* It is rather old-fashioned.

Other courtesy titles include academic or medical titles, e.g. *Doctor* (*Dr*), *Professor* (*Prof.*); military titles, e.g. *Captain* (*Capt.*), *Major* (*Maj.*), *Colonel* (*Col.*), *General* (*Gen.*); and aristocratic titles, e.g. *Sir, Dame, Lord, Lady. Sir* means that the addressee is a knight, and is always followed by a first name, e.g. *Sir John Brown*, never *Sir J. Brown* or *Sir Brown*. It should not be confused with the SALUTATION *Dear Sir.*

Esq., abbreviation for *Esquire*, is seldom used now. It can only be used instead of *Mr*, and is placed after the name. Do not use *Esq.* and *Mr* at the same time, e.g. *Bruce Hill Esq.*, NOT *Mr Bruce Hill Esq.*

All these courtesy titles, except *Esq.*, are also used in salutations ▶see page 10.

1 Sender's address	**1** Bredgade 51 DK 1260 Copenhagen K DENMARK
2 Date	**2** 6 May 20—
3 Inside address	**3** Compuvision Ltd Warwick House Warwick Street Forest Hill London SE23 1JF UK
4 Attention line	**4** **For the attention of the Sales Manager**
5 Salutation	**5** Dear Sir or Madam
6 Body of the letter	**6** Please would you send me details of your DVD video systems. I am particularly interested in the Omega range.
7 Complimentary close	**7** Yours faithfully
8 Signature	**8** *B. Kaasen* (Ms) B. Kaasen

Note that a full stop is often used at the end of the abbreviation if it takes the form of the first few letters of the word, e.g. *Prof.* (Professor), but is not necessary if it takes the form of the first and last letter of the word, e.g. *Dr* (Doctor). However, some people prefer to write, e.g. *Mr.*, *Mrs.*, with a full stop. Again, whatever you choose to do, you should be consistent throughout your correspondence.

Job title known
If you do not know the name of the person you are writing to, but know their job title, you can use that, e.g. *The Sales Manager, The Finance Director*, in the inside address.

Department known
Alternatively, you can address your letter to a particular department of the company, e.g. *The Sales Department, The Accounts Department*. ▸ **see letter on page 43**.

Company known
Finally, if you know nothing about the company and do not know which person or department your letter should go to, you can simply address the letter to the company itself, e.g. *Compuvision Ltd, Messrs Collier, Clark & Co.*

Order of inside address
After the name of the person and / or company receiving the letter, the recommended order and style of addresses in the UK is as follows:
— Name of house or building
— Number of building and name of street, road, avenue, etc.
— Name of town or city and postcode
— Name of country

Industrial House
34–41 Craig Road
Bolton
BL4 8TF
UK

In other European countries, the number of the building may be placed after the name of the street. It is also common to substitute the name of the country with an initial before the district code number. These two examples are from Italy and Germany ('*Deutschland*') respectively.

Facoltà di Medicina
Via Gentile 182
I–70100 Bari

Lehrschule für Bodenkunde
Amalienstrasse
D–80000 München 40

It is simplest to follow the above order and style, though variations are possible: for example the name of the county, e.g. *Lancashire*, may, if known, be included on the line below the name of the town or city; the postcode may be written on a separate line; the name of the town, as well as the country, may be in capital letters ▸ **see also page 14**.

Attention line

An alternative to including the recipient's name or job title in the address is to use an ATTENTION LINE ▸ **see letter on page 9**.

Salutation

Dear Sir opens a letter written to a man whose name you do not know.

Dear Sirs is used to address a company. (In American English a letter to a company usually opens with *Gentlemen*.)

Dear Madam is used to address a woman, whether single or married, whose name you do not know.

Dear Sir or Madam (or *Dear Sir / Madam*) is used to address a person when you do not know their name or sex. Notice that Ms Kaasen in the letter on page 9 uses this form, i.e. she does not assume that the sales manager of Compuvision Ltd is a man ▸ **see also page 36**.

When you know the name of the person you are writing to, but do not know them well, the salutation takes the form of *Dear* followed by a courtesy title and the person's surname. Initials or first names are not used with courtesy titles, e.g. *Dear Mr Smith*, NOT *Dear Mr J. Smith* or *Dear Mr John Smith*. Business associates who you know well can be addressed using just their first name, e.g. *Dear John*.

A comma after the salutation is optional, i.e. *Dear Mr Smith,* or *Dear Mr Smith.* (In American English a colon is usually used after the salutation, e.g. *Dear Mr Smith:*, *Gentlemen:*).

Body of the letter

The blocked style is the one most often used for the body of the letter. It is usual to leave a line space between paragraphs.

Complimentary close

If the letter begins *Dear Sir*, *Dear Sirs*, *Dear Madam*, or *Dear Sir or Madam*, the COMPLIMENTARY CLOSE should be *Yours faithfully*.

If the letter begins with a personal name, e.g. *Dear Mr James*, *Dear Mrs Robinson*, or *Dear Ms Jasmin*, it should be *Yours sincerely*.

A letter to someone you know well may close with the more informal *Best wishes*. Note that Americans tend to close even formal letters with *Yours truly* or *Truly yours*, which is unusual in the UK in commercial correspondence.

Avoid closing with old-fashioned phrases, e.g. *We remain yours faithfully*, *Respectfully yours*.

A comma after the complimentary close is optional, i.e. *Yours faithfully,* or *Yours faithfully*.

The complimentary close is usually placed on the left, aligned under the rest of the letter.

Signature

Always type your name and, if relevant, your job title, below your handwritten signature. This is known as the SIGNATURE BLOCK. Even though you may think your handwriting is easy to read, letters such as *a*, *e*, *o*, *r*, and *v* can easily be confused.

It is, to some extent, a matter of choice whether you sign with your initial/s, e.g. *D. Jenkins*, or your full given name, e.g. *David Jenkins*, and whether you include your courtesy title in your signature block as in the letter on page 9. But if you include neither your given name nor your title, your correspondent will not be able to identify your sex and may give you the wrong title when he or she replies.

TITLE	STATUS	COMPLIMENTARY CLOSE
Mr	married or umarried male	Yours sincerely
Mrs	married female	Yours sincerely
Miss	unmarried female	Yours sincerely
Ms	married or unmarried female	Yours sincerely
Sir	male – name not known	Yours faithfully
Madam	female – name not known	Yours faithfully
Sir/Madam	when unsure whether you are addressing male or female	Yours faithfully
medical/academic/military e.g. Dr/Professor/General	these titles do not change whether addressing a male or female	Yours sincerely

LAYOUT 2 ▶

Opposite is the company's reply to the letter from the prospective customer in Denmark. It shows some more features of a typical business letter.

Letterhead

The printed letterhead of a company gives a great deal of information about it.

Type of company

The abbreviation *Ltd* after a company's name indicates that it has LIMITED LIABILITY. This means that the individuals who own the company, or part of it, i.e. the shareholders, are only responsible for their holding (i.e. the capital they have contributed) if the company goes bankrupt. In other words, it indicates to people giving the company credit that in bankruptcy they can only be paid back from what the company owns, and not from the personal funds of its shareholders.

The abbreviation *PLC* (*PUBLIC LIMITED COMPANY*) is used to show that a company's shares can be bought and sold by the public, unlike the shares of private limited liability companies. In the USA the term *INC.* (*INCORPORATED*) is used.

> *Compuvision Ltd*
> *SP Wholesalers plc*
> *Hartley–Mason Inc.*

The abbreviation *AND (&) CO.* indicates that a company is a partnership between two or more people. (*And* is usually written as an ampersand (&) in English company names.) If the company is a family concern, *Son/s*, *Bros* (*Brothers*), or *Daughter/s* may be added. Partnerships may have limited liability or unlimited liability.

> *F. Lynch & Co. Ltd*
> *R. Hughes & Son*

If neither *Ltd* nor *& Co.* appear after a company's name, then it may be a SOLE TRADER, i.e. a person who owns and runs a business on their own.

Board of Directors

The name of the chairman (in the USA, the *president*), who runs the concern, may be given, as well as the names of the directors, who decide the overall policy of the company. The managing director (in the USA, and increasingly in the UK, termed the *chief executive officer* or *CEO*), who takes an active role in the day-to-day running of the company, may be mentioned if he or she is not the same person as the chairman. In the UK, the chairman runs the Board of Directors while the Chief Executive Officer runs the company.

Address

In addition to the address of the office from which the letter is being sent, the letterhead may also give the address of the head office or registered office, if different, and the addresses of any branches or other offices the company owns.

Telephone and fax numbers will also be included and, if relevant, email and website addresses. A cable (telegram) address may also be included. It is important to remember that although the majority of companies are connected to the Internet, there are many countries where fax and cable are still important ways of transmitting information or, where banks are concerned, money.

Registered number

This usually appears in small print, sometimes with the country or city in which the company is registered.

In the UK, the VAT (VALUE ADDED TAX) number may also be given ▶ **see, for example, the letter on page 56.**

References

REFERENCES are often quoted to indicate what the letter refers to (*Your ref.*) and the correspondence to refer to when replying (*Our ref.*).

References may either appear in figures, e.g. *661/17*, where *661* may refer to the number of the letter and *17* to the number of the department, or in letters, e.g. *DS/MR*, as in the letter on page 13, where *DS* stands for Donald Sampson, the writer, and *MR* for his assistant, Mary Raynor.

❶ Letterhead

❷ References

❶ Compuvision Ltd

Warwick House
Warwick Street
Forest Hill
London
SE23 1JF

Telephone +44 (0)20 8566 1861
Facsimile +44 (0)20 8566 1385
Email staff@comvis.co.uk
www.comvis.co.uk

Your ref.	6 May 20—
❷ *Your ref.*	DS/MR
Date	11 May 20—

Ms B. Kaasen
Bredgade 51
DK 1260
Copenhagen K
DENMARK

Dear Ms Kaasen,

Thank you for your enquiry.

I enclose our catalogue and price-list for DVD video equipment . You will find full details of the Omega range on pages 31–35.

Please contact us if you have any further questions or would like to place an order.

We look forward to hearing from you.

Yours sincerely,

Mary Raynor

❸ Per pro
❹ Job title

❺ Enclosure

❸ p.p. Donald Sampson
❹ Sales Manager

❺ Enc.

Chairman John Franks OBE.
Directors S.B. Allen M.SC. N. Ignot R. Lichens B.A.

Note that the *Your Ref.* in the letter on page 13 is a date, as Ms Kaasen did not give any reference in her original letter.

Per pro

The abbreviation *P.P.* sometimes appears in signature blocks. It means *PER PRO*, i.e. *for and on behalf of*, and is used by administrators or personal assistants when signing letters on behalf of their managers.

Job title

When sending a letter or email on behalf of your company, it is a good idea to include your job title in the signature block, especially if your recipient has not dealt with you before.

Enclosures

If there are any documents enclosed with a letter, although these may be mentioned in the body of the letter, it is also common to write *Enc.* or *Encl.* below the signature block. If there are a number of documents, these can be listed, e.g.:

Enc.
Bill of lading (3 copies)
Insurance certificate (1 copy)
Certificate of origin (1 copy)
Bill of exchange (1 copy)

LAYOUT 3 ▶

The final letter in this section shows some further features of a business letter.

Private and confidential

This phrase may be written at the head of a letter and, more important, on the envelope, in cases where the letter is intended to be read only by the addressee.

There are many variations of this phrase, e.g. *Confidential*, *Strictly confidential*, but little difference in meaning.

Subject title

A SUBJECT TITLE at the beginning of a letter, directly after the salutation, provides a further reference, saves introducing the subject in the first paragraph, immediately draws attention to the topic of the letter, and allows the writer to refer to it throughout.

It is not necessary to begin the subject title with *Re.* (*with regard to*), e.g. *Re.: Application for the post of web designer*. When sending email messages this may even be confusing as *RE* is short for *reply* ▶**see page 48**.

Copies

When copies are sent to people other than the named recipient, *c.c.* (*CARBON COPY*) is added, usually at the end of a letter, before the name/s of the recipient/s of the copies.

Sometimes you will not want the named recipient to know that other people have received copies. In this case, *B.C.C.* (*BLIND CARBON COPY*), and the name/s of the recipient/s, are added on the copies themselves, though not, of course, on the top copy.

These abbreviations are used in email, and mean exactly the same thing ▶**see page 21**.

ADDRESSING ENVELOPES

Envelope addresses are written in a similar way to inside addresses ▶**see pages 8–10**. But in the case of letters within or for the UK, the name of the town and the country are written in capital letters, and the postcode is usually written on a line by itself.

Mr G. Penter
49 Memorial Road
ORPINGTON ·
Kent
BR6 9UA

Messrs W. Brownlow & Co.
600 Grand Street
LONDON
WIN 9UZ
UK

Compuvision Ltd

Warwick House
Warwick Street
Forest Hill
London
SE23 1JF

Telephone +44 (0)20 8566 1861
Facsimile +44 (0)20 8566 1385
Email staff@comvis.co.uk
www.comvis.co.uk

Your ref.
Your ref. **DS/MR**
Date **21 September 20—**

Ms B. Kaasen
Bredgade 51
DK 1260
Copenhagen K
DENMARK

① Private and
confidential

① **Private and confidential**

Dear Ms Kaasen

② Subject title

② **Non-payment of invoice 322/17**

It appears from our records that, despite several reminders, the above
invoice remains unpaid. Unless the account is cleared within 14 days from
the date of this letter, we shall take legal action.

Yours sincerely

Donald Sampson

Donald Sampson
Sales Manager

③ Copies

③ c.c. Messrs Poole & Jackson Ltd, Solicitors

Chairman John Franks OBE.
Directors S.B. Allen M.SC. N. Ignot R. Lichens B.A.

Faxes

INTRODUCTION

The word *fax* comes from *facsimile*, which means *an exact copy or reproduction*. Like *email*, the word *fax* can be used as a noun, e.g. *I sent a fax* or as a verb, e.g. *We will fax you when we have the information.*

A fax message is useful when speed is important and the recipient does not have email. It is especially useful for documents containing diagrams or drawings. Like email, a fax can be sent quickly to many different recipients at the same time. However, again like email, fax is an open system, i.e. correspondence can easily be accessed by outsiders, so it should not be used for confidential information.

When sending handwritten fax messages, use a dark colour and make your writing large and clear.

As faxes are copies of documents, they cannot be used when the originals are required. For example, an original BILL OF LADING gives TITLE to goods (i.e. you would own the goods if you had the bill in your possession), and would not be valid if it were a faxed copy.

Faxes have been 'court tested', and they tend to be accepted in legal cases, along with letters, as evidence in certain areas of international trade. However, an email containing similar information might not be considered valid under certain circumstances.

Different fax machines offer a wide range of facilities, including repeat dialling if the receiver's fax machine is engaged; a transmission report which gives details of the time, date, sender, receiver, number of pages, duration, and result; a verification mark at the foot of the page to confirm the fax was sent; and a number memory for frequently used numbers. Check the manual of your fax machine to find out what functions it can perform.

It is also possible to send a fax from a computer.

Preparing for transmission

Check that you have the correct fax number. Check that the paper on which your message is printed or written is suitable. If it is too big, too small, or in poor condition, photocopy the message on paper that can be accepted by the fax machine. Before using the machine, check that you know how to dial, cancel, clear a paper jam, and send.

When you send a fax it is a good idea to use a fax transmission cover form. This will help to ensure that the fax reaches its intended recipient safely. Most companies use their own headed fax transmission form, but you can easily create one for yourself, e.g.:

BRITISH CRYSTAL Ltd.
Glazier House
Green Lane
Derby
DE11RT

FAX MESSAGE
To:
From:
Fax no.:
Subject:
Date:
Page/s:

STYLE

Generally, faxes are similar to letters in style, level of formality, and the use of conventions . However, a fax may be shorter and the language more direct, like an email, as there is a time element in the cost of sending them. As with email messages, beware of using too informal a tone with customers or suppliers you do not know well.

F. Lynch & Co. Ltd

Head Office
Nesson House
Newell Street
Birmingham
B3 3EL

Telephone: +44 (0)21 236 6571
Fax: +44 (0)21 236 8592
Email: pcrane@lynch.co.uk
www.lynch.com

Advice of damaged consignment

This fax is from Lynch & Co, who received a damaged CONSIGNMENT and were told by their supplier, Satex S.p.A., to return it ▸ see page 106.

Fax message

To	D. Causio, Satex S.p.A.
From	L. Crane
Fax no.	(06) 481 5473
Subject	Replacement of damaged order no. 14478
Date	19 October 20—
Page/s	1

This is an urgent request for a consignment to replace the above order, which was damaged during delivery. We informed you about this in our letter of 15 September.

Please airfreight the following items:

Cat. No.	Quantity
R30	50
R20	70
N26	100

The damaged consignment will be returned when we receive the replacement.

Peter Crane

Peter Crane
Chief Buyer

Response to importer's enquiry

This is a fax from British Crystal to their AGENTS, S.A. Importers, in Saudi Arabia ▸see correspondence on pages 174–176.

This fax is quite formal in style as the companies have just started their business relationship. Notice how Mr Oliver 'sells' the product to the importers. ▸See also British Crystal's faxed enquiry to Universal Airways and the letter reply on pages 194–195.

British Crystal Ltd

GLAZIER HOUSE · GREEN LANE · DERBY DE1 1RT
TELEPHONE: +44 (0)1332 45790 · FACSIMILE: +44 (0)1332 51977
Email: oliverh@crystal.com · www.britishcrystal.com

FAX MESSAGE

To	S.A. Importers	From	H. Oliver, Marketing Manager
Fax no.	(966) 134981	Subject	French Empire designs
Date	16 August 20—	Page/s	5, including this one

Thank you for your enquiry about our French Empire range of drinking glasses. There is a revival of interest in this period, so we are not surprised that these products have become popular with your customers.

I am sending with this fax pp. 1–4 of our catalogue with CIF Riyadh prices, as you said you would like an immediate preview of this range. I would appreciate your comments on the designs with regard to your market.

I look forward to hearing from you.

H. Oliver

H. Oliver (Mr)
Marketing Manager

Fax

Nigerian Exploration Company

Block D . Surulere Industrial Road
Ogba . Ikeja . Lagos

Telephone (+234) 1 4836082/3/4/5
Facsimile (234) 1 4837001

To John Malcovitch, Chief Engineer

From Tosin Omosade, United Drilling Inc. Managing Director

Fax 213–890–0740

Topic Drilling Heads

No. of pages 1–5

c.c. Kwame Adeole (Accountant)
Vidal Lamont (Chief Engineer)

Pages 2–4 of this fax are specifications for the exploration drilling heads that we discussed on your visit here in October. Could you please supply these heads as soon as possible?

I am also sending our official Order No. AT 320–1046. I shall make arrangements to open a confirmed letter of credit with the Nigerian International Bank as soon as you have sent me your invoice and details of shipment.

I look forward to hearing from you.

Tosin Omosade

Tosin Omosade (Mr)
Managing Director

With this fax, an importer is sending an official order and specifications for the drills he requires. He says that a CONFIRMED LETTER OF CREDIT will be opened once he has the supplier's COMMERCIAL INVOICE. Notice that the fax is copied to his company's accountant, and also the chief engineer.

Emails

INTRODUCTION

Email (short for *electronic mail*) is a means of sending messages between computers.

To send and receive email you need access to the Internet. An Internet Service Provider (ISP) will provide you with connection software, which is often free. This will give you Internet access, storage for incoming mail, and the capability to read your messages. Finally, you need email software, generally already installed in modern computers, so that you can write, send, receive, and read messages.

Advantages

There are numerous advantages to email. It is personal and easy to use. It can be used both within and between companies, and is an effective way to communicate quickly and easily with people all over the world. It is especially useful for short messages and for everyday correspondence, e.g. setting up a meeting, passing on information, and making or replying to a request.

You can pick up your email messages, even when you are travelling, via a laptop or palmtop. With compatible systems, you can access text and graphic documents, and spreadsheets. And whatever you send or receive can be quickly and easily filed.

Disadvantages

The disadvantages of email include technical problems which may result in the unexpected non-delivery of messages, or attachments arriving in unreadable form. A non-technical disadvantage is that, paradoxically, the ease with which messages can be sent results in large amounts of 'junk' and unnecessary communication, which waste time.

As with faxes, a major drawback is the lack of privacy and security. Do not use email to communicate confidential information. It is sometimes said that an email message is like a postcard – anyone can read what you have written. However, digital signing and encryption (coding data, so that it can only be read by authorized users), which both work along similar lines, make email more secure.

Email and other forms of correspondence

There are several areas of business communication where more traditional forms of correspondence are still the most suitable. For example, personal and sensitive correspondence such as messages of congratulation, condolence, or complaint are usually best done by letter. Confirmation of contracts, memos which are confidential and must be signed to acknowledge receipt, and any correspondence which may be needed for legal or insurance purposes should not normally be sent by email. You might find a job on the Internet, but most companies would still expect your application to consist of a completed form with a covering letter.

Email addresses

Typical email addresses look like this:

dfranks@intchem.co.no
corneyg@kingsway.ac.uk

The first part of the email address is usually the surname and initial of the person you are contacting, or the name if it is a department, or a shortened version of it. The second part, which appears immediately after the @ (at), is the name of the ISP or organization, or again an abbreviation of it. Usually, the last part of the address includes the domain name suffixes referring to the type of organization (e.g. '.co' for 'company', '.ac' ('academic') for a university) and to the country from which the message was sent (e.g. '.no' for Norway, '.uk' for the United Kingdom).

Other examples of domain name suffixes referring to types of organization include:

.biz   *business*
.gov   *government office*
.org   *non-profit-making organization (e.g. a charity)*
.pro   *profession (e.g. medicine, law)*

If the name of a country in its main language differs significantly from its name in English, this is reflected in its domain name suffix, e.g.:

.de   *Deutschland* (Germany)
.es   *España* (Spain)
.za   *Zuid Afrika* (South Africa)

LAYOUT ▼

Below is a typical email message.

Header information

The header gives essential information about the message. In addition to the basic details shown in the sample, it may include:

c.c.
This stands for carbon copies, which means much the same as it does on a letter ▶**see page 14**. Here you insert the email addresses of anyone you want to send copies of the message to.

b.c.c.
This stands for blind carbon copies, which, as in a letter, you should use if you do not want the main recipient to know who has received copies ▶**see page 14**.

Attachments
Icons of any ATTACHMENTS will appear here.

The amount of header information, and the order in which it appears, will vary according to the software being used, so do not worry if the messages you send and receive do not look exactly like the one in the example.

Message text

The presentation of the text in an email is usually less formal than in a letter. In this example Ms Kaasen has used the formal *Dear Sir / Madam*, but she could simply have headed her message *For the attention of the Sales Manager*. Rather than ending with *Yours faithfully*, she uses the less formal *I look forward to hearing from you*.

Signature

This is like the signature block in a letter, although it usually includes more details, e.g. the sender's company or private address, and telephone and fax numbers. You can program your email software to add your signature automatically to the end of outgoing messages.

1

❶ Header information

❷ Message text

❸ Signature block

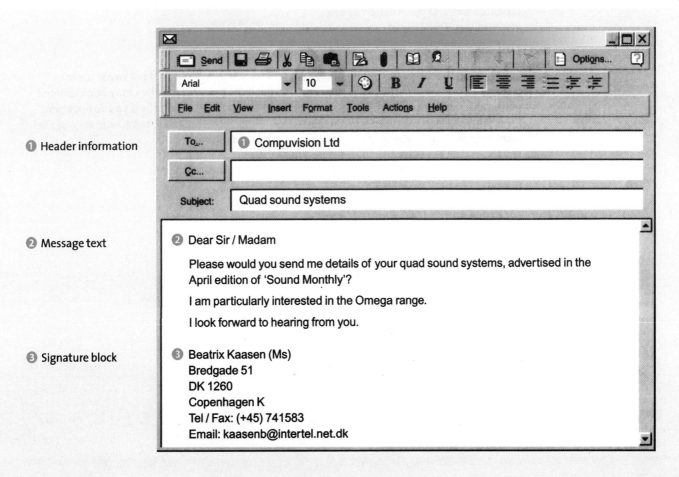

STYLE

Email is a relatively recent development, and because it is perceived as a quick and informal means of communication, people are often unclear about the style and conventions they should use in business situations.

As a general rule, although email correspondence may tend towards informality, it should follow the same principles as any other form of business correspondence.

Here are some basic tips about style:

— In general, email messages follow the style and conventions used in letters or faxes. For example, you can use salutations such as *Dear Mr Pinto* or *Dear Tom*, and complimentary closes such as *Yours sincerely* or *Best wishes*. However, if you know the recipient well, or if you are exchanging a series of messages with one person, you may dispense with the salutation and complimentary close.

— Do not confuse personal messages with business messages. In a business message, the same rules of writing apply as for a letter: write clearly, carefully, and courteously; consider audience, purpose, clarity, consistency, conciseness, and tone.

— Use correct grammar, spelling, capitalization, and punctuation, as you would in any other form of correspondence.

— Do not write words in capital letters in an email message. This can be seen as the equivalent of shouting and therefore have a negative effect. If you want to stress a word, put asterisks on each side of it, e.g. *urgent*.

— Keep your email messages short and to the point. People often receive a lot of emails at work, so conciseness is especially important.

— In general, limit yourself to one topic per message. This helps to keep the message brief and makes it easier for the recipient to answer, file, and retrieve it later.

— Check your email message for mistakes before you send it, just as you would check a letter or a fax message.

Email abbreviations

TLAs (three-letter acronyms)

In order to keep email messages short, people sometimes use abbreviations for common expressions, just as they do in text messaging. These are known as TLAs (three-letter acronyms), although some of them are more than three letters long. Here is a list of some of the most commonly used TLAs:

AFAIK	as far as I know
BFN	bye for now
BTW	by the way
COB	close of business
FYI	for your information
IOW	in other words
NRN	no reply necessary
OTOH	on the other hand

Use TLAs with great care, and only when you have established a friendly, informal relationship with your correspondent. They should not be be used in letters and faxes.

Emoticons

Emoticons (a combination of the words *emotion* and *icon*), also know as *smileys*, are often used in informal email correspondence. They express emotions which may not be evident from the words alone, e.g.:

:-)	a smile
:-(	a frown
;-)	a wink

On the whole, it is better not to use them in business messages, as they may be considered unprofessional, especially if you do not know the recipient well or are not sure that he or she will understand them.

Here is an example of an email asking for an ESTIMATE to refit a store. There are three attachments. Notice that the email is quite short. It is acceptable, as here, to omit the salutation and the complimentary close when the sender and recipient have been in touch with each other previously.

✉   _ □ ✕

⬛ Send | 🖫 🖨 | ✂ 🗎 📋 | 🖳 📎 | 📖 🔍 | ⚕ ↓ ⬗ | 🗎 Options... | 🔲

Arial   ▾ 10 ▾ | 🎨 | **B** *I* <u>U</u> | 🗏 ▤ ▦ ▤ | ▦ ▤ ▦

File   Edit   View   Insert   Format   Tools   Actions   Help

To...	Peter Lane
Cc...	
Subject:	Refit of Halton Road store

Plan of premises   Specification list   Architect's drawings

With reference to our phone conversation this morning, I would like one of your representatives to visit our store at 443 Halton Road, London, SE4 3TN, to give an estimate for a complete refit. Please could you contact me to arrange an appointment?

As I mentioned on the phone, it is essential that work is completed before the end of February 20—, and this would be stated in the contract.

I attach the plans and specifications.

Jean Landman (Ms)
Assistant to K. Bellon, Managing Director
Superbuys Ltd, Superbuy House
Wolverton Road, London SW16 7DN
Tel.: 020 8327 1651
Fax: 020 8327 1935
j.landman@superbuys.com

Making arrangements for an estimate

Peter Lane replies to Jean Landman, copying the message to the surveyor, John Pelham. Notice that this message fulfils the requirements for correspondence dealing with an enquiry, i.e. the reply is sent as soon as possible and covers the points mentioned in the enquiry. The style is quite informal but still polite and businesslike.

The letters RE: appear before the subject title in the header information. This indicates that Peter Lane has selected the 'reply' option. The original message appears below his reply.

To...	Jean Landman
Cc...	John Pelham
Subject:	RE: Refit of Halton Road store

Dear Ms Landman

Our surveyor, John Pelham, is available to inspect the premises and discuss your exact requirements. Could you please contact John on jpelham@wemshop.com, or on his mobile (71292 89541), to arrange a convenient time for him to visit the store?

From your attached specifications, I estimate the work could be completed within the time you give, and we would be willing to sign a contract to this effect.

Peter Lane
Director, Wembley Shopfitters Ltd
Wycombe Road, Wembley, Middlesex HA9 6DA
Telephone: 020 8903 2323
Fax: 020 8903 2349
Email: plane@wemshop.com

— Original message —
From: Jean Landman
Sent:
To: Peter Lane
Subject: Refit of Halton Road store

Dear Mr Lane

With reference to our phone conversation this morning, I would like one of your representatives to visit our store at 443 Halton Road, London, SE4 3TN, to give an estimate for a complete refit. Please could you contact me to arrange an appointment?

As I mentioned on the phone, it is essential that work is completed before the end of February 20—, and this would be stated in the contract.

I attach the plans and specifications.

Jean Landman (Ms)
Assistant to K. Bellon, Managing Director

```
✉                                                    _ □ ✕
  ▭ Send  🖫 🖨 ✂ 🖻 🖹  🖹  📷  📖 🔍  ✓  ❗ ↓ ▿  🖹 Options...  ?
  Arial            ▾  10  ▾ 🎨  B  I  U  🖹 🖹 🖹 🖹 🖹 🖹 🖹
  File  Edit  View  Insert  Format  Tools  Actions  Help
```

To...	Allan Rubain
Cc...	
Subject:	RE: Sato Inc.

Dear Mr Rubain

> Please find answers to your queries below.

How long has the company been in business?
> The company has traded for 24 years under its current name.

How many showrooms does it have?
> It has a chain of 30 showrooms throughout the country.

What is its turnover every year?
> Its registered turnover this year was $410 million.

Will its products compete with mine?
> It specializes in foreign cars – yours will be unique to your country.

How is it regarded in Japan?
> It has an excellent reputation.

I hope this information is useful.

Kyoko Mamura (Ms)
Assistant to Trade Information Officer
Sakuragi Bldg, Minami Aoyama, Minato-ku, Tokyo 109
Tel: (+81) 3 4507 6851
Fax: (+81) 3 4507 8890
Email: mamurak@tcha.com.jp

Asking for information

A company has emailed their local CHAMBER OF COMMERCE to ask for some information about their prospective DISTRIBUTORS, Sato Inc. In this reply, the answers given by the chamber of commerce have been inserted at the relevant points in the original message. They are preceded by the '>' symbol.

Request for goods on approval

Mr Cliff of Homemakers is a furniture manufacturer and supplies Mr Hughes's shop with a wide range of goods. In this example, Mr Hughes wants two new products ON APPROVAL.

1

Example email

To... Richard Cliff

Cc...

Subject: Cat. Nos KT3 and KT14 on approval

Order No B1463

Dear Mr Cliff

A lot of customers have been asking about your bookcase and coffee-table assembly kits (above cat. nos). We would like to test the market and have 6 sets of each kit on approval before placing a firm order. I can supply trade references if necessary.

I attach a provisional order (No. B1463) in anticipation of your agreement. There is no hurry, so you can send these with your next delivery to Swansea.

Many thanks

Robert Hughes
R. Hughes & Son Ltd
Tel: 01792 58441
Fax: 01792 59472
Email: r.hughes@huson.com

Questions

1 Why does Mr Hughes want the goods on approval?

2 What does Mr Hughes think might be required to get goods on approval?

3 What sort of order has been sent, and how has it been sent?

4 Is this an urgent request?

Reply to request
for goods on
approval

Letters, faxes, and emails

1

Example email

☒   _□X

☐ Send   🖫 🖨 ✂ 🖹 🖺 🖼 📋 📖 🔍   ! ↓ ▽   📄 Options...   ?

Arial   ▼   10 ▼   🎨   **B** *I* <u>U</u>   📄 ≡ ≡ ≡ ≣ ≣ ≣

File   Edit   View   Insert   Format   Tools   Actions   Help

To...	Robert Hughes
Cc...	
Subject:	RE: Cat. Nos KT3 and KT14 on approval

Dear Mr Hughes

Thank you for your enquiry about our assembly kits. We'd be pleased to send you 6 of each on approval. They should be with you by noon on Monday.

There's no need to supply references. The provisional order (B1463) you sent is sufficient, but please return any unsold kits in two months.

Let us know if we can be of any further help.

Richard Cliff
Director, Homemakers Ltd
54–59 Riverside, Cardiff CF1 1JW
Direct line: +44 (0)29 20 49723
Fax: +44 (0)29 20 49937
Email: rcliff@homemakers.com

---

1 Does Mr Cliff agree to send the goods on approval?

2 What sort of references are required?

3 What should Mr Hughes do with any unsold kits?

4 What phrase does Mr Cliff use to offer more help?

Points to remember

Letters

Many of these points apply to faxes and emails as well.

1 The layout and presentation of your letter are important as they give the recipient the first impression of your company's efficiency.

2 Write both the sender's and the recipient's address in as much detail as possible and in the correct order.

3 Make sure you use the recipient's correct title in the address and salutation. If in doubt as to whether a woman is single or married, use Ms.

4 Do not write the month of the date in figures.

5 Choose the correct salutation and complimentary close:
Dear Sir / Madam with *Yours faithfully*
Dear Mr / Ms Smith with *Yours sincerely*

6 Make sure your references are correct.

7 Make sure your signature block tells your reader what he or she needs to know about you.

Faxes

1 Fax is an open system, so it should not be used for confidential correspondence.

2 Write clearly when sending handwritten messages.

3 Faxes are copies, and cannot be used when original documents are required.

4 Prepare your transmission carefully before you send it.

5 In general, the language of faxes is much like that of letters, although faxes can be briefer and more direct, like email messages.

Emails

1 Email is very fast and effective, but there are areas where it is preferable to use letters, e.g. personal, confidential, or legal correspondence.

2 Email addresses usually give the name of the person or department, then the @ (at) symbol, followed by the name of the company or institution, and finally the domain names, which indicate the type of organization and the country from which the message was sent.

3 The language of emails can be quite informal, but if you do not know the recipient well, it is better to keep to the usual writing conventions. You can become more informal as you establish a working relationship.

4 It is possible to use special abbreviations, e.g. TLAS and emoticons, but do not confuse your recipient by using abbreviations he or she may not know or understand.

Content and style

2

LENGTH

All correspondence should be long enough to explain exactly what the sender needs to say and the receiver needs to know. You must decide how much information you put in the letter: you may give too much ▶ **see the letter on this page**, in which case your letter will be too long, or too little ▶ **see the letter on page 31**, in which case it will be too short. Your style and the kind of language you use can also affect the length.

The following three letters are written by different people in reply to the same enquiry from a Mr Arrand about their company's products.

Too long

There are a number of things wrong with this letter. Though it tries to advertise the products, and the company itself, it is too wordy. There is no need to explain that stores are buying in stock for Christmas – Mr Arrand is aware of this. Rather than drawing attention to certain items he might be interested in, the letter only explains what he can already see, that there is a wide selection of watches in the catalogue covering the full range of market prices. In addition, the writer goes on unnecessarily to explain which countries the company sells to, to give its history, and to quote its rather unimpressive motto.

Dear Mr Arrand

Thank you very much for your enquiry of 5 November which we received today. We often receive enquiries from large stores and always welcome them, particularly at this time of the year when we know that you will be buying in stock for Christmas.

We have enclosed our winter catalogue and are sure you will be extremely impressed by our wide range of watches. You will see that they include ranges for men, women, and children, with prices that should suit all your customers, from watches costing only a few pounds to those in the luxury bracket priced at several hundred pounds. But whatever price bracket you are interested in, we guarantee all our products for two years.

Enclosed you will also find our price list giving full details of prices to London (inclusive of cost, insurance, and freight) and explaining our discounts, which we think you will find very generous and which we hope you will take full advantage of.

We are always available to offer you further information about our products and can promise you personal attention whenever you require it. This service is given to all our customers throughout the world, and as you probably know, we deal with countries from the Far East to Europe and Latin America. This fact alone bears out our reputation, which has been established for more than a hundred years and has made our motto 'Time for everyone' – familiar worldwide.

Once again, may we thank you for your enquiry and say that we look forward to hearing from you in the near future?

Yours sincerely

Too short

There are a number of problems with this letter:

1 It should have begun *Dear Mr Arrand* and ended *Yours sincerely* as the writer knew Mr Arrand's name from his letter of enquiry.

2 Neither the date nor the reference number of the enquiry are quoted.

3 Ideally, a catalogue should be enclosed with a reply to an enquiry about a company's products or indication of a website if the company has one.

4 When a catalogue is sent, attention should be drawn to items which might be of particular interest to the enquirer. New products should also be pointed out.

5 A price list should be included if prices are not given in the catalogue. Any discounts should be quoted and, if possible, delivery dates.

The right length

Here is a more suitable letter. It is neither too short nor too long. It provides all the relevant information Mr Arrand might need, and draws his attention to some specific products which may be of interest to him.

▶**See page 33 for the plan for this letter**.

Dear Sir

Thank you for your enquiry. We have a wide selection of watches which we are sure you will like. We will be sending a catalogue soon.

Yours faithfully

Dear Mr Arrand

Thank you for your enquiry of 5 November.

We enclose our winter catalogue, and a price list giving details of CIF London prices, discounts, and delivery dates.

Though you will see we offer a wide selection of watches, may we draw your attention to pp. 23–28, and pp. 31–36, where there are styles we think might suit the market you describe? On page 25 you will find our latest designs in pendant watches, which are already selling well.

All our products are fully guaranteed, and backed by our worldwide reputation.

If you need any further information, please contact us. We look forward to hearing from you soon.

Yours sincerely

ORDER AND SEQUENCE

As well as containing the right amount of information, your letter should also make all the necessary points in a logical sequence, with each idea or piece of information linking up with the previous one in a pattern that can be followed. Do not make a statement, switch to other subjects, then refer back to the point you made a few sentences or paragraphs before, as in the example.

2

Unclear sequence

This letter is difficult to understand because there is no clear sequence or logical order.

Clear sequence

Here is a better version of the same letter, in which the ideas and information are in a logical order.

Dear Sir / Madam

We are interested in your security systems. We would like to know more about the prices and discounts you offer.

A business associate of ours, DMS (Wholesalers) Ltd, mentioned your name to us and showed us a catalogue. They were impressed with the security system you installed for them, so we are writing to you about it. Do you give guarantees with the installations?

In your catalogue we saw the Secure 15 which looks as though it might suit our purposes. DMS had the Secure 18 installed, but as we mentioned, they are wholesalers, while we are a chain of stores. We would like something that can prevent robbery and shoplifting, so the Secure 15 might suit us.

How long would it take to install a system that would serve all departments? Could you send an inspector or adviser to see us soon?

If you can offer competitive prices and guarantees we would put your system in all our outlets, but initially we would only install the system in our main branch.

We would like to make a decision on this soon, so we would appreciate an early reply.

Yours faithfully

Dear Mr Jarry

We are a chain of retail stores and are looking for an efficient security system. You were recommended to us by our associates, DMS (Wholesalers) Ltd, for whom you recently installed the Secure 18 alarm system.

We need a system which would give us comprehensive protection against robbery and shoplifting throughout all departments, and the Secure 15 featured in your current catalogue would appear to suit us. However, it would be helpful if one of your representatives could visit us so that we can discuss details of the available systems.

Initially we would test the system we select in our main branch, and, if it proves satisfactory, install it throughout our other branches. Our choice would, of course, be influenced by a competitive quotation and full guarantees for maintenance and service.

Please reply as soon as possible as we would like to make a decision within the next few months.

Yours sincerely

PLANNING

The way to make sure you include the right amount of information, and in the right order, is by planning. Ask yourself what the purpose of the letter is, and what response you would like to receive. Note down everything you want to include before you start writing, then read your notes to check that you have included all the necessary information, that it is relevant, and that you have put it in the right order. Here, for example, is the plan for the letter on page 31.

1st para.	*Acknowledge enquiry*
2nd para.	*Enclose catalogue, price list*
3rd para.	*Draw attention to watches suitable for Arrand, and latest designs*
4th para.	*Mention guarantees and reputation*
5th para.	*Encourage further contact*

First paragraph

The opening sentence or paragraph is important as it sets the tone of the letter and creates a first impression. Generally speaking, you would thank your correspondent for their letter (if replying to an enquiry), if necessary introduce yourself and your company, state the subject of the letter, and set out its purpose. Here are two examples of opening paragraphs.

— *Thank you for your enquiry dated 8 July in which you asked us about our range of cosmetics. As you probably know from our advertising, we appeal to a wide age group from the teenage market through to more mature women, and our products are retailed in leading stores throughout the world.*

— *Thank you for your letter of 19 August, which I received today. We can certainly supply you with the industrial floor coverings you asked about. Enclosed you will find a catalogue illustrating our wide range of products currently used in factories and offices throughout the world.*

Middle paragraphs

The main part of your letter will concern the points that need to be made, answers you wish to give, or questions you want to ask. As this depends on the type of letter that you are writing, these topics will be dealt with in later units. In the middle paragraphs, planning is most important to make sure your points are made clearly, fully, and in a logical sequence.

Final paragraph

At the end of your letter, if it is a reply and you have not done so at the beginning, you should thank your correspondent for writing. If appropriate, encourage further enquiries or correspondence, mentioning that you look forward to hearing from him or her soon. You may want to restate, briefly, one or two of the most important points you made in the main part of your letter. Here are some examples of final paragraphs.

— *Once again thank you for writing to us. Please contact us if you would like any further information. To summarize: all prices are quoted CIF Yokohama, delivery would be six weeks from receipt of order, and payment should be made by bank draft. I look forward to hearing from you soon.*

— *I hope I have covered all the questions you asked, but please contact me if there are any other details you require. If you would like to place an order, may I suggest that you do so before the end of this month so that it can be met in good time for the start of the summer season? I hope to hear from you in the near future.*

— *We are confident that you have made the right choice as this line is a leading seller. If there is any advice or further information you need, we would be happy to supply it, and look forward to hearing from you.*

2

STYLE AND LANGUAGE

Simplicity

Commercial correspondence often suffers from an old-fashioned, pompous style of English which complicates the message and gives readers the feeling that they are reading something written in an unfamiliar language. In this letter, all the writer is trying to do is explain why he delayed paying his account but, because of the style, it is too long and is difficult to understand.

2

Here is a simpler version of the letter. Mr Aldine will be satisfied with it because it tells him – simply and clearly – what he wants to know. First, his customer uses his name. Second, he has apologized. Third, Mr Aldine knows his was not the only account that was not paid when due, and knows why. Finally, he has his cheque.

Courtesy

Your style should not, however, be so simple that it becomes rude. Here is an example of a letter that is too short and simple.

Dear Sir / Madam

I beg to acknowledge receipt of your letter of the 15th inst. in connection with our not clearing our account, which was outstanding as of the end of June.

Please accept our profuse apologies. We were unable to settle this matter due to the sudden demise of Mr Noel, our Accountant, and as a result were unaware of those accounts which were to be cleared. We now, however, have managed to trace all our commitments and take pleasure in enclosing our remittance for £2,120, which we trust will rectify matters.

We hope that this unforeseen incident did not in any way inconvenience you, nor lead you to believe that our not clearing our balance on the due date was an intention on our part to delay payment.

We remain, yours, etc …

Dear Mr Aldine

I am replying to your letter of 15 July asking us to clear our June balance.

I apologize for not settling the account sooner, but due to the unfortunate death of Mr Noel, our Accountant, there have been delays in settling all of our outstanding balances.

Please find enclosed our cheque for £2,120, and accept our apologies for any inconvenience.

Yours sincerely

Dear Mr Rohn

I've already written to you concerning your debt of £1,994. This should have been cleared three months ago. You seem unwilling to co-operate in paying us. We'll sue you if you do not clear your debt within the next ten days.

Yours, etc.

In the version of the same letter, notice the stylistic devices that are used to make it more polite: complex sentences, joined by conjunctions, rather than short sentences (e.g. ... *the balance of £1,194, which has been outstanding* ... rather than ... *your debt of £1,994. This should have been cleared* ...); the use of full rather than abbreviated forms (e.g. *I shall have to consider* ... rather than *We'll sue* ...); and the use of passive forms and indirect language that avoids sounding aggressive (e.g. ... *for the account to be settled* ... rather than ... *if you do not clear your debt* ...).

Idioms and colloquial language

It is important to try to get the right 'tone' in your letter. This means that, generally speaking, you should aim for a neutral tone, avoiding pompous language on the one hand and language which is too informal or colloquial on the other.

You may set the wrong tone by using the wrong vocabulary or idioms, or using short forms inappropriately. Here are a few examples, together with a preferred alternative.

INAPPROPRIATE FORM	PREFERRED ALTERNATIVE
you've probably guessed	*you are probably aware*
you'll get your money back	*the loan will be repaid*
prices are at rock bottom	*prices are very low*
prices have gone through the roof	*prices have increased rapidly*

On the whole, it is better to avoid using colloquial language or slang. Apart from the danger of being misunderstood if your correspondent's first language is not English, he or she may think you are being too familiar.

Dear Mr Rohn

I refer to our previous letter sent on 10 October in which you were asked to clear the balance of £1,994 on your account, which has been outstanding since July. As there has been no reply, I shall have to consider handing over the matter to our solicitors.

However, I am reluctant to do this and am offering a further ten days for the account to be settled.

Yours sincerely

2

CLARITY

Your correspondent must be able to understand what you have written. Confusion in correspondence often arises through a lack of thought and care, and there are a number of ways in which this can happen.

Abbreviations and initials

Abbreviations can be useful because they are quick to write and easy to read. But both correspondents need to know what the abbreviations stand for.

The abbreviations CIF and FOB, for example, are INCOTERMS which mean, respectively, Cost, Insurance, and Freight and Free On Board. But can you be sure that your correspondent knows that *p&p* means *postage and packing*?

Some international organizations, e.g. NATO (North Atlantic Treaty Organization), are known in all countries by the same set of initials, but many are not, e.g. EU (European Union) and UN (United Nations). National organizations, e.g. in the UK, CBI (Confederation of British Industry) and TUC (Trades Union Congress), are unlikely to be familiar to correspondents in other countries.

A range of abbreviations are used in email correspondence **see page 22**, but many of them are not widely known. If you are not absolutely certain that an abbreviation or set of initials will be easily recognized, it is best not to use it.

Numbers

We saw on page 8 that the use of figures instead of words for dates can create problems.

Numerical expressions can also cause confusion. For example, the decimal point in British and American usage is a full stop, but a comma is used in most continental European countries, so that a British or American person would write *4.255* where a French person would write *4,255* (which to a British or American person would mean *four thousand two hundred and fifty-five*).

If there is the possibility of confusion, write the expression in both figures and words, e.g. *£10,575.90 (ten thousand five hundred and seventy-five pounds, ninety pence)*.

Prepositions

Special care should be taken when using prepositions. There is a big difference between *The price has been increased* **to** *£450.00*, *The price has been increased* **by** *£450.00*, and *The price has been increased* **from** *£450.00*.

ACCURACY

Spelling

Careless mistakes in a letter can give readers a bad impression. Spelling, punctuation, and grammar should all be checked carefully. Many people have come to rely on the spellchecker in their computers to ensure that there are no spelling mistakes. But a word spelt incorrectly may form a completely different word, e.g. *Please give it some though* (the writer means *thought*); *I saw it their* (the writer means *there*). A spell checker would miss these mistakes. There is no substitute for carefully reading, or proofreading a letter that you have written.

Titles, names, and addresses

Use the correct title in the address and salutation. Spell your correspondent's name correctly (nothing creates a worse impression than a misspelled name), and write their address accurately.

If you do not know your correspondent, do not assume that they are one sex or the other, i.e. use *Dear Sir / Madam* rather than *Dear Sir* or *Dear Madam*. If you know a correspondent's name but not their sex, use *Mr / Ms*, e.g. *Dear Mr / Ms Barron*.

References

When replying to a letter, fax, or email, quote all references accurately so that it is immediately clear to your reader what you are writing about.

Prices, measurements, etc.

Special care should be taken when quoting prices or giving specifications such as measurements or weights. Quoting these incorrectly can cause serious misunderstandings.

Enclosures and attachments

Always check that you have actually enclosed the documents you have mentioned in your letter, or attached them to your email ▶**see page 14**. Check, too, that you have enclosed or attached the right documents. If, for example, the document you are enclosing is invoice PL/231, make sure you do not enclose invoice PL/213.

When ordering, make sure you quote the order number correctly, especially in international trade where mistakes can be very expensive in both time and money.

Points to remember

1 Include the right amount of information. If you are responding to an enquiry, make sure you have answered all the writer's questions.

2 Plan before you start writing. Make sure you say everything you want to say, and in a logical sequence.

3 Use a simple but polite style of language.

4 Make sure that everything you write is clear and easy to understand. Do not use colloquial language or abbreviations that your reader may not understand. Write numbers in words as well as figures.

5 Accuracy is important. Pay special attention to details such as titles and names, and references and prices, and remember to check enclosures or attachments.

6 Check what you have written when you have finished. Make sure everything is as it should be.

2

Enquiries

MAKING ENQUIRIES

A simple enquiry can be made by email, fax, or cable. The contents of an enquiry will depend on three things: how well you know the supplier, whether the supplier is based in your country or abroad, and the type of goods or services you are enquiring about. There is a difference between asking a computer company about the cost of installing a complex computer network and asking a publisher about the price of a book.

Opening

Tell your supplier what sort of organization you are.
—*We are a co-operative wholesale society based in Zurich.*
—*Our company is a subsidiary of Universal Business Machines and we specialize in ...*
—*We are one of the main producers of industrial chemicals in Germany, and we are interested in ...*

How did you hear about the company you are contacting? It might be useful to point out that you know their associates, or that they were recommended to you by a consulate or trade association.
—*We were given your name by the Hoteliers' Association in Paris.*
—*You were recommended to us by Mr John King, of Lawsom & Davies, Merchant Bankers.*
—*We were advised by Spett. Marco Gennovisa of Milan that you are interested in supplying ...*
—*The British Consulate in Madrid has told us that you are looking for an agent in Spain to represent you.*

It is possible to use other references.
—*We were impressed by the selection of gardening tools displayed on your stand at this year's Hamburg Gardening Exhibition.*
—*Our associates in the packaging industry speak highly of your Zeta packing machines, and we would like to have more information about them. Could you send us ...*

Asking for catalogues, price lists, etc.

It is not necessary to give a lot of information about yourself when asking for CATALOGUES, price lists, etc. This can be done by letter, fax, or email, but remember to give your postal address. It is also helpful to point out briefly any particular items you are interested in.
—*Could you please send your current catalogue and price list for exhibition stands? We are particularly interested in stands suitable for displaying furniture.*
—*We have heard about your latest equipment in laser surgery and would like more details. Please send us any information you can supply, marking the letter 'For the Attention of Professor Kazuhiro', Tokyo General Hospital, Kinuta-Setagayaku, Tokyo, Japan.*
—*I am planning to come and study in London next autumn and would be grateful if you could send me a prospectus and details of your fees. I am particularly interested in courses in computing.*
—*Please would you send me an up-to-date price list for your building materials.*

Asking for details

When asking for goods or services you should be specific and state exactly what you want. If replying to an advertisement, you should mention the journal or newspaper and its date, and quote any BOX NUMBER or department number given, e.g. *Box No. 341*; *Dept 4/128*. And if ordering from, or referring to, a catalogue, BROCHURE, or PROSPECTUS, always quote the reference, e.g. *Cat. no. A149*; *Item no. 351*; *Course BL 362*.
—*I am replying to your advertisement in the June edition of 'Tailor and Cutter'. I would like to know more about the steam presses which you are offering at cost price.*
—*I will be attending the auction to be held at Turner House on 16 February, and am particularly interested in the job lot listed as Item No. 351.*

—*Could you please give me more information about course BL 362, which appears in the language-learning section of your summer prospectus?*

—*I would appreciate more details about the 'University Communications System' which you are currently advertising on your website.*

Asking for samples, patterns, and demonstrations

You might want to see what a material or item looks like before placing an order. Most suppliers are willing to provide samples or patterns so that you can make a selection. However, few would send a complex piece of machinery for you to look at. Instead, you would probably be invited to visit a showroom, or the supplier would offer to send a representative. In any case, if it is practical, ask to see an example of the article you want to buy.

—*When replying, could you please enclose a pattern card?*

—*We would also appreciate it if you could send some samples of the material so that we can examine the texture and quality.*

—*Before selling toys we prefer to test them for safety. Could you therefore send us at least two examples of the 'Sprite' range?*

—*I would like to discuss the problem of maintenance before deciding which model to install in my factory. Therefore I would be grateful if you could arrange for one of your representatives to call on me within the next two weeks.*

—*Where can I see a demonstration of this system?*

Suggesting terms, methods of payment, and discounts

Companies sometimes state prices and conditions in their advertisements or literature and may not like prospective customers making additional demands. However, even if conditions are quoted, you can mention that you usually expect certain concessions and politely suggest that, if your terms were met, you would be more likely to place an order.

—*We usually deal on a 30% trade discount basis with an additional quantity discount for orders over 1,000 units.*

—*As a rule, our suppliers allow us to settle by monthly statement and we can offer the usual references if necessary.*

—*We would also like to point out that we usually settle our accounts on a D/A basis with payment by 30-day bill of exchange.*

—*Could you let us know if you allow cash discounts?*

—*As we intend to place a substantial order, we would like to know what quantity discounts you allow.*

Asking for goods on approval, or on sale or return

Sometimes retailers and wholesalers want to see how a LINE will sell before placing a firm order with a supplier. Two ways of doing this are by getting goods on approval or on a SALE OR RETURN basis. In either case the supplier would have to know the customer well, or would want TRADE REFERENCES. The supplier would also place a time limit on when the goods must be returned or paid for.

—*The leaflet advertising your latest hobby magazines interested us, and we would like to stock a selection of them. However, we would only consider placing an order if it was on the usual basis of sale or return. If this is acceptable, we will send you a firm order.*

—*In the catalogue we received from you last week, we saw that you are introducing a new line in synthetic furs. While we appreciate that increasing pressure from wildlife protection societies is reducing the demand for real furs, we are not sure how our customers would react to synthetic alternatives. However, we would like to try a selection of designs. Would it be possible for you to supply us with a range on an approval basis to see if we can encourage a demand? Three months would probably be enough to establish a market if there is one.*

Asking for an estimate or tender

ESTIMATES are quotations to complete a job, e.g. putting a new roof on a factory or installing machinery. TENDERS are similar quotations, but in written form. They are often used when the job is a large one, e.g. building a complete factory. When the work is for a government, or is a large undertaking, there are often newspaper advertisements inviting tenders.

— ADVERTISEMENT:

The Irish Tourist Organization invites tenders from building contractors to erect seating for 10,000 people for the Dublin Summer Festival. Tenders should be in by 1 March 20—, and will be assessed on price and suitability of construction plans.

— ADVERTISEMENT:

The Zena Chemical Company invites tenders from private contractors for the disposal of chemical waste. Only those licensed to deal with toxic substances should apply. Further details from …

A company may write CIRCULAR LETTERS to several suppliers, inviting offers to complete a construction job, or to do repairs or decorating.

—*We are a large chain of theatres, and would be interested in receiving estimates from upholsterers to re-cover the seats in our two main theatres in Manchester.*

—*We are writing to a number of building contractors to invite estimates for the conversion of Northborough Airfield into a sports and leisure centre. The work will include erecting buildings and providing facilities such as ski slopes and parachute jumps. The deadline for completion is the end of December 20—. If you can provide a competitive estimate please contact us at …*

—*As you may be aware from recent press reports, we have taken over International Motors plc and are in the process of automating their Hamburg factory. We are writing to several engineering designers, including yourselves, who we think may be interested in converting the plant to a fully automated production unit. Enclosed you will*

find the specifications. We would welcome inspection of the site by your surveyors, with a view to supplying an estimate for the reconstruction.

Closing

Usually a simple 'thank you' is sufficient to close an enquiry. However, you could mention that a prompt reply would be appreciated, or that certain terms or guarantees would be necessary.

—*We hope to hear from you in the near future.*

—*We would be grateful for an early reply.*

—*Finally, we would like to point out that delivery before Christmas is essential, and hope that you can offer us that guarantee.*

—*If you can agree to the concessions we have asked for, we will place a substantial order.*

—*Prompt delivery would be necessary as we have a rapid turnover. We would therefore need your assurance that you could meet all delivery dates.*

You can also indicate further business or other lines you would be interested in. If a supplier thinks that you may become a regular customer, they will be more inclined to quote competitive terms and offer concessions.

—*If the product is satisfactory, we will place further orders with you in the future.*

—*If the prices quoted are competitive and the quality up to standard, we will order on a regular basis.*

—*Provided you can offer favourable quotations and guarantee delivery within four weeks from receipt of order, we will place regular orders with you.*

Request for a catalogue and price list

Dear Sir / Madam

Please would you send me your Spring catalogue and price list, quoting CIF prices, Le Havre?

Yours faithfully

F. Raval

F. Raval (M.)

3 Request for a prospectus

Dear Sir / Madam

I would like some information about your courses in English for Business Executives, beginning in July.

Please send me a prospectus, details of your fees, and information about accommodation in London for the period July to December. If possible, I would like to stay with an English family.

Yours faithfully

Y. Iwanami

Y. Iwanami (Ms)

Request for general information

Note that the reference to TRADE PRICES in this letter tells the manufacturer that he is dealing with a RETAILER or wholesaler, not a private individual.

If these examples were sent as email messages, it would be acceptable to remove the salutation and change the complimentary close from *Yours faithfully* to the less formal *Thanking you in advance*.

Dear Sir / Madam

Could you please send me details of your tubeless tyres which are being advertised in garages around the country?

I would appreciate a prompt reply quoting trade prices.

Yours faithfully

Brian Wymer

Brian Wymer

These three short enquiries could be sent by letter, fax, or email.

251 rue des Raimonières
F–86000 Poitiers Cédex

Téléphone (+33) 2 99681031
Télécopie (+33) 2 74102163
Email p.gerard@disc.co.fr

Réf. PG/AL

12 May 20—

The Sales Department
R.G. Electronics AG
Havmart 601
D-50000 Köln 1

Dear Sir / Madam

We are a large music store in the centre of Poitiers and would like to know more about the re-writable and recordable CDs you advertise in this month's edition of 'Lectron'.

Could you tell us if the CDs are leading brand names, or made by small independent companies, and whether they would be suitable for domestic recording? We would appreciate it if you could send us some samples. If they are of the standard we require, we will place a substantial order. We would also like to know if you offer any trade discounts.

Yours faithfully

P. Gérard

P. Gérard (M.)
Manager

Reply to an advertisement

In this letter the customer is replying to an advertisement for CDs in a trade journal. The advertiser gave little information, so the writer asks for details.

3

Example letter

1 Why does M. Gérard say *We are a large music store*?

2 How did he hear about the CDs?

3 What requirements does he suggest must be met before he will place an order?

4 What concession does he ask for?

5 If he had begun the letter *Dear Mr —*, what would the complimentary close be?

6 Which words in the letter have a similar meaning to the following?
   a most important
   b type of product
   c large
   d reduced price

3

Enquiry from a buying agent

Companies often have agents in other countries who sell or buy products for them ▸ **see pages 169–170**. In this email the agent is acting on behalf of her PRINCIPALS in Canada.

To...	John Merton
Cc...	
Subject:	Our ref. 180/MB

Dear Mr Merton

You were recommended to us by your trade association and I am writing on behalf of our principals in Canada, who are interested in importing chinaware from England.

Could you send us your latest catalogue and price list, quoting your most competitive prices?

Our principals are a large chain store in North America and will probably place substantial orders if the quality and prices of your products are suitable.

Many thanks.

Linda Lowe
Director
Sanders & Lowe Ltd
Planter House, Princes Street
London EC1 7DQ
Tel.: +44 (0)20 7 87457
Fax: +44 (0)20 7 87458
Email: l.lowe@sanlo.co.uk

To... Satex S.p.A.

Cc...

Subject: Sales enquiry

Dear Sir / Madam

We are a chain of retailers based in Birmingham and are looking for a manufacturer who can supply us with a wide range of sweaters for the men's leisurewear market. We were impressed by the new designs displayed on your stand at the Hamburg Menswear Exhibition last month.

As we usually place large orders, we would expect a quantity discount in addition to a 20% trade discount off net list prices. Our terms of payment are normally 30-day bill of exchange, D/A.

If these conditions interest you, and you can meet orders of over 500 garments at one time, please send us your current catalogue and price list.

We hope to hear from you soon.

Peter Crane
Chief Buyer
F. Lynch & Co. Ltd
Nesson House, Newell Street, Birmingham B3 3EL
Telephone: +44 (0)21 236 6571
Fax: +44 (0)21 236 8592
Email: pcrane@lynch.co.uk

This email is from the Chief Buyer for a chain of shops in Birmingham to an Italian knitwear manufacturer. The buyer explains how he got to know about the manufacturer, and suggests that a quantity discount and acceptance of his method of payment would persuade him to place an order. He is stating his terms in his enquiry because he feels that as a BULK BUYER he can demand certain conditions. But you will see from the reply ▶ page 58 that, although the Italian manufacturer wants the order, he does not like the terms, and suggests conditions that are more suitable to him.

1 What expression does Peter Crane use to indicate that Lynch & Co. is a large company?

2 What market are Lynch & Co. interested in?

3 Where did Lynch & Co. get to know about Satex?

4 What kinds of discount are they asking for?

5 How would payment be made?

6 How many sweaters are they likely to order?

7 Which words in the letter have a similar meaning to the following?
a selection
b presented
c fixed price
d item of clothing

Points to remember

1 Give details of your own company as well as asking for information from your prospective supplier.

2 Be specific and state exactly what you want. If possible, quote box numbers, catalogue references, etc. to help your supplier identify the product/s.

3 Ask for a sample if you are uncertain about a product.

4 Suggest terms and discounts, but be prepared for the supplier to make a counter-offer.

5 Close with an expression such as *I look forward to hearing from you* and / or indicate the possibility of substantial orders or further business.

Replies and quotations

4

REPLYING TO ENQUIRIES

Opening

In an email reply, the RE: abbreviation in the subject line automatically shows that you are replying to a message. Therefore it is not usually necessary to use a salutation.

▶See pages 20–27 for more on email.

However, letters are different. Mention your prospective customer's name, e.g. if the customer signs his letter *Mr B. Green*, begin *Dear Mr Green*, NOT *Dear Sir*.

Thank the writer for his or her enquiry. Mention the date of his or her letter and quote any other references.

— *Thank you for your enquiry of 6 June 20— in which you asked about…*
— *I would like to thank you for your enquiry of 10 May 20—, and am pleased to tell you that we would be able to supply you with the…*
— *We were pleased to learn from your letter of 10 December that you are impressed with our selection of…*
— *Thank you for your letter, NJ 1691, which we received this morning.*

Confirming that you can help

Let the enquirer know near the start of your reply if you have the product or can provide the service he or she is asking about. It is irritating to read a long letter only to find that the supplier cannot help.

— *We have a wide selection of sweaters that will appeal to the market you specified.*
— *Our factory would have no problem in producing the 6,000 units you asked for in your enquiry.*
— *We can supply from stock and will have no trouble in meeting your delivery date.*
— *I am pleased to say that we will be able to supply the transport facilities you require.*
— *We can offer door-to-door delivery services.*

'Selling' your product

Encourage or persuade your prospective customer to do business with you. A simple answer that you have the goods in stock is not enough. Your customer might have made ten other enquiries, so remember it is not only in sales letters that you need to persuade. Mention one or two selling points of your product, including any guarantees, special offers, and discounts.

— *When you have had the opportunity to see the samples for yourself, we feel sure you will agree that they are of the highest quality; and to see a wide selection online, go to www.bettaware.co.uk.*
— *Once you have seen the Delta 800 in operation we know you will be impressed by its trouble-free performance.*
— *We can assure you that the Alpha 2000 is one of the most outstanding machines on the market, and our confidence in it is supported by our five-year guarantee.*

Suggesting alternatives

If you do not have what the enquirer has asked for, but have an alternative, offer that. But do not criticize the product he or she originally asked for.

— *…and while this engine has all the qualities of the model you asked for, the 'Powerdrive' has the added advantage of fewer moving parts, so reducing maintenance costs. It also saves on oil as it…*
— *The model has now been improved. Its steel casing has been replaced by strong plastic, which makes the machine much lighter and easier to handle.*
— *Of course, leather is an excellent upholstery material, but escalating costs have persuaded many of our customers to look for an alternative which is more competitive in price. Tareton Plastics have produced a high-quality substitute, 'Letherine', which has the texture, strength, and appearance of leather, but at less than a quarter of the cost. We feel confident that the samples enclosed will convince you…*

Referring the customer to another place

You may not be able to handle the order or answer the enquiry. If this is the case, tell the enquirer and, if possible, refer them to another company which can help them.

— *I regret to say that we no longer produce the type of stapler you refer to as there is no longer sufficient demand for it. I am sorry we cannot help you.*

— *The book you mention is not published by us, but by Greenhill Education Ltd. Their address is …*

— *We no longer manufacture pure cotton shirts as their retail prices tend only to attract the upper end of the market. All our garments are now polycotton, which is stronger, needs little ironing, and allows variations in pattern, which you can see on our website at www.elegance.co.uk. However, if you are only interested in pure cotton garments, we advise you to contact Louis Fashions Ltd at …*

Even if you can handle the enquiry, you may still have to refer the enquirer elsewhere.

— *We manufacture the product you require, but we only deal with wholesalers, not retailers. Therefore, I suggest you contact our agent, R. L. Depré SA, rue Montpellier 28, Paris, …*

— *Our agents in Italy are Intal S.p.A, Via Alberto Poerio 79, Rome, Email: <sales@intal.co.it>. They carry the full range of our products.*

Sending catalogues, price lists, prospectuses, and samples

Remember to enclose current catalogues and price lists with your reply. If you are attaching catalogues, price lists, etc. to an email message, make sure you compress them to save your recipient's time when they download the material. If prices are subject to change, let your customer know. It is bad policy suddenly to send a letter telling a customer that prices have been increased by ten per cent after you have quoted a firm price. And if you are sending samples UNDER SEPARATE COVER, let

your customer know when they are likely to arrive.

— *Please find enclosed our current catalogue and price list quoting CIF prices Kobe. The units you referred to in your letter are featured on pp. 31–34 under catalogue numbers Y32–Y37. When ordering could you please quote these numbers? The samples you asked for will follow under separate cover.*

— *We enclose our booklet on the Omega 2000 and are sure you will agree that it is one of the finest machines of its kind. It can be adapted to your specifications (see the section 'Structural changes' on page 12).*

— *We enclose our summer catalogue, which unfortunately is only published in English. However, we have included a German translation for the relevant pages (41–45) and hope this will prove helpful.*

— *… and we have enclosed our price list, but should point out that prices are subject to change as the market for raw materials is very unstable at present.*

Arranging demonstrations and visits

Certain products, e.g. heavy equipment, machinery, and computer installations, may need demonstrating. In these cases the supplier will either send a representative or adviser, or suggest that the customer visits their showroom.

— *We have enclosed full details of the Laren welder, but a demonstration would be necessary to show you its full capabilities. We therefore suggest that you visit our centre in Birmingham, where the equipment is set up, so that you can see the machine in action.*

— *As the enclosed booklet cannot really show the efficiency of this system, we would be happy to arrange for our representative to visit you and give a demonstration. If you are interested in a visit, please fill in the enclosed pre-paid card and return it to us.*

— *The enclosed catalogue will give you an idea of the type of sound equipment we produce, but may we suggest that you also visit our*

agent's showrooms in Rotterdam where you can see a wide range of units? The address is …
— Before installing the equipment, we would like to send Mr Tony Griffith, our Chief Engineer, to look over your plant and prepare a report on the installation, taking your particular requirements into account. We suggest you contact us to arrange a convenient date.

Closing

Always thank the customer for contacting you. If you have not done so at the beginning of the letter or email, you can do so at the end. You should also encourage further enquiries.
— Once again we would like to thank you for writing. We would welcome any further questions you might have.
— Please contact us again if you have any questions, using the above telephone number or email address.
— I am sorry we do not have the model you asked for, but can assure you that the alternative I have suggested will meet your requirements. Please remember that we offer a full three-year guarantee.
— We hope to hear from you again soon, and can assure you that your order will be dealt with promptly.

GIVING QUOTATIONS

In your reply to an enquiry, you may want to give your prospective customer a QUOTATION. Below is a guide to the subjects you should cover.

Prices

When a manufacturer, wholesaler, or retailer quotes a price, they may or may not include other costs such as transport, insurance, and PURCHASE TAX (e.g. VAT (VALUE ADDED TAX) in the UK). Prices which include these extra costs are known as GROSS PRICES; those which exclude them are known as NET PRICES.

— The net price of this article is £100.00, to which VAT must be added at 17.5%, making a gross price of £117.50.
— We can quote you a gross price, inclusive of delivery charges, of £347.50 per 100 items. These goods are exempt from VAT.

A quotation is not necessarily legally binding, i.e. the company does not have to sell you the goods at the price quoted in the reply to an enquiry. However, when prices are unstable, the supplier will say in their quotation that their prices are *subject to change*. If the company makes a *firm offer*, it means they will hold the goods for a certain time until you order, e.g. *firm 14 days*. Again, this is not legally binding, but suppliers generally keep to firm offers to protect their reputation.
— The prices quoted above are provisional, since we may be compelled by the increasing cost of raw materials to raise them. I will inform you immediately if this happens.
— We can offer you a price of £5,200.00 per engine, firm 21 days, after which the price will be subject to an increase of 5%.

Whenever possible you should quote prices in your customer's currency, allowing for exchange fluctuations.
— The price of this model is ¥2,800,000 at today's rate of exchange.
— We can quote you a price of €300 per 100 units, though I regret that, because of fluctuating exchange rates, we can only hold this price for four weeks from today's date.
— The net price of $530.00 per unit is extremely competitive.

Transport and insurance costs

There are a number of abbreviations that indicate which price is being quoted to the customer. These are established by the INTERNATIONAL CHAMBER OF COMMERCE (ICC) and are called INCOTERMS. They are revised regularly, and additional terms may be added, e.g. the phrase *cif Naples Incoterms 2000 landed* means that a consignment is covered under an Incoterm CIF (cost, insurance, and freight) set in the year 2000, up to the time it is landed in Naples.

The main Incoterms are in four groups, which are named after the first letter in the term.

Group C
The seller covers only the costs listed to get the goods to a named destination, e.g. freight and import duties, but not insurance.
Group D
The seller carries all the costs and risks to get the goods to a named destination.
Group E
The buyer pays all costs once the goods have left the seller's premises.
Group F
The seller delivers the goods to a carrier who is appointed by the buyer.

Incoterms are quoted in correspondence in the following way: *£30,000 CFR Hong Kong* (i.e. the price includes all delivery costs to Hong Kong, except for insurance); *$35,000 FOB Rotterdam* (i.e. the price includes delivery costs to when the goods are on board ship at Rotterdam). Abbreviations for Incoterms may also be written in lower case, e.g. *cfr* or *fob*.

Two other terms which should be noted, but which are used mainly in the UK, are:
— CARRIAGE PAID (*c/p*), i.e. charges will be paid by the sender, e.g. *We will send replacements for the damaged goods c/p.*
— CARRIAGE FORWARD (*c/f*), i.e. charges will be paid by the receiver, e.g. *As you are responsible for the damage, we will send replacements c/f.*

Discounts

Manufacturers and wholesalers sometimes allow a discount (i.e. a deduction) on the net or gross price. These are of different kinds, e.g. a trade discount to sellers in similar trades; a quantity discount for orders over a certain amount; a cash discount if payment is made within a certain time; a LOYALTY DISCOUNT when companies have a long association.
— *We allow a 3% cash discount for payment within one month.*
— *The net price of this model is £170.00, less 10% discount for quantities up to 100 and 15% discount for quantities over 100.*
— *We do not normally give discounts to private customers, but because of your long association with our company we can offer you 12% off the retail price.*
— *The prices quoted are CFR Yokohama, but are subject to a 20% trade discount off net price. We can offer a further 10% discount off net prices for orders of more than 2,000 units.*

Methods of payment

When quoting terms, you may require, or suggest, any of several methods of payment, e.g. letter of credit or bill of exchange.
▶**For more on this subject, see pages 78–79, and 147–167.**
— *On receipt of a cheque for the amount quoted, we will send the article by registered mail.*
— *Payment for initial orders should be made by sight draft, payable at Den Norske Creditbank, Kirkegaten 21, Oslo 1, cash against documents.*
— *We are willing to consider open account facilities if you can provide the necessary bank reference.*

INCOTERM	ABBREVIATION	EXPLANATION
Group C		
Cost and FReight	CFR	The seller pays all delivery costs to a named destination, except for insurance.
Cost, Insurance, and Freight	CIF	The same as CFR, except the seller also pays the cost of insurance.
Carriage Paid To	CPT	The seller pays all delivery costs to a named destination. The buyer pays any additional costs after the goods have been delivered to a nominated carrier.
Carriage and Insurance Paid	CIP	The seller pays transport and insurance costs to a named destination, but not import duty.
Group D		
Delivered at Frontier	DAF	The seller pays all delivery costs to the buyer's frontier, but not import duty.
Delivered Ex-Ship	DES	The seller pays all delivery costs on board ship, but does not clear the goods for import at the named port of destination.
Delivered Ex-Quay	DEQ	The seller pays all delivery costs to a port named by the buyer, but does not clear the goods for import at the named port.
Delivered Duty Paid	DDP	The seller pays all delivery costs, including import duty, to a named destination in the importing country.
Delivered Duty Unpaid	DDU	The same as DDP, except that the seller does not pay import duty.
Group E		
EX-Works	EXW	The buyer pays all delivery costs once the goods have left the seller's factory or warehouse.
Group F		
Free CArrier	FCA	The seller pays all delivery costs to the buyer's carrier, and clears the goods for export.
Free Alongside Ship	FAS	The seller pays all delivery costs to the port. The buyer pays for loading the goods on to the ship and all other costs.
Free On Board	FOB	The seller pays all delivery costs to when the goods are on board ship at a named port. The buyer pays all other costs.

Quoting delivery date

If the enquiry specifies a delivery date, confirm that it can be met, or if not, suggest an alternative date. Do not make a promise that you cannot keep as it will give you a bad reputation. If a delivery time is a condition of ordering, the customer could reject the goods or sue you if you break the contract.

— *... and we are pleased to say that we can deliver by November 1, so you will have stock for the Christmas sales period.*

— *As there are regular sailings from Liverpool to New York, we are sure that the consignment will reach you well within the time you specified.*

— *We have the materials in stock and will ship them immediately we receive your order.*

— *As there is a heavy demand for fans at this time of year, please allow at least six weeks for delivery.*

— *We would not be able to deliver within two weeks of receipt of order, as we would need time to prepare the materials. However, we could guarantee delivery within four weeks.*

Fixed terms and negotiable terms

You can quote terms in two ways: state your price and discounts with no room for negotiation, or suggest the customer could discuss them. In the two examples below, the writers make firm quotes, indicating that methods of payment and discounts are fixed.

— *All list prices are quoted FOB Southampton and are subject to a 25% trade discount with payment by letter of credit.*

— *The prices quoted are EXW, but we can arrange freight and insurance (CIP Hong Kong) if required. However, unless otherwise stated, payment should be made by 30-day bill of exchange, documents against acceptance.*

In the next two examples, the use of the adverbs *normally* and *usually* soften the tone of the statements to indicate that, although the company prefers certain terms, these can

be discussed. In the final example the supplier softens the tone further by asking the customer to confirm whether or not the arrangement is satisfactory.

— *We usually offer an 18% trade discount on FOB prices, and would prefer payment by irrevocable letter of credit.*

— *Normally we allow a 23% trade discount off net prices with payment on a documents against payment basis. Please let us know if this arrangement is satisfactory.*

Giving an estimate

Companies which are asked to give an estimate for a particular job may include the estimate in tabulated form in a letter ▶ **see page 59**. More often, however, they will send their official estimate form with a covering letter.

— *As you know, our representative has visited your factory to discuss your proposed extension, and I now have pleasure in enclosing our official estimate.*

— *The enclosed estimate covers labour and parts and carries a six-month guarantee on all work completed.*

4

Reply to a request for a catalogue and price list

▶See page 42 for the request.

Dear Mr Raval

Thank you for your enquiry of 31 January. We enclose our Spring Catalogue and current price list quoting CIF prices Le Havre.

We would like to draw your attention to the trade and quantity discounts we are offering in our Special Purchases section on pp. 19–26, which may be of particular interest to you.

Please contact us if we can be of any further help.

Yours sincerely

Tim Hoad

Tim Hoad

Reply to a request for a prospectus

▶See page 42 for the request.

Dear Ms Iwanami

Please find enclosed our prospectus covering courses from July to December. Details of fees and accommodation in London for that period are covered in the booklet 'Living in London' which accompanies the prospectus.

At present we still have places available for students taking the English for Business Executives course beginning in July, but would ask you to book as soon as possible so that we can reserve a place for you and arrange accommodation with an English family.

We are sure you will enjoy your stay here and look forward to seeing you.

Yours sincerely

M. Preston

M. Preston (Ms)

Reply to a request for general information

▶See page 42 for the request.

Dear Mr Wymer

Thank you very much for your enquiry. I enclose a catalogue giving detailed information about our heavy goods vehicle tyres, including the impressive results we have achieved in rigorous factory and track tests. Please note especially the items on safety and fuel economy – the main selling points of this product.

With regard to trade discounts, we can offer 25% off list prices to bona fide retailers and wholesalers, with quantity discounts for orders over £20,000.00.

We would be pleased to supply any further information you require.

Yours sincerely

Darren Treadwell

Darren Treadwell

Catalogues and samples

M. Gérard wrote to R.G. Electronics to enquire about CDs ▶ **see page 43**. He implied that his store was a large one, that he was only interested in high-quality products, and that he might place a substantial order. This is the reply.

R.G. Electronics AG

Havmart 601
D–50000 Köln 1

Telefon (+49) 221 32 42 98
Telefax (+49) 221 83 61 25
Email gerlachr@rge.co.de
www.rge.de

Your Ref: **PG/AL**

14 May 20—

P. Gérard
Manager
Disc S.A.
251 rue des Raimonières
F-86000 Poitiers Cédex

Dear M. Gérard

Thank you for your enquiry of 12 May in which you asked about the CDs we advertised in this month's edition of 'Lectron'.

I can confirm that they are of high quality, and suitable for domestic recording. They are 'Kolby' products, a brand name you will certainly recognize, and the reason their prices are so competitive is that they are part of a consignment of bankrupt stock that was offered to us.

Because of their low price, and the small profit margin, we will not be offering any trade discounts on this consignment. But we sell a wide range of electronic and computer products and have enclosed a price list giving you details of trade, quantity, and cash discounts.

We have sent, by separate post, samples of the advertised CDs and other brands we stock, and would urge you to place an order as soon as possible as there has been a huge response to our advertisement. Thank you for your interest.

Yours sincerely

R. Gerlach

(Herr) R. Gerlach
Sales Director

Enc. price-list

1 What references does Herr Gerlach quote?

2 Why are the CDs being sold cheaply?

3 Does he offer any discounts on the advertised goods?

4 What other material has he sent to Disc S.A.?

5 Can Disc S.A. order whenever they want to?

'Selling' the product

This is a reply to the buying agent who emailed Glaston Potteries ▶ see page 44 on behalf of her principals in Canada. As the agent made no reference to any particular line of chinaware she was interested in, and did not mention terms, this reply takes the form of a sales letter.

Clayfield | Burnley | BB10 1RQ

GLASTON POTTERIES LTD

Telephone +44 (0)1282 46125
Facsimile +44 (0)1282 63182
Email j.merton@glaston.co.uk
www.glaston.com

10 June 20—

Ms L. Lowe
Sanders & Lowe Ltd
Planter House
Princes Street
London EC1 7DQ

Dear Ms Lowe

We were pleased to receive your enquiry today, and are enclosing the catalogue and price list you asked for.

You will see that we can offer a wide selection of dinner and tea services ranging from the rugged 'Greystone' earthenware breakfast sets to the delicate 'Ming' bone china dinner service. You can choose from more than fifty designs, which include the elegance of 'Wedgwood', the delicate pattern of 'Willow', and the richness of 'Brownstone' glaze.

We would very much like to add your clients to our worldwide list of customers, and could promise them an excellent product with a first-class service. We would be glad to accept orders for any number of pieces, and can mix sets if required.

You will see that our prices are quoted CIF to Eastern Canadian seaboard ports and we are offering a special 10% discount off all net prices, with delivery within three weeks from receipt of order.

If there is any further information you need, please contact us, or go to our website at the address above. Once again thank you for your enquiry.

Yours sincerely

J. Merton

J. Merton (Mr)
Sales Manager
Enc.

Registered No. 716481
VAT Registered No. 133 53431 08

1 How does Mr Merton draw attention to his company's many products?

2 How does he imply that his company has an international reputation?

3 What terms for delivery do Glaston Potteries quote?

4 How does he encourage further enquiries?

5 Which words in the letter have a similar meaning to the following?
a range
b select
c time when order received

A wholesaler is out of
stock of the adapters
that her customer has
asked for, so she offers a
substitute. However, the
new product has not yet
been tested and she
knows nothing about its
performance or safety.

4

✉									_ □ ×

▭ Send	🖫 🖨	✂ 🗈 📋	📄 📎	📖 🔍	❘ ↓ ↘	📄 Options...	❓

Arial	▾	10	▾	⊕	**B** *I* <u>U</u>	▤ ▦ ▦	☰ ☲ ☲

<u>F</u>ile   <u>E</u>dit   <u>V</u>iew   <u>I</u>nsert   F<u>o</u>rmat   <u>T</u>ools   Acti<u>o</u>ns   <u>H</u>elp

To...	Pedro Monteiro
<u>C</u>c...	
Subject:	RE: Enquiry (K153, K157 units)

Dear Sr Monteiro

Thank you for your email. I regret to say that we are out of stock of K153 and K157 units, and
do not expect another delivery until later this month.

We are currently testing a consignment from Taiwan, but these do not have a Belgian
Standards Institute stamp of approval and we would like to complete our tests before putting
them on the market. We will contact you again as soon as our testing is completed, or when
the units you requested are available, whichever date is the earlier.

Diane Charcot (Mme)
Manager
D & S Charcot S.A.R.L.
place du 20 août 79, B–4000, Liège
Tél: (+32) 49–240886
Télécopie: (+32) 49–16592
Email: d.charcot@dscharcot.co.be

1 What is Mme
   Charcot's problem?

2 How does she show
   her customer that she
   is concerned about
   safety?

3 Is Mme Charcot
   relying on her
   customer to contact
   her again?

Quotation of terms

This is a reply to the general enquiry in which Mr Crane, Chief Buyer at F. Lynch & Co, asked for certain concessions ▸**see page 45**. Notice how Sig. Causio of Satex does not turn down his requests but makes a counter-offer.

Satex S.p.A.

Via di Pietra Papa, 00146 Roma

Telefono: +39 (0)6 769910
Telefax: +39 (0)6 6815473
Email: causiod@satex.co.it

Vs.rif.   Vs. rif.: 6 Feb. 20—
Ns.rif.   D/1439

21 February 20—

Mr Peter Crane
Chief Buyer
F. Lynch & Co. Ltd
Nesson House
Newell Street
Birmingham B3 3EL
UK

Dear Mr Crane

We were pleased to receive your enquiry, and to hear that you liked our range of sweaters. We can confirm that there would certainly be no trouble in supplying you from our wide selection of garments.

We can offer you a quantity discount, which would be 5% off net prices for orders over £2,000, but the usual allowance for a trade discount in Italy is 15%, and we always deal on payment by sight draft, cash against documents. However, we would be prepared to review this once we have established a firm trading association with you.

Enclosed you will find our summer catalogue and price list quoting prices CIF London. We are sure you will find a ready sale for our products in England, as have other retailers throughout Europe and America, and we hope very much that we can reach agreement on the terms quoted. Thank you for your interest. We look forward to hearing from you soon.

Yours sincerely

D. Causio

D. Causio (Sig.)
Sales Director

Encs.

Questions

1 Does Sig. Causio agree to all Mr Crane's requests concerning discounts?

2 What sort of payment does he ask for?

3 What does he suggest about the method of payment in the future?

4 What is enclosed with the letter?

5 How does Sig. Causio indicate that his company deals internationally?

6 Which words in the letter have a similar meaning to the following?
a bill paid on presentation
b reconsider
c link or connection

W|S|L

Wycombe Road
Wembley
Middlesex
HA9 6DA

Wembley Shopfitters Ltd.
Telephone: +44 (0)20 8903 2323
Fax: +44 (0)20 8903 2323
Email: plane@wemshop.com

Mr K. Bellon
Superbuys Ltd
Superbuy House
Wolverton Road
London SW16 7DN

22 June 20—

Dear Mr Bellon

Estimate for refitting Superbuys' Halton Road Branch

Our Surveyor, John Pelham, visited the above premises on Wednesday 16 June, and our costing department have now worked out the following estimate for fixtures and fittings. This includes materials and labour.

Fitting 200m of 'Contact' shelving in main shop and store room @ £35.00 per metre	£7,000.00
Erecting 15 steel stands plus shelves 23m x 6m @ £110.00 each	£1,650.00
Laying 3,320 sq.m. 'Durafloor' flooring @ £18.00 per sq.m.	£59,760.00
Rewiring; fixing power points, boxes, etc. 36 'Everglow' light fittings @ £28.00 each.	£1,008.00
Subtotal	£69,418.00
plus VAT @ 17.5%	£12,148.15
TOTAL	£81,566.15

We feel sure you will agree that this is a very competitive estimate, bearing in mind that we use top-quality materials backed by a one-year guarantee. We can also confirm that the job will be completed before the end of February provided that no unforeseen circumstances arise.

If you have any further questions, please contact our Senior Supervisor, Mr Terry Mills, on the above number, ext. 21.
We look forward to hearing from you soon.

Yours sincerely

P. Lane

P. Lane (Mr)
Director

Reg: London 481629
VAT: 314651928

1 What is the subject of this letter?

2 Is the figure £69,418 a net or a gross total?

3 Why does Mr Lane consider this a competitive offer?

4 What might prevent the job from being completed in February?

5 What is Mr Mills's job title?

6 Which words in the letter have a similar meaning to the following?
a buildings
b calculated
c supported

Points to remember

1 In salutations, use the customer's name rather than *Dear Sir / Madam*.

2 Let the customer know early in the letter whether or not you can help them.

3 Make sure that you have supplied all the information you think will help your customer including, if relevant, catalogues and price lists.

4 Thank the customer for contacting you, and encourage further enquiries.

5 When giving a customer a quotation, in addition to the price quote transport and insurance costs, any discounts, method of payment, and delivery date.

6 Do not promise a delivery date that you cannot keep.

Orders

5

5

PLACING AN ORDER

Orders are usually written on a company's official order form ▸ **see page 65 for an example** which has a date and a reference number that should be quoted in any correspondence referring to the order. If the order is telephoned, it should be confirmed in writing, and an order form should always be accompanied by either a COMPLIMENTS SLIP or a COVERING LETTER. A covering letter is preferable as it allows you the opportunity to make any necessary points and confirm the terms that have been agreed.

The guide below is for an outline of a covering letter. You may not want to make all the points listed, but look through the guide to see what could be mentioned.

Opening

Make it clear that there is an order accompanying the letter.
— *Please find enclosed our Order No. B4521 for 25 'Clearsound' transistor receivers.*
— *The enclosed order (No. R154) is for 50 packets of A4 copier paper.*
— *Thank you for your reply of 14 May regarding our email about the mobile phones. Enclosed you will find our official order (No. B561) for …*
— *I would like to place a trial order for the 'Letherine' material we discussed at the trade show last month. Please find enclosed …*

Payment

Confirm the TERMS OF PAYMENT.
— *As agreed you will draw on us at 30 days, D/A, with the documents being sent to our bank, The National Mercantile Bank …*
— *We would like to confirm that payment is to be made by irrevocable letter of credit, which we have already applied to the bank for.*
— *Once we have received your advice, we will send a bank draft to …*
— *… and we agreed that payments would be made against quarterly statements …*

Discounts

Confirm the agreed discounts.
— *We would like to thank you for the 30% trade discount and 10% quantity discount you allowed us.*
— *Finally, we would like to confirm that the 25% trade discount is quite satisfactory.*
— *… and we will certainly take advantage of the cash discounts you offered for prompt settlement.*
— *Although we anticipated a higher trade discount than 15%, we will place an initial order and hope that the discount can be reviewed in the near future.*

Delivery

Confirm the delivery dates.
— *It is essential that the goods are delivered before the beginning of November, in time for the Christmas sales period.*
— *Delivery before 28 February is a firm condition of this order, and we reserve the right to refuse goods delivered after that time.*
— *Please confirm that you can complete the work before the end of March, as the opening of the store is planned for early April.*

Methods of delivery

Many companies use FORWARDING AGENTS ▸ **see page 199** who are specialists in packing and handling the documentation to SHIP goods. Nevertheless, to ensure prompt and safe delivery, it is a good idea to advise the company on how you want the goods packed and sent. This means that if the consignment arrives late, or in a damaged state, your letter is evidence of the instructions you gave.
— *… and please remember that only air freight will ensure prompt delivery.*
— *Please send the goods by express freight as we need them urgently.*
— *We advise delivery by road to avoid constant handling of this fragile consignment.*
— *Could you please ship by scheduled freighter to avoid any unnecessary delays?*

Packing

Advise your supplier how you want the goods packed. Note, in the first example, that crates are often marked with a sign – a diamond, a target, a square, a lion, etc. – that can be recognized by the supplier and customer.

— *Each piece of crockery is to be individually wrapped in thick paper, packed in straw, and shipped in wooden crates marked ◊ and numbered 1 to 6.*

— *The carpets should be wrapped, and the packaging reinforced at both ends to avoid wear.*

— *The machines must be well greased with all movable parts secured before being loaded into crates, which should be clearly marked with your castle logo for easy identification.*

Closing

— *We hope that this will be the first of many orders we place with you.*

— *We will place further orders if this one is completed to our satisfaction.*

— *If our sales targets are met, we shall be placing further orders in the near future.*

— *I look forward to receiving your advice / shipment / acknowledgement / confirmation.*

ACKNOWLEDGING AN ORDER

As soon as a supplier receives an order, it should be acknowledged. This can be done by letter, or by email for speed ▶see page 66. The following examples can be used in both emails and letters.

— *Thank you for your order No. 338B which we received today. We are now dealing with it and you may expect delivery within the next three weeks.*

— *Your order No. 6712/1 is now being processed and should be ready for despatch by the end of this week.*

— *We are pleased to inform you that we have already made up your order, No. 9901/1/5, for 500 bed-linen packets, and are now making arrangements for shipment to Rotterdam.*

ADVICE OF DESPATCH

When the supplier has made up the order and arranged shipment, the customer is informed by means of an advice note. This may be a form ▶see page 70, letter, fax, or email.

Although an advice note can be sent by fax or email, the customer may need to present original documents (e.g. INVOICE, bill of lading, INSURANCE CERTIFICATE) to collect the consignment. Of course these cannot be faxed or sent by email.

— *Your order, No. D/154/T, is already on board the SS Mitsu Maru, sailing from Kobe on 16 May and arriving Tilbury, London, on 11 June. The shipping documents have been forwarded to your bank in London for collection.*

— *We are pleased to advise you that the watches you ordered – No. 88151/24 – will be on flight BA165 leaving Zurich at 11.00, 9 August, arriving Manchester 13.00. Please find enclosed air waybill DC 15161/3 and copies of invoice A113/3, which you will need for collection.*

— *Your order, No. YI/151/C, is being sent express rail-freight and can be collected after 09.00 tomorrow. Enclosed is consignment note No. 1167153, which should be presented on collection. You should contact us immediately if any problems arise. Thank you for your order, and we hope we can be of further service in the future.*

Placing an order: covering letter

F. Lynch & Co. have decided to place an order with Satex S.p.A. ▶see previous correspondence on pages 45 and 58 and are sending a covering letter with the order form.

F. Lynch & Co. Ltd

Head Office
Nesson House
Newell Street
Birmingham
B3 3EL

Telephone: +44 (0)21 236 6571
Fax: +44 (0)21 236 8592
Email: pcrane@lynch.co.uk
www.lynch.com

Your ref: D/1439
Our ref: Order DR4316

9 March 20—

Satex S.p.A
Via di Pietra Papa
00146 Roma
ITALY

Attn. Sig. D. Causio

Dear Sig. Causio

Please find enclosed our official order, No. DR4316.

For this order, we accept the 15% trade discount you offered, and the terms of payment (sight draft, CAD), but hope you are willing to review these terms if we decide to order again.

Would you please send the shipping documents and your sight draft to Northminster Bank (City Branch), Deal Street, Birmingham B3 1SQ.

If you do not have any of the items we have ordered currently in stock, please do not send alternatives.

We would appreciate delivery within the next six weeks, and look forward to your acknowledgement.

Yours sincerely

Peter Crane

Peter Crane
Chief Buyer

Enc. Order No. DR4316

1 On whose terms are F. Lynch & Co. paying?

2 If any of the sweaters they have ordered are out of stock, would they accept alternatives?

3 How soon do they want the sweaters?

F. Lynch & Co. Ltd

Head Office
Nesson House
Newell Street
Birmingham
B3 3EL

Telephone: +44 (0)21 236 6571
Fax: +44 (0)21 236 8592
Email: pcrane@lynch.co.uk
www.lynch.com

Order no.   **DR 4316**

Satex S.p.A
Via di Pietra Papa
00146 Roma
ITALY

Authorized

Peter Crane

Quantity	Item description	Cat. No.	Price (CIF London)
50	V-neck: 30 red + 20 blue	R 432	£30.80 each
30	Roll neck: 15 black + 15 blue	N 154	£20.40 each
30	Crew neck: 15 green + 15 beige	N 157	£23.00 each
40	Crew neck: pattern	R 541	£25.60 each

Note: Subject to 5% quantity discount

Comments   15% Trade Disc. allowed. Pymt. C/D Del. 6 weeks

Date   9 March 20—

1 In the email on page 45, Mr Crane suggested that he might place orders for over 500 sweaters, but this order is for only 150. Why do you think it is relatively small?

2 Which reference identifies the sweaters?

3 What sort of discounts have been agreed?

4 By when should the order be delivered?

5 If F. Lynch & Co. have further correspondence with Satex on this order, what reference would they use?

Acknowledging an order

Satex will now prepare Mr Crane's order, but in the meantime they email him to let him know that the order has been received.

To...	Peter Crane
Cc...	Marco Bonetto
Subject:	Your Order DR 4316

Dear Mr Crane

Thank you for the above order, which we are now making up. We have all the items in stock and will advise you about shipment in the next few days.

Daniele Causio
Sales Director
Satex S.p.A.
Via di Pietra Papa, 00146 Roma
Telefono: +39 06 769910
Telefax: +39 06 6815473
Email: causiod@satex.co.it

This email message
confirms that Satex have
sent the order. When Mr
Crane receives the email,
the Northminster Bank
will issue a DEBIT
AUTHORITY, which
allows them to debit
F. Lynch & Co.'s account.
The shipping documents
will then be sent to
F. Lynch & Co., so that the
goods can be collected.
Remember, this was a
CIF transaction where
the supplier paid cost,
insurance, and freight,
and on a documents
against payment basis.

5

Example email

Send		Options...

Arial — 10 — **B** *I* <u>U</u>

File   Edit   View   Insert   Format   Tools   Actions   Help

To...	Peter Crane
Cc...	Marco Bonetto
Subject:	Your Order DR 4316

Dear Mr Crane

We are pleased to tell you that the above order has been shipped on the SS *Marconissa* and should reach you in the next 10 days.

Meanwhile, our bank has forwarded the relevant documents and sight draft for £3,092.80, which includes the agreed trade and quantity discounts, to the Northminster Bank (City Branch) Birmingham.

We are sure you will be very satisfied with the consignment and look forward to your next order.

Best wishes
Daniele Causio
Sales Director
Satex S.p.A.
Via di Pietra Papa, 00146 Roma
Telefono: +39 06 769910
Telefax: +39 06 6815473
Email: causiod@satex.co.it

Placing an order

This email and the next one follow on from previous correspondence ▶ **see pages 44 and 56**. There are three parties involved: the manufacturers, Glaston Potteries; the buying agents, Sanders & Lowe; and their principals in Canada, MacKenzie Bros. Here, Ms Lowe is writing on behalf of her principals and forwarding their order. Notice the instructions she gives and notice that she has already phoned Glaston Potteries to agree terms of payment, which were not mentioned in their letter on page 56.

To... John Merton

Cc...

Subject: MacKenzie order

Order No. R1432

Dear Mr Merton

Please find attached an order (R1432) from our principals, MacKenzie Bros Ltd, 1–5 Whale Drive, Dawson, Ontario, Canada.

They have asked us to instruct you that the 60 sets of crockery ordered should be packed in 6 crates, 10 sets per crate, with each piece individually wrapped, and the crates marked clearly with their name, the words 'fragile' and 'crockery', and numbered 1–6.

They have agreed to pay by letter of credit, which we discussed on the phone last week, and they would like delivery before the end of this month, which should be no problem as there are regular sailings from Liverpool.

If the colours they have chosen are not in stock, they will accept an alternative provided the designs are those stipulated on the order.

Please send any further correspondence relating to shipment or payment direct to MacKenzie Bros, and let us have a copy of the commercial invoice when it is made up.

Many thanks
Linda Lowe

1 What instructions have been given about packing?

2 What method of payment has been arranged?

3 Why should there be no problem for Glaston Potteries to deliver within four weeks?

4 Will substitutes be acceptable if Glaston Potteries are out of stock of any items?

5 Sanders & Lowe have completed their job, which was to find a supplier. So who must Glaston Potteries write to now?

6 Which words in the email have a similar meaning to the following?
   a cups, saucers, plates, etc.
   b large, wooden boxes
   c easily damaged or broken
   d stated
   e completed

Advice of despatch

Glaston Potteries have made up the MacKenzie order and now advise them of despatch. MacKenzie Bros will already have opened a letter of credit ▶ **see page 155** at their bank, The Canadian Union Trust Bank, in favour of Glaston Potteries. The Canadian bank will now wait until they have confirmation of shipment from their agents in England, Burnley City Bank, and will then transfer the money so that Glaston Potteries can be paid.

														_ □ ✕
	📧 Send	💾 🖨	✂ 🗐 📋	🗐 📎	📖 👤	‼ ↓	▽	📄 Options...	⁇					

Arial   10   🌐   **B** _I_ U   📰 ≡ ≡ ≣ ≣ ≣

File   Edit   View   Insert   Format   Tools   Actions   Help

To...   Richard MacKenzie

Cc...

Subject: Order No. R1432

Dear Mr MacKenzie

The above order has now been completed and sent to Liverpool Docks, where it is awaiting loading on to the SS *Manitoba*, which sails for Dawson, Canada on 16 July arriving 30 July. When we have the necessary documents we will transfer them to Burnley City Bank, your bank's agents here, and they will forward them to the Canadian Union Trust Bank.

We have taken particular care to see that the goods have been packed as per your instructions: the six crates have been marked with your name, and numbered 1–6. Each crate measures 6ft x 4ft x 3ft and weighs 5 cwt.

We managed to get all items from stock with the exception of Cat. No. G16, which is only available in red, but we included it in the consignment as it was of the design you asked for.

If you need any further information, please contact us. Thank you very much for your order.

We look forward to hearing from you again soon.

John Merton
Sales Manager
Glaston Potteries Ltd
Clayfield, Burnley BB10 1RQ
Tel: +44 (0)1282 46125
Fax: +44 (0)1282 63182
Email: j.merton@glaston.co.uk

---

1   How will the consignment be sent?

2   When is it due to arrive in Canada?

3   What will happen to the documents once Glaston Potteries receive them?

4   What did Glaston Potteries do about the item they could not supply?

5   Which words in the email have a similar meaning to the following?
    a   essential
    b   forwarded
    c   in accordance with
    d   apart from

Advice note

Glaston Potteries advised MacKenzie Bros of despatch in an email ▶ **see page 69**. Here, D & S Charcot use a form.

D & S Charcot S.A.R.L.   Advice note

place du 20 août 79 B–4000 Liège
Tél: (+32) 49–240886
Télécopie: (+32) 49–16592
Email: sales@dscharcot.co.be

The Chief Buyer
Caravela
Rua das Ameixoeiras 1291
P–1700 Lisboa

Your order No. D163/9

The following consignment has been sent to you by rail today. Please confirm receipt and quote consignment note No. 8817561 915.

Quantity	Goods (Description)
48	ERC adaptors 13 amp
68	dimmer switches 250 watt
100	1-metre fluorescent fitting with defuser
48	Jacar 4-metre extension leads 3kW (3,000 watt)
72	point fittings 13 amp

Comments   **Paid on pro forma inv. B3171**   Date   **5 September 20—**

DELAYS IN DELIVERY

If goods are held up either before or after they are sent, you must keep your customer informed. State what has happened, how it happened, and what you are doing to put things right. In these cases the speed of email is very useful. If email is not available, then fax or cable should be used as the sooner your customer is informed, the sooner they can take action. It is a good idea to keep copies of any messages you send about delays.

— *I was surprised and sorry to hear that your consignment (Order No. B145) had not reached you. On enquiry I found that it had been delayed by a local dispute on the cargo vessel SS Hamburg on which it had been loaded. I am now trying to get the goods transferred to the SS Samoa, which is scheduled to sail for Yokohama before the end of next week. I shall keep you informed.*

— *I am writing to tell you that unfortunately there will be a three-week delay in delivery. This is due to a fire at our Greenford works which destroyed most of the machinery. Your order has been transferred to our Slough factory and will be processed there as soon as possible. I apologize for this delay, which is due to circumstances beyond our control.*

— *We regret to inform you that there will be a delay in getting your consignment to you. This is due to the cut in supplies from Gara, where, as you may be aware, civil war broke out last week. We have contacted a possible supplier in Lagos and he will let us know if he can help us. If you wish to cancel your order, please let us know as soon as possible. However, I think you will find most manufacturers are experiencing the same difficulties at present.*

REFUSING AN ORDER

There are a number of reasons for a company to refuse an order, and some of the most common are given below. Whatever your reason, you must be polite: the words *reject* and *refuse* have a very negative tone, therefore it is better to use *decline* or *turn down* instead.

Out of stock

You may be out of stock of the product ordered, or you may no longer make it. Note that, in either case, you have an opportunity to sell an alternative product ▸**see page 48**, but remember not to criticize the product you can no longer supply.

— *We are sorry to say that we are completely out of stock of this item and it will be six weeks before we get our next delivery, but please contact us then.*

— *We no longer manufacture this product as demand over the past few years has declined.*

— *Thank you for your order for heavy-duty industrial overalls. Unfortunately we have run out of the strengthened denim style you asked for. As you particularly specified this material, we will not offer a substitute, but will inform you immediately we receive delivery of a new consignment. This will be within the next two months.*

— *We received your order for ACN dynamos today, but regret that due to a strike at the ACN factory we are unable to fulfil it at present. We are aware that other models will not suit your requirements, but hope that the dispute will be settled soon and that we will be able to supply you. We will keep you informed of developments.*

5

Bad reputation

The customer may have a bad reputation for settling their accounts or, in the case of a retailer of, say, electrical or mechanical products, may have offered a poor after-sales service which could in turn affect a manufacturer's or supplier's reputation. In these cases, it is better to indicate terms on which you would be prepared to accept the order, or, as in the last two examples below, find a diplomatic way of saying 'no'.

— *We would only be prepared to supply on a cash basis.*
— *We only supply on payment against pro forma invoice.*
— *As there is heavy demand at present, we have very few of these products in stock and are serving on a rota basis. It is extremely unlikely that we will be able to deliver within the next four months.*
— *As our plant is closing for the summer vacation we would not be able to process your order for the date you have given. Therefore, regretfully, we have to decline it.*
— *I am sorry to say that we must turn down your order as we have full order books at present and cannot give a definite date for delivery.*

Unfavourable terms

The supplier may not like the terms the customer has asked for, either for delivery:
— *Delivery cannot possibly be guaranteed within the time given in your letter.*
— *Two months must be allowed for delivery as we are dependent on our suppliers for raw materials.*

or discount:
— *It would be uneconomical for us to offer our products at the discounts you suggest as we work on a fast turnover and low profit margins.*
— *The usual trade discount is 15% in this country, which is 5% lower than the figure mentioned in your letter.*
— *The discount you asked for is far more than we offer any of our customers.*

or payment:
— *We only accept payment by letter of credit.*
— *We never offer quarterly terms on initial orders, even to customers who can provide references. However, we might consider this sort of credit once we have established a trading relationship.*
— *Our company relies on quick sales, low profits, and a fast turnover, and therefore we cannot offer long-term credit facilities.*

Size of order

The quantity required might be too large:
— *We are a small company and could not possibly handle an order for 20,000 units.*
— *Unfortunately, our factory does not have facilities to turn out 30,000 units a week.*

The quantity required might be too small:
— *We only supply orders for ballpoint pens by the gross, and therefore suggest you try a wholesaler rather than a manufacturer.*
— *The shirts we manufacture are sold by the dozen in one colour. I regret that we never sell individual garments.*
— *Our factory only sells material in 30-metre rolls which cannot be cut up.*

Panton Manufacturing Ltd
Panton Works | Hounslow | Middlesex | TW6 2BQ

TELEPHONE +44 (0)20 8353 0125
FACSIMILE +44 (0)20 8353 6783
EMAIL d.panton@panman.co.uk

8 October 20—

Mr H. Majid
Majid Enterprises
Grant Road
Bombay
INDIA

Dear Mr Majid

I am writing to you concerning your order, No. CU 1154/d, which you placed four weeks ago. At that time we had expected to be able to complete the order well within the delivery date which we gave you of 18 June, but since then we have heard that our main supplier of chrome has gone bankrupt.

It will be necessary to find an alternative supplier who can fulfil all the outstanding contracts we have to complete. As you will appreciate this will take some time, but we are confident that we should be able to deliver consignments to our customers by the middle of next month.

The units themselves have been assembled and only need completing. We regret this unfortunate situation over which we had no control, and apologize for the inconvenience caused. We will understand if you wish to cancel the order, but stress that we are confident that we will be able to complete delivery by the middle of next month.

Please let us know your decision as soon as possible. Thank you for your consideration.

Yours sincerely

D. Panton

D. Panton
Managing Director

Registered No. England
266135

1 Why have Panton Manufacturing not completed the order?

2 How do they intend to overcome the problem?

3 When do they now expect the order to be completed?

4 Can Majid Enterprises cancel the order if they want to?

5 What is the 'decision' referred to in the last paragraph?

6 Which words in the letter have a similar meaning to the following?

a with reference to
b unable to pay one's debts
c certain
d put together
e trouble
f understanding

[Email toolbar]

Send | File Edit View Insert Format Tools Actions Help

Arial | 10 | **B** *I* <u>U</u>

To...	Eric van Gellen
Cc...	
Subject:	Order HU 14449

Attn: Eric Van Gellen

Thank you for your order, No. HU 14449, which we received today. Unfortunately, we cannot offer the 35% trade discount you asked for. 25% is our maximum discount, even on large orders, as our prices are extremely competitive. Therefore, in this instance, I regret that we have to turn down your order.

Denis York
SP Wholesalers plc
King's Lynn, Norfolk
PE30 4SW
Tel.: +44 (0)1553 60841
Fax: +44 (0)1553 60923
Email: d.york@spw.co.uk

---

1 Why does Mr York refuse the order?

2 How does he generalize his refusal?

3 What is the implication of *in this instance* in the last sentence?

Points to remember

1 Even if you use an official order form when placing an order, it is a good idea to send a covering letter confirming terms of payment, discounts, delivery, and packing.

2 Orders should be acknowledged as soon as they are received. Email is a convenient way of acknowledging them quickly.

3 When sending an advice of despatch, remember that, if collection requires original documents, you cannot fax these or attach them to an email message.

4 If there are problems with delivery, tell your customer immediately what you intend to do to correct them. Apologize for the inconvenience.

5 If you turn an order down, be polite, and generalize the terms you use so that the customer does not think this refusal only applies to them.

5

Payment

6

INVOICES AND STATEMENTS

Invoices

INVOICES are one of the main documents used in trading. They are not only requests for payment but also records of transactions which give the buyer and seller information about what has been bought or sold, the terms of the sale, and details of the transaction. An invoice may be accompanied by a short covering letter or email offering additional information the customer might need.

— *Please find enclosed our Invoice No. B1951 for £329.43. The plugs you ordered have already been despatched to you, c/F, and you should receive them within the next few days.*

— *The enclosed invoice (No. D1167) for £723.60 is for 2 'Layeazee' chairs at £540.00 each less 33% trade discount. We look forward to receiving your remittance and will then send the chairs c/F.*

— *Our Invoice, No. TR335116 for €6,780.00 net is attached. We look forward to receiving your cheque, from which you may deduct 3% cash discount if payment is made within seven days.*

Pro forma invoices

A PRO FORMA INVOICE is one with the words *pro forma* typed or stamped on it, and is used:

— If the customer has to pre-pay (i.e. pay for goods before receiving them), they pay against the pro forma

— If the customer wants to make sure a quotation will not be changed, the pro-forma will say exactly what and how they will be charged

— If goods are sent on approval, on sale or return, or on consignment to an agent who will sell them on behalf of the principal

— As a customs document

A covering letter may accompany a pro forma invoice.

— *The enclosed Pro forma No. 1164 for £8,253.76 is for your Order No. C1534, which is now packed and awaiting despatch. As soon as we receive your cheque we will send the goods which should then reach you within a few days.*

— *We are sending the enclosed pro forma (No. H9181) for £3,960 gross, for the consignment of chairs you ordered on approval. We would appreciate it if you could return any unsold chairs by the end of May as agreed.*

— *Pro forma invoice, No. PL7715, is for your order, No. 652 1174, in confirmation of our quotation. The total of £15,351 includes cost, insurance, and freight.*

Statements of account

Rather than requiring immediate payment of invoices, suppliers may offer credit ▶ **see pages 118–136** in the form of open account facilities for an agreed period of time, usually a month but sometimes a quarter (three months). At the end of the period a STATEMENT OF ACCOUNT is sent to the customer, giving details of all the transactions between the buyer and seller for that period. The statement includes the BALANCE on the account, which is brought forward from the previous period and listed as ACCOUNT RENDERED. Invoices and DEBIT NOTES ▶ **see page 111** are added, while payments and CREDIT NOTES ▶ **see page 111** are deducted.

Statements of account rarely have letters with them unless there is a particular point that the supplier wants to make, e.g. that the account is OVERDUE, or that some special concession is available for prompt payment, but a compliments slip may be attached.

Note the expression AS AT (e.g. *as at 31 March*), which means *up to this date*.

— *I enclose your statement as at 31 July. May I remind you that your June statement is still outstanding, and ask you to settle as soon as possible?*

— *Please find enclosed your statement of account as at 31 May this year. If the balance of £161 is cleared within the next seven days, you can deduct a 3% cash discount.*

SETTLEMENT OF ACCOUNTS

Methods of payment: trade within the UK

Here is a list of methods of payment which can be used in trade within the UK.

Bank draft

In the case of a BANK DRAFT, the customer buys a cheque from the bank for the amount he or she wants to pay and sends it to the supplier. Banks usually require two of their directors' signatures on drafts, and make a small charge.

Bank transfer

A BANK TRANSFER is when a bank moves money by order from one account to another.

Bill of exchange

In BILL OF EXCHANGE (B/E) transactions the supplier draws a bill on the customer. The bill states that the customer will pay the supplier an amount within a stated time, e.g. thirty days. The bill is sent direct to the customer or paid through a bank. If the bill is a SIGHT DRAFT, the customer will pay immediately (i.e. on 'sight' or presentation). If the bill is a TERM DRAFT the customer signs (accepts) the bill before the goods are sent and pays later.
▶ **See pages 147–154 for more on bill of exchange transactions.**

Cheque

The customer must have a CURRENT ACCOUNT, or certain types of SAVINGS ACCOUNT, to pay by cheque ▶ **see pages 138–139.** Cheques can take three working days to clear through the commercial banks, and can be open, to pay cash, or closed (crossed), to be paid into an account.

Credit transfer

In the case of CREDIT TRANSFERS, the customer fills out a bank GIRO slip and hands it in to a bank with a cheque. The bank then transfers the money to the supplier.

Debit / credit card payment

DEBIT and CREDIT CARD payments can be made either direct on the phone, or on the Internet.

Letter of credit

A LETTER OF CREDIT (L/C) is a document issued by a bank on a customer's request, ordering an amount of money to be paid to a supplier. Payments by letter of credit can be made within the UK, but this method is more common in overseas transactions ▶ **see page 79.**

Cash on delivery

CASH ON DELIVERY (COD) is a service offered by the Post Office. They will deliver goods and accept payment on behalf of the supplier.

Post Office Giro

The Post Office Giro system allows a customer to send a payment to a supplier, whether they have a Post Office Giro account or not.

Postal order

POSTAL ORDERS can be bought from the Post Office, usually to pay small amounts, and sent to the supplier direct. They can either be CROSSED, in which case the money can only be paid into the supplier's account, or left open for the supplier to cash.

Methods of payment: trade outside the UK

Bank transfer

The customer orders a bank to transfer money to the supplier's account. If telegraphed, this is known as a TELEGRAPHIC TRANSFER (TT). The Society for Worldwide Interbank Financial Communications (SWIFT) offers a twenty-four-hour international bank transfer service. Businesses in European Union (EU) countries often use the SWIFT system. Payments are subject to EU directives, e.g. transfers have to be made within six days.

Bill of exchange

The procedure is the same as that for trade in the UK, but shipping documents usually accompany bills when the bank acts as an intermediary in international transactions.

Cheque

It is possible to pay an overseas supplier by cheque, but it takes a long time before they get their money. In a transaction between businesses in Germany and the UK, for example, the supplier could wait up to three weeks for payment.

Documentary credit

When a letter of credit is accompanied by shipping documents it is called a DOCUMENTARY CREDIT. The money is credited to the supplier's account as soon as confirmation of shipment is made.

See pages 155–166 for more on documentary credit transactions.

International bank draft

An INTERNATIONAL BANK DRAFT is a cheque which a bank draws on itself and sells to the customer, who then sends it to their supplier. The supplier's bank should usually have either an account or an agreement with the customer's bank.

International money order

INTERNATIONAL MONEY ORDERS (IMOs) can be bought at most banks in the UK and are paid for in sterling or dollars. The bank fills out the order for the customer then, for a small charge, hands the IMO over, and the buyer sends it to the supplier. IMOs can be either cashed or credited to the supplier's account.

International Post Office Giro

Payment by International Post Office Giro can be made when either the customer or supplier, or both, do not have bank accounts. An order for the amount to be paid is filled out at a Post Office, which forwards it to the Giro Centre. The Giro Centre will send the amount to a Post Office in the supplier's country, where the supplier will receive a postal cheque. They can then either cash it, or pay it into a bank account. Giros are charged at a flat rate.

Promissory note

A PROMISSORY NOTE is, strictly speaking, not a method of payment but simply a written promise from a customer to a supplier that the former will pay the amount stated, either on demand or after a certain date. In effect, a promissory note is an IOU (*I owe you*).

Advice of payment

Correspondence advising payment, particularly in the UK, tends to be short and routine.

— *We have pleasure in enclosing our postal order / cheque / bank draft for £—— in payment of your statement Invoice No. —— dated …*
— *I have instructed my bank today to transfer £1,161.00 to your account in payment of your 31 May statement.*
— *We have drawn a cheque for £267.00 in payment of your Invoice No. L231 dated 2 August. This can be paid into your account or cashed at any Post Office.*

Correspondence confirming payment in trade transactions outside the UK may be more complicated if you want to make specific points.

— *Thank you for your prompt delivery. Please find enclosed our draft for £4,341 drawn on Eastland City Bank, Sommerville. Could you please acknowledge receipt?*
— *We would like to inform you that we have arranged for a credit transfer through our bank, the Hammergsbank, Bergen, for £3,120 in payment of Invoice No. R1641. Could you confirm the transfer has been made as soon as the correspondent bank advises you?*
— *We have pleasure in enclosing our bank draft for £5,141.53 as payment on Pro forma Invoice No. 5512. Please advise us when the goods will be shipped and are likely to reach Barcelona.*
— *You will be pleased to hear that we have accepted your bill and now have the documents. We shall collect the consignment as soon as it arrives in Bonn and pay your bill on the date agreed.*
— *Our bank informs us that they now have the shipping documents, and will be transferring the proceeds of our letter of credit to your account.*

6

Acknowledgement of payment

Correspondence acknowledging payment also tends to be short.

— *Thank you for your draft / credit transfer for £—— in payment of our statement / invoice No. —— dated …*

— *Our bank advised us today that your transfer of £3,761.00 was credited to our account. Thank you for paying so promptly, and we hope to hear from you again soon.*

— *We received your Giro slip today informing us that you had paid £1,126.00 into our account in settlement of invoice No. L231. Thank you for letting us know, and we look forward to hearing from you again in the near future.*

— *Thank you for sending your draft for invoice No. 11871 so promptly. We feel sure you will be pleased with the consignment and look forward to receiving your next order.*

— *We received advice from our bank this morning that your transfer for invoice No. RE1641 has been credited to our account. We would like to thank you, and would be pleased to help if you need further information, or would like to place another order.*

— *Our bank informed us today that you accepted our bill (No. BE 2255) and the documents have been transferred to you. We are sure you will be pleased with the consignment.*

— *The Nippon Bank in Tokushima have told us that the proceeds of your letter of credit have been credited to our account. Thank you for your custom, and we hope you will be in touch with us again. We have pleasure in enclosing our new summer catalogue.*

D & R Electrical Ltd

Invoice

35 Hill Street
Seacroft
Leeds
LS14 1ND

Telephone +44 (0)113 640181
Facsimile +44 (0)113 643782
Email accounts@drelec.co.uk

Invoice No. 81951

To P. Gwent & Co. Ltd
43 Ring Road
Leeds LS16 2BN

Your order No. L57/5

Date 1 May 20—

Number	Description	Total
40	RVA 250 volt plugs @ 65p. each	£26.00
	Add VAT 17.5%	£4.55
	Add p&p	£4.00
		£34.55

E&OE

Registered London No. 115662
VAT Reg. No. 154 6627 19

Invoice 1

This is a relatively simple invoice. Note the addition for Value Added Tax (VAT) and POSTAGE AND PACKING (P&P). The letters E&OE at the bottom mean ERRORS AND OMISSIONS EXCEPTED; in other words, if there is a mistake on the invoice, the supplier has the right to correct it by asking for more money or giving a refund.

Invoice 2

This invoice is rather more complicated. It is from Glaston Potteries to their Canadian customers, MacKenzie Bros. It would be sent with copies and shipping documents to The Canadian Union Trust Bank via the Burnley Bank, who are MacKenzie's agents in the UK. These documents prove that a shipment has been made from Glaston Potteries to MacKenzie Bros so that the Canadian bank can now release the money that MacKenzie Bros said they would pay in their letter of credit. There will also be additional charges that MacKenzie Bros will pay their bank for handling the transaction.

It might be helpful to refer back to enquiry, reply, order, and advice ▶see pages 44, 56, 68, and 69.

You will see from the invoice that CIF charges have been deducted from the gross price. This is because under UK law the customer must be told exactly what they are paying for. And in this case CIF has also been deducted so that the 10% special discount can be taken off the net price.

Clayfield | Burnley | BB10 1RQ

GLASTON POTTERIES LTD

Telephone +44 (0)1282 46125
Facsimile +44 (0)1282 63182
Email j.merton@glaston.co.uk
www.glaston.com

Invoice No. 1096/A3   11 July 20—

MacKenzie Bros Ltd
1–5 Whale Drive
Dawson
Ontario
CANADA

Your order No. R1432

Quantity	Description	Cat. No.	£ each	£		
35	Earthenware	R194	@ 55.00	set	1,925.00
10	Wedgwood	W161	@ 47.50	set	475.00
15	Bone/Tea	T21	@ 23.00	set	345.00
10	Staffordshire Red	S73	@ 52.60	set	526.00
	CIF	3,271.00			3,271.00
	Less Cost & Freight Liverpool–Dawson	347.00			
	Less Insurance	292.00			
10% discount off net price	2,632.00		Less Disc.		263.20
			Total		2,368.80

E & OE

Registered No. 716481
VAT Registered No. 133 53431 08

1 Which reference would MacKenzie Bros use when referring to this invoice?

2 What does the sign @ mean in the calculations?

3 What is the net total of the invoice?

4 What charges have been taken off the gross price?

5 How have Glaston Potteries indicated they have the right to correct the invoice if there is a mistake?

Seymore Furniture Ltd

Telephone: +44 (0)1628 26755
Fax: +44 (0)1628 26756
Email: accounts@seymore.co.uk
Registered No. 18514391 London
VAT No. 231 6188 31

C.R. Méndez SA
Avda del Ejército 83
E-48015 Bilbao

Statement

Tib Street
Maidenhead
Berkshire
SL6 5D2
UK

31 May 20—

Date	Item	Debit	Credit	Balance
20—	£	£	£	£
1 May	Account Rendered			270.00
2 May	Inv. L8992	260.00		530.00
8 May	D/N 311	52.00		582.00
12 May	Cash		100.00	482.00
14 May	Inv. L8995	720.00		1,202.00
20 May	C/N C517		80.00	1,122.00
25 May	Cash		600.00	522.00

E. & O. E. Cash Disc. 3% if paid within 7 days

Statement of account

This statement is an account of the transactions that took place over the month of May between Seymore Furniture and their customer, C.R. Méndez. You will see that a debit note (D/N 311) and a credit note (C/N C517) are listed as well as the invoices they corrected. There are also two payments which are listed here as cash, although the word *cheque* can also be used in this context.

1 How much did C.R. Méndez owe at the beginning of the month?

2 How much was the error in their favour?

3 What did they pay during the month?

4 What was the total amount of their purchases during May?

5 How will their 1 June statement open?

6 Is there an allowance for payment within a certain time?

Advice of payment 1

This letter continues previous correspondence ▸ see page 45 (enquiry), page 58 (reply and quotation), pages 64–65 (order), and pages 66–67 (the email messages acknowledging the order and advising despatch). The customer, Mr Crane of F. Lynch & Co., uses this confirmation of payment to ask for the terms of payment to be revised ▸ see also page 118. If you look back to page 58, you will see that Satex S.p.A. said they would review the terms after a while. Notice how the letter begins with confirmation of payment, then states the present arrangement, and finally makes the next order subject to Mr Causio accepting the new terms. The letter is firm, but still polite. For this kind of correspondence a letter is more appropriate than an email message.

F. Lynch & Co. Ltd

Head Office
Nesson House
Newell Street
Birmingham
B3 3EL

Telephone: +44 (0)21 236 6571
Fax: +44 (0)21 236 8592
Email: pcrane@lynch.co.uk
www.lynch.com

Your ref:
Our ref: Order 14463

16 June 20—

Satex S.p.A.
Via di Pietra Papa
00146 Roma
ITALY

Attn Mr D. Causio

Dear Mr Causio

Thank you for being so prompt in sending the documents for our last order, No. 14463. We have accepted the sight bill, and the bank should send you an advice shortly.

We have been dealing with you on a cash against documents basis for over a year and would like to change to payment by 40-day bill of exchange, documents against acceptance.

When we first contacted you last February you told us that you would be prepared to reconsider terms of payment once we had established a trading association. We think that sufficient time has elapsed for us to be allowed the terms we have asked for. If you need references, we will be glad to supply them.

As we are planning to send another order within the month, could you please confirm that you agree to these new terms of payment?

Yours sincerely

Peter Crane

Peter Crane
Chief Buyer

```
✉                                                            _ □ ×
   ▭ Send   🖫 🖨 ✂ 🖻 🖻  🖹 📎  📖 👤           🖹 Options...  ❓

   [          ▾]  [    ▾] 🎨 B I U  📄 ▤ ▤ ▤ ▥ ▥

   File  Edit  View  Insert  Format  Tools  Actions  Help
```

To...	John Merton
Cc...	

Subject: Payment; packing

📄W

Breakages

Dear Mr Merton

We have instructed our bank to arrange for a letter of credit for £6,158.92 to be paid against your pro forma invoice No. G1152/S. The proceeds will be credited to you as soon as Canadian Trust receive the documents.

We usually ask you to wrap each piece of crockery individually and pack no more than ten sets into a crate to allow for easy and safe handling. This was not done with our last consignment and as a consequence there were breakages (see attached list). We would like either replacements to be included in our next shipment, or your credit note.

Richard MacKenzie

Advice of payment 2

This email also continues previous correspondence ▶see page 44 (enquiry) page 56 (reply), page 68 (order), page 69 (advice of despatch), and page 82 (invoice). MacKenzie Bros use the email both to confirm payment and to make a complaint about the packing ▶see also pages 100–116. Note that MacKenzie Bros will accept either replacements for the broken crockery or a credit note. Glaston Potteries will claim on their insurance company for the breakages, although they might not get compensation as they have been negligent in their packing.

6

DELAYED PAYMENT

Asking for more time to pay

This is an area of correspondence where you must use your own judgement about how confidential the information is. Would an open system like email or fax be satisfactory, or should you send a letter? These situations can be sensitive.

If you are writing to a supplier to explain why you have not cleared an account, remember that they are mainly interested in when the account will be paid. So, while you must state why you have not paid, you must also explain when and how you intend to pay.

Begin the letter with your creditor's name (this should always be done once correspondence has been established, but it is essential in this case: if you owe someone money, you should know and use their name). Refer to the account and apologize in clear, objective language (i.e. do not use over-elaborate language like *Please forgive me for not settling my indebtedness to you*). Notice the verbs *clear* and *settle* (an account) are used rather than *pay*.

— *I am sorry that I was not able to clear my July account.*
— *We regret we were unable to send a cheque to settle our account for the last quarter.*

Explain why you cannot clear the account, but do not be dramatic.

— *The dock strike which has been going on for the past six weeks has made it impossible to ship our products, and as our customers have not been able to pay us, we have not been able to clear our own suppliers' accounts yet.*
— *A warehouse flood destroyed the majority of the Zenith 900 components. We are waiting for our insurance company to settle our claim so that we can renew our stock and pay our suppliers.*
— *We were not able to settle the account because of the bankruptcy of one of our main customers. The debt was considerable and its loss has made it difficult for us to pay our suppliers.*

Notice in the last example above that there is no reference to the bankrupt customer's name, nor how much they owed. It would be unethical to give this sort of information. Also notice how the debtor generalizes the situation, explaining that other suppliers have not been paid yet.

You may be able to pay some money ON ACCOUNT, i.e. to pay part of what you owe. This shows a willingness to clear the debt, and will gain your creditor's confidence.

— *We will try to settle your invoice within the next four weeks. Meanwhile the enclosed cheque for £2,500.00 is part payment on account.*

If you cannot offer a part payment, give as precise a date of payment as you can.

— *Once the strike is over, which should be within the next few days, we will be able to clear the balance.*
— *As soon as the insurance company sends us compensation, we will settle the account. We expect this to be within the next two weeks.*

Replying to requests for more time

There are three possible ways in which you might reply to a request from a customer for more time to settle an account: you may agree to their request, refuse it, or suggest a compromise.

If you agree to the request, a short letter is all that is needed.

— *Thank you for your letter concerning the outstanding balance on your account. I sympathize with the problem you have had in clearing the balance and am willing to extend the credit for another six weeks. Would you please confirm that the credit will be settled then?*
— *I was sorry to hear about the difficulties you have been experiencing in getting components to complete orders, and realize that without sales it is difficult to settle outstanding accounts. Therefore your account has been extended another month, but I will have to insist on payment by the end of July.*

If you refuse the request, you will need to explain, politely, why you are refusing.

— *Thank you for your letter explaining why you cannot clear your January statement for £2,167.54. I appreciate your difficulty, but we ourselves have to pay our own suppliers and therefore must insist on payment within the next ten days. We look forward to receiving your remittance.*

— *With reference to your letter of 6 August in which you explained why the outstanding invoice, No. YR 88190 C, has not been cleared, we understand the problems you have been facing in the current recession. However, it was because of the present economic climate that we allowed you a two-month period to settle, and while we would like to offer you more time to clear the balance, our own financial position makes this impossible. Therefore, we must ask you to settle the account within the next fortnight.*

An offer of a compromise (for example paying part of the money) will also need an explanation.

— *Thank you for writing to let us know why the May account is still outstanding. Unfortunately, we cannot extend the credit any longer as we allowed a considerable discount for prompt payment. Nevertheless, in view of the difficulties you have been having with your two major customers, we are prepared to compromise and suggest that you clear half the outstanding balance immediately by sending a cheque for £4,871.00, and clear the remainder by the end of next month. We look forward to your remittance and confirmation that the balance of the account will be cleared in July.*

— *I was sorry to hear about the strike which has held up production in your plant for the past few weeks and understand why you need more time to clear your account. Nevertheless, when we allowed open account terms, we emphasized this was on condition balances were cleared promptly on due dates as credit facilities put a strain on our own cash flow situation. However, because of your previous custom with us we are quite willing to allow you to clear half the balance, £5,189, by sending us a sight draft, see enclosed B/E No. 898101, and clear the outstanding amount by accepting the enclosed draft B/E No. 898108, drawn at 30 days. We look forward to receiving your acceptance and confirmation.*

REQUESTS FOR PAYMENT

First request

Never immediately assume your customers have no intention of paying their account if the balance is overdue. There may be a number of reasons for this: they may not have received your statement; they may have sent a cheque which has been lost; or they may have just overlooked the account. Therefore, a first request should take the form of a polite enquiry. Try to make the letter impersonal. You can do this by using the definite article, e.g. *the* outstanding balance instead of **your** outstanding balance; using the passive voice, e.g. *to be cleared* instead of *which you must clear*; and modifying imperatives, e.g. *should* instead of *must*. The first example will give you an idea of this style.

— *We are writing concerning the outstanding October account for £3,171.63 (copy enclosed), which should have been cleared last month. Please could you contact us and let us know why the balance has not been paid?*

— *We think you may have overlooked invoice No. 5A 1910 for £351.95 (see copy) which was due last month. Could you please let us have a cheque to clear the amount as soon as possible? If payment has already been sent, please disregard this letter.*

Second request

If a customer intends to pay, they usually answer a first request immediately, offering an apology for having overlooked the account, or an explanation. But if they acknowledge your request but still do not pay, or do not answer at all, then you can make a second request. As with first requests, you should include copies

of the relevant invoices and statements, and mention any previous correspondence.
— *We wrote to you on 3 March concerning our January statement, which is still outstanding. Enclosed you will find a copy of the statement and our letter.*
— *This is the second letter I have sent you with regard to your March account, which has not yet been cleared. My first letter, dated 21 April, asked why the account had not been paid, and you will see from the enclosed that …*

State that you have not received payment, if this was promised in the reply, or that no reply has been received.
— *Since I wrote we have not received either a reply or remittance from you.*
— *I would like to know why you have neither replied to my letter nor sent a cheque to clear the outstanding balance.*
— *In your reply to my letter of 21 April, you promised that the account would be cleared by the end of May, yet I have not received your remittance or an explanation.*

Insist that you receive payment or an answer within a certain time.
— *We must now insist that you clear this account within the next seven days, or at least offer an explanation for not clearing it.*
— *As we have traded for some time, we have not pressed for payment. However, we must now insist that either you settle the account before the end of this month or offer a reasonable explanation for not doing so.*
— *I would appreciate receiving your remittance by return of post, or failing that, your reasons for not clearing this account.*

Third request (final demand)

Review the situation from the time the account should have been paid.
— *We have written you two letters, dated 22 September and 19 October, and have sent copies of the outstanding invoices with them, but have not received either a reply or remittance.*
— *I wrote to you twice, on 8 May and 4 June, concerning your balance of $15,934.00, which has been outstanding since April, but as yet have not received a reply.*
— *I am writing to you about your June account which I had hoped would have been cleared by now. On 5 July and 12 August, I sent letters with copies of invoices and statements, asking you to clear the balance or at least offer an explanation of why you have not sent a remittance.*

Explain that you have been patient.
— *When we arranged terms, we offered you payment against monthly statements, yet it has been three months since you wrote promising the account would be cleared. We now, reluctantly, assume that you have no intention of clearing the balance.*
— *We had expected this matter to have been settled at least two months ago, but you have shown no indication of cooperating with us.*

Let the customer know what you are going to do, but do not threaten legal action unless you intend to take it, as it will make you look weak and indecisive. In the two examples below legal action is not threatened.
— *We feel that you have been given sufficient time to clear this balance and now insist on payment within the next ten days.*
— *We must now press you to clear this outstanding account. Please send your remittance immediately.*

In the next two examples legal action is threatened. Notice the language used to do this. Do not use obscure language (e.g. *We will take other steps* or *We will use other methods to enforce payment*), and do not try to sound like a lawyer (e.g. *Unless payment is forthcoming, we will be obliged to take steps to enforce our claims*). A direct, clear statement is more effective.
— *We were disappointed that you did not bother to reply to either of our letters asking you to clear your account, and you have left us with no alternative but to take legal action.*
— *We are giving you a further seven days to send your remittance after which we will hand over the matter to our solicitors.*

D. van Basten SA

Heidelberglaan 2
Postbus 80.115
NL–3508 TC
Utrecht

Telefoon (+31) 30–532 044
Fax (+31) 30–581 617
Email vanBasten.d@vanBasten.co.nl
www.vanBasten.com

Request for more time

D. van Basten write to their suppliers to warn them that payment will be delayed.

6

Example letter

15 January 20—

Herr Dieter Schubert
Director
DVB Industries GmbH
Correnstrasse 250
D–40000 Münster

Dear Herr Schubert

I am sorry that we were not able to clear your November statement for €5,850 and December invoice, No. 7713, for $1,289. We had intended to pay the statement as usual, but a large cash shipment to one of our customers in Australia was part of the cargo destroyed in the fire on the *Tippa* when she docked in Bombay in late November.

Our insurance company have promised us compensation within the next few weeks. Once we have received this, the account will be paid in full.

We feel confident that you will appreciate the situation and hope you can bear with us until the matter is settled.

Yours sincerely

D. van Basten

D. van Basten (Ms)
Director

1 What is the total outstanding balance?

2 What explanation is given for non-payment?

3 Why is Ms van Basten confident that she can clear the account?

4 Which words in the letter have a similar meaning to the following?

a pay
b planned
c goods carried in a ship or aircraft
d payment to reduce the effects of loss or damage
e understand

Agreeing to more time

This is a reply to the previous letter. Herr Schubert accepts the request and asks for payment as soon as possible.

DVB Industries GmbH

Correnstrasse 250
D–40000 Münster

Tel: (+49) 251–86613
Fax: (+49) 251–90271
Email: schubd@dvb.co.de

20 January 20—

Ms D. van Basten
Director
D. van Basten S.A.
Heidelberglaan 2
Postbus 80.115
NL–3508 TC
Utrecht

Dear Ms van Basten

Thank you for your letter of 15 January regarding our November statement and December invoice No. 7713.

We were sorry to hear about the difficulties you have had, and understand the situation. However, we would appreciate it if you could clear the account as soon as possible, as we ourselves have suppliers to pay.

We look forward to hearing from you soon.

Yours sincerely

Dieter Schubert

Dieter Schubert
Director

L. Franksen plc

Prince of Wales Road
Sheffield
S9 4EX

Telephone +44 (0)742 24789
Fax +44 (0) 742 25193
Email franksenl@frank.co.uk

Request for an extension

In this letter the customer asks for his bill of exchange to be extended for another sixty days.

6

Example letter

19 May 20—

Mr D. Bishkin
Zenith S.A.
Haldenstrasse 118
3000 Bern 22
SWITZERLAND

Dear Mr Bishkin

I regret to inform you that I will not be able to meet my bill, No. B/E 7714, for 35,498.00SF due on 6 June.

My government has put an embargo on all machine exports to Zurimba, and consequently we have found ourselves in temporary difficulties as we had three major cash consignments for that country. However, I am at present discussing sales of these consignments with two large Brazilian importers, and am certain that they will take the goods.

Could you allow me a further 60 days to clear my account, and draw a new bill on me, with interest of, say, 6% added for the extension of time?

I would be most grateful if you could help me in this matter.

Yours sincerely

Leo Franksen

Leo Franksen
Director

1 What expression does Mr Franksen use instead of *pay*?

2 What is an *embargo*?

3 How does Mr Franksen intend to get the money for the cargo he cannot sell to Zurimba?

4 What solution does he suggest to the problem?

5 Which words in the letter have a similar meaning to the following?

a not permanent
b large
c a quantity of goods
d prepare (e.g. a bill of exchange / cheque)

Offer of a compromise

In this case Mr Bishkin, the supplier, has the legal right to present the bill to his bank for payment, then if it is not paid, call a lawyer to PROTEST the bill, i.e. prevent Mr Franksen DISHONOURING it (denying that it was presented for payment). The costs of this procedure are paid by the customer. However, the customer in this case has not said they *will not* pay, but *cannot* pay at present. If Mr Bishkin forced Mr Franksen to pay, the result might be bankruptcy, and all Mr Bishkin would get is a percentage of his customer's debts like the other creditors. This could be as small as five per cent of the total debt. So he does not want to force the bill on Mr Franksen yet. On the other hand, he has waited long enough for his money, and cannot be expected to wait another sixty days, even with the interest offered. In his reply to Mr Franksen he offers a compromise.

Haldenstrasse 118 | 3000 Bern 22 | Switzerland

Zenith S.A.

Tel +41 31 30172
Fax +41 31 82357
Email bishn@zenith.co.ch

23 May 20—

Mr L. Franksen
L. Franksen plc
Prince of Wales Road
Sheffield S9 4EX
UK

Dear Mr Franksen

Bill No. B/E 7714

I was sorry to learn about the embargo your government has placed on exports to Zurimba and of the problems this has created. However, the above bill already allows credit for 40 days, and although I appreciate your offer of an additional 6% interest on the outstanding 35,498.00SF, it is impossible for me to allow a further 60 days' credit as I myself have commitments.

I think the following solution might help us both.

You need not add interest on the present amount, but I have enclosed a new draft (B/E 7731) for 17,749.00SF, which is half the outstanding balance, and will allow you 40 days to pay it. But I expect you to pay the remaining 17,749.00SF by banker's draft.

Please confirm your acceptance by signing the enclosed bill and sending it to me with your draft by return of post.

I hope that your negotiations with the Brazilian importers have a positive outcome and trust that this setback will soon be resolved.

Yours sincerely

N. Bishkin

N. Bishkin (Mr)
Director

Enc. Bill B/E 7731

---

1 Is Mr Bishkin sympathetic to Mr Franksen's problem?

2 Why does he say he cannot wait a further sixty days for payment?

3 Does he want the six per cent interest added on?

4 What compromise does he suggest?

5 How will he know that Mr Franksen has accepted his offer?

HOMEMAKERS

54–59 Riverside, Cardiff CF1 1JW
Telephone: +44 (0)29 20 49721
Fax: +44 (0)29 20 49937
Email: rcliff@homemakers.com
Registered No. C135162

20 November 20—

R. Hughes & Son Ltd
21 Mead Road
Swansea
West Glamorgan 3ST 1DR

Dear Robert

I am writing concerning our invoice No. H931 for £919.63, a copy of which is enclosed. It appears that this invoice has not yet been settled.

I see from our records that since we began trading you have cleared your accounts regularly on the due dates. That is why I wondered if any problems have arisen which I might be able to help you with? Please let me know if I can be of assistance.

Yours sincerely

Richard Cliff

Richard Cliff
Director

Reply to first request

You will see from Mr Hughes' reply to Mr Cliff's letter that the invoice had been paid, not by cheque, which was Mr Hughes' usual method of payment, but by credit transfer. If Mr Cliff had looked at his bank statement, he would have seen that the money had been credited. However, as Mr Hughes changed his method of payment, he should have informed his supplier as banks do not always advise credit transfers. This is a good example of why you should not assume that a customer has failed to pay an account. Remember that this type of correspondence is best handled by letter, not email or fax.

R. Hughes & Son Ltd

21 Mead Road, Swansea
West Glamorgan 3ST 1DR
Telephone: +44 (0)1792 58441
Fax: Swansea +44 (0)1792 59472
Email: r.hughes@huson.co.uk

24th November 20—

Mr R. Cliff
Homemakers Ltd
54–59 Riverside
Cardiff CF1 1JW

Dear Richard

I was surprised to receive your letter of 20 November in which you said you had not received payment for invoice No. H931.

I instructed my bank, The Welsh Co-operative Bank, Swansea, to credit your account in Barnley's Bank, Cardiff, with the £919.63 on 2nd November.

As my bank statement showed the money had been debited to my account, I assumed that it had been credited to your account as well. It is possible that your bank has not advised you yet. Could you please check this with Barnley's, and if there are any problems let me know, so that I can make enquiries here?

Yours sincerely

Robert Hughes

Robert Hughes

VAT NO. 215 2261 30

INGENIEROS INDUSTRIALES SA

Barrio de Ibaeta s/n   E–20009   San Sebastian

Tel: (+34) 943 212800	Fecha: **30 August 20—**
Fax: (+34) 943 618590	Su ref:
Email: r.costello@ingenieros.co.es	Ns. ref: **613/02**

Sig. D. Giordianino
Omega S.p.A.
Via Agnello 2153
20121 Milano
Italy

Dear Sig. Giordianino

With reference to my letter of 10 August, I enclose copy invoices which made up your June statement, the balance of which still remains outstanding.

Having dealt with you for some time, we are concerned that we have neither received your remittance nor any explanation as to why the balance of €6,000.00 has not been cleared. Please would you either reply with an explanation or send us a cheque to clear the account within the next seven days?

Yours sincerely

R. Costello

R. Costello (Sr)
Credit Controller
Encl.

This is an example of a second request for payment, but you will see that, even though this is a second letter, Sr Costello still avoids an unfriendly tone.

Reply to second request

Here is Sig. Giordianino's reply to Sr Costello's letter.

 **Omega**

Omega S.p.A.
Viale Mortidio 61269 I—10125 Torino

Telefono (+39)—11—5981461
Telefax (+39)—11—628351
Email giordiand@omega.co.it
www.omega.it

Vs. rif. **613/02**
Ns. rif. **SG/DA**

Date 1 September 20—

Sr R. Costello
Credit Controller
Ingenieros Industriales SA
Barrio de Ibaeta s/n
E-20009 San Sebastian

Dear Sr Costello

First let me apologize for not having cleared our June statement or replying to your letter of 10 August. However, I am surprised that you did not receive our circular letter informing all our suppliers that we were moving from Milan to Turin. I have checked our post book, and find that a letter was sent to you on June 30.

As you will see from the copy enclosed, we warned suppliers that there might be some delay in clearing accounts and replying to correspondence as the move would involve employing new staff who needed time to get used to our accounts and filing systems.

You will be pleased to hear that we have now settled into our new offices and will have a fully trained staff by the end of next month. Meanwhile, I am enclosing a cheque for €20,000 on account, and will send a full settlement of your June statement within the next few days.

Could you please note our new address for future reference?

Yours sincerely

D. Giordianino

D. Giordianino (Sig.)
Accountant

Enc. Bank Draft No. 427322 for €20,000

1 Why hadn't Omega cleared their June statement?

2 What has Sig. Giordianino done about the outstanding account, and what will he do in the near future?

3 What has he asked Sr Costello to do to ensure that letters get to him?

Delta Computers Ltd
Bradfield Estate
Bradfield Road
Wellingborough
Northamptonshire
NN8 4HB

Telephone +44 (0)1933 16431/2/3/4
Fax +44 (0)1933 20016
Email millarj@delta.com
www.delta.com

Your Ref:
Our Ref:

9 December 20—

P. Theopolis SA
561 3rd September Street
GR–I04 32
Athens

Dear Mr Theopolis

Account No. TYG 99014

We wrote to you on two occasions, 21 October and 14 November, concerning the above account, which now has an outstanding balance of £3,541.46 and is made up of the copy invoices enclosed.

We have waited three months for either a reply to explain why the balance has not been cleared, or a remittance, but have received neither.

We are reluctant to take legal action to recover the amount, but you leave us no alternative. Unless we receive your remittance within the next ten days, we will instruct our solicitors to start proceedings.

Yours sincerely

J. Millar

J. Millar (Mrs)
Chief Accountant

Enc. invoice copies

Reg. England 1831713
VAT 2419 62114

1 What is enclosed with the letter?

2 How long has the balance remained unpaid?

3 Do Delta Computers plan to take legal action?

4 What phrase is used which has a similar meaning to *take legal action*?

6

Points to remember

1 Invoices are records of transactions as well as requests for payment. An invoice may be accompanied by a short covering letter or email.

2 Pro forma invoices are used in the case of pre-payment, when they are needed for documentation, or to inform the customer of the price.

3 Statements of account are sent monthly or quarterly, and include details of all transactions within the period.

4 There are various methods of payment available through banks and the Post Office.

5 Letters advising and acknowledging payment tend to be short and routine, but they may be used to propose new terms of payment or to make complaints.

6 If you are asking for more time to pay, you should apologize for not having cleared the account on the due date, explain why you have not paid, and when and how you intend to clear the balance. Remember, your creditors are more interested in when they will get their money than in good excuses.

7 Three steps are usually taken by a supplier to recover a debt. The first is to write a polite letter which accepts that there may be a good reason why the account has not yet been cleared. The second is a more insistent request which refers to the letter you have already sent, and encloses copies of invoices and statements. You can, in the second request, state that you expect payment or a reply within a reasonable time. A final demand must be handled with restraint. Review what has happened, explain the balance has been outstanding for a long period, and if necessary threaten legal action if the account is not paid within a specified period.

Complaints and adjustments

7

UNJUSTIFIED COMPLAINTS

Before you complain, make absolutely sure your facts are right.

If you have to respond to an unjustified complaint, be polite and remember that anyone can make a mistake. Below are two examples of unjustified complaints, and the replies to them. Notice how restrained the replies are.

— *Dear Sir*

I strongly object to the extra charge of £9.00 which you have added to my statement. When I sent my cheque for £256.00 last week, I thought it cleared this balance. Now I find …

— *Dear Mr Axeby*

We received your letter today complaining of an extra charge of £9.00 on your May statement. I think if you check the statement you will find that the amount due was £265.00 not £256.00 which accounts for the £9.00 difference. I have enclosed a copy of the statement and …

— *Dear Sir*

I could not believe it when I read that your prices have now been increased by £30.00. To have to pay £55.00 for an article that was £25.00 only a few months ago is outrageous! The government is fighting inflation …

— *Dear Mr Richardson*

Thank you for your letter. I checked the item you referred to, the Scriva Pen, catalogue No. G14 on our price-list. The price of the pen has been increased from £25.00 to £30.00, not by £30.00, and I think you will agree that for a fountain pen this is not an unreasonable increase considering that the cost of our materials has doubled in the past few months.

MAKING GENERAL COMPLAINTS

When sending a complaint, you will need to decide whether it is appropriate to use fax or email, where privacy cannot be guaranteed, or to write a letter. Some complaints, e.g. a mistake in a small payment or in the number of goods despatched, can be faxed or emailed, but a letter should be used for larger or more serious complaints.

Opening

Do not delay. Complain as soon as you realize a mistake has been made; delay weakens your case and can complicate the matter as details may be forgotten. There is no need to open by apologizing for the need to complain (*We regret to inform you …, I am sorry to have to write to you about …*) as this also weakens your case. Simply begin:

— *We would like to inform you …*
— *I am writing to complain about …*
— *I am writing with reference to Order No. P32, which we received yesterday.*

The language of complaints

Emotional terms like *disgusted, infuriated,* or *amazed* have no place in business. You can express dissatisfaction by saying:

— *This is the third time this mistake has occurred and we are far from satisfied with the service you offer.*
— *Unless you can fulfil our orders efficiently in the future we will have to consider changing to another supplier.*
— *Please ensure that this sort of problem does not arise again.*

Do not be rude or personal. In most cases correspondence between companies takes place between employees in various departments. Nothing is gained by being rude to the individual you are writing to. You may antagonize someone who has probably had nothing to do with the error and, rather than getting it corrected, he or she could become defensive and difficult to deal with. Therefore, do not use sentences like:

— *You must correct your mistake as soon as possible.*
— *You made an error on the statement.*
— *You don't understand the terms of discount. We told you to deduct discount from net prices, not CIF prices.*

Use the passive and impersonal structures mentioned earlier ▸ **see page 87**.
— *The mistake must be corrected as soon as possible.*
— *There appears to be an error on the statement.*
— *There seems to be some misunderstanding regarding terms of discount. Discount is deducted from net prices, not CIF prices.*

Do not use words like *fault* (*your fault, our fault*) or *blame* (*you are to blame*) – these expressions are rude and childish. Do not write:
— *It is not our fault. It is probably the fault of your despatch department.*

Instead, write:
— *The mistake could not have originated here, and must be connected with the despatch of the goods.*

Never blame your own staff, and finally, while writing the complaint remember that your supplier will almost certainly want to help you and correct the mistake. Suppliers are not in business to irritate or confuse their customers but to offer them a service.

Explaining the problem

If you think you know how the mistake was made, you may politely point this out to your supplier. Sometimes, when a mistake occurs several times, you may be able to work out why it is happening more quickly than the company you are dealing with.
— *Could you tell your despatch department to take special care when addressing consignments? My name and address are C. J. Schwartz, Bergstr. 101 Köln. But there is a C. Schwartz, Bergstr. 110 Köln who also deals in electrical fittings.*
— *Could you ask your accounts department to check my code carefully in future? My account number is 246–642, but they have been sending me statements coded 642–246.*
— *I think the reason that wrong sizes have been sent to me is because I am ordering in metric sizes, and you are sending me sizes measured in feet and inches. I would appreciate your looking into this.*

Suggesting a solution

If you think you know how the mistake can be corrected, let your supplier know.
— *If I send you a debit note for €984.00 and deduct it from my next statement, that should put the matter right. The best solution would be for me to return the wrong articles, charging you P&P.*
— *Rather than send a credit note you could send six replacements, which would probably be easier than adjusting our accounts.*

REPLYING TO LETTERS OF COMPLAINT

Opening

Acknowledge that you have received the complaint, and thank your customer for informing you.
— *Thank you for your letter of 6 August informing us that ...*
— *We would like to thank you for informing us of our accounting error in your letter of 7 June.*
— *We are replying to your letter of 10 March in which you told us that ...*

Asking for time to investigate the complaint

Sometimes you cannot deal with a complaint immediately, as the matter needs to be looked into. Do not leave your customer waiting but tell them what you are doing straight away. In this case, an email or fax message is appropriate as the customer then knows immediately that you have received the complaint and are doing something about it.
— *While we cannot give you an explanation at present, we are looking into the problem and will contact you again shortly.*
— *As we are sending out orders promptly, I think these delays may be occurring during transit. I shall get in touch with the haulage contractors.*
— *Would you please return samples of the items you are dissatisfied with, and I will send them to our factory in Düsseldorf for tests.*

Explaining the mistake

If the complaint is justified, explain how the mistake occurred but do not blame your staff. You employed them, so you are responsible for their actions.

— *The mistake was due to a fault in one of our machines, which has now been corrected.*
— *There appears to have been some confusion in our addressing system, but this has been sorted out.*
— *It is unusual for this type of error to arise, but the problem has now been dealt with.*

Solving the problem

Having acknowledged your responsibility and explained what went wrong, you should put matters right as soon as possible, and tell your customer that you are doing so.

— *We have now checked our accounts and find that we have been sending you the wrong statement due to a confusion in names and addresses. The database has been adjusted and there should be no more difficulties. Please contact us again if a similar situation arises, and thank you again for pointing out the error.*
— *The paintwork on the body of the cars became discoloured because of a chemical imbalance in the paint used in spraying the vehicles. We have already contacted our own suppliers and are waiting for their reply. Meanwhile we are taking these models out of production and calling in all those that have been supplied.*
— *The fabric you complained about has now been withdrawn. The fault was in the weave of the cloth, which was due to a programming error in the weaving machines. This has now been corrected and replacement fabric will be sent to you.*

Rejecting a complaint

If you think the complaint is unjustified, you can be firm but polite in your answer. But even if you deny responsibility, you should always try to give an explanation of the problem.

— *We have closely compared the articles you returned with our samples and can see no difference between them. Therefore, in this case we are not willing either to substitute the articles or to offer a credit.*
— *Our factory has now inspected the unit you returned last week, and they inform us that the circuits were overloaded. We can repair the machine, but it will be necessary to charge you as incorrect use of the unit is not covered by our guarantee.*

Closing

It is useful when closing your letter to mention that the mistake, error, or fault is an exception, and it either rarely or never happens. You should also, of course, apologize for the inconvenience your customer experienced.

— *In closing we would like to apologize for the inconvenience, and also point out that this type of fault rarely occurs in the Omega 2000.*
— *Finally, may we say that this was an exceptional mistake and is unlikely to occur again. Please accept our apologies for the inconvenience.*
— *Replacements for the faulty articles are on their way to you, and you should receive them tomorrow. We are sure that you will be satisfied with them and there will be no repetition of the faults. Thank you for your patience in this matter, and we look forward to hearing from you again.*

Complaint about wrong delivery

The reply to this email message ▶ page 104, will explain why complaints should be carefully written and Mr Hughes should not assume that Mr Cliff is responsible for the mistake. The companies concerned here have dealt regularly with one another, so an email message is quite appropriate, as this is not particularly confidential.

To... Richard Cliff

Cc...

Subject: Wrong delivery (order No.1695)

Dear Richard

I received a consignment of dressing tables, Cat. No. DT154, to the above order yesterday. However, the delivery consisted of six heavy mahogany-finished dressing tables instead of the light pine-finished units I asked for.

As I have firm orders for the design I asked for, I would be grateful if you could send my consignment as soon as possible, and collect the wrongly delivered goods. Thank you in advance.

Robert Hughes

Reply to complaint about wrong delivery

Notice the contractions *I'll* and *there's*, and the informal style in this message. However, it is still polite and efficient in tone. In this case it is important that the mistake, regardless of whose fault it is, is corrected as soon as possible. And notice that the invoice – an important document in this transaction – is sent with the next delivery and the catalogue is sent by separate post, neither of them as attachments to the email message.

To...	Robert Hughes	
Cc...		
Subject:	Re: Wrong delivery (order No.1695)	

Dear Robert

Thank you for yesterday's email concerning the above wrong delivery.

I have looked into it and find that our current winter catalogue lists the dressing tables you wanted under DT189. I think you must have used last summer's catalogue.

I have instructed one of our drivers to deliver the pine-finished dressing tables tomorrow and pick up the other consignment.

Rather than sending you a credit note, I'll cancel invoice No. D4451 and include another, No. D4487, with the delivery.

There's also a winter catalogue on its way to you, by post, in case you have mislaid the current one.

Richard Cliff

1 Why did Mr Hughes receive a wrong delivery?

2 What will Mr Cliff do about it?

3 Why is Mr Cliff not going to send a credit note?

4 How will Mr Cliff help Mr Hughes not to make the same mistake again?

5 Which words in the email have a similar meaning to the following?
a investigated
b told
c collect
d lost

Complaint about damage

You have already seen a complaint about breakages in MacKenzie's email to Glaston Potteries ▶ **page 85**. This letter also deals with damage.

F. Lynch & Co. Ltd

Head Office
Nesson House
Newell Street
Birmingham
B3 3EL

Telephone: +44 (0)21 236 6571
Fax: +44 (0)21 236 8592
Email: pcrane@lynch.co.uk
www.lynch.com

Your ref:
Our ref: Order No. 14478
Date: 15 August 20—

Satex S.p.A.
Via di Pietra Papa
00146 Roma
ITALY

Attn. Sig. Daniele Causio

Dear Sig. Causio

Our Order No. 14478

I am writing to you to complain about the shipment of sweaters we received yesterday against the above order.

The boxes in which the sweaters were packed were damaged, and looked as if they had been broken open in transit. From your invoice No.18871 we estimate that thirty garments have been stolen, to the value of £550.00. Because of the rummaging in the boxes, quite a few other garments were crushed or stained and cannot be sold as new articles in our shops.

As the sale was on a CIF basis and the forwarding company were your agents, we suggest you contact them with regard to compensation.

You will find a list of the damaged and missing articles enclosed, and the consignment will be put to one side until we receive your instructions.

Yours sincerely

Peter Crane

Peter Crane
Chief Buyer
Encl.

1 How did the damage occur?

2 Why can't many of the garments be sold?

3 Why does Mr Crane suggest that Mr Causio has to deal with compensation?

4 What is enclosed with the letter?

5 What does Mr Crane intend to do with the damaged consignment?

6 Which words in the letter have a similar meaning to the following?
  a during transportation
  b assess
  c get in touch with

Reply to complaint about damage

Because Satex sells goods to their retailers on a CIF basis, and in this case there was no special instruction to send the goods in a particular way, they will have to find out what happened and whether they can get compensation. Sig. Causio could have asked Mr Crane to keep the undamaged garments and return those which could not be sold. However, he wants the shipping company to inspect the whole consignment in case they do not accept that the damage was caused by thieves.

Satex S.p.A.

Via di Pietra Papa, 00146 Roma

Telefono: +39 (0)6 769910
Telefax: +39 (0)6 6815473
Email: causiod@satex.co.it

Vs.rif.: Order 14478
Vs.rif.: Ns. rif.: D/1162

24 August 20—

Mr L. Crane
Chief Buyer
F. Lynch & Co. Ltd
Nesson House
Newell Street
Birmingham B3 3EL
UNITED KINGDOM

Dear Mr Crane

Thank you for informing us about the damage to our consignment (Inv. No. 18871).

From our previous transactions you will realize that this sort of problem is quite unusual. Nevertheless, we are sorry about the inconvenience it has caused you.

Please would you return the whole consignment to us, postage and packing forward, and we will ask the shipping company to inspect the damage so that they can arrange compensation. It is unlikely that our insurance company needs to be troubled with this case.

If you want us to send you another shipment as per your order No. 14478, please let us know. We have the garments in stock and it would be no trouble to send them within the next fortnight.

Yours sincerely

Daniele Causio

Daniele Causio
Sales Director

Superbuys Ltd
Superbuy House
Wolverton Road
London
SW16 7DN

Telephone +44 (0)20 8327 1651
Facsimile +44 (0)20 8327 1935
Email k.bellon@superbuys.com
www.superbuys.com

Date: 7th July 20—

Mr P. Lane
Wembley Shopfitters Ltd
Wycombe Road
Wembley
Middlesex HA9 6DA

Dear Mr Lane

'Superbuys', 443 Halton Road, London SE4 3TN

I am writing to you with reference to the above premises which you refitted last February.

In the past few weeks a number of faults have appeared in the electrical circuits and the flooring which have been particularly dangerous to our customers.

With regard to the electrical faults, we have found that spotlights have either failed to work, or flicker while they are on, and replacing the bulbs has not corrected the fault.

The flooring which you laid shows signs of deterioration, and some areas are worn through to the concrete, creating a hazard to our customers. I would be grateful if you could come and inspect the damage and arrange for repairs within the next week. The matter is urgent as we can be sued if any of our customers are injured. I would also take this opportunity to remind you that you have guaranteed all your fixtures and fittings for one year.

I look forward to hearing from you soon.

Yours sincerely

Keith Bellon

Keith Bellon
Managing Director

Reg. No. 94116 London
VAT No. 516 8410 30

Complaint about bad workmanship

When bad workmanship is involved the customer can only complain as the faults arise, but they should still complain as soon as possible. In earlier correspondence ▶ **pages 23–24 and 59**, Superbuys, a supermarket chain, asked Wembley Shopfitters to refit one of their shops. The work was completed, but some months later faults began to appear.

W | S | L

Wembley Shopfitters Ltd.
Telephone: +44 (0)20 8903 2323
Fax: +44 (0)20 8903 2323
Email: plane@wemshop.com

Wycombe Road
Wembley
Middlesex
HA9 6DA

10 July 20—

Mr Keith Bellon
Superbuys Ltd
Superbuy House
Wolverton Road
London SW16 7DN

Dear Mr Bellon

'Superbuys', 443 Halton Road, London SE4 3TN

The damage you described in your letter of 7 July has now been inspected.

The faults in the wiring appear to have been caused by dripping water from the floor above. The electrical contractor, who put the wiring in in February, tells me that the wall was dry at the time he replaced the old wires. However, we will arrange for repairs to be made and seal off that section.

Durafloor is one of the most hardwearing materials of its kind on the market and we were surprised to hear that it had worn away within six months, so we made a close inspection. We noticed that the floor had been cut into and this seems to have been the result of dragging heavy metal boxes across it. The one-year guarantee we offer on our workmanship is against 'normal wear and tear', and the treatment the floor appears to have been subjected to does not come into this category. I am quite willing to arrange for the surface to be replaced, but we will have to charge you for the materials and work involved. If I may, I would like to suggest that you instruct your staff to use trolleys when shifting heavy containers.

I am sorry about the inconvenience you have experienced and will tell the fitters to repair the damage as soon as I have your confirmation that they can begin work.

The floor repairs should not come to more than £890 and the work can be completed in less than a day. Perhaps you could ring me to arrange for a convenient time for the work to be carried out?

Yours sincerely

Peter Lane

Peter Lane
Director

Reg: London 481629
VAT: 314651928

Questions

1 What does Mr Lane think caused the faulty wiring, and what does he intend to do about it?

2 What does he think caused the problem with the flooring, and what does he say he will do about it?

3 How does Mr Lane suggest the damage to the floor can be avoided?

4 How long will the repairs to the floor take?

5 Which words in the letter have a similar meaning to the following?
a looked at
b durable
c everyday use
d moving

FORHAM VEHICLES PLC

Lever Estate
Scarborough
Yorkshire
YO11 3BS

Telephone: +44 (0)1723 16952
Fax: +44 (0)1723 81953
Email: m.blackburn@forham.co.uk

Date: 20 June 20—

Herr R. Zeitman
E.F. Baden AG
Zülpicher Str. 10–20
D-40000 Düsseldorf 11

Dear Herr Zeitman

Order No. VC 58391

We are writing to you with reference to the above order and our letter of 22 May in which we asked when we could expect delivery of the 60 dynamos (Artex model 55) you agreed to supply on 3 June for an export order. We have tried to contact you by phone, fax, and email but no-one in your organization seemed to know anything about this matter.

It is essential that we deliver this consignment to our Greek customers on time as this was an initial order from them and would give us an opening in the Greek market. Our deadline is 28 June, and the lorries have been completed except for the dynamos that need to be fitted.

Unless we receive the components within the next five days, our customers will cancel the order and place it elsewhere. We would like to make it clear that we are holding you to your delivery contract, and if any loss results because of this late delivery we will take legal action.

Yours sincerely

Michael Blackburn

Michael Blackburn
Director

Reg. England: 8969135
VAT. 462 321 17

Complaint about non-delivery

In this case the customer, Forham Vehicles, makes lorries for export. They placed an order with E.F. Baden to supply them with sixty dynamos for a shipment of lorries to be exported to Greece. Baden have neither delivered the order nor replied to Forham's previous letter urging them to make delivery, so Forham send a strong complaint.

Reply to complaint about non-delivery

Note how this letter is apologetic but firm. Though E.F. Baden accept responsibility for the problems Forham Vehicles face in delivering their consignment to their Greek customers, Herr Zeitman rejects the threat of legal action by drawing Mr Blackburn's attention to a clause in their contract stating that the company will not be responsible for *unforeseen circumstances*. However, Herr Zeitman is flexible enough to realize he must not antagonize his customer, so he allows Mr Blackburn the opportunity to cancel the order if he can make other arrangements.

This letter illustrates two main points: first, do not commit yourself to contracts unless you are absolutely certain they can be fulfilled; second, always try and be as flexible as possible with customers or associates even if you are in a strong position – it will improve your business reputation.

E.F. Baden AG

29 June 20—

Mr M. Blackburn
Forham Vehicles plc
Lever Estate
Scarborough YO11 3BS

Dear Mr Blackburn

Thank you for your letter of 20 June concerning your order (No. VC 58391), which should have been supplied to you on 3 June.

First, let me apologize for your order not being delivered on the due date and for the problems you have experienced in getting in touch with us. Both are the result of an industrial dispute which has involved our administrative staff and employees on the shop floor, and has held up all production over the past few weeks.

The dispute has now been settled and we are back to normal production. There is a backlog of orders to fill, but we are using associate companies to help us fulfil all outstanding commitments. Your order has been given priority, so we should be able to deliver the dynamos before the end of this week.

May I point out, with respect, that your contract with us has a standard clause stating that delivery dates would be met unless unforeseen circumstances arose, and we think you will agree that an industrial dispute is an exceptional circumstance. However, we understand your problem and will allow you to cancel your contract if it will help you to meet your commitments to your Greek customers. But we will not accept responsibility for any action they may take against you.

Once again let me say how much I regret the inconvenience this delay has caused, and emphasize that it was due to factors we could not have known about when we accepted your delivery dates.

Please let me know if you wish us to complete your order or whether you would prefer to make other arrangements.

I look forward to hearing from you.

Yours sincerely

Rolf Zeitman
Managing Director

ACCOUNTING ERRORS AND ADJUSTMENTS

Many letters of complaint arise out of accounting errors, which can be corrected by adjustments. Debit notes and credit notes are used for this purpose.

Debit notes

DEBIT NOTES are a second charge for a consignment and become necessary if a customer has been undercharged through a mistake in the calculations on the original invoice. An explanation for the charge must be included on the debit note:
— *Undercharge on invoice C293. 10 Units @ £12.62 each = £126.20, NOT £16.20*
— *Invoice No. P.32, one line omitted viz. 100MB Zip Disks @ £8.40 each = £840.00*
— *VAT should have been calculated at 17.5%, NOT 15%. Difference = £81.86*

Once a buyer has settled an account, it is annoying to be told that there is an additional payment. An apology should always accompany a debit note.
— *We would like to apologize for the mistake on invoice No. C293, which was due to an oversight. Please could you send us the balance of €795.00?*
— *I am sorry to trouble you, particularly since you were so prompt in settling the account, but I would be grateful if you would let us have the additional amount of €340.00 as itemized on the enclosed debit note.*
— *I regret that we miscalculated the VAT and must now ask you to forward the difference of £51.86.*

Credit notes

CREDIT NOTES are sent because of accidental overcharges:
— *10 copies of International Commerce @ £16.50 = £165.00 NOT £195.00*
— *Invoice L283. Discount should have been 12%, not 8%. Credit = ¥5,140.00.*

A credit note may also be issued when a deposit is refunded (e.g. on the cartons or cases which the goods were packed in) or when goods are returned because they were not suitable or were damaged.
— *Received 3 returned cases charged on Invoice No. 1436 @ £7.00 each = £21.00.*
— *Refund for 4 copies of International Commerce £16.50 each (returned damaged) = £66.00.*

As with a debit note, in the case of mistakes a covering letter of explanation and apology should be sent with a credit note.
— *I have pleasure in enclosing a credit note for €240.00. This is due to a miscalculation on our invoice dated 12 August. Please accept our apologies for the error.*
— *Please find enclosed our credit note No. C23 for €165.60 which is a refund for the overcharge on invoice No. L283. As you pointed out in your letter, the trade discount should have been 12%, not 10%, of the gross price. We apologize for the inconvenience.*

This note is necessary because the suppliers, Seymore Furniture, have made a mistake in their calculations and have undercharged their customer, C.R. Méndez.

Seymore Furniture Ltd

Telephone: +44 (0)1628 26755
Fax: +44 (0)1628 26756
Email: accounts@seymore.co.uk
Registered No. 18514391 London
VAT No. 231 6188 31

Debit Note

NO. 311

Tib Street
Maidenhead
Berkshire
SL6 5D2
UK

31 May 20—

C.R. Méndez S.A.
Avda del Ejército 83
E-48015 Bilbao

5 May 20—	Invoice No. L 8992. UNDERCHARGE.	
	The extension should have read:	
	6 Chairs @ £ 35.00 each = £210.00	
	NOT	
	6 Chairs @ £ 25.00 each = £150.00	
	We apologize for the error and ask if you would please pay the difference of £60.00.	£60.00

Seymore Furniture Ltd

Telephone: +44 (0)1628 26755
Fax: +44 (0)1628 26756
Email: accounts@seymore.co.uk
Registered No. 18514391 London
VAT No. 231 6188 31

C.R. Méndez S.A.
Avda del Ejército 83
E-48015 Bilbao

Credit Note
NO. C517

Tib Street
Maidenhead
Berkshire
SL6 5D2
UK

20 May 20—

10 May 20—	Invoice No. L8995. OVERCHARGE. The invoice should have read: 15% off gross price of £800.00 = £120.00 NOT 10% off gross price of £800.00 = £80.00 Refund = £40.00. Please accept our apologies.	£40.00

Credit note

Seymore Furniture have made a mistake on another invoice and must now send a credit note. Note that the form for a credit note is the same as that for a debit note, except for the heading. Credit notes, however, are often printed in red.

Complaint about accounting errors

M. Lancelot (a builders' supplier) has received a statement which contains several accounting errors.

M. LANCELOT SARL

703 rue Métairie de Saysset
F–34000 Montpellier

Télephone
(+33) 4 843 1031
Télécopie
(+33) 4 843 1037
Email
m.lancelot@lancelot.co.fr

5 August 20—

Mr K. Winford
K. Winford & Co. Ltd
Preston New Road
Blackpool
Lancashire FY4 4UL

Dear Mr Winford

I have received your July statement for £3,280.64 but notice it contains a number of errors.

1 Invoice Y1146 for £256.00 has been debited twice.

2 No credit has been listed for the wallpaper (Cat. No. WR114) which I returned in July. Your credit note No. CN118 for £19.00 refers to this.

3 You have charged for a delivery of paintbrushes, invoice No. Y1162 for £62.00, but I neither ordered nor received them. Could you check your delivery book?

I have deducted a total of £337.00 from your statement and will send you a draft for £2,943.64 once I have your confirmation of this amount.

Yours sincerely

Maurice Lancelot

Maurice Lancelot
Director

Telephone
+44 (0)1253 61290/1/2
Fax
+44 (0)1253 61378
Email
wink@winford.co.uk

K. Winford & Co. Ltd

Preston New Road
Blackpool
Lancashire
FY4 4UL

7 August 20—

M. Maurice Lancelot
Director
M. Lancelot SARL
703 rue Métairie de Saysset
F-34000 Montpellier

Dear M. Lancelot

Thank you for your letter of 5 August in which you pointed out that three mistakes totalling £337.00 had been made on your statement.

I apologize for the errors. These were due to a software fault which has now been fixed. I have enclosed another statement for July, which shows the correct balance of £2,943.64.

Yours sincerely

K. Winford

K. Winford

Enc. Statement

Reg. No. 31162531
VAT No. 8314003 36

7

Points to remember

1 Minor complaints can be faxed or emailed, but use letters when dealing with more serious ones.

2 Before writing a letter of complaint, make sure you have got your facts right.

3 Complaints are not accusations, they are requests to correct mistakes or faults. They should be written remembering that the supplier almost certainly wants to put things right.

4 Never make the complaint personal (e.g. *your mistake, your fault, you are to blame*). Use an impersonal tone (e.g. *the mistake, it must have happened because…, the error*).

5 When answering a complaint, thank your customer for pointing out the problem. If the complaint is justified, explain how the problem occurred and how you intend to deal with it.

6 If you need more time to investigate the complaint, tell your customer.

7 If the complaint is unjustified, politely explain why, but sympathize about the inconvenience it has caused.

FORMS OF CREDIT

Credit arrangements between trading companies take two forms:
- BILLS OF EXCHANGE, or BANK DRAFTS, by which the supplier gives credit to the customer for the period specified, e.g. thirty, sixty, or ninety days.
- OPEN ACCOUNT FACILITIES, by which the customer is allowed to pay for goods against monthly or quarterly statements.

In order to control a transaction, a supplier may send a *quality and delivery fax* to the customer shortly after despatch of the goods, stating that they were despatched on the date of the invoice; that they met the quality conditions of the contract; that the supplier would like to be informed if the goods arrived intact or were damaged on delivery; and that the supplier looks forward to prompt payment on the due date.

As a rule, all areas of credit dealing should be considered confidential, so open correspondence like email and fax should be used carefully.

REQUIREMENTS FOR GRANTING CREDIT

CREDIT FACILITIES will only be granted by a supplier if the customer can satisfy one or more of these three requirements:

1 Reputation – Credit may be given to firms which have an established reputation, i.e. are well known nationally or internationally.
2 Long-term trading association – If a customer has been trading with a supplier over a period of time and has built up a good relationship by, for example, settling accounts promptly, they may be able to persuade the supplier to grant credit facilities on this basis alone.
3 REFERENCES – Normally, when asking for credit, a customer will supply references, i.e. the names of concerns or companies which will satisfy the supplier that the customer is reputable and CREDITWORTHY. Banks will supply references, though these tend to be brief, stating the company's capital and who its directors are. TRADE ASSOCIATIONS, i.e. organizations which represent the company's trade or profession, also give brief references telling the enquirer how long the company has been trading and whether it is large or small. References can also be obtained from, e.g. the customer's business associates and the commercial departments of embassies.

ASKING FOR CREDIT

Opening

When asking for credit facilities, it is best to go straight to the point and specify what form of credit you are looking for.
- *I am writing to ask if it would be possible for us to have credit facilities in the form of payment by 60-day bill of exchange.*
- *Thank you for your catalogue and letter. As there was no indication of your credit terms, could you let me know if you would allow us to settle on monthly statements?*
- *We appreciate your prompt answer to our enquiry. As I pointed out in my letter, our suppliers usually allow us open account facilities with quarterly settlements, and I hope this method of payment will be acceptable to you.*

Convincing your supplier

As mentioned above, your supplier will only grant credit if they are convinced that you will not DEFAULT, so mention your previous dealings with them.
- *As we have been dealing with you for more than a year, we feel that you know us well enough to grant our request.*
- *We believe we have established our reliability with you over the past six months and would now like to settle accounts on a quarterly basis.*
- *During the past few months we have always settled promptly, and therefore we feel we can ask for better credit facilities from you.*

Mention your reputation, and offer references.

— *We are a well-established company and can offer references, if necessary.*

— *We can certainly pay on the due dates, but if you would like confirmation concerning our creditworthiness, please contact any of the following who will act as our referees: …*

— *We deal with most of our suppliers on a quarterly settlement basis and you may contact any of those listed below for a reference.*

Closing

— *We hope for a favourable decision and look forward to your reply.*

— *We hope you will follow up the references we have submitted. We look forward to your confirmation that payment by 30-day bill of exchange is acceptable.*

— *As soon as we receive your confirmation that you will allow the open account facilities we have asked for, we will send our next order.*

REPLYING TO REQUESTS FOR CREDIT

Agreeing to credit

If the supplier does not think it necessary to take up references, they may grant credit immediately.

— *As we have been trading for over a year, references will not be necessary. You may clear your accounts by 30-day bill of exchange, which will be sent to Burnley's Bank (Queens Building, Cathays Park, Cardiff CF1 9UJ) with shipping documents for your acceptance.*

— *We are pleased to inform you that the credit facilities you asked for are acceptable, and as we know the reputation of your company there will be no need for us to contact any referees. I would just like to confirm that we agreed settlement will be made against monthly statements. We look forward to receiving your next order.*

If references are considered necessary, however, the supplier will acknowledge the request ▶ **see page 120** and then reply in full when references have been received.

— *We have now received the necessary references and are pleased to inform you that, from your next order, payment can be made on a quarterly basis against statements.*

— *The referees you gave us have replied and we are able to tell you that as from next month you may settle your account on a documents against acceptance basis by 60 D/S B/E.*

Refusing credit

When refusing credit facilities, the writer must explain why the request has been turned down. There may be various reasons for this. It might be uneconomical to offer credit facilities; you may not trust the customer, i.e. the customer has a bad reputation for settling accounts; or it might simply be company policy not to give credit. Whatever the reason, the reply must be worded carefully so as not to offend the customer.

— *Thank you for your letter of 9 November in which you asked to be put on open account terms. Unfortunately, we never allow credit facilities to customers until they have traded with us for over a year. We are very sorry that we cannot be more helpful at present.*

— *We regret that we are unable to offer open account terms to customers as our products are competitively priced, and with small profit margins it is uneconomical to allow credit facilities.*

— *We are sorry that we cannot offer credit facilities of any kind at present owing to inflation. However, if the situation improves we may be able to reconsider your request.*

— *We have considered your request for quarterly settlements, but feel that with our competitive pricing policy, which leaves only small profit margins, it would be uneconomical to allow credit on your present purchases. However, if you can offer the usual references and increase your purchases by at least 50%, we would be willing to reconsider the situation.*

8

Negotiating

Sometimes a supplier will not offer as much credit as the customer wants, but will negotiate a compromise.

— *I regret that we cannot offer you credit for as long as three months, since this would be uneconomical for us. However, we are prepared to offer you settlement against monthly statements. Perhaps you would let me know if this is acceptable?*

— *Though we do not usually offer credit facilities, we would be prepared to consider partial credit. In this case you would pay half your invoices on a cash basis, and the rest by 30-day bill of exchange. If this arrangement suits you, please contact us.*

Reply while waiting for references

In some cases you will not be able to grant credit without making further investigations. In particular, you may want to take up the references your customer has offered. In these cases, your reply will be little more than an acknowledgement of the request.

— *Thank you for your letter in which you asked for credit facilities. At present we are writing to the referees you mentioned and will let you know as soon as we hear from them.*

— *In reply to your email of 8 June, we will consider your request to pay by 30-day bill of exchange and will contact you by letter as soon as we have reached a decision.*

— *With reference to your letter of 15 March, in which you asked for open account facilities, I will contact you as soon as the usual enquiries have been made.*

— *As we have only just received your letter asking for credit facilities, would you allow us a little time to consider the matter? I will be in touch with you again within the next couple of weeks.*

R. Hughes & Son Ltd

21 Mead Road, Swansea
West Glamorgan 3ST 1DR
Telephone: +44 (0)1792 58441
Fax: Swansea +44 (0)1792 59472
Email: r.hughes@huson.co.uk

18 July 20—

Mr R. Cliff
Homemakers Ltd
54–59 Riverside
Cardiff CF1 1JW

Dear Richard

I have enclosed an order, No. B 1662, for seven more 'Sleepcomfy' beds which have proved to be a popular line here, and will pay for them as usual on invoice. However, I wondered if in future you would let me settle my accounts by monthly statement as this would be more convenient for me?

As we have been dealing with one another for some time, I hope you will agree to trade on the basis of open account facilities. I can, of course, supply the necessary references.

Yours sincerely

Robert

Robert Hughes

Enc. Order No. B1662

VAT NO. 215 2261 30

Request for open account facilities

Mr Hughes, some of whose correspondence we looked at in previous units ▸ **see pages 26–27, 93–94, and 103–104,** asks his supplier if he will allow him open account facilities. Although some of their exchanges have been by email, the topic of credit is more sensitive and would be dealt with by letter. Mr Hughes makes his request while sending an order rather than making his next order conditional on Mr Cliff's acceptance. Compare this with the letter in which F. Lynch & Co. made their next order conditional on revised terms ▸ **see page 84.**

Reply granting open account facilities

In his reply, Mr Cliff says he is prepared to give credit, even though he feels it may not be in Mr Hughes' best interests.

HOMEMAKERS

54–59 Riverside, Cardiff CF1 1JW
Telephone: +44 (0)29 20 49721
Fax: +44 (0)29 20 49937
Email: rcliff@homemakers.com

24 July 20—

Mr R. Hughes
R. Hughes & Son Ltd
21 Mead Road
Swansea
West Glamorgan 3ST 1DR

Dear Robert

Thank you for your order, No. B1662, which will be sent to you tomorrow. I have taken the opportunity to enclose the invoice, DM1113, with this letter.

With regard to your request for open account facilities, settlement against monthly statements, I feel there would be more advantage for you in claiming the 3% cash discounts offered for payment within seven days of receipt of invoice. Nevertheless, I am quite prepared to allow monthly settlements, and there will be no need to supply references as you are a long-standing customer.

The enclosed invoice will be included in your next statement.

Yours sincerely

Richard

Richard Cliff
Director

Enc. Invoice DM1113

Registered No. C135162

Questions

1 Why does Mr Cliff think it would be better for Mr Hughes to settle invoices within seven days?

2 What form of open account facilities is Mr Cliff offering?

3 Why doesn't Mr Cliff need any references from Mr Hughes?

4 When should Mr Hughes pay invoice DM1113?

251 rue des Raimonières
F–86000 Poitiers Cédex

Téléphone (+33) 2 99681031
Télécopie (+33) 2 74102163
Email p.gerard@disc.co.fr

Réf. PG/AL

3 December 20—

Herr R. Gerlach
R.G. Electronics AG
Havmart 601
D-50000 Köln 1

Dear Herr Gerlach

I intend to place a substantial order with you in the next few weeks and
wondered what sort of credit facilities your company offered?

As you know, over the past months I have placed a number of orders with
you and settled promptly, so I hope this has established my reputation with
your company. Nevertheless, if necessary, I am willing to supply references.

I would like, if possible, to settle future accounts every three months with
payments against quarterly statements.

Yours sincerely

P. Gérard

P. Gérard (M.)
Manager

In this reply, R.G. Electronics turn Disc S.A.'s request down, even though the two companies have traded for some time.

R.G. Electronics AG

Havmart 601
D–50000 Köln 1

Telefon (+49) 221 32 42 98
Telefax (+49) 221 83 61 25
Email gerlachr@rge.co.de
www.rge.de

Your Ref: PG/AL

8 December 20—

M. P. Gérard
Disc S.A.
251 rue des Raimonières
F-86000 Poitiers Cédex

Dear M. Gérard

Thank you for your letter of 3 December in which you enquired about credit facilities.

We appreciate that you have placed a number of orders with us in the past, and are sure that you can supply the necessary references to support your request. However, as you probably realize, our products are sold at extremely competitive prices. This allows us only small profit margins and prevents us offering any of our customers credit facilities.

We are very sorry that we cannot help you in this case and hope you understand our reasons.

Once again, thank you for writing, and we look forward to hearing from you soon.

Yours sincerely

R. Gerlach

R. Gerlach
Sales Director

1 How does Herr Gerlach assure M. Gérard that his firm's reputation has nothing to do with the rejection?

2 What reason does Herr Gerlach give for refusing credit facilities?

3 Is it only in M. Gérard's case that credit has been refused?

4 How does Herr Gerlach encourage further correspondence?

```
File  Edit  View  Insert  Format  Tools  Actions  Help
```

To...	John Merton
Cc...	
Subject:	Terms of payment

Dear Mr Merton

Our bank has advised us that the proceeds of our letter of credit against your invoice, No. G1197/S, have now been credited to your account.

Although we have paid for some time on this basis, it does not really suit our accounting system, and as we feel you know us well enough by now, we would like to make future payments on quarterly statements by international banker's draft.

If you require a reference, please contact either Mr M. Pierson or Mr J. Tane at our other suppliers, Pierson & Co, Louis Drive, Dawson, Ontario, who will be happy to vouch for us.

Please confirm that these new terms are acceptable to you.

Richard MacKenzie

Request for a change in the terms of payment

As we have seen in previous units, MacKenzie Bros of Canada import chinaware from Glaston Potteries in England. They currently pay by letter of credit ▶ see pages 68 and 85, but now want to pay on quarterly statements by international banker's draft. This involves fairly long-term credit, so they supply references.

```
File  Edit  View  Insert  Format  Tools  Actions  Help
```

To...	Richard MacKenzie
Cc...	
Subject:	RE: Terms of payment

Dear Mr MacKenzie

Thank you for your email of 9 February in which you asked to change your terms of payment to settlement by banker's draft on quarterly statements.

We are taking up the reference you offered, and provided it is satisfactory, you can consider the new arrangement effective from your next order.

John Merton
Sales Manager
Glaston Potteries Ltd
Clayfield, Burnley BB10 1RQ
Tel: +44 (0)1282 46125
Fax: +44 (0)1282 63182
Email: j.merton@glaston.co.uk

Notification of taking up references

Glaston Potteries are sympathetic to Mr MacKenzie's request, but decide to take up the reference offered.

8

ASKING ABOUT CREDIT RATING

The guide below gives you an outline of how to take up references and to ask about a company's CREDIT RATING.

Opening

Say who you are and why you want the information. Make it clear that the name of the company you are writing to has been given to you as a reference by your customer. If this is not the case, you are unlikely to get a reply ▶ **see page 127**.

— *We are a furniture wholesalers and have been asked by L. R. Naismith & Co. Ltd of 21 Barnsley Road, Sheffield to offer them open account facilities with quarterly settlement terms. They have given us your name as a reference.*

— *We are a glass manufacturers and have recently begun to export to the UK. D. R. Mitchell & Son, who are customers of yours, have placed an order with us, but want to pay by 30-day bill of exchange. They have informed us that you would be prepared to act as their referees.*

— *Your branch of the Eastland Bank was given to us as a reference by I.T.S. Ltd, who have placed a substantial order with us, and want to settle by 40-day draft. Could you give us a guide to I.T.S.'s credit rating?*

Details

Say exactly what you want to know.

— *We would like to know if the company is creditworthy and has a good reputation.*

— *We would be grateful if you could tell us if the company is reliable in settling its accounts promptly.*

— *Could you let us know if this company is capable of repaying a loan of this size within the specified time?*

— *Could you tell us if the company has a good reputation in your country; whether they can be relied on to settle promptly on due dates; and what limit you would place or have placed on credit when dealing with them?*

If the amount of credit is known, it is usually mentioned.

— *The credit will be about £6,000.*

— *We do not expect the credit to exceed £4,000.*

— *The draft is for £926.00.*

— *It is unlikely that they will ask for more than a £1,000 credit at this stage.*

Closing

Thank the company in advance for giving you the information, and tell them you will reciprocate if the opportunity arises. Also, let them know that whatever they say in their letter will be treated as confidential.

— *We would like to thank you in advance for the information and can assure you that it will be treated in the strictest confidence.*

— *Your help will be appreciated, and the information will be held in confidence. We will return the favour should the opportunity arise.*

— *We can assure you that the information will not be disclosed. Thank you for your assistance in this matter. If we can reciprocate in a similar situation, please do not hesitate to contact us.*

Using an enquiry agency

Business associates may give more information than banks and trade associations, who will usually only give brief references ▶ **but see page 127**. An enquiry agency will give much more detail about a company, and for a fee, will research its financial background, its standing, creditworthiness, and ability to repay loans or fulfil obligations. When writing to an enquiry agency, therefore, you can ask for more information.

— *We have been asked by D. F Rowlands Ltd of Milton Trading Estate, Peterborough, to provide them with a credit of up to £5,000 by allowing them to settle by quarterly statements. As we have no knowledge of this company, would it be possible for you to give us detailed information of their trading activities over, say, the past three years?*

— The company named on the enclosed slip has written to us asking if we would allow them to settle by 60-day bill of exchange. Our trading with them so far has only been up to £1,500.00. As we know nothing about them or their creditworthiness, could you investigate their business activities over the past few years and give us a detailed report?

REPLYING TO ENQUIRIES ABOUT CREDIT RATING

In most countries there are laws which protect a company from having its reputation damaged by anyone saying or writing anything that could harm its good name, and this should be considered when giving details of a company's creditworthiness or commenting on its standing.

Refusing to reply

There are a number of reasons why you may not wish to reply to an enquiry. If, for example, the company writing to you does not state that you have been named as a REFEREE by their customer, and you do not want to risk offending a business associate, it would be better not to make any comment.

— Thank you for your letter concerning our customer, but we cannot give you any information until we get permission from the customer. Could you therefore ask the person mentioned in your letter to write to us asking us to act as referees? We would then be happy to give you the necessary information.

— As we have not been asked by the person mentioned in your letter to write a reference on their behalf, we cannot supply any information about them.

If you do not know enough about the company to comment, then it is better to say so.

— With reference to the company you mentioned in your letter of 9 October, we are sorry to say we know little about them as we have only supplied them on a couple of occasions. Therefore we cannot give you any details of their trading record or credit standing.

— Thank you for your letter, which we received today. Unfortunately, we know nothing about the company as our only dealings with them have been on a cash basis. We are sorry that we cannot help you in this matter.

Sometimes you may simply not want to give any information about a customer, whether you know their reputation or not. In this case a polite refusal, generalizing your statements, is the best course of action.

— With reference to your letter of 16 October in which you asked about the credit standing of one of our customers, we regret that it is our policy never to give information about customers to inquirers. As business associates of ours, we are sure you will appreciate this. Perhaps an enquiry agency would be more helpful?

Replying unfavourably

If you give an unfavourable reply, do not mention the name of the company. Give only the facts as they concern you. Do not offer opinions, and remind the company you are writing to that the information is strictly confidential. It is advisable not to use an open system like fax or email for this kind of communication.

— With reference to your letter of 19 April in which you asked us to act as referees for the customer mentioned, we have only dealt with them on a few occasions but found they tended to delay payment and had to be reminded several times before their account was cleared. But we have no idea of their trading records with other companies. We are sure you will treat this information in the strictest confidence.

— In reply to your letter of 14 September concerning the customer you enquired about, we regret that we cannot recommend the firm as being reliable in their credit dealings, but this information is based only on our own experience of trading with them. We offer this information on the strict understanding that it will be treated confidentially.

8

8

Replying favourably

Even in a favourable reply, you should still not mention the customer's name if possible. You can state that you have allowed credit facilities and, if you are sure, you could mention the customer has a good reputation within your trade. In the examples below you will see that the reference should still be considered confidential, and that the referee takes no responsibility for how the information is used.

— *We are pleased to inform you that in our experience the company mentioned in your letter of 7 November is completely reliable and can be trusted to clear their balances promptly on due dates. However, we take no responsibility for how this information is used.*

— *With regard to the company mentioned in your letter of 8 December, we can assure you that they have an excellent reputation in dealing with their suppliers, and though we have not given them the credit terms they have asked you for, we would allow them those facilities if they approached us. Please treat this information as confidential.*

GLASTON POTTERIES LTD

Clayfield | Burnley | BB10 1RQ

Telephone +44 (0)1282 46125
Facsimile +44 (0)1282 63182
Email j.merton@glaston.co.uk
www.glaston.com

Your ref:

16 February 20—

Mr M. Pierson
Pierson & Co.
Louis Drive
Dawson
Ontario
CANADA

Dear Mr Pierson

We are suppliers to MacKenzie Bros Ltd, 1–5 Whale Drive, Dawson, Ontario, who have asked us to give them facilities to settle their statements on a quarterly basis.

They told us that you would be prepared to act as their referee, and while we have little doubt about their ability to clear their accounts, we would like confirmation that their credit rating warrants quarterly settlements of up to £8,000.

We would be very grateful for an early reply, and can assure you that it will be treated in the strictest confidence.

Yours sincerely

John Merton

John Merton
Sales Manager

Registered No. 716481
VAT Registered No. 133 53431 08

Letter to a referee 1

As notified in their email ▶ see page 125, Glaston Potteries take up the reference offered by MacKenzie Bros.

1 What do Glaston Potteries want Mr Pierson to do?

2 Why have they asked Mr Pierson to do this?

3 What assurance do they give Mr Pierson about the information they want?

4 Which words in the letter have a similar meaning to the following?
a every three months
b saying that something is true
c justifies
d payments

8

Example letter

Pierson & Co.

Louis Drive | Dawson | Ontario | Canada

Telephone (+1) 614 295 1682
Facsimile (+1) 614 295 1471
Cable PIERCO
Email m.pierson@pierco.co.uk

Date 28 February 20—

Mr J. Merton
Glaston Potteries Ltd
Clayfield
Burnley BB10 1RQ
UK

Dear Mr Merton

I am replying to your enquiry of 16 February in which you asked about
MacKenzie Bros of Dawson, Ontario.

I contacted them yesterday and they confirmed that they wanted us to act
as their referees, and I am pleased to be able to do so.

The company has an excellent reputation in North America for both service
and the way they conduct their business with their associates in the trade.

We have given them credit facilities for at least ten years and have always
found that they have paid on due dates without any problems. I might also
add that our credit is in excess of the one mentioned in your letter.

You can have every confidence in offering this company the facilities they
ask for.

Yours sincerely

Malcolm Pierson

Malcolm Pierson
Director

Questions

1 What did Mr Pierson
do before he wrote
the reference?

2 What is his opinion of
of MacKenzie Bros?

3 What does he mean
by *they have paid on
due dates*?

4 How does he explain
that they are
creditworthy?

5 Which words in the
letter have a similar
meaning to the
following?
a more than
b feeling of certainty

Satex S.p.A.

Via di Pietra Papa, 00146 Roma

Telefono: +39 (0)6 769910
Telefax: +39 (0)6 6815473
Email: causiod@satex.co.it

Vs. rif.:
Ns. rif.: DC/AA

4 July 20—

Mr T. Grover
Grover Menswear Ltd
Browns Lane
Rugeley
Staffordshire WS15 1DR

Dear Mr Grover

Your name was given to us by Mr L. Crane, the chief buyer of F. Lynch & Co.
Ltd, Nesson House, Newell Street, Birmingham B3 3EL, who have asked us to
allow them to settle their account by 40-day B/E.

They told us that you would be prepared to act as their referee. We would be
grateful if you could confirm that this company settles promptly on due
dates, and are sound enough to meet credits of up to £5,000 in transactions.

Thank you in advance for the information.

Yours sincerely

Daniele Causio

Daniele Causio
Sales Director

Here is another example
of taking up references,
this time from Satex,
the Italian manufacturer
we have met in previous
units. Their customer,
F. Lynch & Co., asked to
be allowed to settle their
accounts by 40-day bill
of exchange, documents
against acceptance
▶ **see page 84**. F. Lynch
& Co. offered references,
which Satex are taking
up.

Referee's reply 2

Note how Mr Grover says he will take no responsibility for how the information he provides is used, and reminds Satex that the letter is confidential.

GM

Grover Menswear

Browns Lane
Rugeley
Staffordshire
WS15 1DR

Telephone +44 (0)1889 431621
Fax +44 (0)1889 431622
Email t.grover@menswear.co.uk

9 July 20—

Mr D. Causio
Satex S.p.A.
Via di Pietra Papa
00146 Roma
ITALY

Dear Mr Causio

We have received confirmation from F. Lynch & Co. Ltd that they want us to act as referees on their behalf, and can give you the following information.

We have been dealing with the company for ten years and allow them credit facilities of up to £4,000, which they only use occasionally as they prefer to take advantage of our cash discounts. However, we would have no hesitation in offering them the sort of credit you mentioned, i.e. £5,000, as they are a large reputable organization and very well-known in this country.

Of course, we take no responsibility for how you use this information, and would remind you to consider it as confidential.

Yours sincerely

T. Grover

T. Grover (Mr)
Director, Grover Menswear

1 What did Mr Grover do before contacting Satex?

2 What expression is used to mean *for them*?

3 Why does F. Lynch & Co. only sometimes use Grover Menswear's credit facilities?

4 How does Mr Grover explain that his company will not be liable for Satex's decision?

5 Which words in the letter have a similar meaning to the following?
a trading with
b respected
c private

In this letter, the writer refuses to reply because he does not have the company's permission.

Dear Mr Stevens

I am replying to your letter of 10 August in which you asked about one of our mutual business associates.

I regret that I cannot give you the information you asked for as it would be a breach of confidence. If, however, you can get the company to write instructing us to act as their referee, then we may be able to help you.

Yours sincerely

Mark Chapman

Mark Chapman

The reply in this case is unfavourable. Notice how the writer does not refer to the company by name.

Dear Mr Scrutton

I am replying to your enquiry about the company mentioned in your letter of 3 May.

In the past we have allowed that company credit, but nowhere near the amount you mentioned, and we found they needed at least one reminder before clearing their account.

This information is strictly confidential and we take no responsibility for how it is used.

Yours sincerely

Sarah Wentworth

Sarah Wentworth

The writer of this letter is unable to supply the information his correspondent wants because he has little knowledge of the company.

Dear Mr Cox

In reply to your letter of 10 August, I regret that we cannot offer you any information concerning the company you asked about in your letter. We have had very little dealing with them and they have never asked us for credit of any kind.

I am sorry we cannot help you in this matter.

Yours sincerely

H.F. Edgley

H.F. Edgley (Mr)

Letter to an enquiry agent

Checking on a customer's credit rating with an enquiry agency allows you to be more specific about the details you want concerning the customer.

P.MARLOW & CO. LTD

M

31 Goodge Street
London
EC4 4EE

Telephone: +44 (0)20 7583 6119
Fax: +44 (0)20 7583 7125
Email: p.marlow@pmarlow.co.uk

9 April 20—

Mr S. Spade
Credit Investigations Ltd
1 Bird Street
London E1 6TM

Dear Mr Spade

You were recommended to me by a previous client of yours, S. Greenstreet & Co. Ltd.

I would like information about Falcon Retailers Ltd, who have asked us to allow them open account facilities with quarterly settlements and credits of up to £8,000.

Would you please tell us if this company has had any bad debts in the past; if any legal action has been taken against them to recover overdue accounts; what sort of reputation they have amongst suppliers in the trade; whether they have ever traded under another name, and if they have, whether that business has been subject to bankruptcy proceedings?

Please would you make the necessary enquiries, and let us know your fee.

Yours sincerely

Pat Marlow

Pat Marlow (Ms)
Director

Registered in England 221359
VAT 240 7225 03

1 How does Ms Marlow ask if the company has ever owed money before?

2 Why would the supplier want to know if the company has ever traded under another name?

3 Which words in the letter have a similar meaning to the following?
   a late payments
   b legal action to close the business

Credit Investigations Ltd

1 Bird Street
London
E1 6TM

Telephone +44 (0)20 7623 1494
Fax +44 (0)20 7623 1965
Email spades@credit.co.uk

26 April 20—

Ms Pat Marlow
P. Marlow & Co. Ltd
31 Goodge Street
London EC4 4EE

Dear Ms Marlow

As requested in your letter of 9 April we have investigated Falcon Retailers Ltd.

It is a private limited company with a registered capital of £10,000 and consists of two partners, David and Peter Lorre. It has an annual turnover of £400,000 and has been trading since October 1993. As far as we know, neither the company nor its directors have ever been subject to bankruptcy proceedings, but the company was involved in a court case to recover an outstanding debt on 17 January 20—. The action was brought by L.D.M. Ltd and concerned the recovery of £3,650, which Falcon eventually paid. We ought to point out that L.D.M. broke a delivery contract which accounted for the delayed payment.

From our general enquiries we gather that some of Falcon's suppliers have had to send them second and third reminders before outstanding balances were cleared, but this does not suggest dishonesty so much as a tendency to overbuy, which means the company needs time to sell before they can clear their accounts.

We hope this information proves useful. If you have any further enquiries, please contact us.

You will find our account for £475.00 enclosed.

Yours sincerely

S. Spade

S. Spade
Credit Investigations Ltd

Enc. Account

Reg. London 3121561

1 How many people run Falcon Retailers?

2 What are their annual sales?

3 Have they ever gone out of business?

4 Have legal proceedings ever been taken against them?

5 Does the company settle its balances on due dates?

6 What does Mr Spade think Falcon Retailers' problem is?

7 Which words in the letter have a similar meaning to the following?
   a researched
   b get back
   c unpaid

Points to remember

1 Credit is only given if the supplier knows that the customer has a sound reputation, knows the customer well, and / or has a reference from a bank or business associate of the customer.

2 When asking for credit, say why you want it and convince your supplier that you will pay on due dates. State how long you have been dealing with the company and offer supporting references.

3 When refusing credit, you should give reasons and convince your customer that the refusal does not discriminate against them in particular. Using generalizations can help, e.g. *We usually / as a rule / normally do not offer credit facilities*.

4 When taking up a reference, tell the company who you are and who you are enquiring about. Tell them the type of credit involved, e.g. bill of exchange, monthly settlements, and let them know how much the credit is for. Assure them that the information will be treated in confidence and that you will reciprocate should the occasion arise.

5 When writing an unfavourable reply, if you do not want to comment on a company's reputation, simply write that you do not give information about any of your customers. Alternatively, be brief, stating only the facts as they concern you. Do not give opinions or mention the name of the company.

6 When writing a favourable reference, state that you have allowed the company credit facilities but do not mention its name. Tell the enquirer the information is given in confidence and without responsibility.

9

Banks in the UK

TYPES OF BANK

These can be divided into three main groups: MERCHANT BANKS, COMMERCIAL BANKS, and PRIVATE BANKS. (BUILDING SOCIETIES, which are MUTUAL institutions where people can save and borrow money, primarily to buy a home, also exist in the UK, but many of them have converted to public limited companies and now compete with commercial banks in offering domestic services like current accounts, loans, MORTGAGES, and insurance, and will act as TRUSTEES and EXECUTORS, like banks. However, FOREIGN EXCHANGE, discounting services, and negotiating documents are still primarily dealt with by banks.)

Merchant banks

Merchant banks tend to encourage larger organizations to use their services, and while the facilities they offer are similar to those of the commercial banks, merchant banks specialize in the areas of international trade and finance, discounting bills, confirming the CREDIT STATUS of overseas customers through CONFIRMING HOUSES, acting in the NEW ISSUE MARKET, and in the BULLION and EUROBOND MARKETS. They are, in addition, involved in the shipping, insurance, and FOREIGN EXCHANGE MARKETS.

Commercial banks

Commercial banks, also known as CLEARING BANKS, offer similar services but are particularly interested in private customers, encouraging them to use their current, deposit, and savings accounts, and credit facilities. They will lend money, against SECURITIES, in the form of OVERDRAFTS and loans, pay accounts regularly by standing order, and transfer credits through the bank giro system. Essentially the differences between the merchant and commercial banks are the latter's availability to customers with their numerous branches and lower charges, and the laws which govern the way each type of organization handles its affairs.

As well as local branches in towns and cities, the commercial banks offer:
— TELEPHONE BANKING, which provides a twenty-four-hour service and allows customers to obtain details of their account, transfer money between accounts, pay bills, etc.
— ONLINE BANKING, which allows customers to make payments, transfer funds, and access information about their accounts using the Internet.

Private banks

Private banks offer similar facilities to the commercial banks but tend to be more expensive to use.

COMMERCIAL BANK FACILITIES IN THE UK

Current accounts

A current account can be opened by anyone in the UK provided they can prove their identity with, e.g. a driving licence, international ID card, or passport. The advantages of this type of account include being able to make payments by cheque. For extra security the customer, when paying by cheque, is required to use a CHEQUE CARD, which makes the bank responsible for the cheque passed, up to the limit stated on the card. This also acts as a CASH CARD allowing money to be drawn from cash dispensers even when the bank is closed.

Although cheques can be drawn immediately, it can take three working days before the amount is DEBITED or CREDITED to an account.

When depositing cash or cheques, a PAYING-IN SLIP is used to record the deposit. Its COUNTERFOIL, with the bank's stamp and cashier's initials, acts as proof that the deposit was made.

It is possible to OVERDRAW a current account, i.e. take out more money than there is in credit. Many banks offer current accounts where overdraft facilities are automatically included, sometimes at no extra charge. However, large overdrafts require the bank manager's agreement.

Many companies have more than one current account, e.g. a Number 1 account for paying wages and OVERHEADS, and a Number 2 account for paying suppliers.

Deposit accounts

Banks offer several types of DEPOSIT ACCOUNT, e.g. instant access accounts, where money can be withdrawn at any time, and notice accounts, where advance notification has to be given for withdrawal, e.g. thirty, sixty, or ninety days.

Credit and debit cards

CREDIT CARDS offer credit facilities to customers buying goods or services in shops, by mail order, or on the Internet. There is a limit to the amount the customer can spend on most cards, and credit card companies charge a basic fee plus monthly interest.

DEBIT CARDS use EFTPOS (Electronic Funds Transfer from Point of Sale) technology which allows the shop to 'swipe' the card, transferring money out of the customer's account into the shop's account directly.

The increasing use of credit and debit cards has resulted in a decline in the use of cheques.

Standing orders and direct debits

Customers making regular payments, such as rent, or mortgage repayments, can ask the bank to transfer the money to the payee on a particular day every month. A STANDING ORDER or a DIRECT DEBIT are two ways of doing this. For a standing order, the amount to be paid is specified in advance. For a direct debit, the bank pays the amount charged by the payee.

Loans and overdrafts

Loans and overdrafts for large amounts usually require a formal agreement. A loan will usually be covered by NEGOTIABLE SECURITIES, e.g. shares, with repayment specified on the agreement. In the UK, interest is not controlled by law but by market forces. The money for a loan is immediately deposited in the customer's account. In the case of an overdraft, the customer is given permission to overdraw an account up to a certain limit.

Administrative correspondence

The examples overleaf, and others in this unit, could also be handled by a telephone call to the bank. The bank employee will in most cases have a template form on-screen which he or she will fill out for the customer after obtaining their password or security number and details of their business. However, it may be advisable for the customer to follow up a telephone conversation with a letter, fax, or email so that there is a written record of the transaction.

9

Opening a current account

In this example, the owner of a fashion shop is applying to open a current account. The bank manager will acknowledge the letter, tell the customer that the account has been opened and the money credited, and either enclose a chequebook or let her know that one is being prepared.

Dear Mr Day

I would appreciate it if you could open a current account for me under my trading name R & S Fashions Ltd. Enclosed you will find two specimen signatures, my own and that of my partner Ms Catherine Sidden. Both signatures will be required on all cheques. I also enclose a reference from Mr Stephen Young, who banks with your branch, and a cheque for £357.00 with a paying-in slip.

Yours sincerely

Anne Roberts

Anne Roberts (Mrs)

Change of signature

The bank must be informed of any change of address and, as here, of a change in the signatures required on cheques.

Dear Mr Winston

Please note that as from 11 August 20— the two signatures that will appear on cheques for our Number 1 and 2 accounts will be mine and that of our new accountant, Mr Henry Lloyd, who is taking over from Ms Dianne Knibbs.

I enclose a specimen of Mr Lloyd's signature and look forward to your acknowledgement.

Yours sincerely

Frank Wearing

Frank Wearing

Dear Sir / Madam

Account No. 33152 110 9501

We have just moved to new premises at the above address and would like to pay our monthly rent of £1,574.00 to our landlords, Richards & Long, 30 Blare Street, London SW7 1LN, by standing order.

Would you please arrange for £1,574.00 to be transferred from our No. 2 account to their account with Dewlands Bank, Leadenhall Street, London EC2, on the 1st of every month, beginning 1 May this year?

Please would you confirm that the arrangement has been made.

Yours faithfully

G.K. Archer

G.K. Archer (Mr)

| ✉ | | | | | | | | | | | | | _ □ × |

| 🖃 Send | 🖬 🖨 | ✂ 🗐 🖺 | 🖺 | 🖉 | 📖 🔍 | ! ↓ ✇ | 🗋 Options... | 🔲 |

| Arial | ▼ | 10 | ▼ | 🎨 | **B** *I* U | 🖹 🖹 🖹 | ☲ ☲ ☲ |

| File | Edit | View | Insert | Format | Tools | Actions | Help |

To...	Stephen Mathers
Cc...	
Subject:	Cheque cancellation

Dear Mr Mathers

Please cancel cheque No. 17892165001 for £1,672 in favour of B. Gelt Ltd.
The cheque appears to have been lost in the post and I am sending another in
its place.

B. Steward
Accountant

Advice of an overdrawn account

Banks prefer not to STOP cheques because of the embarrassment it can cause the customer, but if there is no arrangement for overdraft facilities, and the cheque, in the bank manager's opinion, is too large, it may be stopped. In the case of Mr Hughes, however, the bank manager lets the credit transfer go through. Naturally, the manager would not use an email for this confidential transaction.

Telephone +44 (0)1792 469008 (10 lines)
Facsimile +44 (0)1792 431726
Email collisd@welshcoop.co.uk

Welsh Co-operative Bank

Seaway House
Glendower Road
Swansea
West Glamorgan
8RN 1TA

8 August 20—

Mr R. Hughes
R. Hughes & Son Ltd
21 Mead Road
Swansea
West Glamorgan 3ST 1DR

Dear Mr Hughes

Account No. 0566853 01362

I am writing to inform you that you now have an overdraft of £1,358.63 on your current account.

We passed your last credit transfer to Homemakers Ltd as you have a substantial credit balance on your deposit account. If you require overdraft facilities on your current account, I suggest that you contact me and we can discuss a formal arrangement.

Yours sincerely

David Collis

David Collis
Manager

Chairman
A.C.M. Conway
Directors
R.M. Lloyd
C.R. Gymre A.I.S.

Reg. No: Swansea 385 1623

1 Why has Mr Collis passed Mr Hughes' cheque although it led to an overdraft?

2 What does he advise Mr Hughes to do if he wants an overdraft in future?

3 Why wouldn't the bank manager use an email in this case?

Reply to advice
of an overdrawn
account

R. Hughes & Son Ltd

21 Mead Road, Swansea
West Glamorgan 3ST 1DR
Telephone: +44 (0)1792 58441
Fax: Swansea +44 (0)1792 59472
Email: r.hughes@huson.co.uk

10 August 20—

Mr D. Collis
Manager
Welsh Co-operative Bank
Seaway House
Glendower Road
Swansea
West Glamorgan 8RN 1TA

Dear Mr Collis

Thank you for your letter of 8 August. I apologize for not being aware that I had a debit balance on my current account.

I have now checked into this and discover that the reason for my account being overdrawn was that I had received a post-dated cheque for £1,700.00 from a customer, and this had not been cleared. However, to avoid a repetition I have transferred £1,500.00 from my deposit account into my current account, and this should ensure against overdrawing in future.

Thank you for passing the credit transfer to Homemakers despite the debit balance it created.

Yours sincerely

Robert Hughes

Robert Hughes

Mr Hughes is aware
that the credit transfer
could have been stopped,
which would have been
embarrassing for him,
especially as he had
recently arranged
monthly settlements
with Homemakers
▶ **see pages 121–122**
and there had earlier
been a problem over
a credit transfer
▶ **see pages 93–94.**

VAT No. 215 2261 30

1 Why was Mr Hughes' account overdrawn?

2 Why hadn't the £1,700 cheque been cleared?

3 How has he made sure it won't happen again?

Request for an overdraft or loan

In this letter, Mr Cliff of Homemakers wants to obtain either an overdraft or a loan to expand his furniture factory. He asks for an appointment to discuss this, and explains why he needs the money. As it is an important matter, a letter is more appropriate than a telephone call, fax, or email.

HOMEMAKERS

54–59 Riverside, Cardiff CF1 1JW
Telephone: +44 (0)29 20 49721
Fax: +44 (0)29 20 49937
Email: rcliff@homemakers.com
Registered No. c135162

18 September 20—

Mr I. Evans
Barnley's Bank Ltd
Queens Building
Cathays Park
Cardiff CF1 9UJ

Dear Mr Evans

I would like to make an appointment with you to discuss an overdraft or a loan to enable me to expand my business.

I have been testing the market with a new line of furniture assembly kits, and have found that demand for these kits, both here and overseas, has exceeded my expectations. In the past six months alone I have had over £60,000 worth of orders, half of which I have been unable to fulfil because of my limited resources.

I would need a loan for about £18,000 to buy additional equipment and raw materials. I can offer £8,000 in ordinary shares, and £3,000 in local government bonds as part security. I estimate it would take me about nine months to repay a loan of this size.

I enclose an audited copy of the company's current balance sheet, which I imagine you will wish to inspect prior to our meeting.

I look forward to hearing from you.

Yours sincerely

Richard Cliff

Richard Cliff
Director

Enc.

1 Why does Mr Cliff need an overdraft or loan?

2 What new line does he want to put on the market?

3 What security does he offer?

4 What evidence does he offer to show his company is in a healthy state?

5 What is a balance sheet?

6 Which words in the letter have a similar meaning to the following?

a talk about
b enlarge
c been greater than
d meet (orders)
e assess
f checked (by an accountant)

Granting a loan

Mr Cliff and Mr Evans have now had their meeting and Mr Evans has checked Homemakers' accounts. He has considered the matter of the overdraft or loan, and is now replying.

BARNLEY'S BANK plc

Head Office Queens Building · Cathays Park · Cardiff CF1 9UJ

Telephone +44 (0)29 20 825316
Fax +44 (0)29 20 613625

Email ievans@barnleys.co.uk
www.barnleys.com

Date **27 September 20—**

Mr Richard Cliff
Homemakers Ltd
54–59 Riverside
Cardiff CF1 1JW

Dear Mr Cliff

With reference to our meeting on 23 September, I am pleased to tell you that the credit for £18,000 which you requested has been approved.

We discussed an overdraft, but agreed it would be better if the credit were given in the form of a loan at the current rate of interest (—%), calculated on half-yearly balances.

The loan must be repaid by 30 June 20—, and we will hold the £8,000 ordinary shares and £3,000 local government bonds you pledged as security. We agreed that the other £7,000 would be guaranteed by Mr Y. Morgan, your business associate. I would appreciate it if you could ask him to sign the enclosed guarantor's form, and if you could sign the attached agreement.

The money will be credited to your current account and will be available from 30 September subject to your returning both forms by that time.

I wish you success with the expansion of your business and look forward to hearing from you.

Yours sincerely

Ian Evans

Ian Evans
Manager

Enc

1 What does Mr Evans offer Mr Cliff?

2 How is the interest on the credit to be charged?

3 Which account will the loan be paid into?

4 When will the credit be available from?

5 Which words in the letter have a similar meaning to the following?
   a paid back
   b a person who guarantees something
   c contract

Refusing an overdraft

Mr Ellison's company owns a chain of petrol stations and garages. He is also a customer of Barnley's Bank and has also asked for an overdraft, but in his case the bank is not willing to lend him the money.

BARNLEY'S BANK plc

Head Office Queens Building · Cathays Park · Cardiff CF1 9UJ

Telephone +44 (0)29 20 825316
Fax +44 (0)29 20 613625

Email ievans@barnleys.co.uk
www.barnleys.com

Date 19 November 20—

Mr P. Ellison
Ellison & Co. Ltd
Bridgend Road
Bridgend CF31 3DF

Dear Mr Ellison

I regret to inform you that we will not be able to offer the credit of £85,000 you asked for at our meeting on 14 November in order to expand your business.

You have had a £26,000 overdraft this year, and this has partly influenced our decision. The current credit squeeze, which has particularly affected loans to the service sector of the economy, was also a factor. May I suggest that you approach a finance corporation as this type of organization might be in a better position to help in the current financial climate?

I am sorry that we have to disappoint you in this matter, and hope that we may be of more help in the future.

Yours sincerely

Ian Evans

Ian Evans
Manager

1 Why did Mr Ellison want the credit?

2 What two things influenced Mr Evans's decision not to allow credit in this case?

3 What alternative does Mr Evans suggest to Mr Ellison?

International banking

On page 78 we looked at various methods of payment used in trade outside the UK. Here we look in detail at two methods of payment, bills of exchange and documentary credits, and the way in which they involve banks at home and abroad.

BILLS OF EXCHANGE

A BILL OF EXCHANGE (B/E) is an order sent by the DRAWER (the person asking for the money / exporter) to the DRAWEE (the person paying / importer) stating that the drawee will pay, on demand or at a specified time, the amount shown on the bill. If the drawee accepts the bill, they will sign their name on the face of it and date it ▶**see the example on page 150**.

The bill can be paid to a bank named by the drawer, or the drawee can name a bank they want to use to clear the bill ▶**see the example on page 150**. In the latter case, the bill will be kept at the drawer's bank until it is to be paid. When the bill is due it is presented to the paying bank. Such bills are said to be *domiciled* with the bank holding them.

It is possible to send the bill direct to the drawee, if they are well-known to the drawer.

A SIGHT BILL or SIGHT DRAFT is paid on presentation. In a DOCUMENTS AGAINST PAYMENT (D/P) transaction, the sight bill is presented to the importer with the shipping documents, and the importer pays immediately, i.e. *on presentation* or *at sight*.

A bill paid DAYS AFTER SIGHT (D/S) can be paid on or within the number of days specified on the bill. For example, *30 days after sight* (or *30 D/s*) means that the bill can be paid thirty days after it has been presented. A bill which is paid after a period of time is called a *usance*.

In a DOCUMENTS AGAINST ACCEPTANCE *(D/A)* transaction, the bank will ask the drawee to accept the bill before handing over the shipping documents.

In the UK, bills of exchange drawn or payable in another country are known as FOREIGN BILLS, and those used within the country in which they are drawn up as INLAND BILLS. A CLEAN BILL is one that is not accompanied by shipping documents.

The advantage to the exporter of payment by bill is that the draft can be DISCOUNTED, i.e. sold to a bank at a percentage less than its value, the percentage being decided by the current market rates of discounting. So even if the bill is marked *90 days after sight*, the exporter can get their money immediately by selling it to a bank. The bank, however, will only discount a bill if the buyer has a good reputation. The advantage for the importer is that they are given credit, provided the bill is not a sight draft.

Bills can be negotiable if they are ENDORSED (signed on the back) by the drawer. For example, if Mr Panton, the drawer of the bill on page 150, wanted to pay another manufacturer, he could sign on the back of the bill, i.e. endorse it, and the bill would become payable to the person who owned it. Mr Panton can endorse it *specifically*, i.e. make it payable only to the person named on the bill.

A DISHONOURED bill is one that is not paid on the due date. In this case the exporter will PROTEST the bill, i.e. they will go to a lawyer, who will, after a warning, take legal action to recover the debt.

There is also a Cash Against Documents transaction (CAD), where the documents are handed over to the importer when cash has been paid. In these transactions, of course, there is no bill of exchange and the importer (buyer) is not given credit.

9

A typical bill of exchange

Bills of exchange vary in layout from company to company. ►**See page 150 for another example.**

```
Number                              __(2)__

Exchange for __(1)__
At __(3)__ pay this __(4)__ Bill of Exchange
__(4)__ to the order of

__(5)__
__(6)__
Value received __(7)__ placed to account

To __(8)__                           __(9)__
                                     __(9)__
```

1 Currency and value of the bill of exchange in figures
2 Date the bill is completed
3 When payment is due, e.g. sight; D/s after sight; on a particular date, e.g. 12 October 20—
4 If only one bill of exchange is required, you write *sola*. If more than one is required, write *first*; and on the second line before the words *to the order of*, write *second of same tenor and date unpaid*. This means there are two copies of this bill, i.e. a second (tenor) copy. The drawee only signs (*accepts*) one copy of the bill.
5 Name of seller writing the bill (the drawer) or the name of another nominated person
6 Write in words the currency (e.g. *euros* or *yen*) and the amount, e.g. *twenty thousand* written in (1)
7 Left blank unless there is a specified form of words to be written, e.g. *payable at the current rate of exchange for banker's drafts in London*
8 Name and address of the person or company the bill is being drawn on, i.e. the drawee
9 Enter the name of the company (the drawer's name); name and position of the person signing the bill (the signatory)

Panton Manufacturing Ltd
Panton Works | Hounslow | Middlesex | TW6 2BQ

TELEPHONE +44 (0)20 8353 0125
FACSIMILE +44 (0)20 8353 6783
EMAIL d.panton@panman.co.uk

2nd March 20—

Advising despatch
of a bill

Panton Manufacturing
have completed an order
for a Dutch customer.
They now advise the
customer that the
agreed bill of exchange
has been sent.

9

Example letter

Mrs B. Haas
B. Haas B.V.
Heldringstraat 180–2
Postbus 5411
Amsterdam 1007
The Netherlands

Dear Mrs Haas

Order No. 8842

Thank you for the above order which has now been completed and is
being sent to you today.

As agreed we have forwarded our bill, No.1671 for £3,860.00, with the
documents to your bank, Nederlandsbank, Heldringstraat, Amsterdam.
The draft has been made out for payment 30 days after sight, and the
documents will be handed to you on acceptance.

Yours sincerely

Donald Panton

Donald Panton
Managing Director

Registered No. England
266135

1 Where has the bill of
   exchange been sent?

2 When should the bill
   be paid?

3 How can Mrs Haas
   obtain the shipping
   documents?

Bill of exchange

Here is the bill mentioned in the previous letter. It has already been accepted by the drawee, who has named a bank in London which she wants to use to clear it.

B/E No. 1671   5 March 20—

30 days after sight pay to the order of
   Panton Manufacturing Ltd London
   Three thousand eight hundred and sixty pounds only (sterling)
value received payable at the current rate of exchange for Banker's sight drafts on London.

To B. Haas B.V.
Heldringstraat 180–2
Amsterdam 1007

Accepted payable at Mainland Bank, London

B. Haas

Signed .... *Donald Panton*
Managing Director

Advising despatch of a sight bill

The bill on page 150 was for payment thirty days after sight. If the supplier wants immediate payment or does not have time to check the customer's creditworthiness, they may send a sight bill, as in this example.

To...	Jan Lindquist
Cc...	
Subject:	Advice Order No.8540

Dear Jan

The above order is now on board the *Leda*, sailing for Copenhagen tomorrow, arriving Thursday.

As there was no time to check references, we drew a sight draft for the total amount of £4,150 (four thousand, one hundred and fifty pounds sterling). This was sent to Nordbank, Garnes Vej, Copenhagen, and will be presented to you with the documents for payment.

If you can supply two business references before your next order, we will put the transaction on a documents against acceptance basis with payment 40 days after sight.

Best wishes
Donald Panton
Managing Director
Panton Manufacturing Ltd
Tel: +44 (0)20 8353 0125
Fax: +44 (0)20 8353 6783
Email: d.panton@panman.co.uk

Exporters sometimes
ask their banks to
forward bills to
importers' banks.

Panton Manufacturing Ltd
Panton Works | Hounslow | Middlesex | TW6 2BQ

TELEPHONE +44 (0)20 8353 0125
FACSIMILE +44 (0)20 8353 6783
EMAIL d.panton@panman.co.uk

6 July 20—

The Manager
Mainland Bank plc
Portman House
Great Portland Street
London W1N 6LL

Dear Sir

Please send the enclosed draft for £4,163.00 on J.K.B. Products Pty and
documents to the National Australian Bank, 632 George Street, Sydney,
Australia, and instruct them to release the documents on acceptance.

Yours faithfully

Donald Panton

Donald Panton
Managing Director

Enc.

Registered No. England
266135

J.K.B. PRODUCTS PTY

Bridge House
183-9 Kent Street
Sydney
NSW 2000

Telephone: +61 (0)2 279611
Facsimile: +61 (0)2 279642
Email: lcorey@jkb.com.au

Date: **18 July 20—**

The Manager
National Australian Bank
632 George Street
Sydney NSW 2000

Dear Sir

You will shortly receive a bill of exchange for £4,163 and relevant documents
from Panton Manufacturing Ltd, Hounslow, UK. Would you please accept
the draft on our behalf, send us the documents, and debit our account?

Yours faithfully

L. Corey

L. Corey
J.K.B. Products Pty

President
D. Bruce
Managing Director
L. Thompson
Directors
I. R. Marsh
T. L. Bradman

**Request to a bank
to accept a bill**

The Australian importer
mentioned in the
previous letter now
writes to their bank to
tell them to accept the
bill.

Non-payment of a bill

If a customer cannot pay a bill, they should inform their supplier immediately ▶ **see page 91**. When a bill is not paid and no notice has been given, the supplier usually writes to the customer before protesting the bill, as here. Note the expression *Refer to drawer*, which means the bank is returning the bill to the drawer. This expression is also used when a dishonoured cheque is returned. Also notice that a formal protest is to be made, which means that the drawer will contact a lawyer to handle the debt if payment is not made within the specified time.

Panton Manufacturing Ltd
Panton Works | Hounslow | Middlesex | TW6 2BQ

TELEPHONE +44 (0)20 8353 0125
FACSIMILE +44 (0)20 8353 6783
EMAIL d.panton@panman.co.uk

10 April 20—

Mrs B. Haas
B. Haas B.V.
Heldringstraat 180–2
Postbus 5411
Amsterdam 1007
The Netherlands

Dear Mrs Haas

B/E No. 1671

The above bill for £3,860.00 was returned to us from our bank this morning marked 'Refer to Drawer'.

The bill was due on 5 April and appears to have been dishonoured. We are prepared to allow you a further three days before re-presenting it to the bank, in which time we trust that the draft will have been met.

If the account is still not settled, we will have to make a formal protest. We hope this will not be necessary.

Yours sincerely

Donald Panton

Donald Panton
Managing Director

Registered No. England
266135

DOCUMENTARY CREDITS

A bill of exchange might be DISHONOURED, as we saw in the example on page 154, or an order might be cancelled. However, these risks can be reduced by issuing a letter of credit, which is a more binding form of payment.

LETTERS OF CREDIT (L/C) have been used for centuries in one form or another to enable travellers to obtain money from foreign banks. The process begins with the traveller asking their bank to open a letter of credit in their favour, i.e. for a specific amount of money to be debited to their account. The bank then drafts a letter, which will allow the traveller to draw money on foreign banks with whom the traveller's home bank has an agreement. The foreign banks will then draw on the home bank to recover their payments.

For individual travellers, credit cards, EUROCHEQUES, and TRAVELLER'S CHEQUES have largely replaced this method of obtaining money, but DOCUMENTARY CREDITS (letters of credit accompanied by documents) are widely used in foreign trade.

There are two types of letter of credit: REVOCABLE, i.e. those that can be cancelled, and IRREVOCABLE, i.e. those that cannot be cancelled except with the agreement of the seller. The first type is very rarely used these days.

Documentary credits are governed by the International Chamber of Commerce code of practice, known as the Uniform Customs and Practice for Documentary Credits. The current code is ICC publication No.500 and is generally referred to as UCP500.

Shipping documents

The following are the essential documents which accompany a documentary credit:
— bill of lading
— commercial invoice
— insurance certificate

Other documents which, in specific cases, it might also be necessary to include are:
— customs form
— CERTIFICATE OF ORIGIN (i.e. a certificate showing where goods were made, which is used to prevent goods from outside coming into a free trade area or customs union without being taxed)
— CONSULAR INVOICE (i.e. an invoice, or sometimes a stamp on the commercial invoice, giving permission for goods to be imported, issued by the consulate in the importing country)
— certificate of inspection (i.e. a certificate signed by agents to ensure the customer is getting goods of the type and quality he ordered
— health certificate

With Electronic Data Interchange (EDI) many of the relevant documents can be completed on computer templates to the exporter's specific requirements and transferred by email. In this case payment is made by SWIFT, the international bankers' computerized transfer of funds.

The stages in a documentary credit transaction

The stages in an irrevocable documentary credit transaction are as follows:

1 The importer (buyer) asks their bank to issue a letter of credit in favour of the exporter (seller). The importer applies for a letter of credit by filling out a form. This gives the following details:
— type of credit (i.e. revocable or irrevocable)
— beneficiary (the person receiving the money)
— amount
— how long the credit will be available for (i.e. valid until a certain date)
— documents involved in the transaction (e.g. bill of lading, insurance certificate, commercial invoice)
— description of goods

2 The importer's bank (called the ISSUING BANK as it issues the letter of credit) asks a bank in the seller's country to advise the seller that a letter of credit has been issued in

their favour. The issuing bank may also ask the bank in the seller's country to *confirm* the letter of credit (i.e. promise to see that the conditions of payment are fulfilled). For these reasons the bank in the seller's country is called the CONFIRMING or ADVISING BANK.

3 The exporters despatch the consignment to the importers and present the shipping documents (bill of lading, commercial invoice, insurance certificate, etc.) to the confirming bank.

4 The exporters draw a bill of exchange on the confirming bank. The bank pays the exporters against the bill and then sends the shipping documents to the issuing bank.

5 The issuing bank checks the documents and pays the confirming bank.

6 The issuing bank releases the shipping documents to the importers and debits their account.

7 The importers collect the consignment by presenting the shipping documents to the shipper.

Standby letter of credit

Exporters may require a guarantee to make sure that they are paid. This is frequently done by means of a STANDBY LETTER OF CREDIT where the bank will pay the exporters if, for any reason, the importers do not pay. It is often used when there is a contract involving several shipments and the exporters want to get part of, or all, of their payment at once. In some countries, the USA for example, standby letters of credit are preferred to bank guarantees and have the advantage of being subject to the Uniform Customs and Practice for Documentary Credits (UCP500).

BUYER/IMPORTER	ISSUING BANK	ADVISING/CONFIRMING BANK	SELLER/EXPORTER
1 Asks his or her bank to open a letter of credit in favour of the seller.	2 Asks bank in buyer's country to advise or confirm the shipping documents.	3 Advises seller of the transaction and may confirm payment against a B/E drawn on it, if that has been arranged.	4 Despatches consignment to the buyer and presents the shipping documents to the advising/confirming bank.
7 The buyer gets the consignment by presenting the shipping documents to the shipping company.	6 Releases the shipping documents to the buyer or agent bank in his or her country against payment.	5 Pays seller or discounts B/E drawn on it, and sends the shipping documents to the issuing bank in the buyer's country.	

N.Z. BUSINESS MACHINES PTY

100, South Street · Wellington | Directors: C.M. Perimann · L.F. Drozin
Telephone: (+64) 4 8617 Fax: (+64) 4 3186 Email: m.tanner@nzbm.co.nz

3 May 20—

Ian Close
New Zealand Bank
Takapuna House
Takapuna Street
Wellington 8

Dear Mr Close

Please open an irrevocable documentary credit for £22,000 in favour of Delta Computers Ltd, Wellingborough, UK. I have enclosed your application form with all the relevant details completed.

Please inform me when you have made arrangements with your agents in London.

Yours faithfully

Michael Tanner

Michael Tanner
Export Manager
N.Z. Business Machines Pty

Enc. Application for documentary credit

From the
importers to the
issuing bank

N.Z. Business Machines,
of Wellington, New
Zealand, who are
importing a
consignment of
computers from Delta
Computers, based in the
UK, ask their bank to
issue a letter of credit in
Delta's favour.

9

Example letter

Application form for documentary credit

Here is a specimen application form. The form filled in by Mr Tanner for his bank in New Zealand would be similar to this.

9

Example form

Please complete all areas in black ink and block capitals

- Original mail instructions
- Original fax instructions

Fax codeword
Date

Party details

Customer (Applicant)

Applicant's reference
Contact name
Telephone number
Fax number
Customer Trade ID

(See note 2)

(See note 3)

Beneficiary

Beneficiary's
Telephone number

Transaction details

Amount and currency   *(In words and figures)*

- Up to
- About ± (specify)   %

Goods description
(Avoid excessive details; you may include a reference to proforma invoice(s) though such documents may not be attached)

Payment terms
- Sight
- For   days after (specify)
          % of invoice value (eg. 100%)

Shipment terms
- Ex works   - FOB/FCA   - CFR/CPT
- CIF/CIP   (specify)
Last shipment date   *(See note 4)*

Documents to be presented within   days of shipment but within the validity of the credit
Expiry date
Transportation
From
To   *(See note 5)*

Partshipment
- Allowed
- Not allowed

Transhipment
- Allowed
- Not allowed

Documents required

Transport documents   *(Tick one box)*
- Sea   Full Set Clean on board Port to Port Bills of Lading   - Air   Airway Bill
- Sea/Road   Full Set Multimodal Transport Documents   - Road   CMR Road Transport Document
- Sea/Air   Full Set Multimodal Transport Documents   - Other   (please specify)

Consignee
- Bland endorsed (B/L only)
- Other
- Other

Original/Copies
Original Copy (State number of originals and/or copy documents)
- Invoice
- GSP Form A
- Other (specify)

Insurance
(See condition d) for shipment terms CIF/CIP/CE&I (or other terms requiring the beneficiary to be responsible for insurance) please indicate cover required.
Orig. Copy
- Insurance Policy/Certificate Endorsed in blank for the Invoice value
plus   %

Marked notify
- Applicant
- Other

Original Copy
- Packing list
- Certificate of Origin
- Other (specify)

Covering
- Institute cargo clauses 'A'
- War risks
- Strikes, riots and civil commotions
- Warehouse to warehouse
- Other (specify)

Other conditions
NB No document will be demanded for non-documentary conditions unless specifically requested (See note 8.)

Settlement   *(On receipt of documents in order/at maturity)*
Branch sort code   -   -
- Debit our Sterling Account number
- Debit our Currency Account number
- Utilise Forward Contract number:
          Maturing   Rate
- Forward cover being arranged

Commission and charges   *(If different)*
- Debit our Sterling Account number
- Debit our Currency Account number

We request you to issue your Irrevocable Import Letter of Credit for our account in accordance with the above instructions and subject to the conditions printed overleaf.   (See note 1)

Stamp and signature(s) on behalf of customer in accordance with mandate held by Bank.

Commissions and charges   *(See condition f)*
- All our account
- All beneficiaries account
- All charges outside UK for beneficiary remainder ours

Fax codeword
Date

From the importers to the exporters

At the same time as they open the credit at their bank, N.Z. Business Machines email their supplier. Notice that Mr Tanner mentions the confirming bank in London.

To... James Millar

Cc...

Subject: Order No.8815

Official order 8851

Dear Mr Millar

We are placing the attached order for 12 (twelve) C3001 computers, your Catalogue No. 548. We have instructed our bank, New Zealand Bank, Takapuna St, Wellington, to open an irrevocable letter of credit for £22,000.00 (twenty two thousand pounds sterling) to cover the consignment, shipment (CIF Wellington), and bank charges. The credit is valid until 10 June 20—.

You will receive confirmation from our bank's agents, Eastland Bank Ltd, 401 Aldgate, London, EC1 2DN, and you can draw on them at 60 (sixty) days for the full amount of the invoice. When submitting your draft, please enclose the following documents.

Bill of Lading (3 copies)
Invoice CIF Wellington (2 copies)
AR Insurance Policy for £24,000.00 (twenty four thousand pounds sterling)

Please fax or email us as soon as you have arranged shipment.

Michael Tanner
Export Manager
N.Z. Business Machines Pty
100, South Street, Wellington
Phone: +64 4 8617
Fax: +64 4 3186
Email: m.tanner@nzbm.co.nz

1 How does Mr Tanner specify which computers he requires?

2 What sort of shipment is this?

3 When does the letter of credit expire?

4 What should Delta Computers do to get their money?

5 What is the name of the confirming bank?

6 What is attached to the email?

7 Why do you think the insurance amount is greater than the invoice amount?

Eastland Bank, London, acting for New Zealand Bank, now inform Delta Computers that a letter of credit has been opened for them. The documents listed in the letter are the essential shipping documents.

Eastland Bank plc

CHAIRMAN Lord Seaforth
MANAGING DIRECTOR I.P. Raimer

401 Aldgate | London | EC1 2DN

DIRECTORS R. Lichen M.SC., B.A.,
S.D. Harrisman O.B.E., P.R. Akermann B.SC.,
N.L. Renut

Telephone +44 (0)20 7635 2217 (10 lines)
Facsimile +44 (0)20 7635 2226
Email p.medway@eastland.com
www.eastland.com

15 May 20—

Delta Computers Ltd
Bradfield Estate
Bradfield Road
Wellingborough
Northamptonshire NN8 4HB

Dear Sir

Please find enclosed a copy of the notification we received yesterday from the New Zealand Bank, Wellington, to open an irrevocable letter of credit in your favour for £22,000 which will be available until 10 June 20—.

You may draw on us at 60 days against the credit as soon as you provide evidence of shipment. Please would you include the following documents with the draft:

Bill of lading (three copies)
Commercial invoice CIF Wellington (two copies)
AR Insurance certificate for £24,200

Your draft should include our discount commission which is 5%, and our charges listed on the attached sheet.

Yours faithfully

P. Medway

P. Medway
Documentary Credits

Enc. Irrevocable Credit No. 2/345/16

BARCLAYS BANK PLC
DOCUMENTARY CREDITS DEPARTMENT

BARCLAYS BANK PLC

LONDON TRADE SERVICES CENTRE
PO BOX 36495, GROUND FLOOR
ST SWITHIN'S HOUSE
11/12 ST SWITHIN'S LANE
LONDON EC4N 8YB UK
PHONE: 020 7200 3200 FAX NO: 0870 607 3601
ANSWERBK: BARCGB G TELEX: 418319

SPECIMEN

date 20 July 2002

IRREVOCABLE CREDIT No: - ENDC 70844
To be quoted on all drafts and correspondence

BENEFICIARY
SPIERS AND WADLEY LIMITED
ADDERLEY ROAD
HACKNEY
LONDON E.8.

ADVISED THROUGH

APPLICANT
WOLDAL INCORPORATED
PO BOX 666, BROADWAY
HONG KONG

IN ACCORDANCE WITH INSTRUCTIONS RECEIVED FROM THE DOWNTOWN BANK & TRUST CO. WE HEREBY ISSUE IN YOUR FAVOUR A DOCUMENTARY CREDIT FOR GBP4106 (FOUR THOUSAND ONE HUNDRED AND SIX POUNDS STERLING) AVAILABLE BY YOUR DRAFTS

AT SIGHT

FOR 100% CIF   INVOICE VALUE ACCOMPANIED BY THE FOLLOWING DOCUMENTS: -

1) SIGNED INVOICE IN TRIPLICATE
2) FULL SET OF CLEAN ON BOARD SHIPPING COMPANY'S BILLS OF LADING MADE OUT TO ORDER AND BLANK ENDORSED, MARKED "FREIGHT PAID" AND "NOTIFY WOLDAL INC., PO BOX 666, BROADWAY, HONG KONG"
3) INSURANCE POLICY OR CERTIFICATE IN DUPLICATE, COVERING MARINE AND WAR RISKS UP TO BUYER'S WAREHOUSE, FOR INVOICE VALUE OF THE GOODS PLUS 10%

COVERING THE FOLLOWING GOODS: -

400 ELECTRIC POWER DRILLS

TO BE SHIPPED FROM   LONDON   TO   HONG KONG CIF

NOT LATER THAN   10TH AUGUST 2002

PARTSHIPMENT NOT PERMITTED   TRANSHIPMENT   NOT PERMITTED

THIS CREDIT IS AVAILABLE FOR   PRESENTATION TO US   UNTIL 31ST AUGUST 2002

DOCUMENTS TO BE PRESENTED WITHIN 21 DAYS OF SHIPMENT BUT WITHIN CREDIT VALIDITY.

DRAFTS DRAWN HEREUNDER MUST BE MARKED "DRAWN UNDER BARCLAYS BANK PLC LONDON T.S.C. CREDIT NUMBER ENDC70844

WE UNDERTAKE THAT DRAFTS AND DOCUMENTS DRAWN UNDER AND IN STRICT CONFORMITY WITH THE TERMS OF THIS CREDIT WILL BE HONOURED.

UNLESS OTHERWISE STIPULATED ALL DOCUMENTS SHOULD BE ISSUED IN THE ENGLISH LANGUAGE OTHERWISE THEY MAY BE DISREGARDED.

THIS CREDIT IS SUBJECT TO THE UNIFORM CUSTOMS AND PRACTICE FOR DOCUMENTARY CREDITS (1993 REVISION), ICC PUBLICATION NUMBER 500

Notification of documentary credit

The notification forwarded to Delta Computers by Eastland Bank will have been similar to this one. Instead of a form like this, many banks ask importers to fax the application form ▸ see page 158 to them and then prepare the letter of credit to suit the importer's requirements.

Questions

1 Who will receive the money?
2 Which documents are involved besides the letter of credit?
3 What special clause is mentioned in the insurance policy?
4 Can the goods be moved from one ship to another?
5 What is the value of the credit?
6 When is the letter of credit valid until?
7 Who is the issuing bank?
8 Who opened the letter of credit?
9 Can the exporters ship the consignment in different lots?
10 What does the consignment consist of?

From the exporters to the confirming bank

Delta Computers now acknowledge Eastland Bank's letter, and send them the documents they asked for and their draft.

Delta Computers Ltd
Bradfield Estate
Bradfield Road
Wellingborough
Northamptonshire
NN8 4HB

Telephone +44 (0)1933 16431/2/3/4
Fax +44 (0)1933 20016
Email millarj@delta.com
www.delta.com

Your Ref: 15/5/20—
Our Ref: NS/OM

24 May 20—

Mr P. Medway
Eastland Bank plc
401 Aldgate
London EC1 2DN

Dear Mr Medway

Thank you for your advice of 15 May. We have now effected shipment to our customers in New Zealand and enclose the shipping documents you asked for and our draft for £23,100 which includes your discount, commission, and charges.

Will you please accept the draft and remit the proceeds to our account at the Mainland Bank, Oxford Street, London W1A 1AA.

Yours sincerely

N. Smith

N. Smith
Senior Shipping Clerk

Enc. Bill of lading (3 copies)
Commercial invoice CIF Wellington (2 copies)
AR Insurance certificate for £24,200
Draft 2152/J

Reg. England 1831713
VAT 2419 62114

From the exporters
to the importers

Delta Computers notify
N.Z. Business Machines
that the consignment is
on its way to them.

To...	Michael Tanner
Cc...	
Subject:	Shipment of your order No.8815

Dear Mr Tanner

The above order has been shipped clean aboard the *Northern Cross*, due in Wellington 12 June.

The shipping documents have been passed to the Eastland Bank, London, and will be forwarded to the New Zealand Bank, Wellington, who will advise you.

As agreed we have drawn on the Eastland Bank at sixty days after sight for the net amount of £23,100.00 (twenty three thousand, one hundred pounds sterling) which includes the bank's discount, commission, and charges.

Neil Smith
Senior Shipping Clerk
Delta Computers Ltd
Wellingborough, NN8 4HB, UK
Tel.: +44 (0)1933 16431/2/3/4
Fax: +44 (0)1933 20016
Email: smithn@delta.com

1 When is the consignment likely to arrive in New Zealand?

2 What has happened to the shipping documents?

3 How has the Eastland Bank earned money on the transaction?

From the importers' bank to the importers

The New Zealand Bank now advises N.Z. Business Machines that their account has been debited, and that the documents are ready for collection. When he has the documents, Mr Tanner will be able to take delivery of the computers.

Send | Options...

Arial | 10 | **B** *I* <u>U</u>

File Edit View Insert Format Tools Actions Help

To... | Michael Tanner

Cc... |

Subject: | Delta Computers

Dear Mr Tanner

In accordance with your instructions of 3 May, our agents, Eastland Bank, London, accepted a draft for £23,100 drawn by Delta Computers Ltd on presentation of shipping documents for a consignment sent to you on 24 May.

We have debited your account with the amount plus our charges of $NZ 350. The documents are now with us and will be handed to you when you call.

Ian Close
New Zealand Bank

This email, from the importers, International Boats, in London to the exporters, Lee Boatbuilders, in Hong Kong, is the first step in our second example of a documentary credit transaction. Note that International Boats ask for a certificate of origin, which they need since they intend to re-export the dinghies to France, which is an EU country. Note also that they will use their bank's agents – the confirming bank –to verify the quality of the boats.

To...	John Lee
Cc...	
Subject:	Our order 90103

Order No. 90103

Dear Mr Lee

We met your representative, Mr Tom Chai, at the Earls Court Boat Show in London last week, and he showed us a number of your dinghies, and informed us of your terms and conditions.

We were impressed by the boats, and have decided to place a trial order for ten of your craft, Catalogue No. NR 17. The attached order, No. 90103, is for delivery as soon as possible.

As Mr Chai assured us that you could meet any order from stock, we have instructed our bank, Northern City Ltd, to open a confirmed irrevocable letter of credit for £10,300 in your favour, and valid until 1 June 20—.

Our bank informs us that the credit will be confirmed by their agents, Cooper & Deal Merchant Bank, Pekin Road, Hong Kong, once you have contacted them. They will also supply us with a certificate of quality when you have informed them that the order has been made up and they have inspected it.

You may draw on the agents for the full amount of the invoice at 60 days, and your draft should be presented with the following documents:

Six copies of the bill of lading
Five copies of the commercial invoice, CIF London
Insurance certificate for £10,540 (A.R.)
Certificate of origin
Certificate of quality

The credit will cover the invoice, discounting, and any other bank charges. Please cable us confirming that the order has been accepted and the dinghies can be delivered within the next six weeks.

Regards
Andy Valour
International Boats Ltd
Email: valoura@intboat.co.uk

From the exporters to the importers

Northern City, who are International Boats' bankers, have now notified their agents in Hong Kong, Cooper & Deal, who have in turn advised Lee Boatbuilders that the credit is available. Meanwhile Lee Boatbuilders have emailed International Boats confirming that they have accepted the order and can deliver within six weeks. They follow this by sending a fax, advising shipment.

Dock 23, Mainway
Hong Kong
Telephone +852 385162
Fax +852 662553

Facsimile

Lee Boatbuilders Ltd

From	J. Lee
To	Andy Valour, International Boats Ltd, London
Fax	+44 (0)20 8834 4431
Subject	Your order No. 90103
Date	6 May 20—
No of pages	2

Dear Mr Valour

Order No. 90103

We are pleased to inform you that the above order has been loaded on to the MV *Orient*, which sails tomorrow and is due in Tilbury on 3 June. The dinghies and their equipment have been packed in polystyrene boxes in ten separate wooden crates marked 1–10, and bearing our brand ⚠.

The shipping documents (see list attached) have been handed to Cooper & Deal, Hong Kong, with our draft for £10,300.50 at 60 D/S. This covers all charges and discounting. Cooper & Deal will forward the documents to Northern City Bank, who will advise you within the next few weeks.

We have supplied the certificate of origin that you asked for. However, we wondered if this was for re-exporting purposes? We should point out that your customers would only be covered by the guarantee if the boats are not modified in any way, as this would be outside the guarantee's terms.

Please confirm delivery when you receive the consignment.

Thank you for your order, and we hope you will contact us again in the future.

Yours sincerely

John Lee

John Lee
Director

Questions

1 When is the consignment likely to arrive in London?

2 How have the dinghies been packed?

3 What does *60 D/s* mean?

4 Who are Cooper & Deal, and what role do they play in the transaction?

5 What will the Northern City Bank advise International Boats?

6 What shipping document (apart from the bill of lading, commercial invoice, and insurance certificate) do International Boats require?

7 What restrictions do Lee Boat Builders put on their guarantee?

8 Which words in the fax have a similar meaning to the following?
  a small open boat
  b provided
  c warranty
  d altered

Points to remember

Banks in the UK

There are various types of bank in the UK which offer a wide range of banking facilities for domestic customers, businesses, and international trade.

International banking

1 The two main methods used in settling accounts in international trade are bills of exchange and documentary credits. These involve banks in both the importers' and the exporters' countries.

2 Bills of exchange can be *at sight*, i.e. payable on presentation, or *after sight*, i.e. payable at a stipulated date in the future. The exporters can send the bill to the importers direct, or to their bank with the documents, and will obtain either payment on presentation or acceptance against the bill.

3 The advantages of bills of exchange are that exporters can get the money immediately if the bill is discounted, and importers can obtain credit if the bill is not a sight draft. The disadvantages are that a bill of exchange may be dishonoured, and it is relatively easy to cancel an order.

4 A confirmed irrevocable documentary credit cannot be cancelled, and the importers' bank and its agent guarantee payment. With discounting facilities, exporters do not have to wait for their money if the bank agrees that they can draw against the credit. Importers are protected by the shipping documents, e.g. a certificate of inspection.

10

TYPES OF AGENCY

AGENTS and AGENCIES usually represent companies. There are many kinds of representation, but in this unit we deal mainly with buying and selling agencies. However, it is useful to look as well at other areas where companies act on behalf of their clients, as these will be referred to later.

Brokers

BROKERS usually buy or sell goods for their PRINCIPALS (the companies they represent) but rarely handle the consignments themselves. There are various types of broker:

— *Brokers / DEALERS on a STOCK EXCHANGE* buy and sell shares for their clients. The clients ask the broker to buy or sell shares for them, and the broker takes a commission on the purchase or sale.
— *Shipbrokers* arrange for ships to transport goods for their clients. They operate from their offices, or on the Baltic Exchange or one of its branches. ▶**See pages 197–199 for more on this topic.**
— *Insurance brokers* arrange insurance COVER with UNDERWRITERS, who pay compensation in the event of a loss. ▶**See pages 222–239 for more on this topic.**
— *Commodity brokers* buy and sell bulk commodities, e.g. cocoa, tea, coffee, and rubber on the COMMODITY MARKETS on behalf of their clients. Metal brokers do the same on the Metal Exchange.

There are other exchanges where companies use brokers to represent them, either because the company does not have membership of that exchange, or they want to use the broker's specialized knowledge of the market.

Buyers, sellers, and brokers communicate by means of telephone, email, cable, or fax as prices in the markets tend to fluctuate quickly – even by the minute in the case of bullion and foreign currency.

Confirming houses

CONFIRMING HOUSES receive orders from overseas, place them, and arrange for packing, shipment, and insurance. They sometimes finance or purchase the goods themselves, then resell them to the client. They may act ON COMMISSION, but if buying ON THEIR OWN ACCOUNT will make a profit on the difference between the ex-works price (the price from the factory) and the resale price they quote the importer.

Export managers

If a company does not have a branch in the country it is exporting to, they can appoint an export manager, who will deal under their own name but use the address of the company represented. The export manager's job is primarily to develop the market for the exporter, and managers may charge a fee for this service or arrange for a profit-sharing scheme with the exporter.

Factors

FACTORS can buy and sell ON THEIR OWN ACCOUNT (i.e. in their own names), receive payment, and send accounts to their principals. They often represent companies exporting fruit or vegetables.

FACTORING is the process whereby a company buys the outstanding invoices of a manufacturer's customers, keeps the accounts, and then obtains payment. NON-RECOURSE FACTORING involves the buying up of outstanding invoices and claiming the debts. If the buyer (the manufacturer's customer) goes bankrupt, the factor has no claim. In RECOURSE FACTORING, the factor will claim from the manufacturer if the customer cannot pay.

Distributors

DISTRIBUTORS buy goods from an exporter then sell them on their own account for a profit. The advantage of this is that the exporter has only one customer in that market to worry about. However, the exporter has to be careful in selecting distributors in order to ensure the best sales.

A distributor is expected to keep the exporter informed about the market and not to sell products which compete with the exporter's. Distributors are also expected to have a network in the area, provide training for technical staff, and supply after-sales service when and where necessary. An exporter might make enquiries about a distributor before signing a contract.

The exporter will refer all enquiries to the distributor, supply conditions of sale to distributors and their customers, offer promotional material, and provide INDEMNITIES (insurance) for guarantees on the goods the distributor sells.

Commercial agents

Another name for a COMMERCIAL AGENT is a COMMISSION AGENT. A commercial agent never takes title to the goods, i.e. never owns them like a distributor, but is the intermediary or 'middleman' between the exporter and the customers.

Commercial agents represent a manufacturer, obtaining goods and then reselling them. They may buy the goods from the manufacturer on consignment: this means that they do not own the goods but sell them on for a commission. Commercial agents can be SOLE or EXCLUSIVE AGENTS, i.e. the only agent allowed to sell a particular manufacturer's products in a specified country or area.

Buying agents

BUYING AGENTS, or BUYING HOUSES, buy goods on behalf of a principal and receive a commission. They are employed to get the best possible terms for their principals, and will try to find the most competitive rates in shipping and insurance for them. Buying houses often act on behalf of large stores.

The orders sent to buying agents are called INDENTS and are of two types: OPEN INDENTS, where the agents choose their supplier, and CLOSED or SPECIFIC INDENTS, where the supplier is named by the principal.

FINDING AN AGENT

It is possible to find an agent through the Internet, or by advertising in TRADE JOURNALS. Other methods include contacting government DEPARTMENTS OF TRADE in your own country or the country you wish to export to, or consulting CHAMBERS OF COMMERCE, CONSULATES, TRADE ASSOCIATIONS, or banks. The guide below provides some suggestions for ways of dealing with this kind of correspondence.

Opening

Tell the organization who you are.
— *We are a large manufacturing company specializing in …*
— *We are one of the leading producers of …*
— *You probably associate our name with the manufacture of chemicals / textiles / business machines / furniture …*

Explaining what you want

— *We are looking for an agent who can represent us in …*
— *We would like to appoint a sole agent in Taiwan to act on our behalf selling …*
— *Our aim is to identify an established company who can represent us …*

Closing

Close by saying that you would be grateful for any help.
— *We would be grateful if you could supply us with a list of possible agents.*

— We hope you can help us, and look forward to hearing from you.
— Thank you in advance for your help. We look forward to receiving your recommendations.

OFFERING AN AGENCY

Once you have obtained the names and addresses of prospective agents, you can write to them direct. Below is a guide for manufacturers offering terms to a prospective agent.

Opening

Tell the agent how you obtained their name.
— You were recommended to us by the Saudi Trade Commission in London.
— Mr Eric Stoleman of the Swiss Export Department has told us that…

Explain who you are.
— We are an established company manufacturing…
— We are the leading exporters of…
— We are one of the main producers of chemicals / textiles / business machines / furniture…

Convincing the prospective agent

Convince the agent that the products you make are worth handling and will sell in their market.
— You will see from our catalogue that we offer a wide range of well-designed products which are hardwearing, light, easy to use, and fully guaranteed for one year.
— Our prices are extremely competitive for a product of this quality. Our research shows us that there is a growing demand for this product in your country, and we are sure that once our brand is established it will become a market-leader.
— The Zenith 2000 is the result of many years' research and development, and we are confident that it will quickly overtake sales of the competing brands at present available in the Swedish market.

Sole or exclusive agency

— We will not restrict the agent by offering a sole agency as we have found that this limits our own sales and, in addition, is sometimes awkward for the agent.
— We are offering an exclusive agency, ensuring that you will not have competition from other agents operating in the area specified in the contract.
— We cannot offer an exclusive agency for Austria at present. However, if the agency is successful, we may reconsider the situation in the future.

It should be established whether you are going to deal with your agent on a CONSIGNMENT BASIS, when the agent will not own the products you send but will sell them for a commission, or whether you want to supply the agent as a distributor to re-sell to customers on their own account, in which case the agent will decide on resale prices and take the profits from the sales.
— Generally, we do not deal on a consignment basis, but prefer our agents to buy our products on their own account. They usually prefer this method as it proves more profitable for them and allows them greater freedom in determining prices.

Note that the use of the word generally in the above example leaves the offer open to negotiation.

Area to be covered

Make it clear what area the agency is for.
— You will have sole distribution rights for the whole of France, which will give you an excellent opportunity to establish a highly profitable market.
— Initially, we will give you a sole agency for the Lazio region, but if sales are successful, we will extend that to other regions.
— As exclusive agents you will have no competition in Northern Germany, therefore with effective selling you should be guaranteed a substantial return.

10

Commission

Some firms offer terms straight away in an initial enquiry, while others wait until they have had a reply from the prospective agent. When offering terms, you should make them sound as inviting as possible.

— *The agency we are offering will be on a commission basis, and as we are very interested in getting into the French market, we are prepared to offer 15%, plus a substantial advertising allowance.*
— *As this will be a sole agency, we are prepared to offer a generous commission as compensation, and a reasonable allowance for expenses.*
— *As an inducement to the agent we appoint, we will be offering a 12% commission on net prices.*

Settlement of accounts

— *Orders should be sent to us direct for shipment, and we will arrange for customers to pay us. You may issue us with quarterly / monthly statements of account, which will be paid by sight draft at the bank of your choice.*
— *Customers should pay us direct on each sale by letter of credit, and we will remit your commission by bill on submission of your monthly / quarterly account. Credit is not to be offered without our express consent.*

Support from the principal

Prospective agents will want to know what support you will give them in their efforts to sell your products.

— *Our products carry a one-year guarantee and we will replace any faulty item carriage paid.*
— *As you know, our company offers a full after-sales service, which is essential in establishing the reputation of our brands, and your customers need have no worries about spare parts or maintenance.*
— *We can offer you additional expenses of £15,000 per annum for advertising. This will be reviewed after a year and increased if we think sales warrant it.*

Delivery

Exporters should always allow some time for unforeseen problems caused by delays, public holidays, etc. It is always best to quote a realistic delivery time.

— *Providing there are no unforeseen delays, we will be able to deliver within six weeks from receipt of order.*
— *We would like you to maintain adequate stocks of our three main ranges, bearing in mind that we will be able to deliver between two and four weeks of receiving orders.*
— *Delivery should not take longer than three weeks if we have the items in stock.*

Duration of the contract

The length of time for the contract is usually discussed after the agency has been agreed.

— *The contract will be from 1 March for one year, and provided both parties agree, will be renewed for a further year in 20—.*
— *We feel that nine months should be enough time to decide whether this arrangement is likely to be successful, and will draw up the first contract accordingly.*
— *Subject to our mutual agreement, the contract will be renewed annually.*

Disagreements and disputes

Provision is usually made for disagreements and disputes. This, too, would not appear in an initial letter, but in correspondence confirming the agency, and, of course, in the contract.

— *In the case of disagreement over conditions or payments, the matter will be settled by arbitration.*
— *We agree that disputes over contracts should be decided according to American law.*

Note: ARBITRATION is when a neutral organization settles problems between the principal and agent. A chamber of commerce or trade association often acts as arbitrator.

Del credere agents

DEL CREDERE AGENTS guarantee a customer's debt 'del credere' (in the belief that) the customer can pay the exporter. In other words, if the customer cannot pay the exporter, the agent is responsible for the debt. For this guarantee, the agent is paid a DEL CREDERE COMMISSION.

— *We are prepared to offer an additional 2.5% del credere commission if you are willing to guarantee customers' debts.*
— *In addition to the 12% commission on net sales, we will offer a further 3% del credere commission if you are willing to deposit £10,000 as a security to guarantee all customers' debts.*

ASKING FOR AN AGENCY

Below is a guide to correspondence when offering to act as a manufacturer's agent.

Opening

Explain who you are and how you found out about the manufacturer's product.

— *You were recommended to us by our associates, Lindus Products Ltd, of Lagos, who told us that you were looking for an agent to represent you in Nigeria.*
— *We are contacting suppliers of medical equipment in your country with a view to acting as their representatives here in Saudi Arabia. Your name was given to us by the British Consul in Jeddah. We already import medical supplies from a number of different countries, but are particularly interested in the EEG machines and scanners you manufacture.*

Convincing the manufacturer

You need to convince the manufacturer that there is a market for their product in your country or area, and that you are the best person to develop it.

— *As you know, Germany is extending its farming areas with the aid of EU grants to farmers. We have many contacts in the government who will direct us to large-scale farms and enterprises which are in the market for your products.*
— *Because we have already established business relationships with hospitals and clinics in Saudi Arabia, we are confident that we are the best company to represent you. The development of the health service means that generous grants to clinics and hospitals have increased the demand for the type of equipment that you manufacture.*

Suggesting terms

You may want to leave discussion of terms until you know that the principal is interested in your request. But there is no harm, even in an initial enquiry, in describing the terms on which you normally operate and asking if they would be acceptable.

— *May we suggest the terms on which we usually operate to give you an idea of the sort of agency contract we have in mind? We generally represent our principals as exclusive distributors for Germany, buying products on our own account, with an initial contract running for one year, renewable by mutual agreement. We expect manufacturers to offer advertising support in the form of brochures – in German and English – and catalogues, and in return we promise our customers a full after-sales service and two-year guarantees on all products. Therefore, we would expect a first-class spare-parts service with delivery for both products and spare parts within six weeks of receipt of order. We would pay you direct by 40-day bill of exchange, documents against acceptance.*

If this type of agency interests you, please contact us so that we can draw up a draft agreement.

Offer of an agency

Mr Jay describes his company, their products, and the type of agency he is offering. Note how he 'sells' the agency.

British Crystal Ltd

GLAZIER HOUSE · GREEN LANE · DERBY DE1 1RT
TELEPHONE: +44 (0)1332 45790 · FACSIMILE: +44 (0)1332 51977
Email: jayn@crystal.com · www.britishcrystal.com

4 May 20—

S.A. Importers Ltd
Al Manni Way
Riyadh
SAUDI ARABIA

Dear Sirs

Mr Mohamed Al Wazi, of the Saudi Arabian Trade Commission in London, informed us that you may be interested in acting as our agent in your country.

As you will see from the enclosed catalogue, we are manufacturers of high-quality glassware. We produce a wide selection of products from moderately priced tableware in toughened smoked glass to ornate Scandinavian and Japanese designed light coverings.

We already export to North and South America and the Far East, and would now like to expand into the Middle Eastern market, where we know there is an increasing demand for our products.

The type of agency we are looking for will be able to cover the whole of Saudi Arabia. We are offering a 10% commission on net list prices, plus advertising support. There would be an additional 2.5% del credere commission if the agent is willing to guarantee the customer's accounts, and he may offer generous credit terms once we have approved the account.

This is a unique opportunity for someone to start in an expanding market and grow with it. Therefore, if you believe you have the resources to handle a sole agency covering the area mentioned, and feel that you can develop this market, please write to us as soon as possible.

Yours faithfully

Nicholas Jay

Nicholas Jay
Managing Director

Enc. Catalogue

1 Who recommended the agency to British Crystal?

2 Where does British Crystal export to at present?

3 What commissions could the prospective agent earn?

4 Are British Crystal offering the prospective agent any additional help?

5 What must happen before the agent can offer good credit terms to customers?

6 What do you think Mr Jay means by 'resources to handle a sole agency'?

7 Which words in the letter have a similar meaning to the following?
a to get bigger
b range
c special

Agent's reply,
asking for more
details

Agents and agencies

10

Example email

```
✉                                                          _ □ ✕
  📧 Send  💾 🖨  ✂ 📋 📋 📧  🗐 📎  📖 🔍  ❗ ⬇ ⌦  🗐 Options...  🔲
  Arial              ▾  10  ▾  🌐  B  I  U  ▤ ▤ ▤ ▤ ▤ ▤
  File   Edit   View   Insert   Format   Tools   Actions   Help
```

To...	Nicholas Jay
Cc...	
Subject:	Agency offer

Dear Mr Jay

Thank you for your letter of 4 May in which you offered us a sole agency for your products in Saudi Arabia.

First, let me say that we can handle an agency of the type you describe, and we agree the demand for good quality chinaware is increasing here. However, before we can take your offer further we need the following information:

1. Payment of accounts. Would customers pay you direct in the UK, or would they pay us, and we in turn settle with you after deducting our commission? How would payment be arranged? Bill of exchange, letter of credit, or bank draft?

2. Delivery. Would we hold stock or would you supply customers direct? If you supply direct, how long would it take for an order to be made up and shipped once it had been received?

3. Advertising. You mentioned that you would help with advertising. Could you give us more details?

4. Disputes. If a disagreement arises over the terms of the contract, who would be referred to in arbitration?

5. Length of contract. How long would the initial contract run? In our view, three years would allow us to estimate the size of the market.

If you can send us this information, and possibly enclose a draft contract, we could give you our answer within the next few weeks.

Mohamed Kassim
Director
S.A. Importers Ltd
Riyadh
Tel: (+966) 1 35669
Fax: (+966) 1 34981
m.kassim@saimp.co.sa

1 What sort of agency is British Crystal offering?

2 Is Mr Kassim confident about selling British Crystal's products in his country?

3 Does he suggest a method of payment?

4 How long does he want the agency to run?

5 What is a *draft contract*?

6 Which words in the email have a similar meaning to the following?
  a subtracting
  b argument
  c first

175

Manufacturer's reply, giving more details

Mr Jay provides the information Mr Kassim asked for, and encloses a draft contract.

British Crystal Ltd

GLAZIER HOUSE · GREEN LANE · DERBY DE1 1RT
TELEPHONE: +44 (0)1332 45790 · FACSIMILE: +44 (0)1332 51977
Email: jayn@crystal.com · www.britishcrystal.com

6 June 20—

Mr M. Kassim
S.A. Importers Ltd
Al Manni Way
Riyadh
SAUDI ARABIA

Dear Mr Kassim

Thank you for your email. As you requested, we enclose a draft contract for the agency agreement.

You will see that we prefer our customers to pay us direct, and usually deal on a letter of credit basis.

You would not be required to hold a large stock of our products, only a representative selection of samples. We can meet orders from the Middle East within four weeks of receipt.

Advertising leaflets and brochures would be sent to you, but we would also allow £7,000 in the first year for publicity, which could be spent on the type of advertising you think most suitable for your market. In our other markets we have found that newspapers and magazines are generally the best media.

The initial contract would be for one year, subject to renewal by mutual agreement. Disputes would be settled with reference to EU law.

If you have any further questions with regard to the contract, or anything else, please contact me.

I look forward to hearing from you.

Yours sincerely

Nicholas Jay

Nicholas Jay
Managing Director

Enc. Draft contract

1 How would customers pay British Crystal?

2 Would customers be supplied from S.A. Importers' warehouse?

3 What sort of advertising material does Mr Jay offer?

4 How long would the agency run initially?

5 What does *mutual agreement* mean?

6 Which words in the letter have a similar meaning to the following?
a typical
b fulfil
c depending on

Allison & Locke Importers Ltd.

Rooms 21–28
Rothermede House
Eastgate Street
London
WC1 1AR

Telephone +44 (0)20 7636 9010/1/2/3/4
Fax +44 (0)20 7636 9271
Email mallison@allock.co.uk
Cable ALLOCK London

Reply to an offer of an agency

This letter is a reply to an offer of an agency, but the prospective agent is asking for the terms to be changed.

17 October 20—

Sr F. Iglasis
Iglasis Leather Manufacturing SA
Enrique Granados 109
Barcelona
Spain

Dear Sr Iglasis

We are interested in the offer you made to us in your letter of 8 October to act as sole agents for your leather goods in this country.

While we agree that there is a steady demand for high-quality leather cases and bags here, in our opinion the annual turnover you suggest is too optimistic. We estimate that half the figure you quoted would be more realistic. In view of this, the 6% commission you offer is rather low, and we would expect a minimum of 10% on net invoice totals.

With regard to payments, we feel it would be preferable for customers to settle with us direct, and we would remit quarterly account sales deducting our commission. However, we are prepared to leave this matter open for discussion.

Finally, we would be willing to hold the stock you suggest, but if there is a rush of orders, as there may be now we are nearing Christmas, you would need to shorten the delivery date you quoted from six weeks to three weeks from receipt of order.

If these conditions are acceptable, then we would be pleased to take on an initial one-year contract to act as your sole agents.

I look forward to hearing from you.

Yours sincerely

M. Allison

M. Allison (Mr)
Director

Directors M. Allison, B. Locke
Reg. No. London 897032
VAT No. 232 6165 73

1 What sort of agency is Sr Iglasis offering?

2 Why does Mr Allison think a six per cent commission is rather low?

3 Which matter is he prepared to negotiate?

4 Why might delivery dates be a problem?

5 How long would the initial contract run?

6 If you were Sr Iglasis, what concessions do you think you could make to meet Mr Allison's terms?

7 Which words in the letter have a similar meaning to the following?
   a the least amount
   b send money
   c reduce

Request for an agency

In this email, Brian Glough, Director of a British motorcycle retail chain, is asking an American motorcycle manufacturer, Hartley-Mason Inc., if he can represent them in the UK. Mr Glough describes his company, tells Mr Mason where he saw his product, convinces him that there is a market, and suggests terms.

Send | | | | | | | | | | | | Options...

Arial | 10 | B | I | U

File Edit View Insert Format Tools Actions Help

To... | Jack Mason

Cc...

Subject: | UK representation

Dear Mr Mason

We are a large motorcycle retail chain with outlets throughout the UK, and are interested in the heavy touring bikes displayed on your stand at the Milan Trade Fair recently.

There is an increasing demand here for this type of machine. Sales of larger machines have increased by more than 70% in the last two years, especially to the 30–50 age group, which wants more powerful bikes and can afford them.

We are looking for a supplier who will offer us an exclusive commission agency to retail heavy machines. At present we represent a number of manufacturers, but only sell machines up to 600cc, which would not compete with your 750cc, 1000cc, and 1200cc models.

We operate on a 10% commission basis on net list prices, with an additional 3% del credere commission if required, and we estimate you could expect an annual turnover in excess of £2,000,000. With an advertising allowance we could probably double this figure.

Our customers usually settle with us direct, and we pay our principals by bill of exchange on a quarterly basis.

You can be sure that our organization would offer you first-class representation and excellent sales, and guarantee the success of your products in this country.

I look forward to hearing from you.

Brian Glough
Director
Glough & Book Motorcycles Ltd
Nottingham NG1 3AA, UK
Tel. +44 (0)115 77153
Fax: +44 (0)115 48865
Email: b.glough@gloughbook.co.uk

Mr Mason is interested
in Mr Glough's proposal,
but would prefer him to
act as a distributor.

✉															_ □ ✕
📧 Send	💾 🖨	✂ 📋 📑	📇 📎	📖 👤		↑		↗	📄 Options...	❓

Arial	10	🌐	**B** *I* U̲	≣ ≡ ≡ ≡	≣ ⋲ ⋲

File   Edit   View   Insert   Format   Tools   Actions   Help

To... | Brian Glough

Cc... |

Subject: | RE: UK representation

Dear Mr Glough

Thank you for your email of 1 March. We were pleased to hear of your interest in our heavy
touring machines.

Regarding the type of agency you suggest, I should point out that we never use exclusive or
commission agencies as we have found that they tend to be rather restrictive both for
ourselves and our customers. We rely on distributors who buy our products on their own
account and then retail them at market prices in their country. We offer a 30% trade discount
off net list prices and a further 5% quantity discount for sales above $100,000. Our terms of
payment are 60 D/S bills, D/A if the customer can provide trade references.

As far as publicity is concerned, you may be interested to hear that we have arranged for an
extensive campaign in Europe. It begins next month and features our heavy machines. We
are sending dealers throughout Europe brochures, leaflets, and posters, and this will be
followed up by TV advertising in May.

I hope you will be interested in the terms outlined here, and look forward to hearing from you.

Best regards
Jack Mason
President
Hartley–Mason Inc.
Chicago, Ill.
Telephone: (+1) 312 818532
Fax: (+1) 312 349076
Email:j.mason@hartley-mason.com

---

1 Why doesn't
Hartley–Mason offer
sole agencies?

2 What are they
planning to do in
Europe?

3 What are their usual
terms of payment?

4 Which words in the
email have a similar
meaning to the
following?

a sell direct to the
public
b prices charged in a
competitive
market
c continued with

This letter is from a buying agent in the UK asking if they can represent a French store. Good buying agents have a first-class knowledge of a country, its products, and the most competitive prices on the market for goods, freight, and insurance. For this reason they often take a commission on CIF invoice values rather than NET INVOICE VALUES.

L. Dobson & Co. Ltd

Royal Parade
Plymouth
PL1 4BG

Telephone +44 (0)1752 31261
Fax +44 (0)1752 31708
Email l.dobson@dobco.uk

8 June 20—

Vivas S.A.R.L.
138 rue Cimarosa
F–75006 Paris

For the attention of the Chief Buyer

Dear Sir / Madam

I am replying to your advertisement in the trade magazine *Homecare* for a buying agent in the UK to represent your group of stores in France.

My company already acts for several companies in Europe and America. We specialize in buying domestic appliances and other household goods for these markets. We have contacts with all the leading brand manufacturers, so are able to obtain heavily reduced export prices for their products. In addition, we can offer excellent terms for freight and insurance.

Our usual commission is 5% on CIF invoice values, and we make purchases in our principals' names, sending them accounts for settlement.

We can keep you well informed of new products that come on to the market, sending you any information or literature that we think may be helpful.

I have enclosed our usual draft contract for you to consider. I hope you will be interested in our terms, and look forward to hearing from you.

Yours faithfully

Leonard Dobson

Leonard Dobson
Managing Director

Enc. Draft agreement

Reg. No. 81561771

Reply to a buying agent's offer

The French company is interested in taking on L. Dobson & Co., but is not happy with their proposal to charge five per cent commission on CIF invoiced values.

VIVAS S.A.R.L.

138 rue Cimarosa · F–75006 Paris

Tél: (+33) 1 46 0313 09
Fax: (+33) 1 46 0319 31
Email: varenne.m@vivas.com

23 June 20—

Mr Leonard Dobson
L. Dobson & Co. Ltd
Royal Parade
Plymouth PL1 4BG
UK

Dear Mr Dobson

Thank you for your letter in reply to our advertisement in *Homecare*. Although we are interested in your proposition, the 5% commission you quote on CIF invoice values is higher than we are willing to pay. However, the other terms quoted in your draft contract would suit us.

We accept that you can get competitive rates in freight and insurance. Nevertheless, we do not envisage paying more than 3% commission on net invoice values, and if you are willing to accept this rate we would sign a one-year contract to be effective as from 1 August. We can assure you that the volume of business would make it worth accepting our offer.

Yours sincerely

Marie Varenne

Marie Varenne (Mme)
Chief Buyer

1 Does Mme Varenne concede that Dobson & Co.'s usual commission is justified?

2 If Mr Dobson accepts Mme Varenne's counter-proposal, how long would the contract be for?

3 How does Mme Varenne suggest that her offer is worth considering?

4 Which words in the letter have a similar meaning to the following?
a business offer
b foresee
c come into operation

Agent's report

Here is a report from an agent who is sending an account sales to a British publisher for books she has sold on his behalf in South-East Asia. The agent takes advantage of the letter to make an enquiry.

511 Silom Road
Bangkok
Thailand

International Trading Co. Ltd

Telephone +66 2 87549
Facsimile +66 2 4853
Cable Intrad
Email l.chailing@intrad.co.th

Your Ref:
Our Ref: LC/PC
Date: 4 April 20—

Mr J. Trevor
Educational Books Ltd
187 Springfield Road
Chatham
Kent ME4 6SN
UK

Dear Mr Trevor

We are submitting our account sales for the consignment delivered ex-*Orianna*. You will find our draft for £4,196.60 enclosed, which is for the total sales less our commission at 10% and charges.

A number of booksellers here have enquired about the availability of scientific textbooks and classic fiction written in a simplified form of English and suitable for intermediate-level students.

If you publish any books of this kind, please would you send us details? If not, we would appreciate it if you could put us in touch with a publisher that specializes in this kind of book.

Yours sincerely

L. Chailing

L. Chailing (Ms)

Enc. Account sales and draft

ACCOUNT SALES

By **International Trading Co. Ltd**

511 Silom Road | Bangkok | Thailand

4 April 20—

In the matter of books ex-MV *Orianna*, sold for the account of Educational Books Ltd, Chatham, Kent, England.

No. of copies	Title	Price per copy	
100	English Dictionary	£14.00	£1,400
50	Adv. Eng. Studies	£12.00	£600
100	International English	£10.00	£1,000
80	Eng. for Proficiency	£10.50	£840
70	Eng. for 1st Cert.	£9.60	£672
90	Beginning English	£10.40	£936
			£5,448

Less Charges		
Ocean Freight	£260.00	
Dock Dues, etc.	£154.00	
Marine Insurance	£189.60	
Customs Tariff	£103.00	
Commission @ 10% on £5,448.00	£544.80	
LESS		£1,251.40
FINAL TOTAL		£4,196.60

Signed

L. Chailing

Account sales

This shows the amount International Trading Co. received for selling books on behalf of Educational Books, less charges and commission.

10

Example form

Points to remember

1 If you are offering an agency, convince the agent that your products are worth selling and will find a market in their area.

2 Be clear about the type of agency you are offering, for example exclusive or non-exclusive, on a consignment basis on the agent's account.

3 Offer terms and suggest ways of settling accounts. Be positive about the support that you, the principal, can provide for your agent.

4 If you are asking for an agency, convince the manufacturer that their products will be well represented.

10

Transportation and shipping

11

Road, rail, and air transport

The three main methods of transporting goods, apart from shipping which we will deal with in a separate section, are road, rail, and air. However, consignments can be transferred from one form of transport to another, especially when containers are used. The term MULTIMODAL (or INTERMODAL) indicates units that can be transferred between systems (or *modes*), e.g. containers being moved from truck to ship or train to truck.

CHARACTERISTICS

Road transport

Road transport tends to be cheaper and more direct than rail, especially for the transportation of small consignments. Its advantages include door-to-door service, quick loading and unloading in containers, and the use of roll-on roll-off (ro-ro) facilities on ferry crossings, where the truck can drive onto and off the ferry or a semi-trailer can be driven onto a ferry by one truck and driven off at the destination docks by another.

TIR (Transports Internationaux Routiers) vehicles, which are sealed, can go through customs without being searched. CABOTAGE LAWS permit carriers to transport third-country goods, e.g a French carrier can take goods from Spain to Italy.

Rail transport

Rail transport tends to be more economical than road transport for BULK CONSIGNMENTS (e.g. oil, grain, and coal). There are often links between road and rail carriers, e.g. many of the European services which use the Channel Tunnel.

Air transport

Some goods lose value or deteriorate over a short period of time, e.g. newspapers and flowers. For this kind of consignment air transport is used for speed, particularly over long distances. Insurance tends to be cheaper as consignments spend less time in transit. However, in the case of bulk consignments, air can be much more expensive than other forms of transport as charges are by weight (airfreight tonnes) or volume, whichever is the greater cost.

DOCUMENTATION

Road transport

A ROAD CONSIGNMENT NOTE (CMR) is the main document used in road transport. It is issued by the carrier and is the CONSIGNOR'S (person sending the goods) RECEIPT. It usually states that the goods are *in good condition* when the carrier receives them, but if there is something wrong with them, there may be a clause which states what this is. There are three original copies.

A CMR cannot be a DOCUMENT OF TITLE, i.e. it does not give ownership of the goods to the person named on the document.

DELIVERY NOTES are sent with consignments. They can be signed by the CONSIGNEE (person receiving the goods) stating either *contents have been examined*, which means the consignee has seen the goods and is accepting them in good condition, or *contents not examined*, as a precaution against receiving damaged goods.

Rail transport

Rail transport is covered by a RAIL CONSIGNMENT NOTE (CIM). Like a CMR, it is a receipt and not a document of title.

Air transport

The main document used in air transport is the AIR WAYBILL, which consists of twelve copies: one is sent to the airline, one to the consignor, and one to the consignee, each being accepted as originals. The other copies are sent to customers and handling. Unlike the bill of lading ▶ **see page 198**, the air waybill is only a receipt and cannot be transferred to another person. It acknowledges that the goods were received in *apparent good order*.

Only the consignee named on the air waybill can claim the goods, and they will need to quote the bill number. When a FORWARDING AGENT uses CONSOLIDATION SERVICES ▶**see page 199**, each consignee receives their own HOUSE AIR WAYBILL, and will need to quote the numbers of both the master air waybill and house air waybill.

General

Consignment notes and air waybills are obtained from the freight company by the consignor (sender) filling out an instructions for despatch form and paying the freight charges. Charges are calculated by size (volume), weight, or value, and sometimes also risk.

Most freight companies are private carriers, and are responsible for taking proper care of the goods and getting them to their destination on time.

Correspondence in transport is generally between consignors and freight companies, or consignors and forwarding agents, who send goods on behalf of the consignor. Customers are kept informed about consignments by means of *advice notes*, which can be sent by ordinary mail or email. They give details of packing and when goods will arrive.

In the European Union (EU) and European Free Trade Association (EFTA), MOVEMENT CERTIFICATES are used, especially for container shipments ▶**see page 211** where the consignment is taken through different customs posts to member countries.

In the EU, the SINGLE ADMINISTRATIVE DOCUMENT (SAD), an eight-part set of forms for export declarations, incorporates what were previously several customs forms. The SIMPLIFIED CLEARANCE PROCEDURE (SCP) is used to make documentation easier for exporters and agents.

No customs documents are required for trade between EU member countries.

Request for a
quotation for
delivery by road

In this example Mr Cliff
of Homemakers, the
furniture manufacturer
we met in earlier units,
faxes a road haulage
firm to ask for a
quotation to deliver
furniture to a customer,
R. Hughes & Son. He
describes the packing
(note that size rather
than weight will be the
main concern of the
carrier in this case),
states the value of the
consignment, and
mentions a delivery
time.

HOMEMAKERS

54–59 Riverside | Cardiff | CF1 1JW
Telephone: +44 (0)29 20 49721
Fax: +44 (0)29 20 49937

FACSIMILE MESSAGE

To	Cartiers Ltd
Fax	029 20 498315
From	R. Cliff
Date	10 November 20—
Subject	Quotation for Swansea delivery
Pages	1

Please quote for collection from the above address and delivery to:
R. Hughes & Son Ltd, 21 Mead Road, Swansea.

- 6 divans and mattresses, 700cm x 480cm

- 7 bookcase assembly kits packed in strong cardboard boxes, each measuring 14m³

- 4 coffee-table assembly kits, packed in cardboard boxes, each measuring 10m³

- 4 armchairs, 320 x 190 x 260cm

The divans and armchairs are fully protected against knocks and scratches by polythene and corrugated paper wrapping, and the invoiced value of the consignment is £4,660.50.

I would appreciate a prompt reply, as delivery must be made before the end of next week.

Richard Cliff

Richard Cliff
Director

CARTIERS LTD

516–519 CATHAYS PARK · CARDIFF CF1 9UJ
Telephone +44 (0)29 20 821597/8/9
Facsimile +44 (0)29 20 498315

Fax

To	R. Cliff
Fax	029 20 49937
From	H. Weldon (Ms)
Subject	Quotation for Swansea delivery
Date	10 November 20—
Page(s)	2

Dear Mr Cliff

In reply to the fax you sent today, we can quote £272.20 for picking up and delivering your consignment to the consignee's premises. This includes loading and unloading, plus insurance, and is valid with immediate effect until 14 December 20—.

If you would like to go ahead, please complete the Despatch Note with this fax, and let us know two days before you want the delivery to be made. Our driver will hand you a receipt when he collects the consignment.
If you have any queries, please do not hesitate to contact me.

H. Weldon

H. Weldon (Ms)

Quotation for delivery by road

In her reply to Mr Cliff's fax, notice how Ms Weldon refers to the consignment note as a *receipt*. She includes *loading and unloading* the consignment in her quote. (Carriers may quote for delivery on a time basis, as here, i.e. how long it will take to load or unload the vehicle.)

Advice of delivery

Homemakers Ltd now
advise their customer
by email.

```
✉                                                                      _ □ X

  🖾 Send   💾 🖨  ✂ 📋 📑  📧  📎  📖 🔍      ↑  ↓  ↕    📄 Options...   ?

  Arial              ▼  10  ▼  🎨  B  I  U   ≡ ≡ ≡ ≡ ≡ ≡ ≡

  File  Edit  View  Insert  Format  Tools  Actions  Help

   ┌─────────┐   ┌──────────────────────────────────────────────────┐
   │  To...  │   │  Robert Hughes                                     │
   └─────────┘   └──────────────────────────────────────────────────┘
   ┌─────────┐   ┌──────────────────────────────────────────────────┐
   │  Cc...  │   │                                                    │
   └─────────┘   └──────────────────────────────────────────────────┘
    Subject:     ┌──────────────────────────────────────────────────┐
                 │  Order No. B1517                                   │
                 └──────────────────────────────────────────────────┘
```

Invoice No. DM2561

Dear Robert

As our own driver is ill, I have arranged for Cartiers Ltd to deliver the above order on
Wednesday 18 November. Before signing the Delivery Note, could you please check that the
consignment is complete and undamaged?

I have attached the invoice, No. DM2561, and will add it to your monthly statement as usual.

Richard Cliff
Director, Homemakers Ltd
54–59 Riverside, Cardiff CF1 1JW
Tel.: +44 (0)29 20 49721
Fax: +44 (0)29 20 49937
Email: rcliff@homemakers.com

Complaint of damage in delivery by road

In this example the goods were sent by road, at the consignee's request, and were received damaged. Disc S.A., the customer, is emailing their supplier to complain.

To... | Rolf Gerlach

Cc... |

Subject: | Consignment Note 671342 158

Dear Herr Gerlach

Yesterday we received the above consignment to our order No. 02/310, but found that the CDs in boxes 4, 5, and 6 were damaged – either scratched, split, or warped.
The goods cannot be retailed, even at a discount, and we would like to know whether you want us to return them or hold them for inspection.

Regards
Pierre Gérard
Manager
Disc S.A.
251 rue des Raimonières
F–86000 Poitiers Cédex
Tél: (+33) 2 99681031, Télécopie: (+33) 2 74102163
Email: p.gerard@disc.co.fr

1 In what ways are the CDs damaged?

2 Were all the boxes damaged?

3 Is there any chance of selling the goods?

4 Is M. Gérard going to return the consignment?

R.G. Electronics AG

Havmart 601
D–50000 Köln 1

Telefon (+49) 221 32 42 98
Telefax (+49) 221 83 61 25
Email gerlachr@rge.co.de
www.rge.de

Your Ref:

17 August 20—

P. Gérard
Manager
Disc S.A.
251 rue des Raimonières
F-86000 Poitiers Cédex

Dear M. Gérard

I was sorry to hear about the damage to part of the consignment, No. T1953, that we sent you last week.

I have checked with our despatch department and our records show that the goods left here in perfect condition. Our checker's mark on the side of each box – a blue label with a packer's number and date on it – indicates this.

As you made the arrangements for delivery, I am afraid we cannot help you. However, I suggest you write to Gebrüder Bauer Spedition, and if the goods were being carried at 'carrier's risk', as they usually are in these cases, I am sure they will consider compensation.

I have enclosed a copy of the receipt from their goods depot at Köln. Please let me know if we can supply any other documents to help you with your claim.

Yours sincerely

Rolf Gerlach

Rolf Gerlach
Sales Director

Enc.

1 What does Herr Gerlach quote in the letter?

2 Why is he sure the goods were in perfect condition when they left his company?

3 Why doesn't he take responsibility for the consignment?

4 What help does he offer M. Gérard?

5 Which words in the letter have a similar meaning to the following?
a harm
b place from which goods are sent
c provide

251 rue des Raimonières
F–86000 Poitiers Cédex

Télephone (+33) 2 99681031
Télécopie (+33) 2 74102163
Email p.gerard@disc.co.fr

Réf. PG/AL

14 September 20—

Gebrüder Bauer Spedition
Mainzerstrasse, 201–7
D–50000 Köln 1

Dear Sirs

Consignment Note 671342 158

The above consignment was delivered to our premises, at the above address, on 6 September. It consisted of eight boxes of read / write CDs, three of which were badly damaged.

We have contacted our suppliers, and they inform us that when the goods were deposited at your depot they were in perfect condition. Therefore we assume that damage occurred while the consignment was in your care. The boxes were marked FRAGILE and KEEP AWAY FROM HEAT. However, the nature of the damage to the goods (the CDs were scratched, warped, or split) suggests that the consignment was roughly handled and left near a heater.

We estimate the loss on invoice value to be €500.00, and as the goods were sent 'carrier's risk' we are claiming compensation for that amount.

You will find a copy of the consignment note and invoice enclosed, and we will hold the boxes for your inspection.

Yours faithfully

P. Gérard

P. Gérard
Manager

Complaint to the carrier

Disc S.A. write to the carrier. On receipt of this letter, the carrier will inspect the goods and decide whether the damage was due to negligence. If it was, the customer will receive compensation.

Questions

1 What did the consignment consist of?

2 What condition were the goods in when delivered to the carrier's depot?

3 How does M. Gérard think the damage was caused?

4 What compensation is M. Gérard asking for?

5 Why does M. Gérard feel he has a right to claim compensation?

6 What is being sent with the letter?

7 Which words in the letter have a similar meaning to the following?
  a place of business
  b accept as true
  c easily damaged
  d keep

Request for a quotation for delivery by air

British Crystal fax an airline to find out how much it would cost to send glassware to their agents in Saudi Arabia.
▶**See pages 174–176 for previous correspondence.**

British Crystal Ltd

GLAZIER HOUSE · GREEN LANE · DERBY DE1 1RT
TELEPHONE: +44 (0)1332 45790 · FACSIMILE: +44 (0)1332 51977
Email: felthams@crystal.com · www.britishcrystal.com

FAX MESSAGE

To	Universal Airways Ltd	**From**	S. Feltham (Export Manager)
Fax no.	020 7638 55555	**Subject**	Shipment enquiry
Date	15 June 20—	**Page/s**	1

We would like to send ex-Heathrow to Riyadh, Saudi Arabia, 12 crates of assorted glassware, to be delivered within the next 10 days.

Each box weighs 40 kilos, and measures 0.51m³. Could you please quote charges for shipment and insurance?

S. Feltham

S. Feltham (Ms)
Export Manager

Universal Airways Ltd
Airline House
Palace Road
London SW1

Telephone +44 (0)20 7638 4129
Fax +44 (0)20 7638 5555
Cable UNIWAY
Email cargo@universalair.com
www.universalair.com

Ms S. Feltham
Export Manager
British Crystal Ltd
Glazier House
Green Lane
Derby DE1 1RT

Dear Ms Feltham

Thank you for your enquiry of 15 June.

We can send your consignment to Riyadh within 24 hours of delivery
to Heathrow. The cost of freight Heathrow–Riyadh is £10.60 per kilo, plus
£8.00 air waybill, and £54.00 customs clearance and handling charges.
You will need to arrange your own insurance.

Please fill in the despatch form and return it to us with the consignment
and commercial invoices, one of which should be included in the parcel
for customs inspection.

Please contact us for any further information.

Yours sincerely

R. Laden

R. Laden (Mr)
Cargo Manager

Reg. No: London 281395
VAT No: 8511625915

Quotation for delivery by air

Here is the airline's reply to Ms Feltham. We saw on page 187 that airlines calculate freight charges by weight or volume. In this case both will have been taken into account.

1 What other charges are there besides the freight charges?

2 Why should a copy of the invoice be included in the parcel?

3 Who will arrange insurance?

4 What form must be completed?

125		3043 3174		CSR/EC1		125- 3043 3174

Shipper's Name and Address | **Shipper's Account Number**

Not negotiable

Air Waybill

Issued by
British Airways London
Member of IATA

BRITISH AIRWAYS WORLD CARGO

Copies 1, 2 and 3 of this Air Waybill are originals and have the same validity

Consignee's Name and Address | **Consignee's Account Number**

It is agreed that the goods herein are accepted in apparent good order and condition (except as noted) for carriage SUBJECT TO THE CONDITIONS OF CONTRACT ON THE REVERSE HEREOF. ALL GOODS MAY BE CARRIED BY ANY OTHER MEANS INCLUDING ROAD OR ANY OTHER CARRIER UNLESS SPECIFIC CONTRARY INSTRUCTIONS ARE GIVEN HEREON BY THE SHIPPER, AND SHIPPER AGREES THAT THE SHIPMENT MAY BE CARRIED VIA INTERMEDIATE STOPPING PLACES WHICH THE CARRIER DEEMS APPROPRIATE. THE SHIPPER'S ATTENTION IS DRAWN TO THE NOTICE CONCERNING CARRIER'S LIMITATION OF LIABILITY. Shipper may increase such limitation of liability by declaring a higher value for carriage and paying a supplemental charge if required.

ISSUING CARRIER MAINTAINS CARGO ACCIDENT LIABILITY INSURANCE

Telephone Number

Issuing Carrier's Agent Name and City | Accounting Information

Agent's IATA Code | Account No.

Airport of Departure (Addr. of First Carrier) and Requested Routing

To | By First Carrier Routing and Destination | to | by | to | by | Currency | CHGS Code | WT/VAL PPD COLL | Other PPD COLL | Declared Value for Carriage | Declared Value for Customs

Airport of Destination | Flight/Date For Carrier Use Only Flight/Date

Handling Information

CANCELLED - SPECIMEN COPY

CSI

No. of Pieces RCP	Gross Weight	kg lb	Rate Class / Commodity Item No.	Chargeable Weight	Rate / Charge	Total	Nature and Quantity of Goods (incl. Dimensions or Volume)

Prepaid | Weight Charge | Collect | Other Charges

Valuation Charge

Tax

Total Other Charges Due Agent

Total Other Charges Due Carrier

Shipper certifies that the particulars on the face hereof are correct and that insofar as any part of the consignment contains dangerous goods, such part is properly described by name and is in proper condition for carriage by air according to the applicable Dangerous Goods Regulations.

Signature of Shipper or his Agent

Total Prepaid | Total Collect

Currency Conversion Rates | CC Charges in Dest. Currency

Executed on (date) at (place) Signature of Issuing Carrier or its Agent

For Carriers Use only at Destination | Charges at Destination | Total Collect Charges

125- 3043 3174

M. 197 – 9th

ORIGINAL 3 (FOR SHIPPER)

Questions

1 Which airline is the carrier?

2 How many original copies would the consignor get?

3 What international association is the carrier a member of?

4 Is this a document of title?

5 Can the air waybill be transferred to another person or company?

6 How is the consignee referred to?

7 Which two signatures are required?

8 How does the air waybill refer to what the goods consist of and how much is being shipped?

9 Shipping goods by air can be charged in two ways. What are they?

Shipping

TYPES OF VESSEL

A variety of vessels are used to transport goods:

— *BULK CARRIERS* transport bulk consignments such as grain, wheat, and ores.
— *TANKERS* transport liquid bulk consignments, usually oil.
— *Container vessels* have special lifting gear and storage space for the containers (large steel boxes) that they transport.
— *Passenger cargo vessels* concentrate on cargoes, but also carry passengers. They offer more facilities for loading and unloading than passenger liners.
— *Passenger liners* follow scheduled routes and concentrate on passenger services, but can also carry cargo.
— *Roll-on roll-off (Ro-Ro) ferries* are vessels constructed with large doors at each end so that cars and trucks can drive on at one port and off at another without having to unload and reload their cargo.
— *Lighters* are used for taking goods from a port out to a ship, or vice versa. They can also do the same work as a barge.
— *Barges* are large flat-bottomed boats which are used to transport goods inland along rivers and canals.

SHIPPING ORGANIZATIONS

Exporters can choose whether they use a company which is a member of the SHIPPING CONFERENCE group, or one that is listed on the BALTIC EXCHANGE.

The Shipping Conference

The Shipping Conference is an international organization of shipowners who meet periodically to set prices for transporting goods or passengers. There are several advantages for their customers. The costs of shipping are steady, i.e. they do not fluctuate over a short period, and universal, i.e. the same price is quoted by all members. Also, vessels registered with the Shipping Conference keep to scheduled routes, so bookings can be made some time in advance. Finally, customers can claim rebates (discounts) by shipping in bulk or for regular shipments.

NON-CONFERENCE SHIPS, as the term suggests, are not registered with the Shipping Conference. They travel anywhere in the world on unscheduled routes, picking up and delivering cargo. The old term for this kind of ship is a *tramp*.

The airline industry has an organization similar to the Shipping Conference. This is the International Air Transport Association (IATA).

The Baltic Exchange

Among its other functions the Baltic Exchange has a freight market which offers facilities for exporters to CHARTER (hire) ships and aircraft through SHIPBROKERS. Shipbrokers work on a commission and are specialists with a knowledge of the movement of ships and aircraft, and the most competitive rates available at any one time.

Once a broker is contacted they will find a shipowner who is prepared to hire a vessel on either a VOYAGE CHARTER or a TIME CHARTER basis. Voyage charter charges, i.e. charges for taking freight from port A to port B, are calculated on the TONNAGE VALUE of the cargo. For example, if an exporter ships 500 tons of grain at £4.20 per ton, the cost of the charter will be £2,100. Time charter charges are calculated on the tonnage (size) of the ship plus its running costs, excluding wages. So the larger the ship, the more the hirer pays, regardless of whether the cargo is 500 tons or 5,000 tons. A contract between a shipowner and a hirer is known as a CHARTER PARTY.

Ships listed on the Baltic Exchange do not run on scheduled routes and freight charges vary from company to company depending on supply and demand. Telephone, fax, or cable are used for speedy communication between hirers and brokers, and brokers and owners, and letters to confirm transactions.

SHIPPING DOCUMENTATION

The main documents used in shipping are described below.

Freight account

A FREIGHT ACCOUNT is an invoice sent by the shipping company to the exporter stating their charges.

Standard shipping note

A STANDARD SHIPPING NOTE is a document completed by the exporter. It is sent to the forwarding agent, an INLAND CLEARANCE DEPOT (ICD), or the docks. It is used as a delivery note or receipt and gives information about the goods. When the goods are delivered to the docks, the driver hands over copies to the shipping company. One copy goes with the goods to the consignee; two are for customs; one remains at the dock office of the carrier; and one is used by the shipping company to prepare the bill of lading.

Bill of lading

A BILL OF LADING, often abbreviated to B/L ▶ **see page 202**, is the most important document in shipping and describes the consignment, its destination, and who it is for. It can be a document of title, i.e. it gives ownership of the goods to the person named on it. If the words TO ORDER are written in the consignee box, it means that it is a NEGOTIABLE DOCUMENT and can be traded. In this case it will be ENDORSED (i.e. the exporter will sign it on the back). If it is not endorsed, there are no restrictions on ownership. In a letter of credit transaction the advising / confirming bank will usually ask for the bill of lading to be made out to them when they pay the exporter, and then transfer it to the customer when the customer pays them.

Bills of lading can be made out singly or in signed sets of two, three, or more original (negotiable) copies, with further unsigned copies kept for records. As soon as one of the originals is used as a document of title, the other original copies become void.

A SHIPPED BILL OF LADING is signed when the goods have been loaded onto the ship. Sometimes the words *shipped on board* are used to mean the same thing.

Bills of lading are marked CLEAN to indicate that the consignment was taken on board in good condition, or CLAUSED to indicate that on inspection there was something wrong with it, e.g. the goods were damaged, or there were some missing. The statement *claused* protects the shipping company from claims that they were responsible for any damage or loss.

In CIF and CFR transactions the words *freight prepaid* are used to signify that the costs of shipment have been paid.

Bills of lading can be made port to port, i.e. from the exporting port to the importing port. When containers are used and are trans-shipped from one mode of transport to another, e.g. truck to ship and then to train, a MULTIMODAL BILL OF LADING is used. This is also known as a THROUGH or COMBINED TRANSPORT BILL.

The Bolero Project is developing full computer-to-computer shipping and bank documents, making paperless documentation available. In this case a bill of lading is referred to as a *Bolero bill of lading*.

Letter of indemnity

A LETTER OF INDEMNITY is used if the bill of lading is lost or missing. The importer gives details of the consignment on company headed paper, and confirms that they will be responsible for the debts to the carrier against their assets.

Packing list

In addition to the bill of lading, a PACKING LIST may be required. Like a bill of lading, this gives details of the consignment. Banks use them in letter of credit transactions and the customs in some countries insist on them.

SHIPPING LIABILITIES

The Hague–Visby Rules, amended by the Brussels Protocol of 1968, govern liability for loss or damage to cargo carried by sea under a bill of lading. They state levels of compensation and the limitations of the carrier's responsibility for goods. The carrier is not responsible under the following conditions:

— acts of war, riots, civil disturbances
— *FORCE MAJEURE*, i.e. exceptional dangers such as severe storms
— negligence, i.e. when the goods have not been properly packed or were in bad condition when packed
— INHERENT VICE, i.e. when goods are subject to deterioration because of their content or nature, e.g. fish can go bad, wood can be attacked by parasites, metal can oxidize

The Hamburg Rules of 1978 extend the shipping companies' liability for damage or delay to goods in their charge, unless they can prove they took all measures to avoid problems.

To be safe, most companies insure their consignments under ALL RISKS (AR) cover, which protects them against most contingencies, but special war insurance is necessary for particularly dangerous zones.

FORWARDING AGENTS

Forwarding agents are used to arrange both import and export shipments. In the case of export shipments, their services include collecting the consignment, arranging shipment and, if required, packing and handling; also all documentation, including making out the bill of lading, obtaining insurance, sending commercial invoices and paying the shipping company for their clients. They are involved in the logistics of transportation, finding the most effective and economical route. They also inform the importer's forwarding agent that the shipment is on its way by sending an advice note.

The importer's forwarding agent, in turn, informs the client, sends the goods on, or arranges for them to be stored until collected. Many forwarding agents in importing countries also act as CLEARING AGENTS, ensuring that the goods are CLEARED through customs and sent to the importer.

Because forwarding agents handle large numbers of shipments, they can use consolidation and collect consignments for the same destination and get competitive GROUPAGE RATES for sending several consignments in one shipment.

11

Request for freight rates and sailings

Lee Boat Builders of Hong Kong fax Far Eastern Shipping Lines to ask about freight rates and sailings.
▶ See the correspondence on page 165 for the beginning of this transaction.

Dock 23, Mainway
Hong Kong
Telephone +852 385162
Fax +852 662553

Facsimile

Lee Boatbuilders Ltd

From	John Lee
To	Far Eastern Shipping Lines
Fax	852 602135
Subject	Your order No. 90103
Date	21 April 20—
No. of pages	1

Dear Sir / Madam

We intend to ship a consignment of dinghies and their equipment to London at the beginning of next month. The consignment consists of ten boats which have been packed into wooden crates marked 1–10, each measuring 4 x 2 x 2.5 metres and weighing 90 kilos.

Could you inform us which vessels are available to reach London before the end of next month, and let us know your freight rates?

I look forward to your reply.

John Lee

John Lee
Director

FAR EASTERN SHIPPING LINES

31–4 Park Road . Hong Kong

Telephone (+852) 421897
Facsimile (+852) 602135
Email mwhang@fareast.com
www.fareast.com
Cable FREAST

24 April 20—

Mr J. Lee
Lee Boatbuilders Ltd
Dock 23
Mainway
Hong Kong

Dear Mr Lee

Thank you for your fax of 21 April. Enclosed you will find details of our sailings from Hong Kong to Tilbury for the end of this month and the beginning of next.

You will see that the first available vessel we have will be the MV *Orient*, which will accept cargo from 3 May to 7 May, when she sails. She is due in Tilbury on 3 June.

Our freight rate for crated consignments is £91.00 (ninety-one pounds) per tonne, and I have attached our shipping instructions to the enclosed itinerary.

Yours sincerely

M. Whang

M. Whang (Mrs)
Director

Enc. Itinerary
Shipping instructions

Directors
S. Chung, M. Whang, L. Grover

Reply to request for freight rates and sailings

If Mr Lee is satisfied with this reply, Far Eastern Shipping Lines will send him a freight account and a standard shipping note for completion, from which they will then complete the bill of lading. When the goods have been loaded, Mr Lee will send an advice to his customer informing him of shipment ▸ **see page 166.**

▸ see page 166.

---

1 When is the earliest that Mr Lee's cargo will leave Hong Kong?

2 How much does Far Eastern Shipping Lines charge for freight?

3 What has Mrs Whang enclosed with the letter?

4 Which words in the letter have a similar meaning to the following?
a information
b ship
c leaves port
d expected

Bill of lading

▶ See page 198 for details of this document.

Bill of Lading for Combined Transport shipment or Port to Port shipment

| Shipper | B/L No.: |
| | Reference: |

P&O Nedlloyd

Consignee or Order (for U.S. Trade only: Not Negotiable unless consigned 'To Order')

| Notify Party/Address (It is agreed that no responsibility shall attach to the Carrier or his Agents for failure to notify (see clause 20 on reverse)) | Place of Receipt (Applicable only when this document is used as a Combined Transport Bill of Lading) |

| Vessel and Voy. No. | Place of Delivery (Applicable only when this document is used as a Combined Transport Bill of Lading) |

| Port of Loading | Port of Discharge |

Undermentioned particulars as declared by Shipper, but not acknowledged by the Carrier (see clause 11)

| Marks and Nos; Container Nos; | Number and kind of Packages; Description of Goods | Gross Weight (kg) | Measurement (cbm) |

VOID VOID VOID VOID VOID

VOID VOID VOID VOID VOID

| * Total No. of Containers/Packages received by the Carrier | Movement | Freight payable at |

Received by the Carrier from the Shipper in apparent good order and condition (unless otherwise noted herein) the total number or quantity of Containers or other packages or units indicated in the box above entitled "Total No. of Containers/Packages received by the Carrier" for Carriage subject to all the terms and conditions hereof (INCLUDING THE TERMS AND CONDITIONS ON THE REVERSE HEREOF AND THE TERMS AND CONDITIONS OF THE CARRIER'S APPLICABLE TARIFF) from the Place of Receipt or the Port of Loading, whichever is applicable, to the Port of Discharge or the Place of Delivery, whichever is applicable. If the acknowledged tally is of Containers, this indicates that the Container has been packed and sealed by the Merchant at his premises without the Carrier being represented and able to check or verify either the tally of Goods or the stowage, which are consequently unknown to him (See Clause 8). The Merchant accepts that, except by special arrangement or pursuant to Clause 9 hereof, Containers are not weighed by the Carrier at any time. If the Carrier so requires, before he arranges delivery of the Goods one original Bill of Lading, duly endorsed, must be surrendered by the Merchant to the Carrier at the Port of Discharge or at some other location acceptable to the Carrier. In accepting this Bill of Lading the Merchant expressly accepts and agrees to all its terms and conditions whether printed, stamped or written, or otherwise incorporated, notwithstanding the non-signing of this Bill of Lading by the Merchant. Without prejudice to the generality of this reference, attention is drawn, inter-alia, to Clauses 12 (Shipper's/Merchant's Responsibility), 19 (Dangerous Goods) and 24 (Law & Jurisdiction).

| Number of Original Bills of Lading | Place and Date of Issue | IN WITNESS of the contract herein contained the number of originals stated opposite has been issued, one of which being accomplished the other(s) to be void |

EXCESS VALUATION: REFER TO CLAUSE 7 (3) ON REVERSE SIDE (U.S. TRADE ONLY). . . .   **ORIGINAL**   FOR P&O NEDLLOYD LTD, AS CARRIER:*

426188

CANCELLED - SPECIMEN COPY

2/DRS B/L4 10/98

*OPERATING IN PARTNERSHIP WITH P&O NEDLLOYD BV

1 Which words make the bill of lading negotiable?

2 What does *combined transport shipment* mean?

3 Where would you put the name of the ship?

4 Who usually signs the bill of lading?

5 Where would you list details of the consignment?

6 How would consignees identify the goods when they arrived?

7 Who is the bill of lading's issuing company?

8 What would it mean if the bill of lading was *claused*?

9 Which part of the bill of lading would the consignee use to collect the goods?

10 Where would you write the place for the goods to be unloaded?

This email is from Delta
Computers to their
forwarding agents, Kent,
Clarke & Co. Ltd,
instructing them to pick
up a consignment of
twenty computers
which is to be sent to
their customers NZ
Business Machines Pty.
See pages 157–164 for
previous
correspondence.

| Send | | | | | | | | | | | | | | | | Options... | |

Arial — 10 — B I U

File Edit View Insert Format Tools Actions Help

To... John Simpson

Cc... Oliver Wentworth

Subject: NZ consignment

Dear Mr Simpson

Could you please pick up a consignment of 20 C2000 computers and make the necessary arrangements for them to be shipped to Mr M. Tanner, NZ Business Machines Pty, 100 South Street, Wellington, New Zealand?

Please handle all the shipping formalities and insurance, and send us five copies of the bill of lading, three copies of the commercial invoice, and the insurance certificate. We will advise our customers of shipment ourselves.

Could you handle this as soon as possible? Your charges may be sent to us in the usual way.

Neil Smith
Senior Shipping Clerk
Delta Computers Ltd
Wellingborough, NN8 4HB, UK
Tel.: +44 (0)1933 16431/2/3/4
Fax: +44 (0)1933 20016
Email: smithn@delta.com

1 What documents are
involved in this
shipment?

2 Who will let the
customer know about
shipment?

3 Who will pay the
charges?

4 Which words in the
email have a similar
meaning to the
following?
    collect
    transported
    deal with
    inform

Forwarding agent's enquiry for freight rates

Kent, Clarke & Co. fax International Shippers.

KENT, CLARKE & CO. LTD

SOUTH BANK HOUSE·BOROUGH ROAD·LONDON SE1 0AA
TELEPHONE: +44 (0)20 7928 7716 · FACSIMILE: +44 (0)20 7928 7111
Email: simpsonj@kencla.com

Facsimile

To	International Shippers Ltd
Fax	020 7312 6117
From	J. D. Simpson
Date	13 May 20—
Pages	1
Subject	NZ consignment

We have packed and ready for shipment 20 C2000 computers which our clients, Delta Computers, Wellingborough, want forwarded to Wellington, New Zealand.

The consignment consists of 4 wooden crates, each containing 5 machines in their cases. Each crate weighs 210 kilos and measures 94 x 136 x 82 cm.

Please let us know by return the earliest vessel leaving London for New Zealand, and let us have your charges and the relevant documents.

J. D. Simpson

J. D. Simpson (Mr)
Supervisor

CHAIRMAN: LORD MATHERSON
DIRECTORS: B. KENT A.C.A., C.D. CLARKE H.N.D., R.P. DILLER
REG NO: LONDON 3395162
VAT NO: 41618231 59

International Shippers Ltd

City House
City Road
London
EC2 1PC

Telephone +44 (0)20 7312 5038
Facsimile +44 (0)20 7312 6117
Email pollardy@intership.com
www.intership.com

14 May 20—

Mr J. D. Simpson
Supervisor
Kent, Clarke & Co. Ltd
South Bank House
Borough Road
London SE1 0AA

Dear Mr Simpson

In reply to your fax of 13 May, the earliest vessel due out of London for New Zealand is the *Northern Cross*, which is at present loading at No. 3 Dock, Tilbury, and will accept cargo until 18 May, when she sails. She is due in Wellington on 25 June. The freight rate for cased cargo is £612.00 (six hundred and twelve pounds) per ton or 10 (ten) cubic metres.

I have enclosed our standard shipping note and bill of lading for you to complete and return to us.

Yours sincerely

Yvonne Pollard

Yvonne Pollard
Shipping Manager

Enc. Standard shipping note
Bill of lading

Chairman Sir Donald Low
Directors P.R. Castle, D.S.M. Bracking, R.T. Kitson

Reg No. England 4513869
VAT No. 12 63154123

1 What is the *Northern Cross*'s closing date for cargo?

2 What other words could be used instead of *due out of* and *due in*?

3 What are the shipping charges?

4 Which two documents will Mr Simpson receive, and what should he do with them?

Confirmation of shipment

Kent, Clarke, & Co. have informed Delta Computers that a vessel is available and have quoted the cost of shipment. Delta have confirmed that the sailing time and rate is acceptable. Kent, Clarke, & Co. now return the completed standard shipping note and bill of lading to International Shippers with this covering letter.

KENT, CLARKE & CO. LTD

SOUTH BANK HOUSE·BOROUGH ROAD·LONDON SE1 0AA
TELEPHONE: +44 (0)20 7928 7716 ·FACSIMILE: +44 (0)20 7928 7111
Email: simpsonj@kencla.com

17 May 20—

Yvonne Pollard
International Shippers Ltd
City House
City Road
London EC2 1PC

Dear Ms Pollard

We have arranged for the consignment of computers (see our fax of 13 May) to be sent to Tilbury for loading on to the *Northern Cross*, which sails for New Zealand on 18 May.

Enclosed you will find the completed standard shipping note and bill of lading (6 copies), 4 copies of which should be signed and returned to us. I have also attached a cheque in payment of your freight account.

Yours sincerely

J. D. Simpson

J. D. Simpson
Supervisor

Enc. Standard shipping note
Bill of lading (6 copies)
Cheque No. 0823146

CHAIRMAN: LORD MATHERSON
DIRECTORS: B. KENT A.C.A., C.D. CLARKE H.N.D., R.P. DILLER
REG NO: LONDON 3395162
VAT NO: 41618231 59

HARTLEY–MASON INC.

618 West and Vine Street / Chicago / Illinois
Telephone (+1) 312 818532
Fax (+1) 312 349076
Email t.hackenbush@hartley-mason.com

Fax Message

To	Eddis Jones
Fax	0151 88970
Date	19 April 20—
Ref.	Invoice EH 3314
Pages	1

The following consignment will arrive on the *America*, due in Liverpool on 27 April.

20 'Lightning' 1000cc motorcycles. Packed 1 machine per wooden crate. Weight 1.25 tons gross. Size 6' x 3' x 2'. Markings Cases numbered 1–20 I–M. Value £9,840.00 each. (Insurance Chicago–Nottingham England AR.) CIF invoiced value £203,000.

Could you please arrange for the consignment to be delivered to your clients, Glough & Book Ltd, Nottingham? If there are any problems, please contact us immediately.

Thomas N. Hackenbush

Thomas N. Hackenbush
Export Manager

In this fax, Hartley–Mason Inc. is advising a British importing agent that a consignment of motorcycles is being sent for them to forward to their customers, Glough & Book.
▶ **See pages 178–179 for previous correspondence.**

Advice of shipment to importer

Hartley–Mason now inform Glough & Book that their consignment has been shipped. Glough & Book will accept the bill that the American company has DRAWN ON them and send the documents to Hartley–Mason's bank's agents. They, in turn, will hand the documents to Glough & Book's forwarding agents in Liverpool, who will then be able to collect the consignment on their behalf.

HARTLEY–MASON INC.

618 West and Vine Street / Chicago / Illinois

Telephone (+1) 312 818532
Fax (+1) 312 349076
Email t.hackenbush@hartley-mason.com

19 April 20—

Mr B. Glough
Glough & Book Cycles Ltd
31-37 Traders Street
Nottingham NG1 3AA
UK

Gentlemen:

Order No. 8901/6

The above order was shipped on 17 April 20— on the *America*, due in Liverpool on 27 April.

We have informed your agents, Eddis Jones, who will make arrangements for the consignment to be sent on to you as soon as they receive the shipping documents for clearance.

Our bank's agents, Westmorland Bank Ltd, High Street, Nottingham, will hand over the documents: shipped clean bill of lading (No. 517302), invoice (No. EH 3314), and insurance certificate (AR 118 4531), once you have accepted our bill.

We are sure you will be impressed by the machines, and that they will find a ready market in your country. Meanwhile, we enclose a catalogue of our new models – see especially pp.103–110.

We look forward to hearing from you again in due course.

Yours truly

Thomas N. Hackenbush

Thomas N. Hackenbush
Export Manager

Enc.

President J.R. Mason D.F.A.
Directors P. Hartley Snr. P. Hartley Jnr.

Who is the agent bank?

2 What must Mr Glough do before he receives the shipping documents?

3 How do we know the consignment is in good condition?

4 Which vessel is the carrier?

5 What are the details of the seller's new products?

6 Who are Glough & Book's forwarding agents?

Send | Arial | 10 | **B** *I* U

File   Edit   View   Insert   Format   Tools   Actions   Help

To... | Yvonne Pollard

Cc... | Neil Smith

Subject: | B/L No. 6715

Dear Ms Pollard

Our clients, Delta Computers, Wellingborough, UK inform us that they have received an email from their customers, NZ Business Machines, Wellington, New Zealand that the *Northern Cross*, which was due in Wellington on June 25, has not yet arrived.

The vessel was carrying a consignment of computers for our clients, shipped B/L No. 6715, and they want to know the reason for the delay and when it is expected to dock. A prompt reply would be appreciated.

John Simpson
Supervisor
Kent, Clarke, & Co. Ltd, London
Tel: +44 (0)20 7928 7716
Fax: +44 (0)20 7928 7111
Email: simpsonj@kencla.com

Delay in arrival of shipment

Goods can be delayed, damaged, or carried over to another port. In such cases the seller or his forwarding agent will contact the shipping company. Here, Mr Simpson of Kent, Clarke & Co., the forwarding agent, emails International Shippers about a delay. ▸ **See pages 203–206 for previous correspondence.**

To...	John Simpson
Cc...	Neil Smith
Subject:	RE: B/L No.6715

Dear Mr Simpson

The *Northern Cross* docked in Wellington within the last 24 hours. It was briefly delayed by engine trouble. I am sure that your customers will now be able to collect their consignment.

We apologize for the delay. You will know from previous experience of shipping with us that our line makes every effort to keep to schedules. This incident was an unfortunate exception.

Please contact us if there is any further information you need.

Yvonne Pollard
International Shippers Ltd
City House, City Road, London EC2 1PC
Telephone: +44 (0)20 7312 5038
Fax: +44 (0)20 7312 6117
Email: pollardy@intership.co.uk

Container services

CONTAINERS

CONTAINERS are large metal boxes with two basic lengths of 20ft (6.1m) and 40ft (12.2m). They are 8ft (2.4m) wide and 8ft 6in (2.6m) high. The cubic capacity of a 20ft container is 33.3m³, and of a 40ft container, 66.9m³. A 20ft container can carry 20 tons and a 40ft one 26 tons. They can be loaded from the top, front, or side. Special equipment is needed to move them.

There are various types of container for carrying individual items, bulk goods such as grain or sugar, or liquids such as oil and chemicals. Containers for carrying perishable goods are refrigerated.

Container stowage is rated in units called TUE, with a 20ft container equal to 1 tue and a 40ft one equal to 2 tue. Containers may be filled as a FULL CONTAINER LOAD (FCL), which is charged at a 'box' rate no matter what its weight or volume. However, shippers or forwarding agents can load smaller consignments from different exporters into a single container. This is known as CONSOLIDATION or GROUPAGE, and each consignment is charged as a LESS THAN FULL CONTAINER LOAD (LCL).

Most ports have facilities for loading and unloading containers. Once a container leaves the ship, it is sent by rail and / or road to the consignee. Container bases for imports are known as CONTAINER FREIGHT STATIONS (CFS).

DOCUMENTATION

For exporting goods

The usual documentation for goods to be exported by container is a CONTAINER WAYBILL. This is not a document of title, but can be used to transfer the goods from one method of transport to another, e.g truck to ship, and ship to train. However, container shipments can also be covered by a multimodal bill of lading. Goods covered by these documents are collected at inland clearance depots (ICDs) and then sent on to their final destination.

A bill of lading can be used as it is in ordinary shipments, with the usual conditions applying, e.g. for a clean shipped bill, naming the port of acceptance (where the goods have been loaded) and port of delivery (where the goods will be unloaded), the shipping company only accepts responsibility for the goods while on board ship. But if a combined transport bill is used, the place of acceptance and place of delivery may be covered, which means the shipping company accepts door-to-door responsibility.

NON-NEGOTIABLE WAYBILLS are also used, but unless instructed, banks will not accept them as evidence of shipment, and they are not documents of title which can be transferred. Although waybills do not have clauses relating to responsibility printed on the back of them, as bills of lading do, container companies will accept the usual liabilities as applying to a waybill.

For importing goods

A freight account is needed if the sea-freight is to be paid in the UK, and this is accompanied by an arrival notification form, which advises the importers that their goods are due. On claiming the goods, the customer has to show a customs clearance form, which allows the goods to be taxed, copies of the certificate of origin, and if necessary, a COMMERCIAL INVOICE, an import licence, and a health certificate for food or animal imports. The bill of lading or waybill also has to be produced to prove ownership of the goods, or if lost, a letter of indemnity. Customs issue an OUT OF CHARGE NOTE once the goods have been cleared by them.

This procedure is used for all forms of importation, not only those in which containers are used. The amount of documentation required is one of the reasons why clearing agents are employed by either exporters, to get their goods accepted quickly in a foreign country, or importers, to clear their goods in their own country.

Transportation and shipping

Enquiry to a container company

Universal Steel fax International Containers about a consignment of steel that they want shipped to Hamburg.

11

Example fax

Telephone +44 (0)114 760271
Fax +44 (0)114 610318
t.pike@unisteel.co.uk
www.unisteel.com

Furnace House . Granville Road . Sheffield S2 2RL

Universal Steel plc

To	International Containers
Fax	020 7387 6655
From	T. Pike, Export Dept
Date	15 March 20—
Reference	Shipment enquiry
Pages	1

We are a large steel company and wish to export a consignment of steel tubing, approximate weight 16 tons, and lengths varying from 2 to 6 metres.

The consignment is destined for Dörtner Industries, Hamburg. Could you pick it up at our works in Sheffield and deliver it to Hamburg by the end of April?

If you can handle this consignment by the date given, please let us have details of your sailings and freight charges. We can promise you regular shipments if you quote a competitive rate.

Thomas Pike

Thomas Pike
Export Department

Chairman H. Eltham
Directors D.E.R. Machin, O.M. Crewit
Reg No. 6217970
VAT No. 31428716

| ✉ | | | | | | | | | | | | Options... | ❓ |

| Arial | ▼ | 10 | ▼ | ◐ | **B** | *I* | U̲ | ▤ | ▤ | ▤ | ▤ | ▤ | ▤ |

File   Edit   View   Insert   Format   Tools   Actions   Help

To...	Thomas Pike
Cc...	
Subject:	Consignment of steel tubing

Tariffs   Export cargo shipping instructions   Export cargo packing instructions

Dear Mr Pike

Thank you for your fax of 15 March.

The *Europe* sails from Tilbury on March 26 and will arrive in Hamburg on March 28, which appears to suit your schedule for delivery. Please note, however, that the vessel closes for cargo on 24 March.

You will see from our list of tariffs that charges are calculated by cubic metre or cubic kilogram and that we offer substantial rebates for regular shipments.

The most suitable container for your consignment would be a half-height container which is 20' x 8' x 4' or, in metres, 6.1 x 2.4 x 1.3. This can carry a payload of 18,300 kg. It has a solid removable top, and will protect the metal against all elements.

I suggest that, as the consignment is to be loaded from lorry to ship and then transferred again, you should use our combined transport bill. This would cover the goods from point of acceptance to point of delivery. If you would like to go ahead on this basis, please complete the attached export cargo shipping instructions and the export cargo packing instructions and return them to us as soon as possible. Although we accept door-to-door responsibility, we would advise you to take out an all-risk insurance policy, and send a copy of this and three copies of the commercial invoice to us.

The cargo should be marked on at least two sides with a shipping mark which includes the destination port. This should correspond with the mark on your shipping documents.

I look forward to receiving your instructions.

David Muner
Customer Service Manager
International Containers plc
London WC1H 9BH
Tel.: +44 (0)20 7387 6815
Fax: +44 (0)20 7387 6655
Email: munerd@incon.co.uk

---

1 How are the freight charges estimated?

2 Is there any advantage in the exporter making regular shipments?

3 When does the *Europe* close for cargo?

4 What type of container does Mr Muner recommend?

5 Why is a combined transport bill suggested rather than a bill of lading?

6 What sort of liability will the shipping company accept?

7 Does the exporter need to insure the cargo?

Certificate of origin

A **CERTIFICATE OF ORIGIN** is used to show where the goods originally came from. Goods from the member state of an economic union of countries, such as the EU and Association of South-east Asian Nations (ASEAN), pay a lower rate of import tax than non-members. It is generally issued and authorized by a chamber of commerce.
▶ See also page 165.

11

Example form

Enquiry for a time charter

A London firm wants to charter a ship to transport grain. They contact a shipbroker. Most of this correspondence is done by fax or email, with letters used to confirm the charter and a charter party signed to confirm the transaction.

London Grain Merchants Ltd

CENTRAL HOUSE · ROWLEY STREET · LONDON EC1
TELEPHONE +44 (0)20 7742 8315
FAX +44 (0)20 7174 2331

FAX TRANSMISSION

To	Charter Dept, Keyser Shipbrokers Ltd
Fax	7671 9873
From	B. Meredrew
Subject	Grain transport to S. America
No. of pages (inc. this page)	1
Date	10 January 20—

This fax is to confirm our telephone conversation this morning in which we asked if you could find a ship of six to seven thousand tons which we could charter for six months to take shipments of grain from Baltimore, North America, to various ports along the South American coast.

We will need a ship that is capable of making a fast turnround and will be able to manage at least ten trips within the period.

B. Meredrew

B. Meredrew (Mr)
Director

CHAIRMAN L. Spencer M.Sc. (Econ.)
DIRECTORS B. Meredrew · L. Oban · C.M. Chirmill

⚓

KEYSER SHIPBROKERS LTD

123–5 LOWLAND STREET, LONDON EC1 2RH
TELEPHONE: +44 (0)20 7671 · FAX: +44 (0)20 7671 9873

FAX MESSAGE

To	Mr B. Meredrew, London Grain Merchants Ltd
Fax number	020 7174 2331
From	Belinda Marston
Subject	Grain transport to South America
Date	12 January 20—
Total pages	1

Dear Mr Meredrew

With reference to your fax of 10 January 20—, we are pleased to inform you that we have identified a vessel that will meet your requirements.

She is the *Manhattan*, and is currently docked in Boston. She is a bulk carrier with a cargo capacity of seven thousand tons. She has a maximum speed of 24 knots, so would certainly be capable of ten trips in the period you mentioned.

Please fax us to confirm the charter and we will send you the charter party.

Yours sincerely

Belinda Marston

Belinda Marston
Charter Department

TELEPHONE +44 (0)20 7467 3149 (10 lines)
FAX +44 (0)20 7467 5959

PUTNEY & RAVEN
MERCHANTS LTD
Dealers House
Cantley Street
London
WC1 1AR

Enquiry for a voyage charter

Putney & Raven
Merchants need a
ship to transport a
consignment of
bauxite.

To	Keyser Shipbrokers
Fax	020 7671 9873
From	David Raven, Shipping Dept
Date	7 July 20—
Subject	Ship charter
Pages	1

We would like to charter a vessel for one voyage from Newcastle, NSW, Australia, to St Malo, Brittany, France, to take a consignment of 4,000 (four thousand) tons of bauxite.

Our contract states that we have to take delivery between 1 and 5 August, so we will need a ship that will be able to load during those dates. Please advise us if you can get a vessel and let us know the terms.

David Raven

David Raven
Shipping Manager

DIRECTORS
M.L. Putney
D. Raven

REG NO. England 615113
VAT NO. 21 371942

⚓

KEYSER SHIPBROKERS LTD

123–5 LOWLAND STREET, LONDON EC1 2RH
TELEPHONE: +44 (0)20 7671 · FAX: +44 (0)20 7671 9873

FAX MESSAGE

To	Putney & Raven
Fax number	7467 5959
From	Belinda Marston
Subject	Option on MS *Sheraton*
Date	10 July 20—
Total pages	1

You should have already received our fax in which we said that we had an option on a vessel, MS *Sheraton*, which is docked in Melbourne, Australia at present. She has a cargo capacity of 7,000 (seven thousand) tons and although she is larger than you wanted, her owners are willing to offer a part charter.

They have quoted £12.30 (twelve pounds, thirty pence) per ton which is a very competitive rate considering you will be sharing the cost.

Could you fax us your decision as soon as possible?

Belinda Marston

Belinda Marston
Charter Department

1 What does an *option* on a vessel mean?

2 Where is the MS *Sheraton* at the moment?

3 Is the ship exactly what Putney & Raven wanted?

4 Why is the chartering cost lower for this shipment?

Adopted by the
Documentary Commitee of the
Chamber of Shipping of the
Unitd Kingdom

CODE NAME:
GENCON.

RECOMMENDED.

Issued to some into force for fixtures on and after 15th September, 1922.

The Documentary Council of The Baltic & White Sea Conference.

UNIFORM GENERAL CHARTER.
AS REVISED 1922.

(Only to be used for trades for which no approved form is in force).

.... 20

Owners.   I. IT IS THIS DAY MUTUALLY AGREED between   1

....   2

Owners of the steamer or motor-vessel   3

of ....tons gross/nett Register and carrying about .... tons of deadweight cargo,   4

Position.   now..   5

and expected ready to load under this Charter about   6

Charterers.   and Messrs   7

of .... as Charterers   8

Where to load.   That the said vessel shall proceed to   9

.... or so near thereto as she may safely get and lie   10

Cargo.   always afloat, and there load a full and complete cargo (if shipment of deck cargo   11

agreed same to be at Charterers' risk) of   12

....   13

....   14

....   15

(Charterers to provide all mats and/or wood for dunnage and any separations required,   16

the Owners allowing the use of any dunnage wood on board if required) which the   17

Charterers bind themselves to ship, and being so loaded the vessel shall proceed to   18

....   19

Destination.   20

....   21

....   22

as ordered on signing Bills of Lading or so near thereto as she may safely get and   23

lie always afloat and there deliver the cargo on being paid freight —on delivered/intaken   24

Rate of freight.   quantity—as follows   25

....   26

....   27

....   28

Points to remember

Road, rail, and air transport

1 In road, rail, and air transport the choice of method depends on whether the main consideration is speed, direct delivery, or economy. These considerations obviously relate to the type of consignment involved.

2 The consignment note is the main form of documentation used in road and rail transport, and the air waybill in the case of air transport. They are receipts, not documents of title, and therefore not negotiable.

Shipping

1 There are various types of vessel available to carry different goods, e.g. bulk carriers, tankers, and container vessels.

2 Shipping companies can either belong to the Shipping Conference, an international organization which sets prices for transporting goods or passengers, or get ships on Baltic Exchange, where ships and aircraft can be chartered through brokers.

3 The bill of lading is the main form of documentation used in shipping. It can be a document of title. It may be *clean* or *claused*, terms used to indicate whether the goods were in perfect condition when taken on board or if there was something wrong with them.

Container services

A convenient method of transporting many types of consignment is containers (large metal boxes) which are taken to the docks and then loaded on to container vessels. Small consignments from different exporters can be loaded into a single container. For documentation, container companies usually use either container waybills or multimodal bills of lading.

12

12

INSURANCE PROCEDURES

Companies and individuals protect themselves against loss, damage, or injury by taking out insurance policies, which are contracts COVERING them against future risks. The usual process of insuring a business or oneself is as follows:

1 A PROPOSAL FORM is completed by the client, i.e. the company or individual who wants insurance COVER. This states what is to be insured, how much it is worth, how long the policy will run, and under what conditions insurance is to be effected, as the policy may not automatically cover the insured against ALL RISKS (AR).

2 The insurance company then works out the PREMIUM, i.e. the price of the insurance. The premium is usually quoted in pence per cent, e.g. pence per hundred pounds. This means that for every £100 of insurance the client would have to pay x pence. So if you insured your computer for £1,500 at 100p%, you would have to pay £15.00 per annum for the premium.

3 If the insurance company is satisfied with the information given on the proposal form, they issue a COVER NOTE to the client. This is not the policy itself, but an agreement that the goods are covered until the policy is ready.

4 When the policy is ready, it is sent to the client. It tells the client that they are INDEMNIFIED against loss, damage, or injury under the conditions of the policy. As insurance is based on the principle of good faith, and supported by laws against fraud, insurance companies accept that the items being insured belong to the client, are not being insured more than once, are of the value stated, and that the client will follow the conditions of the policy. Indemnification means that the insurance company will compensate the client to restore their original position before the loss or damage. Therefore, if you insured your car for £12,000 and three months later it was wrecked, you

would not receive £12,000, but the market price of the car if it had not been damaged. For example, it might have depreciated by 20% to £9,600. The insurance company will also have the right of SUBROGATION, which means they can now claim the wrecked vehicle and sell it for any price they can get. However, insurance companies also offer policies which cover goods at their original prices or may replace the item. Many household policies, for example, offer this guarantee.

In the case of injury or death, or LIFE ASSURANCE, the principle of BENEFIT PAYMENT operates. The injured person (or their dependants if they are killed) is paid compensation. The life assurance BENEFICIARY is paid according to his or her contributions and interest earned on investment.

Insurance companies are large institutional investors on the stock market, and by investing premiums they are able to cover claims for compensation and pay matured life assurance policies.

FIRE AND ACCIDENT INSURANCE

Fire insurance

Fire insurance companies offer three main types of policy:

1 Insurance of home and business premises and their contents

2 *Special perils* policies, which protect the client against loss or damage due to special factors, e.g. floods or earthquakes

3 CONSEQUENTIAL LOSS INSURANCE, which means insurance against losing money as a consequence of an accident, e.g. when a company is unable to produce goods because of fire damage to their factory.

Accident insurance

Accident insurance covers four areas:

1 INSURANCE OF LIABILITY, which covers employers' liabilities for industrial accidents, accidents to people attending functions on company business, and motor insurance.

2 Property insurance, which is part of the service fire insurance companies provide, but also includes a wide range of protection against riots, terrorism, gas explosions, etc. Usually, the client takes out an all risks policy, which offers full protection.

3 Personal accident insurance, which offers compensation in the form of benefit payments to people injured (or their dependants if they are killed) on outings, in sporting accidents, or travelling by train, coach, or air.

4 INSURANCE OF INTEREST, which protects companies against making costly mistakes. For example, publishers might want to cover themselves against libel, i.e. being sued for publishing something which damages someone's reputation. Accountants and lawyers also protect themselves with insurance of interest. FIDELITY BONDS can be included under this heading. These are used by companies to insure against their employees defrauding them or stealing from them.

Claims

Companies and individuals make claims for loss, damage, or accident by filling in a claim form, which tells the insurance company what has happened. If the insurers accept the claim, often after an inspection or investigation, they will pay compensation.

The insurance company will not pay compensation under the following conditions: if the CLAIMANT was negligent; if the claimant suffered the injury or loss outside the terms of the policy; or if the claimant misled the insurers when obtaining insurance, e.g. overvalued the article, insured the same thing twice, or gave false information on the proposal form.

The insurer may, of course, offer less compensation than the claimant is asking for. If the claimant disagrees with the offer, they can call in an independent ASSESSOR, and then, if necessary, take the case to court. But usually insurance companies are quite reasonable in their assessments, and small claims are sometimes paid without question.

12

Request for comprehensive insurance

United Warehouses want to change their insurance company. In this letter they ask Westway Insurance for a QUOTATION.

UW United Warehouses Ltd

Head Office
Bruce House
Bruce Street
Aberdeen
AB9 1FR

Telephone: +44 (0)1224 41615
Fax: +44 (0)1224 62219
Email: daracotb@uniwar.com

Your ref

Our ref N 3162–1

Date 6 April 20—

Westway Insurance Co. Ltd
Society House
Ellison Place
Newcastle-upon-Tyne NE1 8ST

Dear Sirs

We would be grateful if you could quote us for comprehensive cover, i.e. against fire, flood, accident, industrial injury, and theft.

We are a large warehouse selling furnishings to the retail trade, and employing a staff of thirty. The building we occupy belongs to us and is currently valued, along with the fixtures and fittings, at £350,000. At any one time there might be stock worth £250,000 on the premises.

If you are able to supply a quote, please would you take the following into consideration:

Our fire precautions conform to current regulations: we have a fully operational sprinkler system, which is serviced regularly, and fire exits on every floor. In general, our health and safety record is excellent.

Our premises are on high ground, and the only danger from flood would be burst pipes.

Since we began trading six years ago we have never had to claim for industrial injury, and damage to stock has been minimal. Petty theft, which is common in warehouses, has cost us only £800 per annum on average. Our present policy expires at the end of this month, so we would require cover as from 1 May.

We are changing insurance companies because of our present insurers' increase in premium, so a competitive quotation would be appreciated.

Yours faithfully

B. Daracott

B. Daracott (Mr)
Finance Manager

1 What sort of policy is United Warehouses asking for?

2 How many people do they employ?

3 What precautions have they taken against fire?

4 Why are they changing their insurers?

5 Which words in the letter have a similar meaning to the following?
  a full cover against all eventualities
  b maintained and repaired
  c very small
  d stealing things in small quantities
  e insurance protection

Insurance Co. Ltd

Regional Office
Society House
Ellison Place
Newcastle-upon-Tyne
N E1 8ST

Telephone +44 (0)191 326115 Ext: 417
Fax +44 (0)191 501116
Email nsagum@westway.co.uk

Your Ref: N3162–1
Our Ref: 1/34/91
Date: 9 April 20—

Mr B. Daracott
United Warehouses Ltd
Bruce House
Bruce Street
Aberdeen AB9 1FR

Dear Mr Daracott

Thank you for your letter of 6 April in which you enquired about insurance cover.

I enclose leaflets explaining our three fully comprehensive industrial policies which offer the sort of cover you require. Policy A351 would probably suit you best as it offers the widest protection at 45p% with full indemnification. I would stress that this is a very competitive rate.

If you would like one of our agents to call on you to discuss any details that might not be clear, I would be pleased to arrange this. However, if you are satisfied with the terms, please complete the enclosed proposal form and return it to us with your cheque for £3,700.00, and we will effect insurance as from 1 May this year.

I look forward to hearing from you.

Yours sincerely

N. Sagum

N. Sagum (Mr)
District Manager

Enc. Leaflets A351, A352, A353
Proposal form

Chairman Sir David Wedge
Directors M. Orwell I.P.A., C.R. Archer F.I.S., D.F. Clements

Reg. No. England 544712
VAT No. 61 576192

Quotation for comprehensive insurance

In this reply to United Warehouses' request, notice that Westway Insurance has three policies available which offer cover under different conditions. Mr Sagum draws attention to one of them and offers to send an agent to explain the details. The rate of 45p% is mentioned *with full indemnification*, i.e. cover for compensation based on the market values of the client's stock and machinery.

Insurance

12

Example letter

Quotation for bonding an employee

International Credit Cards have asked if Westway would provide a fidelity bond for one of their employees, i.e. insure him against defrauding the company. Here is the reply.

Westway
Insurance Co. Ltd

Regional Office
Society House
Ellison Place
Newcastle-upon-Tyne
N E1 8ST

Telephone +44 (0)191 326115 Ext: 417
Fax +44 (0)191 501116
Email nsagum@westway.co.uk

Your Ref: **A 4517**
Our Ref: **1/47/9165**
Date: **17 August 20—**

Mr E. Brockway
International Credit Cards plc
117–120 Hardman Road
Sheffield S2 2RL

Dear Mr Brockway

Thank you for your letter of 15 August in which you asked about bonding your employee, Mr Alfred Cade.

We have checked the references you gave us and he appears to have an excellent record. Therefore, we are willing to cover Mr Cade for £60,000 on the understanding that he only handles credit cards and customers' accounts. If, however, he is going to deal with cash, would you please inform us at once?

Insurance will be effected as soon as we receive the enclosed proposal form, completed by you.

Yours sincerely

N. Sagum

N. Sagum (Mr)
District Manager

Enc. Proposal form

Chairman Sir David Wedge
Directors M. Orwell I.P.A., C.R. Archer F.I.S., D.F. Clements

Reg. No. England 544712
VAT No. 61 576192

UW United Warehouses Ltd

Head Office	Telephone: +44 (0)1224 41615
Bruce House	Fax: +44 (0)1224 62219
Bruce Street	Email: daracotb@uniwar.com
Aberdeen	
AB9 1FR	

Your ref

Our ref **N 3215–1**

Date **16 October 20—**

Claims Department
Westway Insurance Co. Ltd
Society House
Ellison Place
Newcastle-upon-Tyne NE1 8ST

Dear Sirs,

Policy No. 18465314C

We regret to inform you that a fire broke out in the basement of our warehouse yesterday. Although the blaze was quickly brought under control, we estimate that about £18,000 worth of stock was badly damaged.

The Fire Service has advised us that the blaze was caused by an electrical fault, and is likely to have started at around midnight. Fortunately, their prompt action prevented more extensive damage.

I would be grateful if you could send us the necessary claim forms.

Yours faithfully

B. Daracott

B. Daracott (Mr)
Finance Manager

Chairman B.R. MacDonald A.C.A.
Directors N.S. Souness, A. Gemill M sc., B. Daracott
Registered in Scotland No. 166051
VAT No. 54 901013

Reply to claim for fire damage

When Westway Insurance received United Warehouses' claim, rather than sending a form straight away, they sent a surveyor to inspect the damage, confirm the cause of the fire, and assess whether £18,000 compensation was a fair estimate.

Westway
Insurance Co. Ltd

Regional Office
Society House
Ellison Place
Newcastle-upon-Tyne
NE1 8ST

Telephone +44 (0)191 326115 Ext: 417
Fax +44 (0)191 501116
Email dpruet@westway.co.uk

Your Ref: A 4517
Our Ref: 1/47/9165
Date: 28 October 20—

Mr B. Daracott
United Warehouses Ltd
Bruce House
Bruce Street
Aberdeen AB9 1FR

Dear Mr Daracott

Policy No. 18465314C

I now have the report from our surveyor, Mr McNulty, who visited your premises on 18 October to inspect the damage caused by the fire on 15 October.

From the copy of the report enclosed, you will see that although he agrees that the fire was caused by an electrical fault, he feels that £9,000 is a more accurate evaluation for damage to stock at present market prices. However, he suggests that we also pay a further £2,800 for structural damage to your premises. Consequently, we are prepared to offer you a total of £11,800 compensation under the terms of your policy.

If you accept this assessment, please would you complete the enclosed claim form and return it to us, with a covering letter of confirmation?

Yours sincerely

D. Pruet

D. Pruet (Mr)
Claims Manager

Enc. Claim form

Chairman Sir David Wedge
Directors M. Orwell I.P.A., C.R. Archer F.I.S., D.F. Clements

Reg. No. England 544712
VAT No. 61 576192

1 Who investigated the claim?

2 Why is Westway Insurance offering only £9,000 for the damaged stock?

3 What is the £2,800 compensation being offered for?

4 What must Mr Daracott do if United Warehouses accept Westway's offer?

5 Which words in the letter have a similar meaning to the following?
  a examine
  b current
  c as a result
  d fill in

MARINE INSURANCE

Lloyd's of London

LLOYD'S OF LONDON is not an insurance company but an international insurance market consisting of insurance brokers and UNDERWRITERS who are controlled by Lloyd's Council.

If insurance is to be arranged through a Lloyd's underwriter (and remember, there are other insurance associations), the transaction has to go through a Lloyd's broker who, working for a commission, will contact underwriters on behalf of the client to get a competitive rate. Underwriters finance the insurance, which means they will pay the claims and take the premiums as their fees. They usually work in SYNDICATES in order to spread the risk, with large corporations supporting the syndicates. Syndicates may cover marine insurance or non-marine insurance such as motor and aviation insurance, or life assurance. Members of syndicates write the insurance details on a Lloyd's slip, which is sent to the Lloyd's Policy Signing Office where it is checked and signed on behalf of the syndicate concerned. Underwriters get a percentage of the premiums they guarantee. If, for example, an underwriter accepts 15% of a £10,000 policy, he or she will be responsible for £1,500 compensation in the event of a claim and will receive 15% of the premium.

Lloyd's is responsible for, or associated with, a number of publications:
— *Lloyd's List and Shipping Gazette*, a daily newspaper read throughout the world, which gives details of shipping movements, sea and air accidents, fires, strikes, etc., and essential information concerning shipping and dry cargo markets.
— *Lloyd's Shipping Index* offers daily details of the movements of merchant ships.
— *Lloyd's Loading List* provides UK and European exporters with information on cargo carriers to all parts of the world.

— *Lloyd's Register of Shipping*, though independent of Lloyd's, works closely with the organization to produce vessel classifications giving details of age, ownership, and tonnage. The highest classification as to seaworthiness and condition is 100–A1.

Marine insurance policies

Generally, marine insurance is governed by the International Underwriting Association's (IUA's) three main clauses, called Institute Cargo Clauses. The most common is Clause A, which offers the broadest form of cover on an all-risk basis. This is the most expensive. Clauses B and C offer more limited cover and consequently are cheaper. If the policy is issued by Lloyds, there are also *Lloyd's own* clauses, which offer different types of cover at different rates.

The client must read the clauses carefully to make sure that their particular cargo is covered against all the risks that the shipment might meet. These could include strikes, war, and piracy, as well as collision and sinking.

VALUED POLICIES are based on the value of the invoice plus insurance and freight, with an extra percentage, e.g. 10%, on the value of the goods. There are also UNVALUED POLICIES, where the value of the goods is not agreed in advance but assessed if loss should occur. This means the client will, if their goods are damaged or destroyed, get the market price as compensation. The owner of the bill of lading has the right to claim compensation.

Goods are usually insured for a voyage on an agreed value basis. However, if a client ships regularly with a given company, they might ask for an OPEN COVER POLICY, e.g. for twelve months. The premium would be agreed at the beginning and the client would declare each shipment, without limit on the number of shipments they make. Alternatively, the policy might accept all shipments without declarations. An initial payment would be charged and adjusted according to the number of shipments made over that period.

12

In this case an insurance certificate covers the agreement.

For goods by air, Institute Cargo Clauses provide similar cover to marine insurance. Insurance by air is cheaper than by sea as the time taken to transport goods is shorter.

Claims

Most policies cover GENERAL AVERAGE SACRIFICE, which means that compensation will be paid for goods which have been deliberately thrown overboard (e.g. highly flammable goods if fire broke out), but it is essential that the client checks the clauses of the policy.

As is the case in large claims in non-marine insurance, AVERAGE ADJUSTERS, i.e. assessors, are called in to examine damage and estimate compensation. In a CIF transaction, the exporter transfers their right to compensation to the importer as the importer holds the bill of lading. In FOB and CFR transactions, the importer holds the insurance policy as they arrange their own insurance.

KENT, CLARKE & CO. LTD

SOUTH BANK HOUSE · BOROUGH ROAD · LONDON SE1 OAA
TELEPHONE: +44 (0)20 7928 7716 · FACSIMILE: +44 (0)20 7928 7111
Email: simpsonj@kencla.com

Facsimile

To	Worldwide Insurance Ltd
Fax	020 7263 6925
From	J.D. Simpson
Date	15 May 20—
Pages	3
Subject	Delta shipment

We will be sending on behalf of our clients, Delta Computers Ltd, a consignment of 20 computers to N.Z. Business Machines Pty, Wellington, New Zealand. The consignment is to be loaded onto the *Northern Cross*, ex-Tilbury 18 May due Wellington 25 June.

Details of packing and values are attached. Please quote AR port-to-port rate.

We would appreciate a prompt reply.

J. D. Simpson

J. D. Simpson (Mr)
Supervisor

CHAIRMAN: LORD MATHERSON
DIRECTORS: B. KENT A.C.A., C.D. CLARKE H.N.D., R.P. DILLER
REG NO: LONDON 3395162
VAT NO: 41618231 59

Request for marine insurance quotation

Kent, Clarke & Co. are forwarding agents for Delta Computers ▶ see pages 157–164 and 203–206 for previous correspondence. They fax Worldwide Insurance, asking them to quote a rate for Delta's shipment to New Zealand, which is outside the terms of their open cover policy see page 229. Notice the expressions EX- (from) the port of departure, and DUE (at) the destination port.

Quotation for marine insurance

In this reply to Kent, Clarke, & Co., Worldwide Insurance suggest a valued policy, which would cover the consignment for £22,000 plus 10% against all risks including war, strike, and normal and exceptional damage. The consignment would be insured from the date the ship leaves port to its arrival. A DECLARATION FORM gives the insurance company information about the shipment so they can prepare an INSURANCE CERTIFICATE.

WORLDWIDE INSURANCE Ltd

Worldwide House, Vorley Road, London N19 5HD

Telephone: +44 (0)20 7263 6216
Fax : +44 (0)20 7263 6925
Email: d.adair@worldwide.co.uk

Chairman
A.L. Galvin ACA FIS
Managing Director
P.R. Erwin CIS
Directors
L. Swanne, T.R. Crowe MC
H.B. Sidey MA

FAX

To	J. Simpson – Kent, Clarke & Co.
Ref	3982/13098
Fax	020 7928 7111
Subject	Delta shipment quotation
Pages	2

Dear Mr Simpson

Thank you for your fax of 15 May regarding the above cover.

I notice the net amount of the invoice is £22,000, and payment is by letter of credit. I would therefore suggest a port-to-port AR valued policy for which we can quote £4.35p%.

We will issue a cover note as soon as you have completed and returned the attached declaration form.

Yours sincerely

David Adair

David Adair
Manager
Quotations Department

ORIGINAL

THIS CERTIFICATE
REQUIRES ENDORSEMENT IN
THE EVENT OF ASSIGNMENT

Certificate of Insurance No. C 0000/

This is to Certify that there has been deposited with the Council of Lloyd's a Contract effected by *A. Short & Co. Ltd.*, of Lloyd's, acting on behalf of *Bodgit and Scarpa Ltd.*, with Underwriters at Lloyd's, for insurances attaching thereto during the period commencing the *First day of March, 1997*, and ending the *Twenty-eighth day of February, 1998*, both days inclusive, and that the said Underwriters have undertaken to issue to *A. Short & Co. Ltd.*, Policy/Policies of Insurance at Lloyd's to cover, up to *US$5,000,000 (or equivalent in other currencies)*, in all by any one steamer and/or conveyances, or sending by air and/or post, General Merchandise and/or Goods and/or Equipment of any nature whatsoever including but not limited to Rice, Sugar, Motor Spare Parts, Bicycles, Generator Sets, Raw Jute, Jute Goods, from any port or ports, place or places in the World, to any port or ports, place or places in the World, including all transhipments as and when occurring, and that *Bodgit and Scarpa Ltd.*, are entitled to declare against the said Contract insurances attaching thereto.

Conveyance	From	
Via/To	To	
		for the Council of Lloyd's.
		Dated at Lloyd's, London, 20th May, 1998.
Marks and Numbers		INSURED VALUE/Currency
		Interest

© Lloyd's, 1998

We hereby declare for Insurance under the said Contract interest as specified above so valued subject to the special conditions stated below and on the back hereof.

Institute Cargo Clauses (A) or Institute Cargo Clauses (Air) (excluding sendings by Post) as applicable. Excluding rust, oxidisation, discoloration, twisting and bending.
Institute War Clauses (Cargo) or Institute War Clauses (Air Cargo) (excluding sendings by Post) or Institute War Clauses (sendings by Post) as applicable.
Institute Strikes Clauses (Cargo) or Institute Strikes Clauses (Air Cargo) as applicable.
Institute Classification Clause.
Institute Radioactive Contamination Exclusion Clause.
Institute Replacement Clause.

Underwriters agree losses, if any, shall be payable to the order of BODGIT AND SCARPA LTD., on surrender of this Certificate.

In the event of loss or damage which may result in a claim under this Insurance, immediate notice must be given to the Lloyd's Agent at the port or place where the loss or damage is discovered in order that he may examine the goods and issue a survey report. The survey agent will normally be the Agent authorised to adjust and settle claims in accordance with the terms and conditions set forth herein, but where such Agent does not hold the requisite authority, he will be able to supply the name and address of the appropriate Settling Agent.

(Survey fee is customarily paid by claimant and included in valid claim against Underwriters.)

SEE IMPORTANT INSTRUCTIONS ON REVERSE

This Certificate not valid unless the Declaration be signed by
BODGIT AND SCARPA LTD.

Dated

Brokers : A. Short & Co. Ltd.,
1 London Road, London EC9 1OC.

LLOYD'S

Signed

Authorised Signatory
9406CM

SPECIMEN

Request for open cover

Glaston Potteries have built up a regular trade with customers in North and South America. They now email Worldwide Insurance asking them for open cover insurance for their shipments.

To... David Adair

Cc...

Subject: Open cover

Dear Mr Adair

As you know, we have been insuring individual shipments of our chinaware with you for some time and have now established a firm customer base in both North and South America.

We will continue to be making regular shipments, and wondered if you could arrange open cover for £200,000 against all risks to insure consignments ex-UK to North and South American eastern seaboard ports?

I look forward to hearing from you.

Elaine Goodman
Export Department
GLASTON POTTERIES Ltd
Clayfield, Burnley BB10 1RQ
Tel: +44 (0)1282 46125
Fax: +44 (0)1282 63182
Email: e.goodman@glaston.co.uk

1 Why does Glaston Potteries want the policy changed?

2 What are the destinations for Glaston Potteries' consignments?

3 Do Glaston Potteries want a policy that insures them against any eventuality, or only specific things?

WORLDWIDE INSURANCE Ltd

Worldwide House, Vorley Road, London N19 5HD

Telephone: +44 (0)20 7263 6216
Fax : +44 (0)20 7263 6925
Email: d.adair@worldwide.co.uk

Chairman
A.L. Galvin ACA FIS
Managing Director
P.R. Erwin CIS
Directors
L. Swanne, T.R. Crowe MC
H.B. Sidey MA

Your Ref: 5/3/20—
Our Ref: Ml–C16893
Date: 7 March 20—

Ms Elaine Goodman
Export Department
Glaston Potteries Ltd
Clayfield
Burnley BB10 1RQ

Dear Ms Goodman

In reply to your email of 5 March, I am pleased to say that we can arrange an AR open cover policy for chinaware shipments to North and South American eastern seaboard ports.

As you propose to ship regularly, we can offer you a rate of £4.48p% for a total cover of £200,000. I enclose a block of declaration forms – you would be required to submit one for each shipment giving full details.

I look forward to your confirmation that these terms are acceptable.

Yours sincerely

David Adair

David Adair
Manager, Quotations Department

Enc. Declaration forms

In an open cover policy, the client can be certain that the consignment is insured as soon as they have returned the declaration form to the insurance company. Settlement may either be on a monthly or quarterly basis, or per shipment. When insurance cover is nearly used up, the insurance company will inform the client and ask whether they want to renew the policy.

Clayfield | Burnley | BB10 1RQ

GLASTON POTTERIES LTD

Telephone +44 (0)1282 46125
Facsimile +44 (0)1282 63182
Email e.goodman@glaston.co.uk
www.glaston.com

14 July 20—

Mr David Adair
Worldwide Insurance Ltd
Worldwide House
Vorley Road
London N19 5HD

Dear Mr Adair

Open Cover Policy OC 515561

Please note a shipment we are making to our customers, MacKenzie Bros, Canada. Details are on the enclosed declaration form, No. 117 65913.

Yours sincerely

Elaine Goodman

Elaine Goodman
Export Department

Enc.

Registered No. 716481
VAT Registered No. 133 53431 08

Claim under open cover policy

One of Glaston Potteries' shipments to Canada has been damaged so Elaine Goodman emails Worldwide Insurance claiming under their open cover policy. Notice that she saves the main details for the claim form and states that the goods were *shipped clean on board*, indicating that the bill of lading shows there was no damage when the goods were delivered to the ship.

To... | Francis Korvin

Cc... |

Subject: | Claim

Dear Mr Korvin

Policy No. OC 515561

I am writing to inform you that a number of pieces of crockery were damaged in a recent shipment to MacKenzie Bros of Dawson, Canada. The consignment was shipped clean on board the *Manitoba*, ex-Liverpool 16 September. You have our declaration form No. 117 65916.

I would be grateful if you could send me a claim form.

Elaine Goodman
Export Department
GLASTON POTTERIES Ltd
Clayfield, Burnley BB10 1RQ
Tel: +44 (0)1282 46125
Fax: +44 (0)1282 63182
Email: e.goodman@glaston.co.uk

Reply to claim under open cover policy

Worldwide Insurance are willing to accept Glaston Potteries' claim, but they offer a warning as this is one of a number of claims Glaston have made. Notice how they acknowledge the fact that the bill of lading was *clean*.

WORLDWIDE INSURANCE Ltd

Worldwide House, Vorley Road, London N19 5HD

Telephone: +44 (0)20 7263 6216
Fax : +44 (0)20 7263 6925
Email: f.korvin@worldwide.co.uk

Chairman
A.L. Galvin ACA FIS
Managing Director
P.R. Erwin CIS
Directors
L. Swanne, T.R. Crowe MC
H.B. Sidey MA

Your Ref:
Our Ref: Ml–C16910
Date: 23 October 20—

Dear Ms Goodman

Policy No. OC 515561

I am sending you the claim form you requested in your email of 19 August 20—. We will consider the claim once we have full details.

May I point out that this is the fourth time you have claimed on a shipment under your open cover policy? Though I appreciate your products are fragile, and that in each case the goods have been shipped clean, it would be in your interest to think about new methods of packing. I agree that the claims have been comparatively small, but in future you will have to ask your customers to hold consignments for our inspection to assess the cause of damage.

I should also mention that further claims may affect your premium when the policy is renewed.

Yours sincerely

Francis Korvin

Francis Korvin
Claims Manager

Enc. Claims form

1 When will Worldwide Insurance consider the claim?

2 Why does Worldwide Insurance think Glaston Potteries have made so many claims?

3 What does Mr Korvin mean by *may affect your premium*?

4 Which words in the letter have a similar meaning to the following?
 a think about
 b bring to your attention
 c ways
 d the cost of insurance

WORLDWIDE INSURANCE Ltd

Worldwide House, Vorley Road, London N19 5HD

Telephone: +44 (0)20 7263 6216
Fax : +44 (0)20 7263 6925
Email: f.korvin@worldwide.co.uk

Chairman
A.L. Galvin ACA FIS
Managing Director
P.R. Erwin CIS
Directors
L. Swanne, T.R. Crowe MC
H.B. Sidey MA

Your Ref:
Our Ref: M2–D23140
Date: 28 October 20—

Mr T. Shane
Excelsior Engineering plc
Valley Estate
Birkenhead
Merseyside L41 7ED

Dear Mr Shane

Policy No. AR 661 72241

I have now received our assessor's report with reference to your claim
CF 37568 in which you asked for compensation for damage to two turbine
engines which were shipped ex-Liverpool on the *Freemont* on 11 October, for
delivery to your customer, D.V. Industries, Hamburg.

The report states that the B/L, No. 553719, was claused by the captain of the
vessel, with a comment on cracks in the casing of the machinery.

Our assessor believes that these cracks were the first signs of the weakening
and splitting of the casing during the voyage, and that this eventually
damaged the turbines themselves.

I regret that the company cannot accept liability for goods unless they are
shipped clean (see Clause 26B of the policy).

I am sorry that we cannot help you further.

Yours sincerely

Francis Korvin

Francis Korvin
Claims Manager

Registered in England No. 6 915614   VAT No. 56 341 27

Rejection of claim

In this letter Worldwide
Insurance reject a claim
on the grounds that the
bill of lading was not
clean. Note that the
exporter is entitled to
call in his own assessor
to inspect the damage,
and that if there is a
dispute, the case would
be settled by
ARBITRATION.

12

Points to remember

1 Insurance is designed to cover a business or individual against risks such as loss, damage, or injury. Numerous types of policy are available to offer cover against various eventualities. The client has to decide which hazards apply.

2 Indemnification is the cover which allows compensation because of loss or damage, and is calculated on the market value or depreciation value of goods, not their original value. To be insured, a client completes a proposal form, and the premium is then assessed and quoted (in the UK, in pence per cent). On acceptance, the client is issued with a cover note, which gives cover until the policy is ready.

3 Marine insurance is governed by Institute Cargo Clauses (or Lloyd's Own Clauses if the policy is issued by Lloyd's). Shippers are offered a variety of policies to cover shipments. However, most exporters ship under an all-risks valued policy, which covers them against most eventualities and allows them compensation for loss or damage, plus 10%.

4 Open cover policies are used when exporters make regular shipments. Each shipment is declared and the insurance company covers it under the agreement.

Miscellaneous correspondence

13

RESERVATIONS

Reservations can be made by letter, fax, or email, as appropriate. It is important to check that you have given the correct details.

Air travel

Train travel

Hotel reservation

Dear Mr Wood

This is to confirm our phone conversation this morning.

Please would you make two Business Class reservations, London–Kobe return, in the names of Mr P.R. Dell and Ms B. Newsome. Outward flight DA164, departing Heathrow at 10.05 on Wednesday 12 June, return flight DA165, departing Kobe at 20.30 on Tuesday 18 June.

Please send the tickets for my attention and charge to our account.

Yours sincerely

Beth Cowan

Beth Cowan

Dear Ms Meek

To confirm the arrangements we discussed this morning, would you please book a return ticket, with couchette, in the name of Ms Jean Miles for London–Paris–Zagreb, depart Thursday 18 July, and returning Zagreb–Paris–London, depart Saturday 3 August?

The reservation should be in a non-smoking compartment.

Please send your invoice to Jane Lewis in our Finance Department.

Yours sincerely

S. Mehta

S. Mehta (Mr)

Dear Ms Okada

Please could you reserve two Executive Grade rooms from 3 June to 18 June inclusive for Mr P.R. Dell and Ms B. Newsome?

I would be grateful if you could confirm these reservations by return.

With best regards

Beth Cowan

Beth Cowan

Dear Sir / Madam

We are holding our annual conference this year in Kyoto and are looking for a hotel which can offer us accommodation and conference facilities from Thursday 14 November to about 4.00 p.m. on Sunday 17 November.

We require accommodation and full board for 60 delegates, 15 of whom will be accompanied by their spouses. Therefore, we will need 45 single and 15 double rooms for three nights. We would also like coffee and tea to be served to the delegates mid-morning and mid-afternoon on each day of the conference.

For the sessions we will need a room with full conference facilities (including PowerPoint), that can accommodate 60 to 70 people.

Please would you send us a list of your tariffs and let us know what discounts you allow for block bookings?

Yours faithfully

W. Herron

W. Herron (Ms)

Dear Mr Gomez

Could you contact our Production Director, Mr Norman Luman, to discuss the possibility of setting up a contract for you to supply us with steel over the next year?

He will be in his office all next week, and if you could email or telephone him he would be glad to arrange a meeting with you.

Best wishes

Pat Nash

Pat Nash (Ms)
PA to Production Director

Confirming an appointment

Dear Mr Gomez

Mr Luman has asked me to confirm the appointment you made to see him at our Head Office, 25 City Road, London W1 at 11.30 a.m. on Tuesday 2 August.

He looks forward to meeting you.

Best wishes

Pat Nash

Pat Nash (Ms)
PA to Production Director

Cancelling an appointment

Dear Ms Nash

Unfortunately, Mr Gomez will not be able to keep his appointment with Mr Luman on Tuesday 2 August. An urgent matter has come up in our Lisbon office which needs his immediate attention.

He offers his sincere apologies for the inconvenience, and will contact you as soon as he returns to London.

Best wishes

Maria Ventura

Maria Ventura
Assistant to Diego Gomez

Follow-up after an appointment

Dear Mr Luman

Just a line to say that I was glad we were finally able to meet yesterday.

I am also pleased we were able to work out the main points of our contract so quickly and come to a mutually acceptable agreement.

I will call you in a few weeks to review progress.

With best wishes

Diego Gomez

Diego Gomez

Dear Mr Deksen

Thank you for your last consignment. You will receive our next order in a few weeks.

I am writing to ask if you could offer assistance to our Overseas Sales Manager, Mr Michael Hobbs, who will be visiting Oslo from 1 to 17 May?

You may remember that when you were here a few months ago I mentioned that we intended to expand our export sales. We are now looking at market potential in Scandinavia, and Michael Hobbs's trip is part of this research. It would help us a great deal if you could introduce him to wholesalers and retailers who may be able to advise him about the types of product that we would need to offer in your market. He would also be interested in finding out more about marketing methods and importing procedures.

I understand that you are very busy, but I would much appreciate any assistance you can offer and will, of course, reciprocate as and when the opportunity arises.

Yours sincerely

Frank Welford

Frank Welford
Managing Director

Dear Mr Deksen

Thank you very much for assisting Michael Hobbs while he was in Oslo. I know he has already written to you expressing his gratitude, but I would like to add a word of appreciation myself. The introductions you made for him and information he gained will be extremely useful in our Scandinavian export programme.

If we can return the favour on some future occasion, please let me know.

Yours sincerely

Frank Welford

Frank Welford
Managing Director

HOSPITALITY

Letter, fax, or email can be used. Letters are more appropriate for more personal invitations and replies.

Request for hospitality

A British company, which wants to expand its sales to Scandinavian countries, asks a Norwegian business associate to provide help and hospitality during a visit to Norway by the company's sales manager. Notice that the letter does not open with the request, but with a reminder of the companies' association.

Letter of thanks

Dear Mr Okada

I have pleasure in enclosing an invitation for our annual award ceremony, which will take place on 14 December. As one of our distinguished ex-students, we wondered if you would be willing to distribute the awards, and give a short address beforehand on a subject of your choice?

We would also like to invite you to a formal dinner after the ceremony. This will be held in the Principal's Lodgings, at 6.30 for 7.00 p.m.

We would be delighted if you are able to accept our invitation. I look forward to hearing from you.

Yours sincerely

David Hope

David Hope
Principal

Enc.

Dear Mr Hope

Mr Okada has asked me to write saying he is honoured to accept your invitation to distribute the prizes and speak at your annual award ceremony on 14 December. He also has much pleasure in accepting your kind invitation to the formal dinner afterwards.

He has fond memories of the college and welcomes the chance to visit it again.

He suggests speaking on the topic 'Changing technology in the next decade'. He would appreciate it if you could let him know whether this would be an acceptable theme.

Yours sincerely

Yuko Ito

Yuko Ito
PA to Mr Okada

Dear Ms Lee

Mr van Ek would like to thank you very much for your kind invitation to attend the reception being held next month at your embassy.

Unfortunately he will be in the United States at that time. However, he sends his apologies, and hopes to be able to attend on another occasion.

Yours sincerely

Els Spruit

Els Spruit
PA to Mr van Ek

Dear Mr Corney

I would like to offer my congratulations on your election as Chairman of our Trade Association.

No one has done more to deserve the honour, or has worked harder to promote our interests. You can count on my full support, and that of my colleagues, during your term of office.

I wish you every success for the future.

Yours sincerely

Mike Benson

Mike Benson
Chief Executive Officer

Dear Jack

I'd like to congratulate you on being appointed Department Manager. I know you've worked very hard to achieve this well-deserved promotion. I wish you the very best in a job where I'm sure you will be successful.

Sandra

Sandra

Dear Rob

I am writing to congratulate you on your new appointment and to thank you for your contribution to making this department so successful.

Your future employers are very lucky to have you joining them, and I am sure you will carry your success here over to the challenges of your new position.

With very best wishes

Damien

Damien

SPECIAL OCCASIONS

Notice that this correspondence is often quite brief. When expressing wishes on special occasions, it is better to write simple, sincere messages, and avoid exaggeration. For personal messages, a letter or card is often more appropriate than an email.

Congratulations on an appointment

Congratulations are also best given directly, not by someone on your behalf.

Congratulations on a promotion

The tone you use will depend on how well you know the person. In this note, the people know each other quite well and are on first-name terms.

Leaving

Illness or accident

Dear Yuko

We were very sorry to hear about your illness. Take care of yourself. We all send our best wishes for a swift recovery, and look forward to seeing you back again soon.

With very best wishes from everyone in the Sales Department.

Sue

Sue

Retiring

Dear Jack

I'd like to take this opportunity to thank you for all your dedication and commitment to the work of the Production Department. It will be extremely difficult to replace you.

May I offer you my best wishes for a long and happy retirement.

Martin Shannon

Martin Shannon

Message of condolence

Messages of condolence should never be written by someone else on your behalf. In these circumstances, it is more appropriate to write a letter rather than send an email message.

Dear Mr Watanabe

I was saddened to hear about the death of your partner, Mr Hiroshi Tanaka, and would like to offer my condolences. He was a fine person and a well-liked man who will be greatly missed by all who knew him.

Please pass my sincerest sympathies to his family.

Yours sincerely

Bernard Fell

Bernard Fell

Seasonal greetings

Seasonal greetings often come in the form of greetings cards and messages. Be aware that people in different countries or from different religious or cultural backgrounds may not share your festivals and holidays.

Dear Mr Peters

May I offer my very best wishes for the New Year to you and your staff? I hope you enjoy the holiday and look forward to working with you again next year.

Paul Davies

Paul Davies

Points to remember

1 The conventions of social correspondence are much the same as those for business correspondence. You should consider the relationship between the writer and receiver and choose not only the most appropriate language but also the most suitable medium, e.g. letter, card, or email.

2 Letters of invitation should state clearly where and when the event will take place, and give some indication of its formality so that guests can dress appropriately.

3 When cancelling an appointment, you should say why you are unable to keep it and offer an alternative day / time if possible.

4 Letters of condolence or congratulation should never be written on someone else's behalf.

5 Personal correspondence on special occasions should be short, simple, and sincere.

13

14

MEMOS

Memos are written internal communications which advise or inform staff of company policies and procedures. They are usually quite formal and impersonal in style. *Memorandum* is the full term, but the abbreviated form is usually used.

Memos may be put on a noticeboard for everyone to see, or circulated in internal mail. In the latter case the receiver/s may be asked to sign the memo to acknowledge that they have read it.

Memos may also be posted on internal email (the Intranet). However, as email is an open access system, this method is not suitable for confidential communications. In addition, some employees, e.g. non-administrative staff, might not be able to access email regularly and might not see the memo.

Memos can address many different subjects, from informing staff of a retirement to announcing important administrative or structural changes in the company.

Layout

Companies often use headed paper for memos. This gives less information about the company than the letterhead for external correspondence, but indicates which department has issued the memo.

A memo should state who it is to, who it is from, the subject, and the date. It may also be signed.

Important points or long lists of points are usually best presented using bullets (•) or numbers.

Guide to contents

A guide to the contents of three example memos, (1), (2), and (3), is given below. They could be sent by email, but it might be advisable to put (1) on a noticeboard too, so that it reaches staff who do not have access to email.

Memos should have an appropriate title, not only to indicate their topic, but also for filing purposes.

(1) *Introduction of shiftwork*
(2) *Annual audit*
(3) *Pension scheme*

Introduce the subject in the opening paragraph.

(1) *A shiftwork system is to be introduced next month.*
(2) *The annual audit will begin on 1 March 20—.*
(3) *A contributory pension scheme is to be introduced as from 1 July 20—.*

Explain to staff how they will be affected.

(1) *The shiftwork system will affect all employees in this branch of Halliwell & Fischer and will be introduced on a two-shift basis: 06.00 to 14.00 hours, and 14.00 to 20.00 hours. Your department manager will inform you ...*
(2) *The auditors will require offices, which means that some members of staff will be temporarily transferred to other offices in the building ...*
(3) *Members of staff who join the pension scheme will contribute 6% of their gross monthly salary. The contributions will go towards a retirement benefit plan which at 60 will offer a pension of 70% of gross salary ...*

Employees should be told when changes will take place, or a policy will become effective.

(1) *The scheme will take effect from 1 February 20—.*
(2) *The annual audit will begin on 1 March and should take about three weeks ...*
(3) *Deduction of contributions to the scheme will start in the month ending 28 July 20—.*

State which staff will be affected.

(1) *All production staff, supervisors, and factory managers will be involved ...*
(2) *The audit will affect all branches of the company. Staff will be expected to explain the loss of any equipment or damage to ...*

14

14

(3) *The pension scheme will only affect those members of staff who were employed on or before 1 January 20—. Employees who joined after that date will be included in the scheme as soon as they have completed six months' full-time employment.*

Once you have mentioned *how* and *when* staff will be affected by an event or change, *where* it will operate, and *who* will be involved, you must explain *what should be done.*

(1) *Please see your supervisor or department manager to find out which shift you will be working on for the first month. Another memo will be circulated next week, explaining a bonus scheme which will be introduced as part of the new arrangement.*

(2) *Please see either your supervisor or department manager for further information on what materials the auditors will want to see.*

(3) *Everyone included in the scheme will receive a booklet, PP301, giving details of how the pension plan will work and what benefits they / their beneficiaries will receive. Two copies of a contract will also be enclosed. You should sign both copies, and return one to your department manager before 21 June 20—. Please keep the other for your own records.*

Finally, if you think the memo might not be understood, advise staff where they can go for an explanation and how to communicate their comments or complaints.

(1) *If you have any problems with your shift allocation please contact your supervisor or department manager.*

(2) *If there are any problems you would like to discuss before the auditors arrive, please contact your department manager.*

(3) *The booklet should explain the scheme clearly, but if there is anything you do not understand, or if you are already in a pension scheme that might be affected by this plan, please inform your department manager as soon as possible.*

Length

Memos can be short or long. They can deal with a number of different points but these should be connected to the same topic. For example, a single memo which tried to deal with canteen facilities, punctuality, and a new accounting system might confuse its readers. It would be better to write a separate memo for each topic.

⚓

KEYSER SHIPBROKERS LTD

123–5 LOWLAND STREET, LONDON EC1 2RH
TELEPHONE: +44 (0)20 7671 · FAX: +44 (0)20 7671 9873

MEMORANDUM

To	Department managers
From	The Chairman
Topic	Donald Crayford
Date	26 November 20—

Strictly Confidential
Please sign to confirm receipt.

Donald Crayford has decided to retire from his position as Chief Executive
on 20 December this year. We have considered several candidates for his
replacement, but no firm decision has yet been reached. However, we hope
to make a confidential announcement by the end of this week at a private
meeting of department managers.

Jessica Renfrew   ————————————

Thomas Dillon   ————————————

Francesca Amis   ————————————

William Thornton   ————————————

Travis Shiran   ————————————

1 Why would you not
send this memo by
email?

2 Why do you think the
memo is *strictly
confidential*?

3 What are the
department
managers asked
to do?

4 When will the
Managing Director's
successor probably be
announced?

5 Which words in the
memo have a similar
meaning to the
following?
a secret
b a number of
c people hoping to
get a job

Visit of a customer

Coventry Components
are expecting some
important visitors to
their factory, so they
circulate a memo.

COVENTRY COMPONENTS   MEMO

To	All staff	**Date**	1 July 20—
From	Henry Woodfield		
Topic	Zorbra Industries visit		

From 8 to 11 July Mr Jason Zorbra of Zorbra Industries, Athens, and two of his colleagues, will be visiting the factory. Zorbra Industries has recently placed a three-year contract with us to supply them with components.

Although Michael Hobbs, our Overseas Sales Manager, will escort them, it might be necessary for individual employees to answer questions or explain production procedures in their section. Therefore, please ask your staff to be as helpful and informative as possible. It will also be necessary for lunch hours and breaks to be re-arranged so that there is always someone available in each section.

Your co-operation in this matter is essential and will be appreciated.

1 Who will escort the visitors?

2 What are employees asked to do?

3 Why is their help so important?

4 Which words in the memo have a similar meaning to the following?

a parts of an engine
b ways of doing things
c help
d very important

⚓

KEYSER SHIPBROKERS LTD

123–5 LOWLAND STREET, LONDON EC1 2RH
TELEPHONE: +44 (0)20 7671 · FAX: +44 (0)20 7671 9873

MEMORANDUM

To	All staff
From	The Chairman
Topic	Mr D.G. Crayford
Date	2 December 20—

Donald Crayford will retire as Chief Executive on 20 December.

As many of you may know, Donald Crayford has been with the company for over 20 years. The 10 years during which he has been CEO have seen a period of unprecedented growth, despite difficult economic conditions in some of our overseas markets.

Diana Hawks has been appointed CEO with effect from 2 January 20—.
I am sure you will join me in wishing her every success.

Would all department managers please attend a meeting in the Main Meeting Room on Monday 6 December at 15.30 hours, where they will be introduced to Diana Hawks.

Retirement of a chief executive officer

Notice how this memo covers a number of different points connected to the retirement of a CEO: it announces the retirement, advises everyone of the new appointment, thanks the retiring CEO, welcomes his successor, and announces a meeting.

Panton Manufacturing Ltd
Panton Works | Hounslow | Middlesex | TW6 2BQ

TELEPHONE +44 (0)20 8353 0125
FACSIMILE +44 (0)20 8353 6783
EMAIL d.panton@panman.co.uk

PANTON

MEMO

To	All supervisors
From	The Chief Executive
Date	6 February 20—
Subject	New machinery

As part of the company's expansion programme, we are introducing RS100 and DS100 machines which will increase productivity and reduce costs, thus making us more competitive in overseas markets.

The new machinery will not in any way affect job security, and there will be opportunities for retraining for all production staff.

A full consultation process has taken place with the Union, and cooperation has been agreed in installing and maintaining the new machines.

Please call a meeting of your team members on Wednesday morning at 9.30 a.m. to inform them of these changes.

Questions

1 Why are the machines being introduced?

2 What does the Chief Executive mean by: *The new machinery will not in any way affect job security*?

3 Who have Management consulted about the introduction of the machines?

4 Which words in the memo have a similar meaning to the following?
 a make smaller
 b influence
 c learning new skills

L. Franksen plc
Memo

To	All employees
From	The Chief Executive
Date	15 July 20—
Subject	Cutting output and redundancies

Following the meetings last week I am writing to confirm that, with regret, we have to announce a 10% reduction in the workforce. The reason is that rising production costs and a fall in demand for our products have caused the company to run at a loss for the past three years. The fall in demand is a result of continuing stagnation in the industrial sector.

We are now, therefore, in a period of consolidation, during which time we hope that the necessary reduction can be achieved by voluntary redundancy and early retirement.

Those employees affected will meet individually with their managers over the next two weeks.

1 Why is the company reducing the size of the workforce?

2 How many people will be affected?

3 What does *voluntary redundancy* mean?

4 When will those affected be informed?

Takeover of a company

This faxed memo is to the staff of a company that is about to be taken over. In these circumstances it is essential to explain exactly what is happening and what is going to happen, as employees will naturally want to know about their job security. Notice how the main points are carefully laid out, and that the memo is written almost immediately after the takeover to prevent rumours spreading.

Bedix Calculators Ltd

To	All branches
From	J.L. Bedix, Chairman
Date	21 October 20—
Subject	Control of Bedix Calculators by Prendall Industries

You are probably aware from reports in yesterday's press that Bedix Calculators has been taken over by Prendall Industries and is now part of the Prendall Group.

Details of the takeover and how it will affect employees will be sent to everyone before the end of the week. However, this memo is being circulated to reassure you of the following:

1 There will be no redundancies as a result of the takeover, although there will be some reorganization.
2 Reorganization will take place over the next year. Prendall intend to expand Bedix Calculators' production in order to make us a major electronic component supplier to their own industries.
3 Salaries and other terms and conditions of employment will not be affected.
4 Management positions will not be affected, although external consultants will be looking at our methods of production with a view to improving efficiency.
5 Bedix Calculators will retain its own name and identity, and fulfil all contracts and obligations it was committed to prior to the takeover.

Further information will be made available through supervisors and union representatives in due course.

J.L. Bedix
J.L. Bedix
Chairman

This memo has been posted on internal email, the Intranet. However, copies of memos describing changes in office regulations should also be put on noticeboards to ensure that members of staff who do not have access to email are informed.

☒   _ □ ×

| ⊡ Send | 🖫 🖨 | ✂ 🗈 🖺 | 🖹 📎 | 📖 ⌕ | ↑ ↓ ▽ | 🖹 Options... | ? |

| Arial ▼ | 10 ▼ | 🎨 | **B** *I* U | 🖹 ≣ ≣ ≣ ≣ ≣ |

File   Edit   View   Insert   Format   Tools   Actions   Help

To...	All staff
Cc...	
Subject:	Smoking policy

We have been reviewing our policy on smoking in the workplace, which currently allows staff who have individual offices to smoke unless prohibited by fire regulations. Smoking is also permitted in ten outdoor areas provided that smoke drifting through open windows does not inconvenience other staff.

Since this policy was drawn up ten years ago, there has been much medical research. Passive smoking is now known to be a serious health hazard, significantly increasing the chances of lung cancer in non-smokers.

Bearing in mind both the weight of medical evidence and the legal duty we have to protect the health and safety of employees, we will be making the following change to our smoking policy:

Smoking will no longer be permitted in individual offices with effect from 1 November 20—.

We appreciate that this decision will affect a minority of staff and that for them this change will be difficult. Therefore, we will provide support and practical help to individuals who wish to stop smoking. Please contact my secretary, Madeleine Richards, for further details.

Frances Easton
Health and Safety Officer

REPORTS

Types of report

The two main types of report are:
— *Regular reports*, which companies prepare monthly, quarterly, or annually, and which give information, e.g. about sales, income, credit status, or the company's performance ▶**see page 263**.
— *Ad hoc* or *special purpose* reports, which are written to describe or explain a programme, e.g. the introduction of a new company programme ▶**see page 262**, or the result of a credit investigation.

All reports should be planned carefully and drafted in outline before they are written. You need to consider the purpose of the report so your reader knows what you are trying to achieve. The report should be comprehensive, and aim to include every relevant point; it should be logical and intelligible so the reader can understand it easily; and it should be accurate in all facts and details.

Structure of a report

Whether the report is short or long, the structure will be similar.

Title
This should explain exactly what the report is about.
— *The future of small businesses under the Consumer Protection Acts*
— *The results of an investigation into the damage to two turbine engines covered by policy AR 661 72241*
— *Fossil fuels as a source of energy*

Introduction
This should summarize the content and references of the report, i.e. what it will cover, why it is being written, and possibly the methods used to collect the information. Often it is easier to write the introduction once the body of the report has been completed, when the writer's ideas are clearer.

— *This report defines small businesses as companies with a staff of less than thirty employees and an annual turnover of not more than £4.5 million. … We have been concerned about the effects of the Consumer Protection Acts and the financial position of our members if they are sued. … We investigated the situation covering the years 19— to 20—.*

Main body
This section, in which the topic of the report is examined, will include the facts you have collected and your sources. These can be either PRIMARY SOURCES, which are direct interviews and questionnaires, or SECONDARY SOURCES such as books, magazines, and newspapers.
— *We used two sources of information: a questionnaire sent out to small businesses in the designated areas, and government publications covering the years 19— to 20—. A copy of the questionnaire and a list of publications can be found in the Appendix.*

Conclusions
Conclusions are the ideas you have formed from the evidence examined in the main body of the report. Whereas facts are objective statements, conclusions interpret and comment on the facts and draw together the different aspects of the situation as you see it.
— *From the evidence we have examined it appears that the new legislation will have the following effects:*
  1 Businesses with an annual turnover of not more than £4.5 million will find that …
  2 Customers in groups A, B1, C1, and C2 will try to …
  3 Electrical and mechanical products will certainly …

Recommendations
You may or may not have been asked for recommendations. If you have, you should explain that the conclusions lead you to recommend a particular course, or courses, of action. You might also predict the outcome of following, or not following, a particular course of action.

— *We feel that as consumers' rights are strengthened by the legislation it would be better for small traders to consider more extensive liability insurance. We also believe they should…*

Headings

In a short report you might need only a few headings or even no headings at all. However, in a longer report a more complicated numbering system might be used. Two examples are given below.

— *Introduction*
  Procedures
  Main points
  (a)
  (b)
  (c)
      (i)
      (ii)
  Conclusions
  Recommendations

— *1 Introduction*
  2 Data collection
      2.1 Questionnaires
      2.2 Interviews
      2.3 Focus groups
  3 Main findings
      3.1 Internet users
          3.1.1 Age group 18–30
          3.1.2 Age group 30–50
          3.1.3 Age group 50 +

Long reports may be made up of many different sections. It is best to include a contents list with page numbers for easy reference. They may also include tables, graphs, lists of references, and acknowledgements thanking people who have helped in the writing of the report. There may also be an APPENDIX giving extra information not required in the main body of the report, e.g. a copy of a questionnaire, transcripts of interviews.

Summary

Busy people do not always have time to read all the reports they receive, especially if they are very long or do not affect them directly. However, it may be useful or important for them to know the gist of what the report contains, and so it is a good idea to include a brief summary of not more than one page at the beginning of your report. The summary should explain why the report has been written and contain only the main findings, conclusions, and recommendations.

14

SP Wholesalers plc

Memo

To The Board of Directors

From Derek Logan, Sales Director

Date 15 October 20—

Subject Introduction of Internet sales

The Sales Department research team came to the following conclusions on
the issue of Internet sales. Further statistical and technical data can be
found in the full report (pages 4–30).

Market

Internet sales have expanded steadily in our markets in recent years for
three main reasons: (1) the range of goods we can offer in a virtual
warehouse environment, (2) convenience, and (3) increased security with
the development of digital signatures. The main area of expansion – over
21% in the period concerned – has been in clothes, especially children's
clothes covering the age groups of 4–11 years (see statistical analysis on
page 9).

With regard to sales of linens and general furnishings, there has been a 6.7%
increase in sales over this period. We would like to monitor this over the
next 12 months to see how these markets develop (see pages 28–9).

Finance

If we concentrate on the garment area of the market, supplying all age
groups, we estimate an increase in our annual budget of 4.8%, which
includes administration, warehousing, expanding stock, advertising, and
the capital needed for new technology. This will increase our present
turnover in this area by 7% over a two-year trial period (see pages 15–18).

The Finance Department suggests that this increase in capital investment
should come from share issues rather than loans because, in the case of the
latter, increasing interest rates will reduce profits.

Conclusions

With our main competitors already in this market, and its potential for
international sales, we recommend that we should implement a new
Internet strategy as quickly as possible. I would suggest a meeting before
the end of this financial year.

---

1 Why do the research
team believe there is
a potential market in
Internet sales?

2 Which is the best
market for SP
Wholesalers to enter?

3 What do they want to
do about selling their
other products?

4 How much would the
company need to
invest?

5 Where could the
company obtain the
money to invest in
the project?

6 When does Derek
Logan think the board
should meet to
discuss the project?

7 Which words in the
report have a similar
meaning to the
following?
a information
b created by
computer
c total business in a
given period

Agent's quarterly report

This report has been produced by Mohamed Kassim, who is British Crystal's agent in Saudi Arabia, for Nicholas Jay, the Managing Director of the company.

▶ See pages 174–176.

Send | Options...

Arial | 10 | **B** *I* U

File Edit View Insert Format Tools Actions Help

To... | Nicholas Jay
Cc... |
Subject: | Quarterly report

Accounts   Market research summary

Dear Mr Jay

You will see from the attached accounts that turnover in the past nine months of trading has been disappointing. There are a number of reasons for this:

1 Sales

Although there is a steady demand for the main ornamental lines, I think there is a much larger market potential for tableware, including glasses, jugs, and serving bowls. It might be useful if you could send me a wider range of these products as samples to show customers.

2 Advertising

Our agreed advertising budget of £7,000 is not enough to promote your products, even though we use only newspapers and magazines. It would be useful to double this budget with a view to extending advertising into neighbouring countries, where there are good opportunities to become established. You will see from the attachment concerning the market research I have done through questionnaires to retailers, that there is a positive response in Jordan, Kuwait, and the Emirates.

3 Competition

a As I am sure you are aware, your main competition is from manufacturers in the Far East, who undercut your prices by at least 40%. While they do not sell the same quality products, a number of large companies are becoming established here and are likely to start targeting the upper end of the market with better quality goods. I am monitoring the situation and will let you know of any developments.

b Some competitors copy designs, so it is important for us to get your new designs as quickly as possible and put them on the market first.

4 Finance

a Your credit limit of £2–3,000 should be at least doubled, as this is a very low figure in this market. As your del credere agent I am quite willing to cover the risks involved.

b In my view, the letter of credit payments you require do not allow sufficient time to clear accounts. I would recommend that you consider credit terms and payment over 45 to 60 days by term draft.

I look forward to your comments on this report.

Mohamed Kassim

---

1 How would you describe business for British Crystal in Saudi Arabia?

2 In which part of the market does Mr Kassim suggest there may be opportunities?

3 How much does he recommend the future advertising budget should be?

4 Which other markets is Mr Kassim considering?

5 Where is the competition coming from?

6 What sort of concessions does Mr Kassim recommend Mr Jay should make?

7 What is attached to the email?

8 Which words in the report have a similar meaning to the following?
   a every three months
   b list of questions
   c restriction on money borrowed

Advertising agency's report

This report comes from an outside agency and is written at the request of the company, Katz Electrical, who manufacture domestic appliances. They are losing ground in the market and have employed an advertising agency with market research resources to find out why. The agency has submitted a preliminary report based on their market research, which they hope will persuade Katz Electrical to attend a presentation in which the agency will propose an advertising campaign.

K&G ADVERTISING ASSOCIATES
Thornton House | Kensington Church Street | London W8 4BN

K&G

Date: 10 April 20—

Preliminary Market Research Report for Katz Electrical Ltd

We have completed our market research on testing consumer reaction to your brands, and attach a statistical analysis of the research results. This preliminary report is a summary of our findings, conclusions, and suggestions, which you might like to discuss with us after you have considered the results.

Our survey was based on discussions by a number of focus groups of users and non-users of your products. These were moderated by a psychologist. Using the results of the discussions, we constructed a questionnaire which was presented to a random sample of 500 people reflecting the population distribution of this country. We asked them about their preferences and awareness of your products compared to others on the market, and from this usage and attitude study we produced a profile of your brands compared to those of other companies.

The lists attached show the statistical breakdown in answers to our questions. In summary, they suggest the following:

1   Although your products are stocked in leading stores and your name is well-known, there is a feeling that, in spite of their reliability, they are over-priced and old-fashioned. The 15–25 age group associate your brands with appliances used by their parents, and the 25–35 age group associate your brands with the 1980s.

2   Your name featured very low on the list when people were asked to name a brand of electric fire, vacuum cleaner, iron, and refrigerator. You will see from the attached survey that less than 10% of the sample had heard of your most recent product, the 'Popup' toaster.

We believe that poor marketing is the main reason for the old-fashioned image people have of your products. Also, there is a lack of brand identification, which we are sure can be overcome with a well-planned advertising campaign. We suggest the following action points:

1   Establish a symbol that will be identified with all your products. The most obvious appears to be a cat, a domestic animal for domestic products, which is also associated with your name.

2   Your current advertisements give the impression of functionalism. We suggest glamorizing the ads, maybe with an exotic cat which will always be recognized when seen.

3   Improve the packaging of the products, perhaps by using more fashionable colours and a symbol (see 1 and 2).

4   Improve the targeting of your advertising campaigns. For example, it would be better to concentrate on women's magazines rather than national newspapers.

If, after studying the enclosed information, you are interested in attending a presentation in which we would be able to illustrate these ideas more fully, please let us know. I am confident that if we handled your account we could improve your sales significantly.

Gerry Grover

Gerry Grover
Marketing Director

1   How did K&G Advertising obtain their information about Katz Electrical's products?

2   What does the document attached to the report show?

3   Why do K&G think that Katz does not have a good image, and what do they suggest to improve it?

4   What symbol do they suggest Katz use?

5   What kind of publication do they suggest Katz advertise in?

6   What do K&G say they could do if Katz allows them to handle their account?

7   Which words in the report have a similar meaning to the following?

a   type of product
b   likes and dislikes
c   out of date
d   area of business handled by another organization

Points to remember

Memos

1 Memos are usually quite formal and impersonal in style.

2 They can be addressed to an individual or to a group of people within a company.

3 A memo should clearly indicate at the top who it is to, who it is from, what it is about, and the date it was written.

Reports

1 There are two main types of report, those submitted regularly and those submitted only when they are required.

2 Plan your report carefully: make sure that it proceeds logically and that your points are expressed clearly. In the case of long reports, a brief one-page summary will help busy people.

3 Most reports, regardless of length, consist of a title, introduction, main body, conclusions and recommendations. The headings you use must be clear, and guide readers through your report quickly and easily.

15

APPLYING FOR A JOB

Job advertisements

Advertisements (often shortened to *ads*) for employment appear in all the media, including radio, TV, and the Internet. However, newspapers and magazines are a very common source of vacancies. Some advertisements use abbreviated forms, especially in the *small ad* section, e.g.:

> *Wntd PA. f.t. sml mnfg co. Gd slry. 5-day wk, hrs 9–5, usl bnfts.*

A full-length version of this would read:

> *Wanted, personal assistant for full-time employment in small manufacturing company. Good salary, five days a week, hours of work 9.00 a.m. to 5.00 p.m., usual benefits in terms of conditions and holidays.*

Letters of application

Opening

Generally, the terms *vacancy*, *post*, or *appointment* are used instead of the word *job* in applications. When replying to a job advertisement, as with most correspondence, it is best simply to state what you are doing, and give a date or reference.

— *I would like to apply for the post of Programmer advertised in this month's edition of* Computers.

— *I am writing concerning your advertisement in the* Guardian *of 12 May for a bilingual secretary to work in your Export Department.*

— *I am answering your advertisement for the post of bank trainee, which appeared in yesterday's* Times.

If the advertisement is not clear about how you should apply for the job, it is better to phone the Personnel Department (sometimes called *Human Resources Department*) of the company to find out.

Remember to quote any reference numbers or job titles that are mentioned in the advertisement.

For UNSOLICITED applications, i.e. applying for a job which has not been advertised, you can open like this:

> *I am writing to ask if you might have a vacancy in your —— department for a(n) administrative assistant / salesperson / accounts clerk.*

If someone associated with the company suggested that you write to them, mention this in your opening.

> *I was recommended by ——, who is currently working in your company / who has had a long association with your company / who is one of your suppliers, to contact you concerning a possible post in your —— Department.*

Request for an application form

If you are writing to ask for an application form, give some very brief details about yourself then ask for the form.

These examples can also be used for unsolicited applications.

— *I am 23 years old, and have recently graduated from —— with a diploma / degree in ——. (Give the subject, and mention any special topics you studied that are relevant to the post. You can also mention the class of a degree, and any special honours such as a distinction.)*

— *At present I am working for ——, where I am employed as a —— in the —— Department.*

Closing

There is no need to give any more information at this stage, so you can close the letter:

— *Please could you send me an application form and any other relevant details?*

— *I would be grateful if you could send me an application form. If you need any further details, please contact me at the above address / email address.*

Application forms and CVs

When you receive an application form, always read it through carefully so that you know exactly what information is required. It is a good idea to photocopy it, complete the photocopy, and when you are happy with it, copy the information onto the actual form.

Some companies prefer a CURRICULUM VITAE, usually called a CV (*resumé* in American English), which is your personal and working history **see pages 274 and 275 for examples**.

Application forms and CVs may be emailed, faxed, or sent by post.

Covering letters

You may need to send a covering letter with an application form or CV. If you do, it should briefly explain points that might not be clear. You could also give further details to stress your suitability for the post.

Opening

If the company has sent an application form, remember to thank them.

If you are enclosing a CV, mention it at the beginning of the letter.

Thank you for your letter of —— and the application form for the post of ——. I enclose the completed form / my CV.

Body of the letter

Your covering letter should be short. If you need to develop or emphasize any points, do so briefly and simply.

You will see that I graduated from —— University / College in 20—, where I gained a degree / diploma / certificate in ——. (Mention any parts of your studies relevant to the post.) During my employment with —— my work was specifically concerned with ——. (Mention work relevant to the post you are applying for.)

Reasons for leaving a job

If you need to explain why you left a job, it is best to sound positive. Never say that you wanted a better salary or conditions. You should not say you were bored with your job, and never criticize the company you worked for, their products or services, or your colleagues.

Explanations for leaving a company could include the following:

— *I left* (old employer) *because* (new employer) *offered me a chance to use my (languages, IT training, etc.).*
— *I was offered a chance to join* (company) *where there was an opportunity for further training and experience in ——.*
— *I was offered the post of Senior Technician by* (company) *in (date), and therefore left* (company) *in order to…*
— *I joined* (company) *in (date) as part of their new Eastern Europe sales team. This was an excellent opportunity to…*

Previous experience

Most application forms give some space to describe previous work experience, e.g. what your duties and responsibilities were. Here you have a chance to highlight your achievements, e.g. any special responsibilities or projects you undertook, changes you made, or schemes you introduced.

— *While I was a Team Leader at* (company), *I supervised a team of six technicians and introduced new quality control procedures which resulted in…*
— *During my time at* (company), *I was responsible for marketing software services. A large part of this role involved successfully implementing change in the…*
— *During my time at* (company), *I studied part-time for an MBA, which I completed in 20—. Since then I have gained more management experience in…*
— *As part of my degree course in Business Studies, I worked for three months in the Data Processing Department of a large computer corporation where I gained experience in…*

Reasons for applying

All prospective employers will want to know why you are applying for a specific job. This not only means explaining why you want the job, but why you think your particular skills and experience would be valuable to the company.

— *I am particularly interested in the post as I could apply my previous experience in* (area of work).
— *I am sure I would be successful in this post as I have the skills and experience you describe, as well as …*
— *I believe my background in* (area of work) *equips me for the post you advertise, especially my recent experience of* (specialist area, e.g. project management, website development).
— *I have some experience of* (area of work), *and am enthusiastic about developing a career in this field.*

Closing

At the end of the letter, offer to supply more information if necessary.
— *I look forward to hearing from you. However, if there is any further information you require in the meantime, please let me know.*
— *Please let me know if there are any other details you need. Meanwhile, I look forward to hearing from you.*
— *I would be happy to discuss with you at interview how my skills and experience could be used to your advantage.*

Unsolicited letter

Notice in this letter how the applicant first mentions how he knows of Mitchell Hill (a merchant bank), gives brief details of his education and experience, and then refers to his current employers, who approve of staff spending time abroad. Finally, he tells Mitchell Hill why he wants to join them temporarily, and asks for an application form. Of course, he could also include a CV with the letter, but in this case, he knows that company practice is to send application forms.

Fürstenweg 110
D–30000 Hanover 71

21 June 20—

Mr John Curtis
Manager
Mitchell Hill PLC
11–15 Montague Street
London EC1 5DN

Dear Mr Curtis

I am writing to you on the recommendation of David McLean, Assistant Manager in your Securities Department. We met last month on a course in Hanover, and he suggested that I should contact your company and mention his name. He told me that you often employ people from other countries on one-year temporary contracts, and I am writing to enquire about the possibility of such a post.

I am at present employed by the International Bank in Hanover, in their Securities Department. I have worked here since 20—, when I graduated from the University of Munich with a degree in Economics. In my present position as Assistant to Wolfgang Lüers, Director of the Securities Department, I deal with a wide range of investments from companies throughout Europe, buying shares and bonds for them on a worldwide basis. As well as speaking fluent English, I also have a good working knowledge of French.

I would like to spend a year in the UK to gain further experience in securities investment with a British bank, and believe that my experience, training, and language skills would prove useful to your organization. My employer encourages all its staff to spend a year abroad and Mr Lüers would be willing to give you a reference.

I would be grateful if you could send me an application form and further information about the posts currently available. If you need any further information, I can be contacted by email on bauerm@aol.com.de or telephone on 49 511 506941x155.

Yours sincerely

Marcus Bauer

Marcus Bauer

1 How did Marcus Bauer hear about Mitchell Hill?

2 What is his present post, and what does he do?

3 What are his qualifications?

4 Why do you think his bank encourages employees to work abroad?

5 What does he want Mitchell Hill to send him?

Mitchell Hill plc

11–15 Montague Street
London
EC1 5DN

TELEPHONE +44 (0)20 7625 3311/2/3
FACSIMILE +44 (0)20 7625 4019
CABLE MITHIL (London)
EMAIL McLean@mithil.co.uk

29 June 20—

Marcus Bauer
Fürstenweg 110
D-30000 Hanover 71

Dear Herr Bauer

Thank you for your letter of 21 June 20—. We currently have two vacancies
in the Securities Department which might be of interest to you.

I am enclosing an application form, and a booklet giving details of Mitchell
Hill, including the salary structure and conditions of employment for
trainees on temporary contracts. Would you please complete the
application form and send it to Helen Griffiths, Human Resources
Department, at the above address.

You will see from the form that we require two referees. I suggest that you
include the names and contact addresses of your Director and an academic
referee from the University of Munich.

We look forward to receiving your application.

Yours sincerely

Sheila Burrows

Sheila Burrows (Miss)
p.p. David McLean
Securities Manager

Application form	Ref	**Mitchell Hill plc** Merchant Bank
Post		11-15 Montague Street London EC1 5DN

Personal

Surname (Mr Mrs Miss Ms) **Bauer**		Forename(s) **Marcus**	
Maiden name **—**		Age **28**	Date of Birth **12 Nov 20–**
Marital status **single**		No of children **—** Ages **—**	

Address **Furstenweg 110, D-30000, Hanover 71**

Tel daytime **(49) 511-506941 x155**   Tel evening **(49) 511 251068**

Next of kin **Mr Kurt Bauer, father (see above address)**

Education

School/univ/college	From	To	Address
Secondary **Friedrich-Ebert Gymnasium**	**20–**	**20–**	**Herrenhauser Str. D-30000 Hanover 21**
Higher **Universitat München**	**20–**	**20–**	**Hittorfstr. D-80000 München**

Examinations

Title	Grade	Subject(s)	Date
Diploma	1	Business studies/ Economics	20–
Abitur	1		20–
LCCI Higher		Business English	20–
Cambridge Proficiency	B	English	20–

Have you any of the following skills?

IT skills: (Tick appropriate box)
- ☐ Spreadsheets
- ☐ Wordprocessing
- ☐ Desktop publishing (DTP)
- ☐ PowerPoint
- ☐ Database
- ☑ Keyboard skills
- ☑ Bookkeeping to TB

Accounts:
- ☐ Manual
- ☐ Computerized
- ☑ Telex
- ☑ Customer contact
- ☑ Driving Licence
- ☑ Filing

Languages

	Fluent	Good	Fair
French			✓
English		✓	

Employer's Name and Address	From	To	Position and duties	Salary
International Bank Georgenplatz 108 D-30000 Hannover 1	20–	20–	Assistant to Director of International Securities Dept. Buying and selling securities	£22,000

Names and addresses of two referees

Herr Prof. K. Weil, Universitat München, Hittorfstr., D-80000 München

Herr Wolfgang Lüers, Director, International Securities, International Bank, Harvesthunderweg 7–9, D–60373, Hanover 15

Hobbies/activities

Reading, chess, skiing, swimming, and tennis

Can we approach your Employer for a reference?	☑ Yes ☐ No
When will you not be available for an interview?	Date (s) **before 5 Sept.**

Date **17 July 20–**   Signature

25 Westbound Road
Borehamwood
Herts
WD6 1DX

18 June 20—

Mrs J. Hastings
Personnel Officer
International Computing Services plc
City Road
London EC3 4HJ

Your Ref: KH 305/9

Dear Mrs Hastings

I would like to apply for the vacancy advertised in the *Guardian* on 16 June for a Personal Assistant to the Sales Director.

As you will see from my CV, I am currently Personal Assistant to the Sales Manager of a small engineering company. In addition to the day-to-day administration work, I represent the Sales Manager on some occasions and am delegated to take certain policy decisions in his absence.

I speak good French and Italian, and use both languages in the course of my work.

I am particularly interested in this post as I would like to become more involved with an IT organization and am very familiar with many of your software products.

If there is any further information you require, please contact me. I look forward to hearing from you.

Yours sincerely

Carol Brice

Carol Brice (Ms)

Enc. CV

Covering letter with cv

In this example, notice that the applicant starts by referring to the job advertisement. She then goes on to expand on her present duties and give other information that she feels is relevant to the post. She also explains why she is applying for this particular vacancy. If, on her cv, she gives her current employers as REFEREES, she could mention that she would prefer International Computing Services not to approach them until after an interview.

Curriculum vitae (cv) 1

There are a number of ways of presenting information in a cv. Traditionally, the sequence was name, address, contact details, marital status, education, qualifications, work experience, referees, and interests. However, it is now more common to begin with brief personal details, followed by a short profile or description of yourself (sometimes also called a CAREER SUMMARY). After that, the most important information is recent employment history, and skills and qualifications. In the interests of completeness, you should account for all years since leaving school, but if the information is irrelevant to the position you are applying for or is some years old, you should summarize it as briefly as possible.

These days, it is generally unnecessary to mention marital status, children, age, health, or current salary unless specifically asked to do so, but this will vary according to the law and custom in different countries.

Here is a typical cv for an experienced professional.

Wendy Benson
Chartered Statistician

Address	48 Danbury Road Amersham Bucks HP8 5SM
Telephone	01494 665093
Email	bensonw@amc.co.uk

Profile

— A highly competent qualitative and quantitative market researcher with wide experience in advertising, market research companies, government research, and production and retail organizations in the UK and overseas.
— Highly numerate, with excellent communication skills.
— Analytical, innovative, self-motivating, confident.
— Able to lead or to work as part of a team.
— Welcomes new challenges, especially if they involve implementing and developing schemes.
— Experienced trainer and facilitator.
— Fluent in French and German.
— Computer literate.

Employment
2002–present

Department of Employment
Senior Market Research Officer. Responsible for planning and implementing research on future government manpower requirements; formulated marketing strategies; conducted customer care study; set up database for labour-force survey. Organized statistical training courses for government staff at all levels. Responsible for a team of six market researchers.

1995–2002

Universal Advertising PLC
Assistant Director, Research and Planning Department. Responsible for trade and consumer research; market information systems; market forecasting; trade and consumer analysis of existing and new business for marketing and sales departments. Managed two members of staff.

1991–1995

MMBC Associates
Market Researcher. Involved in research on products and data relating to the retail food and beverage market.

Qualifications

MBA, Open University (part-time)	1995
Diploma of Institute of Statisticians	1991
BSc. (Mathematics and Statistics), University College, London	1990

Publications   See list attached.

Adam Hall

Date of birth:	25 February 19—
Address:	25 Victoria Road, Birmingham B19 2ZK
Tel.:	0121 8953 9914
Email:	adhall@interserve.net.uk

Profile

A highly-motivated, well-travelled, and creative graduate with practical work experience in both sales and TEFL teaching. A 4-month postgraduate residency at the Biosphere 2 Center, Arizona, has given me wide-ranging knowledge of, and insight into, environmental problems and ways of presenting them to the public.

Education

19—–19—	King Edward's School, Birmingham
	O Levels: Art, Biology, Chemistry, English, French, Geography, History, Maths, Spanish

A levels:

Art	A
Environmental Studies	A
Chemistry	B
Spanish	B

20—–20—	Leeds Metropolitan University
	BA Hons Environmental Studies: 2:1
July, 20—	Academy School of English, Leeds Cert CELTA

Work experience

April 19—–July 19—	Weekend sales assistant, Kings Norton Garden Centre, Birmingham
January 20—–May 20—	TEFL tutor, JA School of English, Katowice, Poland

Other information

September 20—–December 20—	4-month residency at the Biosphere 2 Center, Arizona, USA
May 15–16, 20—	Co-presented 'No smoke …' at the Bretton Hall Sculpture Park, University of Leeds. An installation which explored the environmental implications of major forest fires, both natural and man-made.
June 20–24, 20—	Co-presented 'Time microscope' at the Covent Garden Flower Festival. An installation which explored different ways of presenting information about the natural world.

Interests

My main interest outside work, although related to it, is travel. In 19— I took part in a school expedition to the High Atlas mountains in Morocco, and produced a video of the trip. In my gap year I travelled extensively in South America, again documenting the trip by means of sketchbooks and video. I also enjoy World Music, particularly that from countries I have visited, and play the *oud* (Moroccan lute).

References

Prof. T.N. Fagin
Department of Environmental Studies
Leeds Metropolitan University
LS2 3RX

Dr Elzbieta Gordon
Principal
JA School of English
Ulica Czysta 14
Katowice
Poland

1 Where did Adam study environmental problems?

2 What did he do while he was in Poland?

3 Who is Dr Elzbieta Gordon?

4 What do you think Adam's main interest is?

5 Where did Adam graduate from?

6 What commercial experience has he had?

L.B. Richman Associates

27–29 Moore Park Road
Peterborough
PE2 7JB

Tel.: +44 (0)1733 572947
Fax: +44 (0)1733 572948
Email: levina@richman.co.uk

Your ref: **18 June 20—**
Our ref: **KH 305/59**

29 June 20—

Mr Adam Hall
25 Victoria Road
Birmingham
B19 2ZK

Dear Mr Hall

Thank you for your application of 18 June for the post of ———. We would like you to come for interview on Thursday 12 July at 11.00 a.m. Could you phone me on Ext. 217 to confirm that you will be able to attend?

I look forward to hearing from you.

Yours sincerely

Anne Levin

Anne Levin
Recruitment Department

MAKING A DECISION

Turning down an applicant

Companies reject applicants for a variety of reasons, the most common of which are lack of relevant qualifications or experience. However, it is unusual for a candidate to be told why he or she has been rejected.

— *Thank you for attending our selection panel on ——. We regret to inform you that you were not successful in your application.*
— *We regret that we are unable to offer you the position of ——, for which you were interviewed on ——. Thank you for your interest in XYZ Ltd.*
— *We have decided not to appoint any of the applicants who were interviewed for the post of —— on ——, and will be re-advertising the vacancy.*

Offering a post

Letters to successful applicants can vary in length and detail depending on the type of job, whether the company has a standard printed contract, or if for some reason, it is necessary to give details of the terms of employment.

Opening

— *We are pleased to inform you that you were successful in your interview for the post of ——.*
— *We would like to offer you the post of ——.*
— *The selection panel has approved your appointment as ——.*
— *The bank has agreed to accept you for the post of trainee, subject to the usual references.*

Details of employment

As we discussed in your interview, your duties will include … Working hours are from 08.00 to 16.00, Monday to Friday. You are entitled to 25 days' annual leave, plus all public holidays. There is a staff contributory pension scheme, which you will be eligible to join on successful completion of a six-month period of probationary employment. Staff benefits include a subsidized canteen and free

membership of the staff social club. Four weeks' notice of termination of employment is required by both you and the company. Your terms and conditions of employment are as follows:

Title: Trainee Maintenance Engineer.
Commence: 08.30, Monday 9th March 20—.
Duties: Servicing all company products.
Hours: 8.00 a.m. to 4.00 p.m.
Days: Monday to Friday, plus occasional weekends at overtime rate.
Holidays: 25 days' annual leave, plus all public holidays.
Paid sick leave: maximum 28 days per annum.
Annual salary: £——.
Overtime: Time-and-a-half. Double time for public holidays.
Pension: pension scheme at 7% of annual pay.
Benefits: Subsidized staff canteen, membership of staff social club.
Notice: Four weeks' notice of termination of employment must be given.
Your training will commence on Monday, 14 November for a period of one year.
Please find enclosed a copy of the Staff Handbook, which contains full details of the terms and conditions of employment with Mitchell Hill.

Closing

A letter offering a job would invite questions if anything is not clear about the terms and conditions of employment, and ask for written confirmation of acceptance. In the UK, the law requires that companies offer a contract of employment, and two copies of this are often sent with the letter. The applicant would be asked to return one signed copy with their confirmation, and keep the other for their own records.

— *I look forward to seeing you in my office at 09.00 a.m. on Monday 10 January 20—. If you have any questions concerning the enclosed conditions, please contact me immediately. Otherwise, please would you sign the enclosed contract of employment and return it with your letter of acceptance.*

15

— *Two copies of your contract of employment
are enclosed with this letter. Please sign one
copy and return it to the Personnel Officer, Mr
Terence Wright, with a letter confirming you
have accepted the position. Mr Wright will
then get in touch with you with your joining
instructions.*
— *Please report to Reception at 08.30 on
Monday 14 November. You will receive a two-
day induction and orientation course, and
then begin work on Wednesday 16 November.*

Accepting a post

Letters confirming that you accept a post can
be brief, as long as they cover all the relevant
points.

— *Thank you for your letter of 23 December
20— offering me the post of ——. I am
delighted to accept. I look forward to seeing
you at 09.00, on Monday 10 January. As
requested, I enclose one signed copy of the
contract of employment.*
— *I am returning a signed copy of the contract
of employment, which you sent me with your
letter of 15 February. I confirm that I will be
able to begin work on Monday 9 March at
08.00, and look forward to seeing you then.*
— *Thank you for offering me the temporary
position of trainee in your bank, starting on
Monday 14 November. I have read the Staff
Handbook and the relevant details
concerning traineeships, and accept the
conditions of employment.*

L.B. Richman Associates

27–29 Moore Park Road
Peterborough
PE2 7JB

Tel.: +44 (0)1733 572947
Fax: +44 (0)1733 572948
Email: levina@richman.co.uk

Your ref: **18 June 20—**
Our ref: **KH 305/59**
Date: **25 July 20—**

Mr Adam Hall
25 Victoria Road
Birmingham
B19 2ZK

Dear Mr Hall

I have much pleasure in offering you the post of ———.

I can confirm that your starting salary will be £21,000 p.a., and your employment will commence on Monday 15 August 20—.

Please sign both copies of the enclosed contract of employment and return them to Joanna Hastings, Human Resources Department, at the above address, with your acceptance letter. Full details of your employment are in the Staff Handbook, a copy of which I also enclose. Please read the relevant sections of the handbook carefully, and let me know if you have any queries.

Please arrive at Reception at 9.30 a.m. on Monday 15 August, and ask for me.

I look forward to meeting you and welcoming you to the company.

Yours sincerely

Anne Levin

Anne Levin
Recruitment

Enc.: Contract of employment (2 copies)
Staff Handbook

25 Victoria Road
Birmingham
B19 2ZK

27 July 20—

Anne Levin
L.B. Richman Associates
27–29 Moore Park Road
Peterborough
PE2 7JB

Your Ref: KH 305/9

Dear Ms Levin

I am very pleased to accept your offer of the post of ———, starting on
15 August 20—.

As requested, I enclose a signed copy of my contract of employment.
I look forward to meeting you.

Yours sincerely

Adam Hall

Adam Hall

Enc. Contract of employment

Points to remember

1 The word *job* is not usually used either in advertisements or applications. The terms *vacancy, post,* or *appointment* are more appropriate.

2 If requesting an application form, keep the letter brief, but provide essential details about yourself. When returning the form, include a covering letter expanding briefly on details that might not be clear, or pointing out important or relevant qualifications and experience – but keep this short as the application form or cv should contain full details.

3 When writing to a prospective employer, remember to explain why you left your previous post, but do not complain about the salary or conditions. Concentrate instead on your suitability for the post, what you can offer your new employer in terms of experience or expertise, and why you particularly want it.

Unit 1

▸ **page 26**

1 Because he wants to see how well they will sell.
2 Trade references, i.e. assurances from other furniture dealers that Mr Hughes' business has a good reputation.
3 A provisional order; as an email attachment.
4 No, Mr Hughes says the consignment can be sent with the next delivery.

▸ **page 27**

1 Yes.
2 None.
3 Return them to Homemakers within two months of the date of the email.
4 *Let us know if we can be of any further help.*

Unit 3

▸ **page 44**

1 To indicate that he may be able to sell a large quantity of CDs.
2 From an advertisement.
3 He wants leading brands suitable for domestic recording, and some samples.
4 Trade discounts.
5 *Yours sincerely.*
6 a leading b brand c substantial d discount

▸ **page 45**

1 *chain of retailers.*
2 Men's leisurewear.
3 At Hamburg Menswear Exhibition.
4 Quantity and trade discounts.
5 30-day bill of exchange, documents against acceptance.
6 Over 500.
7 a range b displayed c net price d garment

Unit 4

▸ **page 55**

1 The reference of M. Gérard's enquiry, and also the date.
2 They are part of a consignment of bankrupt stock.
3 No.
4 A price-list enclosed with the letter, and also samples of the CDs by separate post.
5 No. Herr Gerlach advises them to order fast as there is strong demand.

▸ **page 56**

1 He refers to some of the products in the enclosed catalogue.
2 He mentions *our worldwide list of customers*.
3 CIF to Canadian seaboard ports.
4 He invites Ms Lowe to contact Glaston Potteries for further information.
5 a selection b choose c receipt of order

▸ **page 57**

1 She is out of stock of the types of unit Sr Monteiro is interested in.
2 She mentions that she is testing another consignment of units.
3 No, she says she will contact him.

▸ **page 58**

1 No, he offers a 15% trade discount, not the 20% which Mr Crane asked for.
2 By sight draft, cash against documents.
3 He says that he would be prepared to review it when a firm trading association has been established.
4 Satex's summer catalogue and price list.
5 He mentions *other retailers throughout Europe and America*.
6 a sight draft b review c association

▸ **page 59**

1 An estimate for refitting Superbuys' Halton Road branch.
2 A net total (it excludes VAT).
3 Because Wembley Shopfitters use best quality materials and offer a one-year guarantee.
4 *unforeseen circumstances*, i.e. problems that were not predicted.
5 Senior Supervisor.
6 a premises b worked out c backed

Unit 5

▸ **page 64**

1 Satex's.
2 No.
3 Within six weeks.

▸ **page 65**

1 The most likely reason is that he wants to see how the order is handled.
2 The catalogue numbers.
3 Trade and quantity discounts.
4 Within six weeks.
5 The order number (DR 4316).

▸ **page 68**

1 The crockery should be packed in 6 crates, 10 sets per crate, each piece individually wrapped, crates marked *MacKenzie Bros Ltd*, *fragile*, and *crockery*, and numbered 1–6.
2 Letter of credit.
3 There are regular sailings from Liverpool to Canada.
4 Yes, provided the designs are those stipulated on the order.
5 MacKenzie Bros.
6 a crockery b crates c fragile d stipulated e made up

▶ **page 69**

1 By sea.
2 On 30 July.
3 Glaston Potteries will transfer them to Burnley City Bank for forwarding to the Canadian Union Trust Bank.
4 They substituted the same design in red.
5 a necessary b sent c as per your d with the exception of

▶ **page 73**

1 Their main supplier of chrome has gone bankrupt.
2 They will find another supplier.
3 By the middle of next month.
4 Yes.
5 Whether or not Majid Enterprises want to cancel the order.
6 a concerning b bankrupt c confident d assembled e inconvenience

▶ **page 74**

1 The customer wants a very large discount.
2 By saying that 25% is his maximum discount.
3 That his refusal only applies to this order.

Unit 6

▶ **page 82**

1 The invoice number (1096/A3).
2 at (each price).
3 £3,271.00
4 Cost, Insurance, and Freight (CIF).
5 By including E & OE (Errors and Omissions Excepted) at the bottom of the invoice.

▶ **page 83**

1 £270.00
2 £80.00
3 £180.00
4 £1,580.00
5 Account rendered £522.00.
6 Yes, 3% discount for payment within seven days.

▶ **page 89**

1 $7,139.00
2 The company are waiting for compensation for cargo lost in a fire.
3 Van Basten's insurance company have promised to pay them compensation within the next few weeks.
4 a clear b intended c shipment d compensation e appreciate

▶ **page 91**

1 meet
2 A government order to stop trade with another country.
3 He plans to sell the consignments to customers in Brazil.

4 He suggests that Zenith should draw a new bill of exchange in sixty days' time, with 6% interest added.
5 a temporary b major c consignment d draw

▶ **page 92**

1 Yes.
2 He has commitments (i.e. suppliers to pay) himself.
3 No.
4 He suggests that Mr Franksen should pay half the outstanding balance immediately, by bank draft, and the other half within forty days.
5 Mr Franksen will send a bank draft for half the amount by return of post, and the signed B/E 7714 for the other half.

▶ **page 96**

1 Because they were moving from Milan to Turin.
2 He has enclosed a cheque as part payment and promises to settle in a few days.
3 To make a note of Omega's new address.

▶ **page 97**

1 Copies of the invoices making up the outstanding balance.
2 Three months.
3 Yes. They plan to instruct their solicitors if payment is not received within ten days.
4 instruct our solicitors to start proceedings

Unit 7

▶ **page 104**

1 Because he ordered from an out-of-date catalogue.
2 Deliver the correct consignment and collect the wrong one.
3 Because he is cancelling the invoice for the wrong consignment.
4 He is sending him a new winter catalogue.
5 a looked into b instructed c pick up d mislaid

▶ **page 105**

1 The boxes were broken open in transit.
2 Because they were crushed or stained.
3 The sale was on a CIF basis, and the forwarding company were Sig. Causio's agents, so he must deal with them.
4 A list of damaged and missing articles.
5 Keep it until Sig. Causio tells him what to do with it.
6 a in transit b estimate c contact

▶ **page 108**

1 He thinks it was caused by dripping water. He will arrange for it to be repaired and seal off the area.

2 He thinks it was damaged by metal boxes being dragged across it. He says he will arrange for it to be repaired, but only if Superbuys pays.
3 By using trolleys to shift metal boxes.
4 Less than a day.
5 a inspected b hardwearing c normal wear and tear d shifting

Unit 8

▶ **page 122**
1 Because he could claim 3% cash discounts.
2 Payment on monthly statements.
3 Because he has been a customer for some time.
4 When he pays his next monthly statement.

▶ **page 124**
1 He says he knows M. Gérard can supply references.
2 He operates on small profit margins.
3 No. Herr Gerlach says he does not offer any of his customers credit facilities.
4 He thanks M. Gérard for writing and says he looks forward to hearing from him again.

▶ **page 129**
1 Confirm that MacKenzie Bros's credit rating is good enough for quarterly settlements of up to £8,000.
2 MacKenzie Bros have said Pierson & Co. would be willing to act as their referees.
3 That it will be *treated in the strictest confidence*.
4 a quarterly b confirmation c warrants d settlements

▶ **page 130**
1 Contacted MacKenzie Bros to confirm that they were happy for Pierson & Co. to act as referees.
2 He has a high opinion of them.
3 They have paid when debts were due.
4 He says that Pierson & Co. give MacKenzie Bros credit facilities *in excess of* those they have asked Glaston Potteries for.
5 a in excess of b confidence

▶ **page 132**
1 He contacted F. Lynch & Co. to confirm that they wanted Grover Menswear to act as their referees.
2 *on their behalf*
3 Because they prefer to take advantage of their cash discounts.
4 He says they will *take no responsibility for how you use this information*.
5 a dealing with b reputable c confidential

▶ **page 134**
1 He asks if they have had *any bad debts in the past*.
2 Because they may have gone bankrupt under another name.

3 a overdue accounts b bankruptcy proceedings

▶ **page 135**
1 Two.
2 £400,000.
3 Not as far as Credit Investigations know.
4 Yes, the company was taken to court by L.D.M. Ltd to recover an outstanding debt.
5 Not always.
6 They tend to overbuy, i.e. buy too much stock.
7 a investigated b recover c outstanding

Unit 9

▶ **page 142**
1 Because he has a large credit balance in his deposit account.
2 He suggests that they discuss a formal arrangement.
3 Because someone else might read it, causing Mr Hughes embarrassment.

▶ **page 143**
1 Because a post-dated cheque had not been cleared.
2 Because it was post-dated, i.e. for a later date.
3 He has transferred £1,500 from his deposit account to his current account.

▶ **page 144**
1 Because he wants to expand his business.
2 Furniture assembly kits.
3 Shares and local government bonds.
4 An audited copy of his company's balance sheet.
5 A document that shows the totals of money received and paid out over a given period, and the difference between them.
6 a discuss b expand c exceeded d fulfil e estimate f audited

▶ **page 145**
1 A loan of £18,000.
2 It is to be calculated on half-yearly balances.
3 Homemakers' current account.
4 30 September.
5 a repaid b guarantor d agreement

▶ **page 146**
1 In order to expand his business.
2 Mr Ellison's previous overdraft and the current credit squeeze.
3 That he approaches a finance corporation.

▶ **page 149**
1 To B. Haas B.V.'s bank.
2 Thirty days after it has been presented.
3 The bank will hand them over to her when she accepts the bill.

▶ **page 150**
1 A bill of exchange paid after a period of time, e.g. thirty days after it is presented to the

importer (buyer), usually by an agent bank in
his country.
2 Panton Manufacturing.
3 Thirty days after presentation.
▶ **page 159**
1 By quoting the number of the model and the
number in Delta's catalogue.
2 Cost, Insurance, and Freight (CIF).
3 10 June 20—.
4 They should draw for the amount of the invoice
on the agent bank and supply the shipping
documents listed in the email.
5 Eastland Bank.
6 Official order 8851.
7 The value of the goods might go up.
▶ **page 161**
1 Speirs and Wadley Limited.
2 Signed invoice in triplicate; full set of clean on
board shipping bills of lading; insurance policy
or certificate in duplicate.
3 Covering marine and war risks up to buyer's
warehouse, for invoice value of the goods plus
10%.
4 No. Transshipment is not permitted.
5 £4,106.00.
6 10 August 2002.
7 Barclay's Bank.
8 The Downtown Bank & Trust Co.
9 No. Partshipment is not permitted.
10 400 electric power drills.
▶ **page 163**
1 On 12 June.
2 They have been sent to the Eastland Bank.
3 By means of discount, commission, and
charges.
▶ **page 166**
1 On 3 June.
2 In polystyrene boxes in ten crates marked 1–10.
3 Sixty days after sight (i.e. days after
presentation of the draft).
4 Cooper and Deal are the importer's
(International Boats) agent bank in Hong Kong.
5 When to collect the documents.
6 A certificate of origin.
7 The boats must not be altered in any way.
8 a dinghies b supplied c guarantee
  d modified

Unit 10

▶ **page 174**
1 Mr Mohamed Al Wazi, of the Saudi Arabian
Trade Commission in London.
2 North and South America, and the Far East.
3 A 10% commission on net list prices, and an
additional 2.5% del credere commission if the

agent is willing to guarantee the customer's
accounts.
4 Yes, advertising support.
5 British Crystal must approve the account.
6 Sufficient capital, contacts, and facilities.
7 a expand b selection c unique
▶ **page 175**
1 A sole agency.
2 Yes.
3 He suggests three: bill of exchange, letter of
credit, or bank draft.
4 Three years.
5 An unsigned version which can be discussed
and altered.
6 a deducting b dispute / disagreement
  c initial
▶ **page 176**
1 Direct, by letter of credit.
2 No, S.A. Importers would only hold samples.
3 Leaflets and brochures.
4 For one year.
5 That both British Crystal and S.A. Importers
agree to renew the contract.
6 a representative b meet c subject to
▶ **page 177**
1 A sole agency.
2 Because he doesn't think sales would be as high
as Sr Iglasis expects.
3 The way in which payments are settled.
4 Six weeks is too long for seasonal demands, e.g.
the Christmas rush.
5 For one year.
6 (For discussion.)
7 a minimum b remit c shorten
▶ **page 179**
1 Because they have found they are restrictive,
both for themselves and their customers.
2 Run a publicity campaign.
3 Sixty D/S (days after sight), D/A (documents
against acceptance).
4 a retail b market prices c followed up by
▶ **page 181**
1 No.
2 For one year.
3 …the volume of business would make it worth
accepting our offer.
4 a proposition b envisage c be effective

Unit 11

▶ **page 191**
1 They are scratched, split, or warped.
2 No, only boxes 4, 5, and 6.
3 No.
4 He asks if they should be returned or kept for
inspection.

▶ **page 192**

1 The consignment number.
2 There is a checker's mark on each box.
3 Because Disc S.A. made the delivery arrangements.
4 He encloses a copy of the carrier's receipt.
5 a damage b goods depot c supply

▶ **page 193**

1 Eight boxes of CDs.
2 In perfect condition.
3 He thinks the consignment was roughly handled and left near a heater.
4 €500.00 – the loss on invoice value.
5 The consignment was sent *carrier's risk*.
6 Copies of the consignment note and invoice.
7 a premises b assume c fragile d hold

▶ **page 195**

1 Air waybill, and customs clearance and handling charges.
2 For customs inspection.
3 British Crystal Ltd.
4 The despatch form.

▶ **page 196**

1 British Airways.
2 Three.
3 IATA.
4 No.
5 No.
6 Receiver/Importer.
7 Shipper or his agent; issuing carrier or its agent.
8 Nature and quality of goods.
9 Pre-paid and collect.

▶ **page 201**

1 On 7 May.
2 £91.00 per ton.
3 Shipping instructions and an itinerary.
4 a details b vessel c sails d due

▶ **page 202**

1 To Order.
2 That the bill of lading covers goods that might be transferred from one kind of transport to another, e.g. ship to train or truck.
3 Under *Vessel and Voy. No.*
4 The ship's captain or a representative of the shipping agency.
5 Under *Number and kind of Packages, Description of Goods*.
6 They would look for the shipping marks on the crates.
7 P&O Nedlloyd.
8 That there was something wrong with the goods.
9 The original document.
10 Port of discharge.

▶ **page 203**

1 The bill of lading, commercial invoice, and insurance certificate.
2 Delta Computers.
3 Delta Computers.
4 a pick up b shipped c handle d advise

▶ **page 205**

1 18 May.
2 *Leaving* or *sailing from*, and *arriving* or *docking in*.
3 £612.00 per ton or ten cubic metres.
4 International Shippers' standard shipping note and bill of lading. He needs to complete them and return them to International Shippers.

▶ **page 208**

1 Westmorland Bank.
2 Accept the bill of exchange.
3 The B/L is clean.
4 The *America*.
5 In the enclosed catalogue, pp103–110.
6 Eddis Jones.

▶ **page 213**

1 By cubic metre or cubic kilogram.
2 Yes, because International Containers would offer substantial rebates (discounts).
3 On 24 March.
4 A half-height container.
5 It would cover the consignment door-to-door.
6 Door-to-door.
7 Mr Muner advises him to do so.

▶ **page 218**

1 A chance to hire it.
2 Melbourne
3 No, she is larger than they wanted.
4 Because her owners are willing to offer a part charter.

Unit 12

▶ **page 224**

1 Comprehensive cover.
2 Thirty.
3 A sprinkler system, and fire exits on every floor.
4 Because their present insurers have raised their rates.
5 a comprehensive cover b serviced
  c minimal d petty theft e cover

▶ **page 228**

1 Mr McNulty, Westway Insurance's surveyor.
2 This is Mr McNulty's valuation of the damaged stock at current market prices.
3 Damage to the premises.
4 Complete the claim form and return it to Westway Insurance.
5 a inspect b present c consequently
  d complete

▶ **page 234**

1 Because they are making regular shipments.
2 North and South American eastern seaboard ports.
3 Against any eventuality, i.e. *all risks*.

▶ **page 238**

1 When they have all the details.
2 Because their packing is inadequate.
3 Worldwide Insurance may raise it.
4 a consider b point out c methods
  d premium

Unit 14

▶ **page 253**

1 Because it is *strictly confidential* and email is an open system.
2 Because if the information was made public before a successor was appointed it might affect the company's shares, credit rating, etc.
3 Sign the memo to confirm they have read it.
4 *by the end of this week*
5 a confidential b several c candidates

▶ **page 254**

1 Michael Hobbs, the Overseas Sales Manager.
2 Be available to answer questions and explain procedures.
3 It will create a good impression of the factory for an important customer.
4 a components b procedures
  c co-operation d essential

▶ **page 256**

1 They will increase productivity and lower production costs, making the company more competitive.
2 No-one will lose their job.
3 Union representatives.
4 a reduce b affect c learning new skills

▶ **page 257**

1 Because it has been losing money for three years.
2 10% of the staff.
3 An employee agrees to give up his / her job.
4 Over the next two weeks.

▶ **page 262**

1 Because they have expanded steadily in SP Wholesalers' markets.
2 Clothes, especially children's clothes.
3 Study the market for the next year.
4 4.8% of their annual budget.
5 Either new share issues or loans.
6 Before the end of the financial year.
7 a data b virtual c turnover

▶ **page 263**

1 Not very good.
2 Tableware.

3 £14,000.
4 Jordan, Kuwait, and the Emirates.
5 Manufacturers in the Far East.
6 He should increase his credit limit and allow term draft payments.
7 Mr Kassim's accounts and a summary of the market research he has done.
8 a quarterly b questionnaire c credit limit

▶ **page 264**

1 They used the results of focus group discussions to construct a questionnaire which they presented to a random sample of 500 people.
2 A statistical breakdown of answers to K&G Advertising's questionnaire.
3 Their products are too expensive, and old-fashioned. They suggest Katz Electrical improve their marketing and brand identification.
4 A cat.
5 Women's magazines.
6 Increase their sales.
7 a brand c old-fashioned b preferences
  d account

Unit 15

▶ **page 270**

1 He met someone who works in Mitchell Hill's Securities Department.
2 He is assistant to the Director of International Bank's Securities Department. He deals in shares and bonds.
3 He has a degree in Economics.
4 To broaden their experience of different working systems.
5 An application form and further information about available posts.

▶ **page 275**

1 In the Biosphere 2 Center, Arizona, USA.
2 He taught English as a Foreign Language.
3 Principal of the JA School of English.
4 The environment.
5 Leeds Metropolitan University.
6 He has worked as a sales assistant.

account rendered Unpaid amount recorded in a statement of account, details of which were in a previous statement. [6]

advice note Document or message informing a customer that a consignment is on its way to them. [5,11]

advising bank Bank in a seller's country that advises the seller that a letter of credit has been issued in their favour, and may also guarantee it. [9]

agency Company that provides a service. [10]

agent Person or company that acts on behalf of a principal, buying or selling goods for them. [1,10]

agent bank Bank representing seller (exporter) usually in the buyer's (importer's) country. The agent bank will hand the shipping documents over to the buyer either when the buyer pays the bank in a *documents against payment* transaction (D/P) or when he or she 'accepts', say, a bill of exchange in a *documents against acceptance* (D/A) transaction. Agent banks are also used in letters of credit transactions in a similar way. [11]

air waybill Document that gives information about goods sent by air, and states whether the buyer or seller is responsible for insurance. [5,11]

all risks (AR) Type of insurance policy that provides cover against all risks except those listed in the policy. [11,12]

and (&) Co. Abbreviation for *and company*, used in company names. [1]

appendix Section of a document, e.g. a report, that contains additional information and is attached to the end. [14]

AR Abbreviation for *all risks*. [11]

arbitration Settling a dispute by means of a third party who is independent of the others rather than by a court of law. [10]

as at *Up to this date.* [6]

as per *According to.* [5]

assessor Person who estimates the value of damage to property for insurance purposes. [12]

asset Anything of value owned by a company that can be sold off. [11]

attachment Separate document attached to an email message. Icons indicating attachments form part of the header information. [1]

attention line Phrase indicating who a letter is for, e.g. *For the attention of the Managing Director.* [1]

average adjuster Assessor specializing in marine insurance claims. [12]

backlog A number of jobs waiting to be done, and which are late, e.g. orders to be filled. [7]

bad debt Debt that is not likely to be paid. [8]

balance Difference between the totals of money coming into and going out of a bank account. [6]

Baltic Exchange An international exchange for freight and shipping, based in London. [11]

bank charges Fees charged by a bank for handling transactions. [9]

bank draft Cheque that a bank draws on itself and sells to a customer. [6,8]

bank transfer Movement of money from one bank account to another. [6]

b.c.c. Abbreviation for *blind carbon copy*, used at the end of copies of a letter or in the header information of copies of an email message to indicate that they are being sent to other people without the named recipient knowing. [1]

B/E Abbreviation for *bill of exchange*. [3,6]

beneficiary Person who receives money from, e.g. an insurance policy or pension scheme. [12]

benefit payment Payment made from a pension fund or a life assurance policy. [12]

bill of exchange (B/E) Method of payment where the seller prepares a bill in the buyer's name ordering them to either pay the amount when the bill is presented, or a specified number of days, e.g. thirty or sixty days, afterwards. [6,8,9]

bill of lading (B/L) Shipping document that gives details of a consignment, its destination, and the consignee. It entitles the consignee to collect the goods on arrival. [1,11]

blind carbon copy (b.c.c.) Similar to carbon copy (c.c.), only there is no indication on the copy of the letter or message sent to the named recipient that copies are being sent to other people. [1]

B/L Abbreviation for *bill of lading*. [1,11]

blocked style Style of writing, e.g. an address, in which each line starts directly below the one above. [1]

box number Number given in a newspaper advertisement as part of the address to which replies should be sent. [3]

brochure Similar to a catalogue, but usually shorter. [3]

broker Person or organization that buys and sells goods, shares, or insurance, for others. [10]

budget Plan of income and expenditure for a particular period of time, e.g. a year. [14]

building society Type of organization originally set up in the UK to provide mortgages, but now offering a wide range of services similar to those offered by commercial banks. [9]

bulk buyer Business or organization that buys goods in large quantities, e.g. a supermarket chain. [3]

bulk carrier Ship that carries very large quantities of freight without packing, e.g. grain, coal. [11]

bulk consignment Consignment of goods carried in large amounts and without packing, e.g. grain, coal. [11]

bullion market Market dealing in gold or silver in bars. [9]

buying agent Agent who buys goods on behalf of a principal and receives a commission. Buying agents can also act as forwarding agents, clearing goods through customs and sending them on to their clients. [10]

buying house Group of buying agents. [10]

cabotage laws Laws that allow a means of transportation, e.g. ship, aircraft, to pick up goods from one country and transport them to another for trade. [11]

CAD Abbreviation for *cash against documents*. [4,5]

career summary Short profile or description of the subject at the beginning of a CV. [15]

carbon copy (c.c.) Exact copy of a letter or email message sent to people other than the named recipient. They are listed at the end of a letter or in the header information of an email message. [1]

c.c. Abbreviation for *carbon copy*, used at the end of a letter or in the header information of an email message to indicate that it is being sent to other people. [1]

carriage forward (CF) Condition of sale where the customer pays for the transport of the goods. [4]

carriage paid (CP) Condition of sale where the seller pays for the transport of the goods. [4]

cash against documents (CAD) A transaction when the *agent bank* (acting for the seller/exporter) in the buyer's country, presents *shipping documents* to the buyer and asks him or her to pay for the shipment before the shipping documents are handed over to the buyer. [4,5]

cash card Card issued by a bank or building society to an account holder that enables him or her to withdraw cash from a cash dispenser. [9]

cash discount Amount taken off the usual selling price of goods when they are paid for by cheque or cash. [3]

cash on delivery (CoD) Condition of sale where the buyer pays immediately the goods are delivered. [6]

catalogue Book or booklet giving details of goods or services offered by a company, usually with a price list. [3]

certificate of origin A document that shows where goods were made. [9,11]

c/F Abbreviation for *carriage forward*. [4]

CFS Abbreviation for *container freight station*. [11]

chamber of commerce Association of business people formed to protect their interests and provide services, e.g. supplying information and setting up recognized standards of trading. [1,10]

charter To hire a means of transport, e.g. a ship or aircraft. [11]

charter party Contract for chartering a ship. [11]

cheque card Card issued by a bank or building society to an account holder guaranteeing that their cheques will be honoured up to an agreed limit. [9]

CIM Abbreviation for *rail consignment note*. [11]

circular letter Letter, either advertising or offering a product or service, circulated to a large number of companies or individuals. [3]

claimant Person who makes a claim for compensation from an insurance company. [12]

claused Term used on a bill of lading to indicate that goods were damaged or incomplete when taken on board. [11]

clean Term used on a bill of lading to indicate that goods were taken on board in good condition. [11]

clean bill Bill of exchange without any accompanying documents. [9]

clear (A) To pay an account. (B) To pass goods through customs. [6 (sense A); 11 (sense B)]

clearing agent Person or organization that clears goods through customs. [11]

clearing bank Another term for *commercial bank*. [9]

closed indent Order that states the source from which the buying agent must buy. [10]

CMR Abbreviation for *road consignment note*. [11]

CoD Abbreviation for *cash on delivery*. [6]

combined transport bill of lading Another term for *multimodal bill of lading*. [11]

commercial agent Person or company that acts on behalf of a manufacturer, selling their goods to retailers. [10]

commercial bank Type of bank that deals mainly with private customers and small companies in domestic and international transactions. [9]

commercial invoice A document that will include the name and address of the seller and buyer, the terms of delivery and payment and a description of the goods being sold. There is a standard SITPRO document, which exporters can use. [1,11]

commission Charge for handling a transaction. [10]

commission agent Another term for *commercial agent*. [10]

commodity market Market in which raw materials and certain manufactured goods (e.g. coffee, copper) are bought and sold in large quantities by brokers and dealers. [10]

compensation Money paid by an insurance company for damage, loss, or injury. [7]

compliments slip Small piece of paper with a company's details on it, and possibly the name of the person sending the slip. Used as a covering note for a longer document. [5]

complimentary close Phrase used at the end of a letter, before the signature, e.g. *Yours faithfully*, *Yours sincerely*. [1]

comprehensive cover Insurance cover against most risks. [12]

confirmed letter of credit The seller's/exporter's bank (acting as an agent bank) in the importer's/buyer's country confirms to the seller that they will guarantee payment for the goods, thus reducing the risk of the buyer/importer not paying the seller/exporter. [1,12]

confirming bank Another term for *advising bank*. [9]

confirming house Agency that receives orders from overseas, places them, and arranges for packing, shipping, and insurance. [9,10]

consequential loss insurance Insurance against loss of money as the result of an accident. [12]

consignee Person or organization to which goods are sent by a consignor. [11]

consignment Quantity of goods sent to supply an order. [1]

consignment basis Basis on which an agent is employed to resell goods for a commission, e.g. as a distributor. [10]

consignment note Document sent with goods, giving details of the goods and sender. It is signed by the person who receives the goods to prove they have arrived. [5]

consignor Person or organization that sends goods to supply a customer's order. [11]

consolidation When small consignments from different exporters are loaded into a single container. [11]

consolidation services When shippers or forwarding agents load small consignments from different exporters into a single container. [11]

consular invoice Invoice, or stamp on a commercial invoice, issued by the consulate in the importing country which gives permission for goods to be imported. [9]

consulate Branch of an embassy that protects the commercial interests of the country it represents. [10]

container Very large metal box in which goods are packed for transportation. [11]

container freight station (CFS) Container depot for imports. [11]

container waybill Document that gives information about goods sent by container, and states whether the buyer or seller is responsible for insurance. [11]

contract Agreement, with legal force, made between two or more people. [7]

correspondent bank Bank that acts as an agent for another bank. [6]

counterfoil Part of a cheque or paying-in slip which can be detached and kept as a record. [9]

courtesy title Title such as *Mr, Mrs,* or *Dr* used before a person's name. [1]

cover (n) Insurance; (vb) Provide insurance. [10,12]

cover note Document that provides cover until the insurance certificate is prepared. [12]

covering letter Letter accompanying a document or goods, explaining the contents. [5]

c/p Abbreviation for *carriage paid*. [4]

credit (n) Sum of money paid into a bank account; (vb) To record in a bank account a sum of money paid in. [9]

credit card Card, issued by a bank or finance company, that guarantees payment for the goods or services the cardholder buys. The cardholder pays the card issuer at a later date. [6,9]

credit facilities Means of allowing credit, e.g. payment by bill of exchange, open account facilities. [8]

credit note Document informing a customer of money owed by a supplier for faulty or returned goods. It can only be used to buy goods from the supplier. [6,7]

credit rating Evaluation of the creditworthiness of an individual or company. [8]

credit status Creditworthiness of an individual or company. [9]

credit terms Rules involved in making a payment, e.g. allowing a certain amount of time, signing a contract, paying by bill of exchange. [8,10]

credit transfer Transfer of money from one bank account to another. [6,9]

creditworthy Capable of paying off the credit offered. [8]

crossed Term used to describe a cheque or postal order that has two lines drawn across it to show that it must be paid into an account and not cashed. [6]

current account Account into which the customer can pay money, and draw it out, without giving notice. [6]

curriculum vitae (CV) Document describing a person's qualifications, work experience, and interests, usually sent with a job application. [15]

CV Abbreviation for *curriculum vitae*. [15]

D/A Abbreviation for *documents against acceptance*. [3]

days after sight (D/S) The number of days within which a bill of exchange must be paid after presentation. [9]

DC Abbreviation for *documentary credit*. [6]

dealer Person who buys and sells shares, goods, or services to make a profit. [10]

debit (n) Sum of money paid out or owed from a bank account; (vb) To record in a bank account a sum of money paid out or owed. [9]

debit card Card issued by a bank that enables payment for goods and services to be taken from the cardholder's account automatically. [6,9]

debit note Document informing a customer of money owed for goods or services supplied. [6,7]

declaration form Form used when an open cover policy is in operation to provide details of individual shipments to the insurer. [12]

default To fail to do something required by law, e.g. repay money owed, keep to the terms of a contract. [8]

del credere agent Agent who guarantees customers' debts. [10]

del credere commission Commission paid to an agent who guarantees customers' debts. [10]

delivery note Document sent with goods to a customer. It is signed by the person who receives the goods to prove they have arrived. [11]

department of trade Government department that provides services to industrial and commercial organizations. [10]

deposit account Type of savings account that requires notice before money can be taken out. [9]

despatch note Document sent with a consignment, giving details of what it contains and any missing items that will be sent later. [11]

direct debit Similar to a standing order, except the amount is specified by the payee. [9]

discount (a B/E) To sell a bill of exchange to a bank at a percentage less than its value. [9]

dishonour To refuse to pay (e.g. a cheque or bill of exchange) because there is not enough money in the account. [6,9]

distributor Person or company that buys goods from a manufacturer and then sells them to retailers. [1,10]

documentary credit (DC) Letter of credit that requires the seller to supply shipping documents to obtain payment from a bank. [6,9]

document of title Document that allows someone to claim the goods specified on it, e.g. a bill of lading. [11]

documents against acceptance (D/A) When a bank will not release shipping documents until a bill of exchange has been signed (accepted) by the person receiving the goods. [3,9]

documents against payment (D/P) When a bank will not release shipping documents until a bill of exchange has been paid by the person receiving the goods. [4,9]

D/P Abbreviation for *documents against payment*. [4]

draw (on) (A) To write a cheque that instructs a bank to make a payment to another person or organization. (B) To write a bill of exchange demanding payment from a person or organization. [11 (sense B)]

drawee Person who must pay a bill of exchange (e.g. the buyer). [9]

drawer Writer of a bill of exchange, who draws the bill on the drawee (e.g. the buyer). [9]

D/S Abbreviation for *days after sight*. [9]

due *Arriving* or *docking in* (a destination port), e.g. *due Hong Kong*. [12]

due date Date by which an account should be settled. [6]

E and (&) OE Abbreviation for *errors and omissions excepted*. [6]

endorse (vb) To transfer a cheque or bill of exchange to someone else by signing it on the back. [11]

errors and omissions excepted (E & OE) Phrase written or printed at the end of an invoice or statement of account to indicate that the seller has the right to correct any mistakes in it. [6]

estimate Price given for work to be done or a service to be provided. [1,3]

eurobond market Market dealing in bonds issued by European governments. [9]

eurocheque Cheque from a European bank that can be cashed at any bank in the world displaying a eurocheque sign. [9]

ex- *From* (a vessel or port of departure), e.g. *ex-SS Orianna, ex-Hamburg*. [10,12]

exclusive agent / agency Another term for *sole agent / agency*. [10]

executor Person or organization appointed by the maker of a will to carry out its terms. [9]

factor Agent who buys and sells for another organization, but in his or her own name. [10]

factoring Process whereby a company buys the outstanding invoices of a manufacturer's customers, keeps the accounts, and then obtains payment. [10]

FCL Abbreviation for *full container load*. [11]

fidelity bond Guarantee against an employee stealing money from a company. [12]

financial year Period used by companies for accounting and tax purposes. In the UK, from 6 April to the following 5 April. [14]

force majeure Term used in insurance policies meaning an outstanding or unusual event, e.g. a violent storm, an earthquake. [11]

foreign bill Term used in the UK for a bill of exchange drawn, or payable, in another country. [9]

foreign exchange Money in a foreign currency. [9]

foreign exchange market Market dealing in foreign currencies. [9]

forwarding agent Person or organization that conveys goods to their destination. Forwarding agents are involved in the logistics of transportation, finding the most effective and economical route. [5,11]

freight account Invoice sent by a shipping company to an exporter. [11]

full container load (FCL) Consignment from a single exporter that fills a container. [11]

general average sacrifice Term used in marine insurance to refer to cargo that has been deliberately thrown overboard, e.g. flammable goods in the case of fire. [12]

giro System for transferring money from one bank to another. [6]

gross price Price of goods including additional costs such as transport, insurance, and purchase tax. [4]

groupage Another term for consolidation. [11]

groupage rates Rate for container shipments when different consignments are put together in a single container. [11]

guarantee (A) A promise that if something goes wrong with a product, the seller will repair it; (B) A promise to repay another's debt. [7]

guarantor Person who undertakes to be responsible for, or to repay, another's debt. [9]

handling charge Freight company's charge to an exporter for dealing with the documentation for a consignment. [11]

house air waybill Air waybill issued to an individual consignee when consignments have been consolidated. [11]

IATA Abbreviation for *International Air Transport Association*. [11]

ICD Abbreviation for *inland clearance depot*. [11]

IMO Abbreviation for *international money order*. [6]

Inc. Abbreviation for *incorporated*, used in company names. [1]

incorporated American term for public limited company. [1]

Incoterm Term established by the International Chamber of Commerce (ICC) indicating which price is being quoted to the customer **see pages 51–52**. [2,4]

indemnify To promise to protect someone against money lost or goods damaged. [12]

indemnity A promise to protect someone against money lost or goods damaged. [10]

indent Order from another country. [10]

inherent vice Term used in insurance policies meaning something in the content or nature of goods which causes deterioration, e.g. fish or fruit can go bad, metal can oxidize. [11]

inland bill Term used in the UK for a bill of exchange payable in the country in which it is drawn up. [9]

inland clearance depot (ICD) Depot where goods are collected and sent on to their final destination. [11]

inside address Address of the person a letter is written to. [1]

instructions for despatch form Consignors fill out this form for transport companies or forwarding agents so the details of the consignment, e.g. contents, packing, measurements, and its departure and arrival dates and places can be put on the relevant transport documents, e.g. the waybills or consignments notes.

insurance certificate Document that an insurance policy is written on. [5,12]

insurance of interest Insurance against making a business mistake. [12]

insurance of liability Insurance of responsibility for loss or damage, e.g. a company's responsibility to compensate employees for injury at work. [12]

intermodal Another term for *multimodal*. [11]

International Air Transport Association (IATA) Association of major airlines that meets regularly to agree on routes and charges for their services. [11]

international bank draft Cheque that a bank draws on itself and sells to a customer, who then sends it to a supplier in another country. [6]

International Chamber of Commerce (ICC) Association of business people that promotes and protects their interests in business affairs. [4]

international money order (IMO) Money order bought from a bank to send to someone in another country. [6]

International Underwriting Association (IUA) Body responsible for Institute Cargo Clauses. [12]

invoice List of goods or services that states how much must be paid for them. [5,6]

irrevocable letter of credit Letter of credit that can only be cancelled with the agreement of the seller. [4,9]

issuing bank Bank that issues a letter of credit. [9]

L/c Abbreviation for *letter of credit*. [6,9]

LCL Abbreviation for *less than full container load*. [11]

less than full container load (LCL) Small consignment that does not fill a container and can therefore be shipped in the same container as other consignments. [11]

letter of credit (L/c) Document issued by a bank on a customer's request that orders an amount of money to be paid to a supplier. [6,9]

letter of indemnity Letter issued by an exporter accepting responsibility for goods lost or damaged during shipping. [11]

letterhead Printed address of the sender, in the UK usually at the top of the page. [1]

life assurance Form of insurance providing for the payment of a specified sum to a named beneficiary if the policyholder dies. [12]

limited liability Company in which the shareholders are only responsible for the capital they have contributed if the company goes bankrupt. [1]

line Particular item made or sold by a company. [3]

Lloyd's of London An association of underwriters and insurance brokers. [12]

Ltd Abbreviation for *limited liability*, used in company names. [1]

long-term credit facilities Credit facilities that allow a buyer a long period of time to pay. [5]

loyalty discount Amount taken off the usual selling price of goods when they are sold to a regular customer. [4]

make up To put together, e.g. an order. [5]

merchant bank Type of bank that specializes in international trade and finance, and deals mainly with large organizations. [9]

mortgage A loan for which property is the security. [9]

movement certificate Usually called a EUR1. This is a customs certificate completed by the exporter and countersigned by Customs to obtain a preferential duty rate for goods coming into the EU from an outside country. It has preferential duty rates with the EU country, e.g. countries that were part of the Lomé Agreement could get a special duty rate. [11]

multimodal Used to describe units for transportation, e.g. containers, that can be transferred between different systems, e.g. truck, train, and ship. [11]

multimodal bill of lading Bill of lading covering more than one means of transport, e.g. road and sea. [11]

mutual Description of a company or institution in which there are no shareholders and in which all profits are distributed to policyholders or members. [9]

negotiable document Document, e.g. a bill of lading, that can be bought or sold. [11]

negotiable securities Securities that can be exchanged for goods, money, etc. [9]

net invoice value Value of an invoice without extra charges such as shipping. [10]

net price Price of goods without additional costs such as transport, insurance, and purchase tax. [4]

new issue market Market dealing in new share issues. [9]

non-Conference ship Ship that is not a member of the Shipping Conference and does not travel on scheduled routes. [11]

non-exclusive agent / agency Person or organization that sells the products of a manufacturer alongside other agents in a particular country or area. [10]

non-negotiable waybill Waybill that cannot be bought or sold. [11]

non-recourse factoring Buying up an outstanding invoice and claiming the debt from the customer. [10]

on approval Term used for goods sent to possible customers to look at or use before buying them. [1]

online banking Using the Internet to transact bank business. [9]

on their own account *In their own name.* [10]

open account facilities Account in which a customer is given an agreed period of time, e.g. three months, to pay for goods. [4,8]

open cover policy Type of marine insurance policy that provides cover for all shipments made by the policyholder over an agreed period, e.g. six months. [12]

open indent Order that allows the buying agent to buy from any source they choose. [10]

option Right to hire a ship. [11]

out of charge note Note issued by customs when goods have been cleared. [11]

outstanding *Unpaid.* [5]

overdraft Loan made by a bank to an account-holder, enabling them to take out more money than is in their account. [9]

overdraw To take out more money than there is in a bank account. [9]

overhead A regular cost of running a company, e.g. wages, rent. [9]

packing list List of goods being sent. This repeats some of the information on a bill of lading, but is a separate document. [11]

p and(&) p Abbreviation for *postage and packing.* [6]

paying-in slip Printed form used by an account holder to record cash or cheques paid into a bank account. [9]

payload The part of a cargo that earns money for the shipping company. [11]

per pro *For and on behalf of.* [1]

PLC Abbreviation for *public limited company*, used in company names. [1]

postage and packing (p&p) Charge for postage and packing goods to be sent to a customer. [6]

postal order (UK) Document bought from a post office that represents a certain amount of money. It is a safe way of sending money by post. [6]

p.p. Abbreviation for *per pro*, used before the sender's name in a signature block to indicate that a letter is signed on behalf of someone else, e.g. a personal assistant signing on behalf of a manager. [1]

premium Payment made to an insurance company in return for cover. [12]

primary source In research, source of first-hand information such as an interview or questionnaire. [14]

principal Person or organization that hires an agent or broker to buy or sell goods for them. [3,10]

private bank Similar to a commercial bank, but owned by one person or a partnership and therefore a much smaller organization. [9]

pro forma invoice Invoice sent in advance of the goods ordered. [5,6]

promissory note Document in which a buyer promises to pay a seller a certain amount of money by a certain date. [6]

proposal form Form completed by a person taking out an insurance policy that states what is to be insured, how much it is worth, how long the policy will run, and under what conditions it is to be effected. [12]

prospectus (A) Similar to a catalogue, but issued by a school or college; (B) Document published by a company, giving details of a new share issue. [3, sense A]

protest To take legal action to obtain payment, e.g. of an outstanding bill of exchange. [6,9]

public limited company (PLC) Company whose shares can be bought and sold by the public. [1]

quantity discount Amount taken off the usual selling price of goods because the buyer is purchasing a large quantity. [3]

quarterly report Report published every three months. [14]

quarterly statement Statement of account sent to a regular customer every three months. [5]

quotation Price given for work to be done or a service to be provided. [4,12]

rail consignment note (CIM) Consignment note sent with goods by rail. [11]

receipt A document showing that goods have been paid for. [11]

recourse factoring Similar to non-recourse factoring, but claiming the debt from the manufacturer if the customer cannot pay. [10]

referee Person who writes a reference (sense B). [8,15]

reference (A) Figures (e.g. date) and / or letters (e.g. initials of sender) written at the top of a letter to identify it, often abbreviated to ref. (B) Written report on a company's creditworthiness or a job applicant's character and suitability for the job. [1(A), 8,15 (B)]

remittance Payment. [6]

retailer Person or company that buys goods from wholesalers or manufacturers to sell to the public. [3]

revocable letter of credit Letter of credit that can be cancelled. [9]

road consignment note (CMR) Consignment note sent with goods by road. [11]

SAD Abbreviation for *single administrative document*. [11]

sale or return Term used when the supplier agrees to take back any goods that the retailer cannot sell. [3]

salutation Opening of a letter, e.g. *Dear Sir / Madam*. [1]

savings account Account with a bank or building society for personal savings. Interest rates are higher than on other types of account, and therefore there are usually restrictions on when money can be drawn out. [6]

SCP Abbreviation for *simplified clearance procedure*. [11]

secondary source In research, source of information such as a book or a report. [14]

securities Items or investments, e.g. shares, that can be bought and sold on a stock exchange. [9]

settle (vb) To pay an account. [6]

settlement Payment of an account. [5]

ship To send goods by any method of transport, i.e. by road, rail, or air as well as by sea. [5]

shipbroker Agent who arranges the transport of cargo by ship. [11]

shipment Consignment. [7]

shipped bill of lading Bill of lading signed when goods are already on board a ship. [11]

shipped clean on board Phrase indicating that the bill of lading was clean, i.e. the goods were taken on board in good condition. [12]

Shipping Conference International organization of shipowners that sets prices for transporting goods or passengers on scheduled routes. [11]

shipping documents The documents used for shipping goods, and usually including – depending on the type of transport – *Bill of Lading* (or *Airway Bill*), *commercial invoice*, *insurance certificate* and any other customs documents that may be required in the shipment, e.g. Health Certificate (for food), EUR1 to get preferential tariffs, Certificate of Origin, etc. [5]

shipping mark Distinctive mark put on the sides of crates and boxes indicating who they belong to. [11]

sight bill Another term for *sight draft*. [9]

sight draft Bill of exchange that must be paid immediately it is presented. [4,6,9]

signature block (A) Name and job title typed below a handwritten signature at the end of a letter; (B) Sender's details that appear below his / her name at the end of an email message. [1]

simplified clearance procedure (SCP) Customs clearance procedure used in the European Union to make documentation easier for exporters and agents. [11]

single administrative document (SAD) Eight-part set of customs forms for export declarations, used in the European Union. [11]

sole agent / agency Person or organization that is the only one allowed to sell the products of a manufacturer in a particular country or area. [10]

sole trader Person who owns and runs a business on their own. [1]

specific indent Another term for *closed indent*. [10]

specimen signature Example of a customer's signature, used by a bank to identify documents as being valid. [9]

standard shipping note Document completed by the exporter that gives information about a consignment. It is used as a delivery note or receipt. [11]

standby letter of credit Bank guarantee to the seller that they will be paid. [9]

standing order Order to a bank to pay someone a specified amount on a regular date, e.g. on the first of every month. [9]

statement of account List of amounts paid and owed sent by a supplier to a customer. [6]

stock exchange Market where stocks and shares are bought and sold. [10]

stop (a cheque) To instruct a bank not to honour a cheque. [9]

subject title Phrase indicating what a piece of correspondence is about, e.g. *CDs damaged in post*. In a letter it is placed directly after the salutation; in a fax or email it forms part of the header information. [1]

subrogation Insurer's right to claim damaged goods for which they have paid compensation. [12]

subsidiary Company of which at least half the share capital is owned by a larger company, but which may trade under its own name. [3]

syndicate Group of people or companies who work together to make money. [12]

take legal action To hand over a matter, e.g. non-payment of a bill, to lawyers. [7]

tanker Ship that carries liquid bulk consignments, usually oil. [11]

tariff List of prices charged for goods or services. [11]

telegraphic transfer (TT) Quick method of transferring money to an account abroad. The sender's bank cables the money to the receiver's bank. [6]

tender Written estimate, usually for a large job. [3]

term draft Bill of exchange that must be paid on a particular date after goods have been sent. [6]

terms of payment Terms the buyer and seller agree regarding discounts, methods of payment, shipment, and documentation. [9]

through bill of lading Another term for *multimodal bill of lading*. [11]

time charter Charter that lasts for a period of time, e.g. six months. [11]

title The legal right of possession. [1]

to account Term used when part of a payment is made. [6]

to order Phrase used to indicate a negotiable document. [11]

tonnage value The cost per ton of cargo for chartering a ship under a *voyage charter*. [11]

trade association Organization that represents and promotes a particular trade. [8,10]

trade discount Amount taken off the usual selling price of goods when they are sold by a manufacturer or wholesaler to a retailer. [3]

trade journal Publication, usually weekly or monthly, specializing in a particular trade or profession. [10]

trade price Price paid for goods by a retailer to a wholesaler or manufacturer. [3]

trade reference Reference in which a person in one company gives their opinion as to the creditworthiness of another company in the same area of business. [3]

traveller's cheque Cheque for a fixed amount, sold by a bank, that can be cashed by the buyer in other countries. [9]

trial order Order, usually for a small quantity of goods, to test the market. [5]

trustee A person or organization that manages money for another person or organization. [9]

TT Abbreviation for *telegraphic transfer*. [6]

tue Unit of container stowage equal to one 20ft (6.1m) container. [11]

turnover Total business done by a company in a given period, e.g. a year. [3]

under separate cover In a separate envelope or parcel. [4]

underwriter Person or organization that examines a risk and calculates the insurance premium to be charged. [10,12]

unsolicited Not asked for, e.g. an application for a post that has not been advertised. [15]

unvalued policy Type of insurance policy in which the value of the goods to be insured is not agreed in advance but assessed if loss should occur. [12]

usance Bill of exchange that is paid after a period of time. [9]

VAT Abbreviation for *Value Added Tax*. [4]

Value Added Tax (VAT) A UK purchase tax. [4]

valued policy Type of insurance policy in which the value of the goods to be insured is agreed in advance. [12]

voyage charter Charter for a particular voyage carrying a particular cargo. [11]

wear and tear Normal deterioration of something as it is used. [7]

wholesaler Person or company that buys goods from manufacturers and sells them to retailers. [3]

Page references in **bold** type indicate examples.

Oxford
Correspondence
Workbook

A. Ashley

OXFORD
UNIVERSITY PRESS

OXFORD

UNIVERSITY PRESS

Great Clarendon Street, Oxford OX2 6DP

Oxford University Press is a department of the University of Oxford.
It furthers the University's objective of excellence in research, scholarship,
and education by publishing worldwide in

Oxford New York

Auckland Bangkok Buenos Aires Cape Town Chennai
Dar es Salaam Delhi Hong Kong Istanbul Karachi Kolkata
Kuala Lumpur Madrid Melbourne Mexico City Mumbai Nairobi
São Paulo Shanghai Taipei Tokyo Toronto

Oxford and *Oxford English* are registered trade marks of
Oxford University Press in the UK and in certain other countries

ISBN 0 19 457214 5

Printed in China

Contents

1
Letters, faxes, and emails

1 Letters: true or false?

Read the following statements and decide which are true and which are false. Mark the true ones 'T' and the false ones 'F' in the spaces provided.

1 ☐ If a letter begins with the *recipient's* name, e.g. *Dear Mr Ross*, it will close with *Yours faithfully*.

2 ☐ The abbreviation *c.c.* stands for *correct carbons*.

3 ☐ If you were writing a letter to Mr Peter Smith, the salutation would be *Dear Mr Peter Smith*.

4 ☐ The head of a company in the UK is known as the *president*.

5 ☐ In *the USA*, it is correct to open a letter with the salutation *Gentlemen*.

6 ☐ In *the UK*, a date written *2.6.05* means *6 February 2005*.

7 ☐ If a secretary signs a letter and the signature is followed by *p.p. Daniel Harris*, it means that the secretary is signing on behalf of Daniel Harris.

8 ☐ The term *plc* after a UK company's name, e.g. *Hathaway plc*, stands for *Public Limited Corporation*.

9 ☐ The term *Ltd* after a UK company's name means *limited liability*.

10 ☐ If you do not know whether a female correspondent is married or not, it is correct to use the courtesy title *Ms* instead of *Miss* or *Mrs*, e.g. *Ms Tessa Groves*.

11 ☐ This address is an example of blocked style.

```
Peter Voss
Oberlweinfeldweg 33
5207 Therwil
Switzerland
```

12 ☐ It is always impolite to close a letter *Best wishes*.

2 Order of addresses

Write out the following names and addresses in the correct order. Use the blocked style.

EXAMPLE   Search Studios Ltd / Leeds / LS4 8QM / Mr L. Scott / 150 Royal Avenue

```
Mr L. Scott
Search Studios Ltd
150 Royal Avenue
Leeds
LS4 8QM
```

1 Warwick House / Soundsonic Ltd / London / 57–59 Warwick Street / SE23 1JF

2 Piazza Leonardo da Vinci 254 / Managing Director / I-20133 / Milano / Sig. D. Fregoni / Fregoni S.p.A. /

3 Bente Spedition GmbH / Herr Heinz Bente / D-6000 Frankfurt 1 / Feldbergstr. 30 / Chairman

4 Sportique et Cie / 201 rue Sambin / The Sales Manager / F–21000 Dijon
5 Intercom / E-41006 Sevilla / 351 Avda Luis de Morales / Chief Accountant /
Mrs S. Moreno
6 Ms Maria Nikolakaki / 85100 Rhodes / Greece / Nikitara 541
7 Excel Heights 501 / Edogawa-ku 139 / 7–3–8 Nakakasai / Japan / Tokyo /
Mrs Junko Shiratori
8 301 Leighton Road / VHF Vehicles Ltd / London NW5 2QE /
The Transport Director / Kentish Town

3 Letters: parts and layout

The parts of the letter below are in jumbled order. Write the numbers of the parts in the correct boxes in the letter plan, and label them with the terms in the box. The first one has been done for you.

letterhead	date	inside address	salutation
body	complimentary close	signature block	enclosure

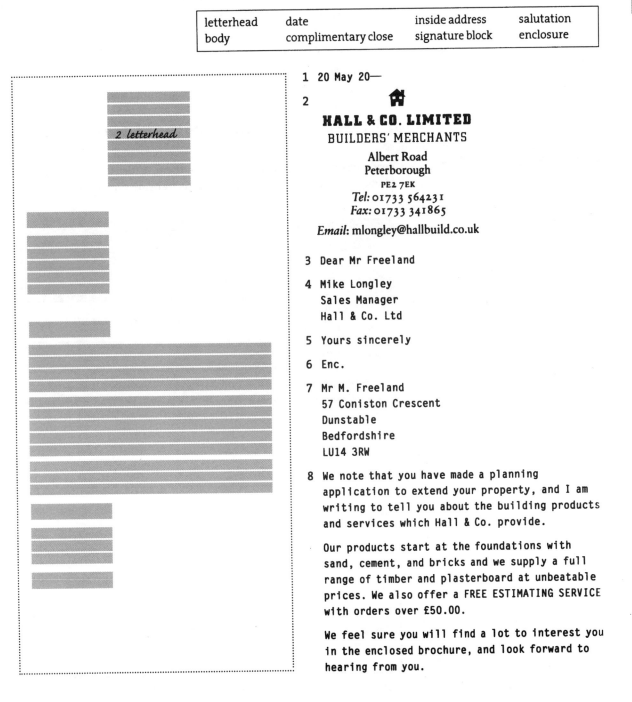

2 letterhead

1 20 May 20—

2   🏠
HALL & CO. LIMITED
BUILDERS' MERCHANTS
Albert Road
Peterborough
PE2 7EK
Tel: 01733 564231
Fax: 01733 341865
Email: mlongley@hallbuild.co.uk

3 Dear Mr Freeland

4 Mike Longley
Sales Manager
Hall & Co. Ltd

5 Yours sincerely

6 Enc.

7 Mr M. Freeland
57 Coniston Crescent
Dunstable
Bedfordshire
LU14 3RW

8 We note that you have made a planning application to extend your property, and I am writing to tell you about the building products and services which Hall & Co. provide.

Our products start at the foundations with sand, cement, and bricks and we supply a full range of timber and plasterboard at unbeatable prices. We also offer a FREE ESTIMATING SERVICE with orders over £50.00.

We feel sure you will find a lot to interest you in the enclosed brochure, and look forward to hearing from you.

4 Faxes and emails: true or false?

Read the following statements and decide which are true and which are false. Mark the true ones 'T' and the false ones 'F' in the spaces provided.

1 ☐ Confidential information should not be sent by fax and email.

2 ☐ If necessary, faxes can be used as substitutes for original documents.

3 ☐ *Fax* is a short form of the word *facts*.

4 ☐ Emails must end with *Yours faithfully* or *Yours sincerely*.

5 ☐ Emoticons can be added to business emails to make them look friendlier.

6 ☐ Using capital letters to write an email is the same as shouting.

7 ☐ @ in an email address means *automatic*.

8 ☐ A letter or card is usually more suitable than an email for a personal message.

9 ☐ In email header information, *c.c.* stands for *confidential copies*.

10 ☐ Emails are usually less formal than letters.

11 ☐ It is not as important to use correct grammar and spelling in a business email as it is in a letter.

12 ☐ The addressee's name comes after the @ sign in an email address.

5 Fax transmission form

Read this internal email from Yvonne Feltham, British Crystal's Export Manager, to her PA. Then complete the fax transmission form.

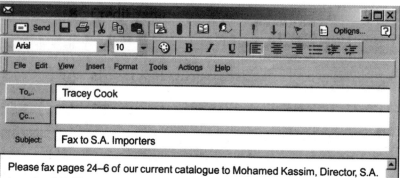

To... Tracey Cook

Cc...

Subject: Fax to S.A. Importers

Please fax pages 24–6 of our current catalogue to Mohamed Kassim, Director, S.A. Importers Ltd, Riyadh (fax no. (+966) 1 34981), subject: Tableware – new lines. No need for covering letter – just write 'As requested. I hope this is helpful. YF' on transmission form. Many thanks. Yvonne.

Yvonne Feltham
17th Sept 20—

Fax

BRITISH CRYSTAL Ltd
Glazier House, Green Lane, Derby DE1 1RT

To: _____

From: _____

Fax no.: _____ Subject: _____

Date: _____ Page/s: _____

6 Email: request for further information

Mohamed Kassim has received Yvonne Feltham's fax. While he was reading the faxed catalogue he made notes about further information he needs. Read his notes and compose his email to Yvonne Feltham.

> 'York' range be available before end Oct?
>
> Approx. sales figures for 'Cambridge' range in other markets?
>
> 'Bristol' range available in green? (can't read fax)
>
> 'Durham' range – dishwasher-proof? (can't read fax)

To...	Yvonne Feltham
Cc...	
Subject:	Your fax, further info.

Dear Yvonne

Many thanks for your fax. Just a few further questions:

_____

_____

_____

_____

_____

_____

Mohamed Kassim
Director, S.A. Importers Ltd
Al Manni Way, Riyadh
SAUDI ARABIA
Tel: (+966) 1 35669
Fax: (+966) 1 34981
m.kassim@saimp.co.sa
18 Sept 20—

7 Email: checking

In this email, Terry Jordan, Manager of the Falcon Grange Hotel, is responding to an enquiry about conference facilities. If he sends it like this, he is in danger of losing a valuable customer – there are fourteen mistakes in it. Check the email, and correct the mistakes.

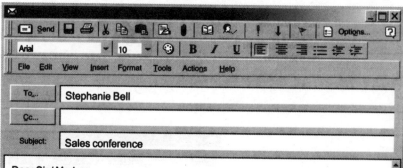

To... | Stephanie Bell

Cc... |

Subject: | Sales conference

Dear Sir / Madam

THANK YOU FOR YOUR ENQUIRY ABOUT CONFERENCE FACILITES

I can confirm that we would be able to accomodate 40 delegates 17 – 19 july, full board, and provide conference facilities including 2 seminar rooms each equiped with PowerPoint. the tarrif per delegate would be £291.00, full board, with coffe and tea served mid-mroning and mid-afternoon.

I hope these terms are aceptable.

Yours sincerly
Terry Jordan
Manager
Falcon Grange Hotel
Tel: 0734 045721
Fax: 0734 045722
Email: jordant@falconhotels.co.uk

17 March 20—

8 Words and definitions

Make words from the jumbled letters and match them with the definitions below.

a LBCDEOK YSETL
b TERSGUANI CLOKB
c ERFCNEREE
d CSRULEENO

e EPITVAR NAD FIDNAILTCOEN
f BOJ TELTI
g SURYO ELERCISNY
h TTCMTHAEAN

1 Document enclosed with a letter.
2 Figures and / or letters written at the top of a letter to identify it.
3 Style of writing in which each line starts directly below the one above.
4 Complimentary close used at the end of a letter when the addressee's name is known.
5 Phrase written on a letter intended only to be read by the addressee.
6 Name and job title typed below a signature.
7 Separate document attached to an email message.
8 The name of someone's job, e.g. *Sales Manager*, *Chief Buyer*.

2
Content and style

1 Typical sentences

Sort out the jumbled words below to make six sentences typical of business correspondence. Add capital letters and punctuation as necessary.

1 grateful / soon / a / as / we / for / would / possible / reply / as / be
2 for / find / please / cheque / £49.50 / a / enclosed
3 further / please / if / us / information / you / any / contact / need
4 april / your / you / letter / thank / 5 / of / for
5 you / we / forward / to / from / look / hearing
6 pleasure / price list / enclosing / have / a / catalogue / our / I / spring / and / in

2 Courtesy

Rewrite the following request for payment in a more polite form.

Dear Sir

You have owed us £567.00 since February, which means you haven t paid us for three months.

We have written to you twice and you haven t bothered to answer us, yet you ve been a customer for years. Anyway, we re not going to put up with this, so if you don t tell us why you haven t paid, or send the money you owe us in ten days, we ll sue you. After all, we ve got bills to pay too, and besides we explained our rules for giving credit, i.e. payment on due dates, some time ago.

Yours, etc.

R Lancaster (Mr)

3 Summarizing

Below is the reply to the letter in Exercise 2. It was opened by Mr Lancaster's secretary, who saw straight away that the letter is wordy and contains a lot of irrelevant information. Pretend you are the secretary and write Mr Lancaster an email summarizing the letter's contents. Try to make your summary no longer than seventy-five words.

```
Dear Mr Lancaster

I am writing to you in reply to your letter dated 9 May,
which we received on 10 May, in which you reminded us of
our outstanding balance, which now amounts to the sum
total of £567.00.

I should like to offer my humblest apologies for our
failure either to settle the account, or to reply to
your two previous communications. However, I feel that
I must explain the cause. We have been the unfortunate
victims of a tragedy. Two months ago, our premises were
almost completely destroyed by fire. Although I am happy
to report that we sustained no casualties, all our
records, stock, orders ready for despatch and so on,
were consumed by the flames.

Now, at last, our fortunes are beginning to rise again,
and our insurance company will shortly be releasing
funds to facilitate our recovery. Let me assure you that
you will be remunerated in full as soon as possible.
In the interim, I would be grateful if you would accept
a small sum towards the settlement of our account, with
my personal promise that the remaining amount will be
forwarded to you as soon as it becomes available.

Please find enclosed a cheque for the sum of £55.00, and
once again, I beg you to accept my deepest apologies for
any inconvenience caused.

Yours sincerely

T. D. Games (Mr)
```

4 Basing a letter on notes

Below is an email from Sarah Barnard, Sales Manager of Barnard Press, to Rosalind Wood, her secretary. Follow the instructions in the email, and write a letter of reply, setting it out in the spaces provided on the opposite page.

To... Rosalind Wood

Cc...

Subject: Reply to Claudio Bini

Please reply to Claudio Bini of International Books.

Address: Via Santovetti 117/9, 00045 Grottaferrata, Rome.

Reference SB/RW.

His letter dated 15 Feb.

He asked about readers for intermediate students of English. Tell him we have nothing in stock at the moment, but we'll be publishing a new series at intermediate level in September. Send him the 'Storyworld' leaflet, and a current catalogue.

Many thanks.
Sarah Barnard

1 March 20—

bp
Barnard Press Limited

183–7 Copwood Road
North Finchley
London N12 9PR
Telephone: +44 (0)20 8239 9653
Facsimile: +44 (0)20 8239 9754
Email: barnards@barnardpress.co.uk
www.barnardpress.co.uk

5 Clear sequence

This is a letter about arrangements for a business trip. At present it is difficult to understand because the ordering of the information is not clear. Rearrange the letter in a clearer sequence.

```
Dear Mr Jackson

NICOSIA COMPUTER TRAINING COURSE

I am writing with information about the arrangements we have made
for your visit.

Unfortunately, Mr Charalambides will not be able to meet you in
Larnaca on Thursday 15 June, as you requested, because he will
be returning from a visit to our subsidiary in Spain. However,
he will be back in the office the following day, so I have
arranged for him to see you at 14.30.

On Friday 9 June your flight to Larnaca will be met by our
driver, who will take you to the Amathus Beach Hotel, where we
have booked you in for the first two nights. The driver will call
for you at 17.00 on Sunday and drive you to the Training Centre
at Nicosia. Most of the trainee operators will have had some
experience of the new program by the time you arrive at the
centre, but they will need a good deal of instruction on the
more complex areas of the system.

We hope you enjoy your weekend at the hotel. The driver will
pick you up from the Training Centre on Wednesday evening, at the
end of the course, and take you back to the Amathus Beach Hotel,
where I have booked you in for a further two nights.

Please could you confirm that you plan to return to London on
the 18.30 flight on Friday 16, and also that the arrangements
outlined here suit you?

Thank you for your letter of 18 May giving us the dates of your
trip. I look forward to hearing from you.

Yours sincerely

Elena Theodorou

Training Manager
```

6 Planning

Mr Jackson is planning his reply to Ms Theodorou (see Exercise 5), using some rough notes he has made. Look at the notes and complete the plan below.

> *How many trainees on course? – London flight on 16 June leaves at 18.00, not 18.30. – Time of meeting with Charalambides OK - 9 June flight arrives Larnaca 15.30 – photocopying facilities at Training Centre?*

paragraph 1   Acknowledge letter
paragraph 2   _____
paragraph 3   _____
paragraph 4   _____
paragraph 5   Thank Ms Theodorou for her help

Now, using your plan, write Mr Jackson's letter.

3
Enquiries

1 Enquiry from a building company

There are no capitals, punctuation, or paragraphs in this fax from a building company to a designer and manufacturer of kitchen units. Write out the fax correctly, dividing the body into four paragraphs.

Fax

Clark Fitzpatrick Builders plc
Dunstable Road
Luton, Bedfordshire
LU2 3LM

To: ms doreen french
From: terry spalding household installations ltd
Fax no: 01582 351711
Subject: kitchen units
Date: 3 april 20—
Page/s: 2

dear ms french

thank you for your letter and the enclosed catalogue giving details of your kitchen units the main item we are interested in is the unit on page 22 it appears to meet all our specifications for the apartment block i described in my letter i am sending herewith a plan of a typical apartment which gives the exact dimensions before placing a firm order we would need samples of all materials used in the manufacture of the units could you please confirm that you guarantee all your products for two years against normal wear and tear i would also be grateful for details of your terms regarding payment and of any trade and quantity discounts if the price and quality of your products are satisfactory we will place further orders as we have several projects at the planning stage

yours sincerely

terry spalding

purchasing manager

2 Words and definitions

Make words from the jumbled letters and match them with the definitions below.

a UEAGTOCLA   e LAOEEHSLWR   i ELSA RO ETRRNU
b METIESAT   f WOSORHOM   j NATYUTQI DSNUOTCI
c ERENTD   g IDISYUSRAB
d ETSMCOUR   h POSSUTCREP

1 Company that is partly owned by a larger one.
2 Person who buys goods or services from a shop or company.
3 Money taken off the usual selling price of goods when the buyer is purchasing a large amount.
4 Place where a company demonstrates its products.
5 Publication giving details of goods or services offered by a company.
6 Price given for work to be done.
7 Written estimate, usually for a large job such as building a factory.
8 Publication giving details about a school or college.
9 Person or company that buys goods from manufacturers and sells them to retailers.
10 Term used when a supplier agrees to buy back unsold goods.

3 Polite requests

John Phillips is telling his PA to write various letters. Change his instructions into an acceptable form for business correspondence. Each sentence has been started for you.

EXAMPLE   John Phillips: 'Ask them for a cash discount.' *Could you...*
PA writes: *Could you offer us a cash discount?*

1 'Tell Rockfords that the consignment must be delivered before the end of September.'
It is essential _____

2 'Ask Schmidt to send us their catalogue and a price list.'
Could you _____

3 'We're going to give them a big order, so find out if they allow quantity discounts.'
As we intend to place a substantial _____

4 'If they can't deliver the goods before Friday, tell Larousse to email us.'
Please could you _____

5 'It would be a lot of help if they could send some samples.'
We would appreciate _____

6 'Say that we'd like Andover to send someone here to give us an estimate.'
We would be grateful if _____

7 'Say we'd like to see a demonstration of both models.'
We would be interested _____

8 'Find out if Weston's will let us have twenty units on approval.'
Would you be _____

9 'Ask when he will let us have the cheque.'
I am writing to enquire _____

10 'Say our suppliers generally let us settle by monthly statement.'
As a rule _____

4 Enquiry to a college

Complete this letter of enquiry to a college with the prepositions from the box.

in (×4) for (×2) to by with at of (×2)

Avda. San Antonio 501
80260 Bellaterra
Barcelona
Spain

12 October 20—

Admissions Department
International College
145—8 Regents Road
Falmer
Brighton BN1 9QN

Dear Sir / Madam

I am a single 23 year-old Spanish student **1**_____ the
University **2**_____ Barcelona doing a Master s Course
3_____ Business Studies, and I intend to spend six
months **4**_____ England, beginning **5**_____ January next
year, preparing **6**_____ the Cambridge First
Certificate.

Your college was recommended **7**_____ me **8**_____
a fellow student and I would like details **9**_____ your
First Certificate courses, including fees and dates.
Could you also let me know if you can provide
accommodation **10**_____ me **11**_____ Brighton **12**_____
an English family?

Thank you for your attention, and I look forward to
hearing from you soon.

Yours faithfully

María Ortega

---

5 An application form

International College have replied to Maria Ortega's letter of enquiry (see Exercise 4) and enclosed an application form. Imagine that you are Maria. You have decided to take the First Certificate course starting on 3 January and finishing on 26 June 20— . You are paying the fees yourself, and today's date is 10 November 20— . Complete the form using the information here and in Maria's letter.

Student Application Form

International College • 145–8 Regents Road • Falmer • Brighton • BN1 9QN

APPLICANT

Family Name: _____

Other Names: _____

Title Mr / Mrs / Miss / Ms: _____   Age: _____

Address: _____

_____

Town / city: _____   Country: _____

Do you have a job or are you a student? _____

Job title / Subject of study: _____

Name of business / university / college: _____ _____

Course applied for: _____

Course dates: _____

Are you paying your own fees, or is your company paying for you?

_____

Will you find your own accommodation or do you want this to be arranged by the

College? _____

Please tick how you found out about International College.

☐ Newspaper   ☐ Friend's recommendation

☐ Through your university / college   ☐ Other source: _____

Signature: _____   Date: _____

6 Enquiry from a retailer

Write the letter of enquiry to which the letter below is a reply. You are M. Morreau, and you saw an advertisement for Glaston Potteries' latest designs for oven-to-table ware in the May edition of *International Homes*.

Clayfield | Burnley | BB10 1RQ

GLASTON POTTERIES LTD

Telephone + 44 (0)1282 46125
Facsimile + 44 (0)1282 63182
Email j.merton@glaston.co.uk
www.glaston.com

Your ref: JFM/PS

2 July 20—

M. J.F. Morreau
Director
Cuisines Morreau S.A.
1150 boulevard Calbert
F—54015 Nancy Cedex

Dear M. Morreau

Thank you for your enquiry of 28 June in which you expressed an interest in retailing a selection of our products in your shops in Nancy.

Please find enclosed our current catalogue and price list. You might also be interested in visiting our website.

In response to your request for a 20% trade discount, we regret that we cannot offer more than 15%. However, we do give a 5% quantity discount on orders over €20,000. In comparison with similar companies in the UK, these terms are extremely competitive. Payment would need to be by sight draft until we have established a business relationship.

Finally, we are confident that we can deliver well within the two-month time limit you require.

Thank you for your interest. We hope to hear from you soon.

Yours sincerely

J. Merton

Sales Manager

Enc.

Registered No. 716481
VAT Registered No. 133 53431 08

4
Replies and quotations

1 Reply to an enquiry

Mr Chan has emailed Hübner GmbH, enquiring about some earth-moving equipment he saw at a trade fair. In his reply, Hübner's Sales Director, Gustav Fest, refers to specific questions asked by Mr Chan. Read Herr Fest's email and tick the items which Mr Chan asked about.

1. ☐ How soon the goods can be delivered
2. ☐ Details of prices
3. ☐ Where the goods can be purchased
4. ☐ After-sales service
5. ☐ How the goods will be transported
6. ☐ Terms of payment
7. ☐ Quantity discounts
8. ☐ Cash discounts
9. ☐ Details of the range of goods available
10. ☐ Which bank will handle the transaction
11. ☐ Guarantees

Send | Arial | 10 | **B** *I* <u>U</u> | Options...

File Edit View Insert Format Tools Actions Help

To... Andy Chan

Cc...

Subject: RE: Earth-moving equipment

Dear Mr Chan

Thank you for your enquiry of 16 August concerning our earth-moving equipment displayed at the International Farm Machinery Fair in Bonn.

In answer to the specific questions in your email, first let me say we are willing to consider substantial discount on orders over €300,000. All our machinery is guaranteed for three years against normal use, and we have several agencies in your country with mechanics trained to service all our products.

With regard to the terms of payment, which you mentioned, we would consider payment by 30-day bill of exchange, documents against acceptance, provided you could offer two referees.

I confirm that we can fulfil orders within three months, unless there are unusual specifications, and you can buy equipment from us direct or through our agents in your country.

As requested, I am sending our current catalogue and price list to you by express mail. I think you will find the equipment on pages 101–15 particularly interesting for the work you have in mind. If you require any further information, please contact me.

Yours sincerely
Gustav Fest

Sales Director
Hübner GmbH
Tel: +49 40 237618
Fax: +49 40 237619
Email: festg@hubner.co.de

18 Aug 20—

2 Question forms

Here are some of the questions Mr Chan asked (see Exercise 1), but the words have been mixed up. Rearrange the words so that the questions makes sense and add the necessary capitals and punctuation.

EXAMPLE offer / do / you / large / a / orders / discount / on
Do you offer a discount on large orders?

1 details / of / can / you / prices / please / me / send / your
2 after-sales / do / an / offer / you / service
3 guaranteed / are / for / how / goods / long / the
4 goods / can / how / delivered / soon / the / be
5 terms / what / payment / your / of / are
6 can / buy / where / the / I / goods
7 you / do / what / quantity / discounts / sort / offer / of
8 can / send / mail / please / your / by / me / you / express / catalogue

3 Words and definitions

Make words from the jumbled letters and match them with the definitions below.

a TMINEROC
b TEN RCIPE
c RIGACREA ROFDRAW
d TNQOAOIUT
e NREDU PATESRAE VREOC
f SORSG IERPC
g LTAYOLY NUTCOSID

1 Condition of sale when the customer pays for the transport of the goods.
2 Internationally used term which indicates which price is being quoted to the customer.
3 Price which does not include additional costs such as transport and insurance.
4 Amount taken off the usual price of goods when they are sold to a regular customer.
5 In a separate envelope or parcel.
6 Price which includes additional costs such as transport and insurance.
7 Price for work to be done or a service to be provided.

4 Reply to a request for information (1)

There are no capitals or paragraphs in this reply to a request for information. Write it out correctly, adding the capitals, and dividing the body of the letter into four paragraphs.

dear mr russell

thank you for your phone call of thursday 4 march enquiring about hiring our delivery vans. my colleague ms angela smith, who took the call, said you were mainly interested in 5-ton vehicles like the 'tobor' so i am enclosing our booklet 'small truck hire' giving you details of our charges. these also appear on our website at www.vanhire.co.uk. you will notice that the summer months of june, july and august are the least expensive and that we offer a 20 per cent discount on weekend hire starting saturday at 08.00 and ending sunday at 20.00. our main offices in the uk are in london and birmingham, but we also have branches in france, germany, and italy. if you are thinking of hiring abroad you will find details on our website. please let me know if i can be of further help.

yours sincerely

michael craddock

transport manager
van hire unlimited

5 Incoterms

Incoterms indicate which price the seller is quoting to the customer, for example DAF (Delivered at frontier) means that the seller pays all delivery costs to the buyer's frontier, but not import duty. In the table below, the explanations have become confused. Match the correct Incoterm to its explanation.

Incoterm	Explanation
1 DDU (delivery duty unpaid)	a The buyer pays all delivery costs once the goods have left the seller's factory or warehouse.
2 CFR (cost and freight)	b The seller pays all delivery costs to the port.
3 CIF (cost, insurance, and freight)	c The seller pays all delivery costs, except for import duty, to a named destination.
4 EXW (ex-works)	d The seller pays all delivery costs to a named destination, except for insurance.
5 FAS (free alongside ship)	e The seller pays all delivery costs to when the goods are on board ship.
6 FOB (free on board)	f The seller pays all delivery costs to a named destination.

6 Reply to a request for information (2)

Read this email from Gerd Busch, Marketing Manager of Busch AG, to his PA. Imagine you are the PA and use the information he gives to write a letter replying to Anne Croft of Shape-up Fitness Centres on Herr Busch's behalf.

```
To...      Birgit Lange
Cc...
Subject:   Shape-up enquiry
```

Birgit

Please reply to this letter. Send Ms Croft a catalogue and price list (tell her that all prices are quoted CIF London). Also mention the following:

5-year guarantee on all our equipment

Highest-quality materials used

No credit terms (our prices highly competitive due to small profit margins)

5% quantity discount off net prices on orders over €5,000

Encourage her to contact us again.

Thanks.
Gerd Busch
14 May 20—

7 An estimate

Steve Smart, of MG Heating Engineers, is telling his secretary to send a customer, Mr Frost, an estimate. As Steve Smart's secretary, write Mr Frost a letter based on the instructions below. Set out the prices in tabulated form, including both subtotal and total with VAT.

'And please send Mr Frost an estimate for upgrading the central heating system in his offices. Thank him for his phone call and tell him that we can fit the seven thermostatic valves at £20 per valve – and the lockshield valve would also cost £20. Drawing down the system before we do the fitting is £40, and filling and balancing it afterwards is £50. Oh, and add VAT at 17.5% to all that. Tell him that we can do it before the end of September, but if he wants it done over a weekend he'll have to pay an additional £80.00 for overtime ... and don't forget to say that all prices quoted include materials and labour. Oh yes – and tell him to contact me if he has any more questions.'

5
Orders

1 Verbs used with *order*

The verbs in the box can all be used with the noun 'order'. Choose the best verb to complete each sentence. Use each verb only once, and in the correct form.

confirm	refuse	ship	despatch
place	make up	cancel	acknowledge

1 We would like to _____ an order with you for 5,000 units.

2 As we are unable to supply the quantity you asked for, we would have no objection if you preferred to _____ your order.

3 I am writing to _____ your order, which we received this morning, for 20 'Omega Engines'.

4 We are pleased to inform you that your order K451 has already been _____ from our depot.

5 Please _____ your order in writing, so that we can inform our distribution depot.

6 Your order was _____ yesterday on the MV *Oxford*.

7 Unfortunately, we shall have to _____ your order unless payment is settled in cash.

8 I would like to reassure you that your order will be _____ in our depot by staff who have experience in handling these delicate materials.

2 Placing an order: accompanying email

In this email Mr Takahashi is placing an order, but the sentences have become confused. Rewrite the email with the sentences in the correct order, starting new paragraphs where appropriate.

To... Daniele Causio

Cc...

Subject: Order No. 49301/231

1 Best wishes

2 If some of the items are out of stock, please do not send substitutes.

3 When you send the order, please make sure all cartons are clearly labelled with our logo and numbered.

4 I can confirm that the 10% quantity discount off net prices that you offered is acceptable.

5 Dear Sig. Causio

6 I attach our order No. 49301/231 for the selection of shirts, trousers, and jackets which we discussed on the phone yesterday.

7 Kosaburo Takahashi

8 As agreed, we will pay by letter of credit - I have already arranged this with the bank.

9 Please note the order must be here by 10 April, in time for the new season.

10 As soon as the bank hands over the shipping documents, the credit will be released.

3 Order form

Read this email from Dieter Faust, a buying manager, to his assistant, Beatrice Mey.

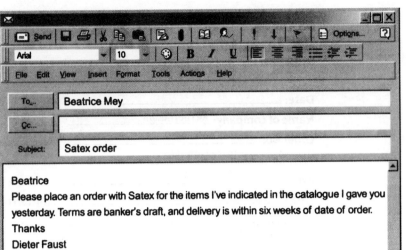

Beatrice
Please place an order with Satex for the items I've indicated in the catalogue I gave you yesterday. Terms are banker's draft, and delivery is within six weeks of date of order.
Thanks
Dieter Faust
17 July 20—

Here is the page from the sales catalogue Dieter Faust mentioned in his email.

Satex S.p.A.
SPRING CATALOGUE

Item		Cat. no.	Price € per item	Quantity
Shirts				
PLAIN	white	S288	€30	50
	blue	S289	€30	50
STRIPED	blue / white	S301	€35	
	white / grey	S302	€35	
	white / green	S303	€35	
Sweaters (V-neck)				
PLAIN	red	P112	€40	20
	blue	P113	€40	20
	black	P114	€40	
PATTERNED	blue	P305	€52	
	black	P306	€52	

As Beatrice Mey, use the information in his email and the catalogue to complete this order form.

Satex S.p.A. ORDER FORM

Via di Pietra Papa, 00146 Roma

Date: _____

Name of company: Reiner GmbH

Order No: W6164

Telephone: +49 541 798252

Fax: +49 541 798253

Email: faustd@reiner.co.de

Address for delivery:
Wessumerstrasse 215–18,

D–4500 Osnabr ck

_____

Authorized: (D. Faust)

Item description	Cat. no.	Price € per item	Quantity	Total €

Amount due: _____

Terms of payment: _____

Requested delivery date: _____

4 Placing an order: covering letter

Dieter Faust emails Beatrice Mey again, reminding her to include a covering letter with the Satex order (see Exercise 3). As she has only recently started working for him, he gives detailed instructions. As Beatrice Mey, write the letter.

To... Beatrice Mey

Cc...

Subject: Covering letter

Beatrice
Please remember to include a covering letter with the Satex order:
- Address it to Sig. Daniele Causio, Sales Director.
- Use the order number as the subject title.
- Thank him for his letter of 1 July, catalogue, and price list.
- Tell him you enclose the above order, and remind him that we expect delivery within six weeks. We will pay by banker's draft when we receive the shipping documents.
- Explain that if items are not available, they should not send substitutes.
- Ask him to email me if there are any problems with delivery.
- Close by saying we look forward to receiving acknowledgement of the order.
Many thanks
Dieter
17 July 20—

5 Acknowledging an order

There are no capitals, punctuation, or paragraphs in this email acknowledging an order. Write it out correctly. Divide the body of the email into two paragraphs.

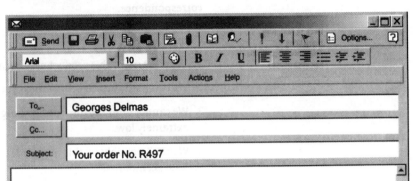

To..: Georges Delmas

Cc...

Subject: Your order No. R497

dear m delmas

thank you for your order (no r497) which we are at present making up the instruments will be packed individually in 8 crates numbered and marked with our logo they will be sent airfreight cif marseille to reach you no later than 18 may our invoice showing the 12% trade and 3% quantity discounts the insurance certificate and the air waybill will be sent to the bank of marseille as requested

harald kjaer
sales manager
dansk industries, kongens nytorv 1, dk–1050 københavn k
tel: +45 367521
fax: +45 367522
email: hkjaer@dansk.co.de
7 may 20—

6 Delay in delivery

Read this extract from a fax apologizing for a delayed delivery, and choose the best words from the options in brackets.

Further to our telephone conversation on Friday, I am writing to you

1_____ (affecting, concerning, changing) your order, No. SX1940,

which was **2**_____ (sold, made, placed) with us on 10 January.

Once again, I must **3**_____ (regret, apologize, speak) for

the delay in processing this order. This was due to a staffing

4_____ (shortage, fault, malfunction). However, since I spoke to you,

we have **5**_____ (dismissed, promoted, taken on) four new

employees at our depot, and I am pleased to tell you that your order is now ready

for despatch. It will **6**_____ (arrive, deliver, reach) you within five

working days.

Special **7**_____ (care, attention, caution) has been taken to ensure

that the **8**_____ (load, crates, consignment) has been packed

9_____ (meeting, according, serving) to your requirements. Each

item will be individually wrapped to **10**_____ (prevent, cause, stop) damage.

7 Refusing an order

All the sentences below give reasons for refusing an order. Match the sentences in column A with sentences in column B with similar meanings. Then put a tick by the sentences which are most suitable for business correspondence.

Column A

1 We don't make this product now because people don't buy enough of it.

2 We can't sell you anything unless you pay cash.

3 We cannot offer the discount you suggest as our profit margins are extremely low.

4 We can't possibly fill this huge order: it's more than our total output for at least six months!

5 Unfortunately, we cannot guarantee delivery within five working days.

Column B

a Unfortunately, we do not have the capacity to supply an order as large as this.

b We can't let you have 15% off because we price our products as cheaply as possible.

c There's no way we can deliver in such a short time.

d We have stopped manufacturing this product as there is no longer sufficient demand.

e We regret that we would only be prepared to supply on a cash basis.

8 Words and definitions

Make words from the jumbled letters and match them with the definitions below.

a SMPOMILCTEN IPLS
b NOVCIIE
c GIFOWRDNRA GNETA
d TSTMTEELEN
e RIA ILWYALB
f IHPS
g VIGCNERO TRTEEL
h CIAVDE TNEO

1 Person or organization that conveys goods to their destination.
2 Letter accompanying a document or goods, explaining the contents.
3 List of goods or services that states how much must be paid for them.
4 Document informing a customer that a consignment is on its way to them.
5 Payment of an account.
6 Small piece of paper with a company's details on it.
7 To send goods by road, rail, air, or sea.
8 Document that gives information about goods sent by air.

6
Payment

1 Invoice

M. Morreau has ordered the following dinner services from Glaston Potteries: ten 'Lotus' at £35 each, catalogue number L305; twenty 'Wedgwood' at £43 each, catalogue number W218. Cost, insurance, and freight are included in these prices. Glaston have offered him a 15% trade discount. Complete the invoice below.

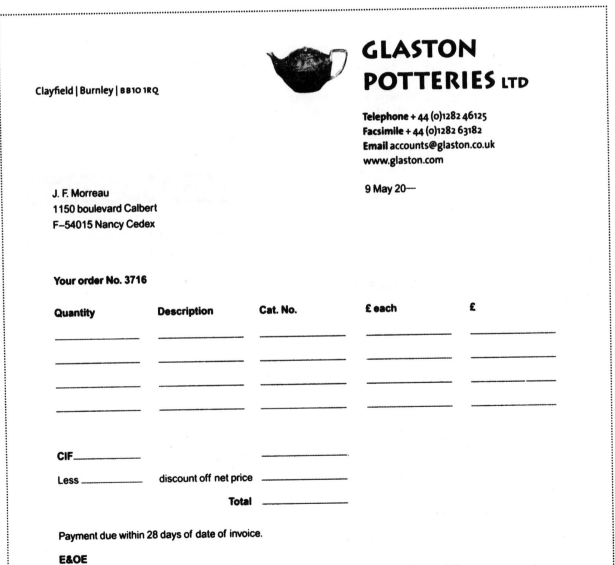

Clayfield | Burnley | BB10 1RQ

GLASTON
POTTERIES LTD

Telephone + 44 (0)1282 46125
Facsimile + 44 (0)1282 63182
Email accounts@glaston.co.uk
www.glaston.com

9 May 20—

J. F. Morreau
1150 boulevard Calbert
F–54015 Nancy Cedex

Your order No. 3716

Quantity	Description	Cat. No.	£ each	£
_____	_____	_____	_____	_____
_____	_____	_____	_____	_____
_____	_____	_____	_____	_____
_____	_____	_____	_____	_____

CIF_____   _____

Less _____ discount off net price _____

Total _____

Payment due within 28 days of date of invoice.

E&OE

Registered No. 716481
VAT Reg. No. 133 53431 08

2 Statement of account

You work in the Accounts Department of Homemakers Ltd, a furniture manufacturer, and are preparing a monthly statement for a regular customer, R. Hughes & Son Ltd. Your first entry is the Account Rendered, i.e. the outstanding balance of £461.00 from last month, which goes in the Balance column. This column also shows a running balance of all the other items. All the money Hughes owes you, including the debit note, goes in the Debit column. All the money he has paid, including the credit note, goes in the Credit column. Complete the May statement using the information below.

Customer: R. Hughes & Son Ltd, 21 Mead Road, Swansea, West Glamorgan 3ST 1DR

Date	Item	Amount
1 May	Account Rendered	£461.00
5 May	Invoice 771/2	£781.00
7 May	Cheque	£300.00
12 May	C/N 216	£285.00
16 May	Invoice 824/2	£302.00
18 May	Cheque	£200.00
23 May	D/N 306	£100.00

The terms at the end of the statement are a Cash Discount of 3% if the statement is paid within 10 days.

HOMEMAKERS

54–59 Riverside, Cardiff CF1 1JW
Telephone: +44 (0)29 20 49721
Fax: +44 (0)29 20 49937

statement

To: _____

Date	Item	Debit	Credit	Balance
1 May	Account Rendered			
Terms:				

3 Request for more time to settle an account

M. Morreau received the consignment from Glaston Potteries (see Exercise 1). Unfortunately he is unable to pay within the period stated on Glaston's invoice. He writes to John Merton, Sales Manager at Glaston, to apologize. Rewrite his letter in less elaborate language: leave out any details which are not relevant.

Dear Mr Merton

I deeply regret that at this moment in time I am unable to settle your invoice dated 9 May for my order No. 3716 for ten Lotus dinner services at £35 each, catalogue number L305, and twenty 'Wedgwood' dinner services at £43 each, catalogue number W218.

The consignment arrived in good condition and as usual I admired the quality and elegance of your products. They always sell very well in my two shops here in Nancy. Unfortunately, two days after the arrival of the consignment, disaster struck. After several centimetres of incessant rain my stockroom was completely flooded and much of the stock damaged or destroyed.

I am waiting with great patience for my insurers to settle my claim, but meanwhile it is with sorrow that I have to tell you that I am unable to pay any of my suppliers. However, on a more optimistic note, I am able to inform you that the aforementioned insurers have promised me compensation within the next four weeks. When I receive this, I will take measures to pay all my suppliers as soon as I possibly can.

Trusting that you will understand this difficult situation, I remain

Your humble servant

Jean Morreau (M.)

4 Crossword

Complete the crossword

ACROSS

1 A _____ note is a form of IOU (*I owe you*).

2 If your supplier has charged too much on an invoice, ask for a _____ .

3 An _____ lists goods or services, and how much must be paid for them.

4 An international money _____ can be bought at the bank to settle an account in another country.

5 A bank _____ is a cheque that a bank draws on itself and sells to a customer.

6 After two requests for payment you might receive a final _____ .

7 _____ is a system for transferring money from one bank or post office to another.

DOWN

8 A _____ _____ invoice is sent in advance of the goods ordered. (2 words: 3, 5)

9 A customer can request a bank to _____ money from one account to another.

5 Request for payment   Choose the best words from the options in brackets in this letter requesting payment.

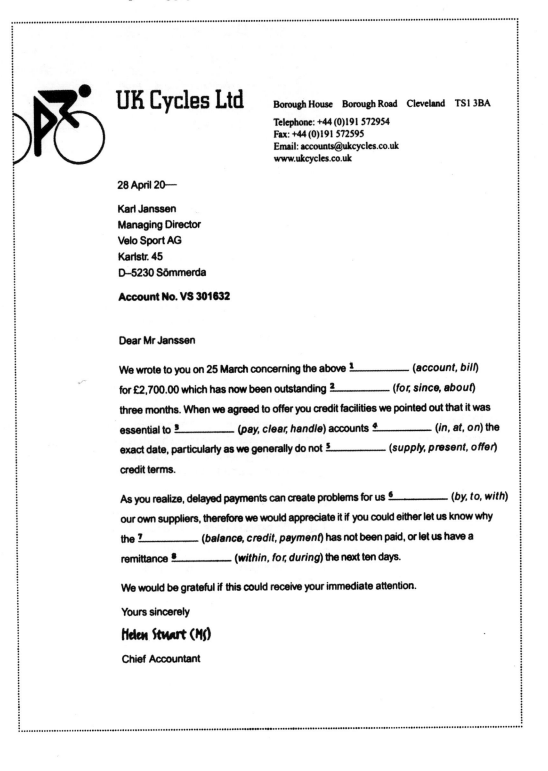

UK Cycles Ltd   Borough House   Borough Road   Cleveland   TS1 3BA

Telephone: +44 (0)191 572954
Fax: +44 (0)191 572595
Email: accounts@ukcycles.co.uk
www.ukcycles.co.uk

28 April 20—

Karl Janssen
Managing Director
Velo Sport AG
Karlstr. 45
D–5230 Sömmerda
Account No. VS 301632

Dear Mr Janssen

We wrote to you on 25 March concerning the above **1**_____ (*account, bill*) for £2,700.00 which has now been outstanding **2**_____ (*for, since, about*) three months. When we agreed to offer you credit facilities we pointed out that it was essential to **3**_____ (*pay, clear, handle*) accounts **4**_____ (*in, at, on*) the exact date, particularly as we generally do not **5**_____ (*supply, present, offer*) credit terms.

As you realize, delayed payments can create problems for us **6**_____ (*by, to, with*) our own suppliers, therefore we would appreciate it if you could either let us know why the **7**_____ (*balance, credit, payment*) has not been paid, or let us have a remittance **8**_____ (*within, for, during*) the next ten days.

We would be grateful if this could receive your immediate attention.

Yours sincerely

Helen Stuart (Ms)

Chief Accountant

6 Reply to request for payment

Karl Janssen emails his PA, Renata Heynold, asking her to draft a reply to Helen Stuart (see Exercise 5). As Renata Heynold, write the reply.

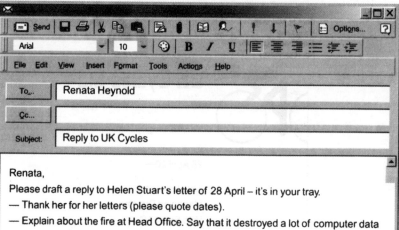

> **To...** Renata Heynold
>
> **Cc...**
>
> **Subject:** Reply to UK Cycles
>
> Renata,
> Please draft a reply to Helen Stuart's letter of 28 April – it's in your tray.
> — Thank her for her letters (please quote dates).
> — Explain about the fire at Head Office. Say that it destroyed a lot of computer data which has disrupted all correspondence with suppliers and customers, and we need time to get back to our normal routine.
> — Request a further 30 days to settle. She's suggested 10, so be as polite as you can. Say our insurers will release compensation within the coming month, so we can pay the outstanding amount in full.
> I'd be grateful if you could let me have it for signature by noon today.
> Thanks, KJ
> 3 May 20—

7 Formal and informal English

Match the sentences in column A with sentences in column B with similar meanings. One sentence in each pair is in formal English (i.e. appropriate for business correspondence), and the other is informal. Write 'F' beside the formal sentences and 'I' beside the informal ones.

Column A

1 ☐ We expect to receive your remittance within seven days.
2 ☐ We are taking you to court to get our money back.
3 ☐ I apologize for not clearing the balance earlier.
4 ☐ It appears that this invoice has not yet been settled.
5 ☐ We would be grateful for another month to settle.

Column B

a ☐ We want you to pay us in less than a week.
b ☐ Sorry I didn't pay you before now.
c ☐ We can't pay you in less than four weeks.
d ☐ Unfortunately, we have no alternative but to take legal action to recover the debt.
e ☐ It looks as though you haven't paid us yet.

8 Words and definitions

Make words from the jumbled letters and match them with the definitions below.

a RTURECN CNATCUO
b HISGT FADTR
c NLACEBA
d KANB NARRSEFT
e TDCRYAMUONE IDERCT
f EUD TAED
g SETTORP
h EMTACNEITR
i EMATTESTN FO TANCOCU
j BEDTI TENO

1 Take legal action to obtain payment.
2 Date by which an account should be settled.
3 Account into which a customer can pay money, or draw it out, without giving notice.
4 Movement of money from one bank account to another.
5 Payment.
6 Difference between the totals of money coming into and going out of a bank account.
7 List of amounts paid and owed.
8 Document informing a customer of money owed.
9 Bill of exchange that must be paid immediately it is presented.
10 Letter of credit that requires the seller to supply shipping documents to the bank to obtain payment.

7
Complaints and adjustments

1 Formal and informal English

All the sentences below could be used in complaints, or replies to them. Match the sentences in column A with sentences in column B with similar meanings. Then put a tick by the sentences which are most suitable for business correspondence.

Column A

1 You should put it right.
2 Please ensure that the problem does not arise again.
3 In this case we are not responsible for the error.
4 Please could you send us a refund.
5 We're sorry about the muddle.
6 We're planning to buy from someone else.
7 Your machine doesn't work.
8 I regret that in this case we are unwilling to offer a refund.

Column B

a We want our money back.
b We would be grateful if you could correct the error.
c We apologize for the confusion.
d We will have to consider changing to another supplier.
e There appears to be a defect in the mechanism.
f We're not giving you your money back.
g This time it's not our fault.
h Make sure it doesn't happen again.

2 Complaint about damage

Complete this letter of complaint about damage with the words and expressions from the box.

wear	crates	rusty
insurers	inspecting	consignment
complain	refund	handled
torn	invoice	carriage forward

C. R. Méndez S.A.

Avda. del Ejército 83
E–48015
Bilbao
Tel: +34 94 231907
Fax: +34 94 245618
Email: mendezc@crmendez.co.es

15 October 20—

Mr B. Harrison
Sales Manager
Seymore Furniture Ltd
Tib Street
Maidenhead
Berks SL6 5DS

Dear Mr Harrison

I am writing to **1**_____ about a shipment of tubular steel garden furniture we received yesterday against **2**_____ No. G 3190/1.

The **3**_____ were damaged on the outside, and looked as if they had been roughly **4**_____ . When we unpacked them, we found that some of the chair legs were bent and **5**_____ , and the fabric on the seating **6**_____ , or showing signs of **7**_____ .

Two further crates from the **8**_____ have not arrived yet, so we have not had the opportunity of **9**_____ them. I have told the shipping company that we cannot accept this consignment from you, and they have contacted your **10**_____ .

As we will be unable to retail this consignment in our stores, we are returning the shipment to you **11**_____ , and we shall expect a full **12**_____ .

Yours sincerely

C. R. Méndez

Managing Director

3 Complaint about late delivery

There are no capitals, punctuation, or paragraphs in this letter of complaint about late delivery to a manufacturer of medical equipment. Write out the letter correctly. Divide the body of the letter into two paragraphs.

ISTITUTO DI MEDICINA

Viale Bracci
1–61001 Siena
Telefono: +39 0586 43-74-25
Fax: +39 0586 43-74-26
Email: clotti@imed.ac.it

15 june 20—

mr h. toda
sales manager
nihon instruments
12–18 wakakusa-cho
hagashi-osaka-shi
osaka-fu
japan

dear mr toda

awb 4156/82

we are writing to point out that the above delivery which arrived yesterday was a week late this is the second time we have had to write to you on this subject and we cannot allow the situation to continue we have already explained that it is essential for medical equipment to arrive on due dates as late delivery could create a very serious problem unless we have your firm guarantee on the promptness of all future deliveries we will have to look for another supplier please could you confirm this before we place our next order

yours sincerely

carlo lotti (sig.)

head of administration

Reply to complaint about damage

Brian Harrison, Sales Manager at Seymore Furniture, emails Jo Hayes, his PA, asking her to draft a reply to Sr Méndez (see Exercise 2). Note that his instructions only concern the letter's content and signature: he assumes that Jo will open and close it in an appropriate way. As Jo Hayes, write the letter.

To... Jo Hayes

Cc...

Subject: Reply to Méndez

Jo,

Could you write a letter replying to the complaint from Sr Méndez? Explain that the goods were checked before they left our warehouse, so the damage must have happened during shipment.

Say that we'll accept the goods C/F, and that we'll send the refund by banker's draft as soon as we receive them – and apologize for the inconvenience caused.

Please don't pp it - I'll sign. Cheers, Brian

PS Ask him about the other 2 crates.

20 October 20—

Reply to complaint about late delivery

The sentences have become confused in Mr Toda's reply to Sig. Lotti's letter (see Exercise 3). Rewrite the letter with the sentences in the correct order, starting new paragraphs where appropriate.

1 **Consignment no. AWB 4156/82**
2 I trust that this will clarify the situation, and look forward to continued good trading with you.
3 However, the two orders you mentioned were sent to our factory rather than our administrative offices at the above address.
4 We would like to take this opportunity of reminding you that to avoid delay in future all orders should be sent to our office address.
5 Sales Manager
6 Thank you for your letter of 15 June concerning late delivery of the above consignment.
7 Hirio Toda (Mr)
8 We understand how important prompt deliveries are to our customers.
9 Dear Mr Lotti
10 Yours sincerely

6 Complaint about accounting errors

1 Find the mistakes and work out the correct figures.
2 Write to Excel Stationers. Your contact is Mrs B. Grevon, Accounts Department.
   — Say what the mistakes are and what the correct version should be.
   — Tell her that you will settle the account when you receive a corrected invoice.
   — Mention that this has happened several times before, and that you will change your suppliers if it happens again.

You work for IT Services plc, King Street, London w8 2MC. Excel Stationers supply your company with stationery. They have sent you the invoice below. The wrong totals have been given for three of the items, which of course results in an incorrect final total.

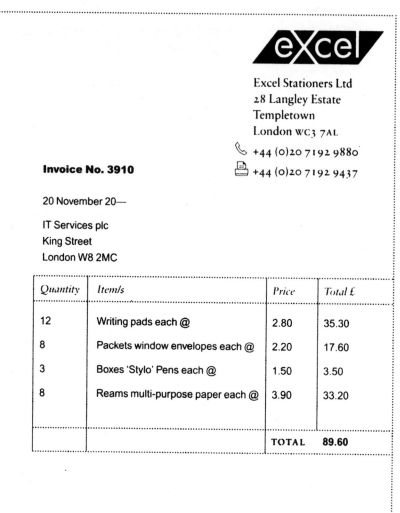

eXcel

Excel Stationers Ltd
28 Langley Estate
Templetown
London WC3 7AL

☎ +44 (0)20 7192 9880
🖶 +44 (0)20 7192 9437

Invoice No. 3910

20 November 20—

IT Services plc
King Street
London W8 2MC

Quantity	Item/s	Price	Total £
12	Writing pads each @	2.80	35.30
8	Packets window envelopes each @	2.20	17.60
3	Boxes 'Stylo' Pens each @	1.50	3.50
8	Reams multi-purpose paper each @	3.90	33.20
		TOTAL	**89.60**

8
Credit

1 Formal and informal English

In the sentences below, the words in italics are not very appropriate for formal correspondence. Choose a more suitable alternative from the box.

inform	overdue	request	promptly	sufficient
elapsed	acceptable	competitive	settle	confidential

1 Thank you for forwarding the documents so *quickly*.
2 We feel that *enough* time has *passed* for you to *pay*.
3 I am writing to *ask for* open account facilities.
4 We would like to remind you that this information is highly *secret*.
5 Your quarterly settlement is three weeks *late*.
6 We are pleased to *tell* you that the credit facilities you asked for are *fine*.
7 Our prices are very *low*.

2 Agreeing to credit

As Alex Rempel, Sales Manager of Rempel GmbH, reply to the email below from Thomas Shaw. Agree to his request for credit, but tell him, politely, that according to your records the period for settlement was 30 days, not 60. Apologize for any misunderstanding. Ask him to confirm that these terms are acceptable and say that, if they are, he will not need to provide references.

To... Alex Rempel

Cc...

Subject: Terms of payment

Dear Mr Rempel

We have been trading with you for the past year and during that time our accounts have been cleared by letter of credit.

However, when we began trading with you, you mentioned that once we had established a business relationship our accounts could be settled by 60-day bill of exchange, D/A.

Please could you let us know, before we place our next order, if these new terms are acceptable?

Yours sincerely

Tom Shaw
Chief Accountant, Fairman Green Ltd
12 May 20 —

3 Request for a reference

Complete the following request for a reference with the correct prepositions.

Antonio Medina S.L.

C/Sagasta 1156
Barcelona 08317
Teléfono: +34 93 478503
Fax: +34 93 479152
Email: pgomez@medina.co.es

18 May 20—

Mr Gerald MacFee
Credit Controller
British Suppliers plc
Hoxteth House
Wrights Way
Glasgow G12 8QQ

Dear Mr MacFee

We are writing **1**_____ you **2**_____ the recommendation **3**_____ Mr David Arnold, Chief Accountant **4**_____ D.L. Cromer Ltd. **5**_____ Staines, Middlesex. He advised us to contact you as a referee concerning the credit facilities which his company has asked us **6**_____.

Could you confirm that the company settles **7**_____ due dates, and is sound enough to meet credits of from £3,000 **8**_____ £5,000?

We would be most grateful **9**_____ a reply **10**_____ your earliest convenience.

Yours sincerely,

Patricia Gómez (Sra.)

Sales Manager

4 Reply to request for a reference

Mr MacFee has made some brief notes before writing a reply to Sra. Gómez's letter (see Exercise 3). As Mr MacFee, write the letter. Include the sender's and inside addresses, and an appropriate date.

> *replying yr. letter 18 May re. D.L. Cromer Ltd.*
> *excellent reputation in UK - customer of ours for a long time*
> *credit limit w. us a little lower than the one you mentioned, but*
> *always settle on or before due dates*
> *grateful if treat this info. in strictest confidence*

5 Unfavourable reply

When replying to enquiries about credit rating, it is better not to mention the company's name or to be too specific in the details you give. Rewrite the letter below considering this advice.

> Dear Ms Allard
>
> I am replying to your enquiry of 19 September about Fit-a-Part Ltd.
>
> We have allowed Fit-a-Part credit in the past three years, but only up to £2,000, not the £10,000 you mentioned. We have also found that they need four or five reminders before clearing their account.
>
> Please treat this information in the strictest confidence.
>
> Yours sincerely
>
> *P.M. Lord*
>
> Accountant

6 Words and definitions

Make words from the jumbled letters and match them with the definitions below.

a DAB TEDB
b TDREIC TAINRG
c LIBL FO CAXNEGEH
d TLAFEDU
e ERECEBNRF
f DERCTI STILFCIIAE

1 Means of allowing credit, e.g. bill of exchange.
2 Debt that is not likely to be paid.
3 Method of payment by which the seller can give the buyer credit for an agreed period, e.g. 30 days.
4 Evaluation of the creditworthiness of an individual or company.
5 To fail to do something required by law.
6 Written report on a company's creditworthiness.

9
Banking

1 Reporting verbs

Read the sentences below. Then find the reporting verb from the box which best fits each situation. The first one has been done for you.

explain	promise	thank	admit
suggest	advise	refuse	apologize

1 I am grateful to you for sending the shipping documents so promptly.
   thank

2 Why don't you think it over for a few days and then get back to me?
   _____

3 Unfortunately, we cannot extend your overdraft.
   _____

4 I think you should consider our terms before making a decision.
   _____

5 I'll definitely let you have the details tomorrow.
   _____

6 It appears that we made an error on your October statement.
   _____

7 We understand that the bank will want about 120% in securities to cover this credit.
   _____

8 I am sorry for the delay in replying to you.
   _____

2 Word forms

Complete the sentences below, using the correct form of the words in brackets. The first one has been done for you.

1 Lack of capital will *endanger* the project. (*danger*)
2 The exporter opens a letter of credit by _____ an application form. (*complete*)
3 The cheque should be made _____ to International Boats Ltd. (*pay*)
4 The shipping documents include bill of lading, _____ certificate, and invoice. (*insure*)
5 I am pleased to inform you that your _____ has now been extended to £4,000. (*overdraw*)
6 Loans can be extended only by _____ with the Branch Manager. (*arrange*)

7 You will receive _____ of payment from our bank. (*confirm*)

8 Your _____ should appear twice on the document. (*sign*)

9 We need a loan to secure the _____ of our company. (*expand*)

10 With _____ to our telephone conversation yesterday, I am writing to confirm our agreement. (*refer*)

3 Bill of exchange

Complete the bill of exchange below with the following information:

- Payment is due 60 days after date.
- There is only one bill, therefore write *sola*. For this reason, there is no need to write anything before the words *to the order of* as there is only one bill (otherwise this line would have *second of the same tenor and date unpaid* to show there was a second copy).
- The bill is for $28,000.
- It was drawn on 28 February 20—.
- The drawer is Hartley–Mason Inc.
- In (6), write in the words of the currency that is being used and the actual words of the amount.
- In *Value Received* write *payable at the current rate of exchange for bankers' drafts in London*.
- The bill is being drawn on Glough & Book Motorcycles Ltd, 31–37 Trades Street, Nottingham, NG1 3AA.
- The drawer's name is Hartley-Mason Inc., 618 West and Vine Street, Chicago, Illinois, and will be signed by Mr J.R. Mason, the President of the Company.

At **1** _____ pay this **2** _____ Bill of Exchange

2 _____ to the order of Number 40031 3021

Exchange for **3** _____ **4** _____

5 _____

6 _____

Value Received **7** _____

placed to account

To
8 _____

For and on behalf of
9 _____

Signed
9 _____

4 Request for a loan

Read the following conversation between a bank manager, John Steele, and a customer, Richard Grey.

JOHN STEELE Good afternoon, Mr Grey. Now, how can I help you?

RICHARD GREY Well, I know my company's been going through a bad time recently, but I would like to expand the fleet by buying another two trucks. I wonder if you could extend my loan to cover the investment?

JOHN STEELE I'm afraid we can't extend your existing loan, but we may be able to offer a bridging loan. How much would you need?

RICHARD GREY Probably around £50,000, I think, to buy two second-hand vehicles. I'm sure that the revenue from the extra trucks would allow me to repay you within a year.

JOHN STEELE What can you offer as security for the loan?

RICHARD GREY Just the trucks themselves.

JOHN STEELE Well, unfortunately, I am not in a position to make an independent decision – I shall have to consult our directors – but I promise I will consult them this week, and let you know as soon as possible.

RICHARD GREY Thank you very much.

As John Steele, summarize the conversation in a memo to the bank's Board of Directors. Try to use some of the reporting verbs from Exercise 1. Remember only to report the details which will help the Board to make a decision. Head the memo 'Strictly confidential', and start like this:

I had a meeting with Mr Richard Grey, of RG Logistics Ltd, on 17 September…

5 Refusing a loan

The bank's Board of Directors has now discussed Mr Grey's request for a loan (see Exercise 4). This is their reply to his memo.

Memo

From: Secretary to the Directors
To: John Steele
Subject: Bridging loan, RG Logistics Ltd
Date: 21 September 20—

STRICTLY CONFIDENTIAL

With reference to your memo dated 19 September concerning the above loan, the Board regret that in this case they are unable to offer Mr Grey the credit requested. They would be grateful if you could inform Mr Grey that it is the bank's policy only to offer substantial loans against negotiable securities such as shares or bonds.

As John Steele write a letter to Mr Grey, explaining that credit has been refused. Suggest that there are other sources he could try, for example a finance corporation, but warn him that their interest rates are likely to be significantly higher than the bank's.

6 Words and definitions

Make words from the jumbled letters and match them with the definitions below.

a SRDNEOE
b TCENRAUOMYD CIERTD
c FIRCETETACI FO IGIRNO
d EALNC LBLI
e SYAD TFARE HSITG
f CHAREMNT NBKA
g AREODVHE
h TGISH TFRDA

1 Transfer a bill or cheque by signing it on the back.
2 Type of bank that specializes in international trade and finance.
3 Document that shows where goods were made.
4 Bill of exchange without any accompanying documents.
5 Letter of credit that requires the seller to supply shipping documents to a bank to obtain payment.
6 Number of days within which a bill of exchange must be paid after presentation.
7 Regular cost of running a company, e.g. rent.
8 Bill of exchange that must be paid immediately it is presented.

7 Abbreviations

Complete the full term for each abbreviation.
The first one has been done for you.

1 B/E   B __ __ l O __   E __ cha __ g __

2 D/P   __ __ c __ __ e n __ __   A __ a __ n s __
       __ __ y __ __ __ t

3 L/C   __ __ tt __ __   O __   __ r __ d __ __

4 D/A   __ o __ um __ __ __ __ s   __ ga __ __ st
       __ c __ ep __ a __ __ __ e

5 E&OE   __ rr __ __ s   an __
       __ mi __ __ __ __ on __   __ xc __ p __ __ d

6 DC   __ o __ um __ __ t __ __ y   __ __ e __ __ t

7 CP   __ ar __ __ ag __   __ ai __

8 D/S   __ __ y __   Af __ __ __ r   __ __ __ gh __

9 IMO   __ nt __ __ __ at __ __ __ __ __ l
       __ __ n __ y   __ r __ er

10 CF   __ __ rr __ a __ e   __ or __ a __ __

8 Documentary credit 1

Letter from the confirming bank to the exporters

Paul Diderot, Documentary Credits Manager of the Banque de Lyon, writes to exporters Château Wines, informing them that a letter of credit has been opened for them. Choose the correct expressions from the box to fill the gaps.

| inform | charges | documents | draw | acting | valid | settle | opened |

500 boulevard Jobert
69000 Lyon
Tél: +33 4 781243
Fax: +33 4 781244
Email: pdiderot@banque-lyon.co.fr

BANQUE DE LYON

8 July 20—

Mr James Freeland
Château Wines
80 rue Gaspart-André
69003 Lyon

Dear Mr Freeland

L/C No. 340895/AGL

We are **1**_____ on behalf of the Eastland Bank, London, and would like to **2**_____ you that the above documentary credit for €5,300 has been **3**_____ in your favour by your customers BestValue Ltd. The credit is **4**_____ until 12 August and all bank **5**_____ have been paid.

Please send the following **6**_____ to the above address:

- Air waybill
- Invoice for full value of the sale CIF London
- Insurance certificate

Would you also **7**_____ a sight draft for the full amount of the invoice on us so that we can **8**_____ this account.

Thank you in advance.

Yours faithfully

Paul Diderot

Manager, Documentary Credits

---

9   Documentary credit 2

Letter from the exporters to the confirming bank

James Freeland of Château Wines has made some notes for his reply to Paul Diderot's letter. Write out the letter in full.

thank for advice of 8 Jly. shipment to BestValue in UK now effected.
encl. shipping documents you request + draft for € 5,300.00.
pl. accept draft and remit proceeds to our account Banque de Commerce,
28 rue Gaspart-André, 69002, Lyon. NB list documents

10
Agents and agencies

1 Find the keyword

Complete the boxes with the missing word from the sentences below to find the keyword down.

ACROSS

1 Shares are bought and sold on a _____ _____ . (2 words: 5,8)
2 _____ houses receive orders from overseas, place them, and make arrangements for packing, shipping, and insurance.
3 A _____ _____ is the only one allowed to sell the products of a manufacturer in a particular area. (2 words: 4,5)
4 An agent who sells products on a _____ basis makes a certain amount of money for each item sold.
5 A _____ is a person or organization that hires an agent to buy or sell goods for them.
6 In non-recourse _____ , a firm buys up outstanding invoices and claims the debts.
7 _____ invoice value is the value of an invoice without extra charges.
8 _____ markets are where items like coffee, cocoa, and rubber are bought and sold.
9 Agents who take the risk of being liable for customers' debts may receive a _____ _____ commission. (2 words: 3,7)
10 A _____ _____ is an organization that buys goods on behalf of a principal. (2 words: 6,5)
11 A prospective agent may need to be convinced that there is a _____ for the principal's products.

DOWN

12 Keyword: The basis on which an agent is employed to resell goods for a commission.

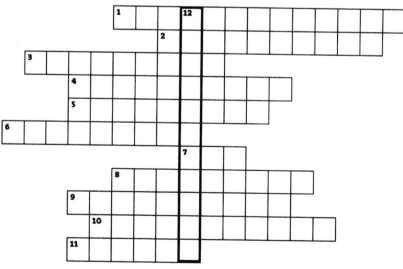

2 Phrasal verbs

Using a word from column A and a word from column B, complete each sentence with a phrasal verb. The first one has been done for you.

A	B
take	in
make	up
work	down
back	out
draw	on
turn	
fill	

1 I am sure it will be possible for us to _work_ _out_ a more satisfactory arrangement for promoting your products.

2 We would be pleased to _____ _____ an initial one-year contract to act as your sole agents.

3 We will _____ _____ a draft agreement and send it to you as soon as possible.

4 We plan to _____ _____ the advertising campaign with supplies of brochures and leaflets to all our dealers.

5 I regret that we must _____ _____ your offer of a sole agency because at present we do not have sufficient resources.

6 Please will you _____ _____ the cheque to Wallis Greene Ltd, our distributors in your area.

7 It will be necessary to _____ _____ the enclosed customs form.

8 As we have been trading for over a year, it will not be necessary for us to _____ _____ references.

3 Offer of an agency

Choose the best words from the options in brackets in this letter offering an agency.

Grazioli S.p.A.

Via Gradenigo 134
50133 Firenze

☏ +39 (0)55 89-65-20
🖨 +39 (0)55 89-65-21
🖳 pgrazioli@ grazioli.co.it

Herr Otto Grassmann
Grassmann AG
Lindenweg 18
D–1000 Berlin 12

23 October 20—

Dear Herr Grassmann

You were recommended to us by the German Chamber of Commerce, who **1**_____ (*said, told, spoke*) you might be interested in representing a leading Italian glass manufacturer in your country.

We have a number of agencies in other European countries who receive products on **2**_____ (*commission, consignment, approval*), then sell them on a 6% commission on ex-works prices. These are **3**_____ (*single, unique, sole*) agencies.

Generally, their customers **4**_____ (*settle, agree, deal*) all accounts with us, then we supply them direct on invoices received from the agent.

In most cases we offer a **5**_____ (*test, proof, trial*) agency for one year, and if the results are good, we **6**_____ (*export, extend, expand*) the agency agreement on a further two-year contract. We would **7**_____ (*offer, suggest, invite*) you support through advertising, brochures, and leaflets in German, the **8**_____ (*cost, value, worth*) of this being shared between us.

Our market **9**_____ (*researchers, reporters, informers*) tell us there is an increasing demand for our line of products in your country, so it would not be difficult to sell our products.

If you would be interested in an agency of this type, we can send you a standard agreement, giving you more details of our terms. Meanwhile, we are enclosing our **10**_____ (*actual, present, current*) catalogue.

Yours sincerely

Pietro Grazioli

Chairman

Encl.

---

4 Reply to an offer of an agency

Choose the phrase or sentence from each group which would be most appropriate in a reply to the letter in Exercise 3. Write out the reply as a letter. Include the inside address, date, salutation, complimentary close, and signature block, and divide it into paragraphs.

1 a Thanks very much for your letter the other day.
   b I was delighted when I received your recent communication.
   c Thank you for your letter of 23 October.

2 a I can confirm that we would be interested in representing you, but not on a sole agency basis, as this would restrict our sales.
   b We might be interested in representing you, but we can't go ahead on a sole agency basis as we've got to sell a lot.
   c Were it not for the sole agency basis you mention, your proposal might be received more favourably.

3 a Not only that, but we want a cut of 10% and three quarters of the ads paid by you.
   b In addition, a 10% commission on ex-works prices and 75% support in advertising are the basis on which we might contemplate negotiating an agreement.
   c Also, our usual terms are a 10% commission on ex-works prices and 75% of the advertising costs.

4 a Notwithstanding, we were overwhelmed by the superlative quality of the products in your catalogue.
   b In spite of our objections about terms, the products in your catalogue look really good.
   c However, we were very impressed by the high quality of the products in your catalogue.

5 a If you are able to revise your terms, we would be interested in receiving a draft contract.
   b Subject to a satisfactory revision of terms, a draft contract would be worthy of our consideration.
   c If you can look at your terms again, send us a contract.

6 a Give us a call sometime, so we can have a chat.
   b I look forward to hearing from you.
   c I remain your humble servant.

5 Request for an agency

Read this request to act as a buying agent from Manfred Kobelt, Managing Director of the Kobelt Agency. Choose the correct words from the box to fill the gaps.

offer	commission	principals
rates	documentation	freight
del credere	recommendation	terms
factory	manufacturers	brochure

The Kobelt Agency

Brauneggerstr. 618
D–4400 Münster
Tel: +49 251 37–25–94
Fax: +49 251 37–25–95
Email: kobeltm@kobeltagency.co.de

24 June 20—

Mrs Cristina Neves
Buying Manager
Portuguese Industrial Importers
Rua dos Santos 179
1200 Lisbon
Portugal

Dear Mrs Neves

We are writing to you on the **1**_____ of the Portuguese Chamber of Commerce, who informed us that you were looking for a buying agent for precision tools in this country.

We have been in this trade for over twenty years and have close contacts with the major **2**_____ both here and overseas.

We would like to give you a brief outline of the **3**_____ we work on. Generally, we place orders for our **4**_____ with our suppliers, and our customers settle direct with the manufacturer. In addition, we arrange all costs, insurance, and **5**_____ facilities for the client, handling consignments from the **6**_____ to the port / airport of the importer's country.

As we have dealt with these agencies for a number of years, we can offer you their most competitive **7**_____ for shipment. In addition, we would take care of all **8**_____ , including customs formalities.

As a rule we operate on a 4.5% **9**_____ on CIF values, but if credit is involved, we could offer **10**_____ services for an additional 2.5% commission, pending the usual inquiries.

If you are interested in this **11**_____ we can assure you of first class, efficient service. Please contact us if you need any more information. I have enclosed our **12**_____ giving you full details of our company.

We look forward to hearing from you in due course.
Yours sincerely

Manfred Kobelt

Managing Director

Enc.

6 Reply to a request for an agency

Cristina Neves has decided to email her reply to Herr Kobelt's letter (see Exercise 5). Draft an email from the notes below. Remember that she does not know him so the style will be quite formal, like a letter.

Kobelt
- Thank for letter – interested in proposals – increasing demand for precision tools here
- In principle, cld. accept either 3% comm. on CIF values or the 2.5% del credere comm.
- Can Kobelt act as clearing and forwarding agency, offering door-to-door facility?
- Kobelt willing to send contact details of 2 companies they act for who can offer references? If yes, we wld. be interested in discussing contract
- Look forward to hearing, etc.

11
Transportation and shipping

1 Two-word terms

Match words from box A with words from box B to make two-word terms used in business correspondence. Then use the terms to complete the sentences below.

A	
shipping	bulk
charter	delivery
air	all
forwarding	shipping

B	
risks	waybill
note	party
agent	note
mark	carrier

1 Packing and shipment will be arranged by our ____ ____ .

2 The freighter *Narvik* is a ____ ____ with a cargo capacity of six thousand tons.

3 When you have confirmed the charter, we will send you the ____ ____ for signature.

4 Before signing the ____ ____ , please check that the consignment has arrived undamaged.

5 The cost of freight London Heathrow – Dubai is £10.00 per kilo, plus £8.00 ____ ____ , and £60.00 customs clearance and handling.

6 Please would you arrange insurance cover for £100,000 against ____ ____ .

7 Enclosed you will find our standard ____ ____ and bill of lading.

8 The ____ ____ on the sides of the crates should correspond with the one on your shipping documents.

2 Formal and informal English

Rewrite these sentences in a more polite form, using the words supplied. The first one has been done for you.

1 Fill in the despatch form and don't forget to let us have it with the parcels. (*please, send, consignment*)
Please fill in the despatch form and send it to us with the consignment.

2 If you don't understand, get in touch with me. (*queries, hesitate, contact*)

_____

_____

3 I've had a word with Despatch, who say there was nothing wrong with the crockery when they sent it off. (*checked, Department, records, perfect condition*)

_____

_____

4 We want a quote for picking up ten armchairs here and taking them to
   R. Hughes & Son Ltd, Swansea.
   (*please, collection, consignment, above address, delivery*)

   _____

   _____

5 The loss on invoice value must be £300.00 and we want our money back.
   (*estimate, claiming compensation, amount*)

   _____

   _____

6 Do you want us to send the goods back to you, or to keep them here for you
   to look at? (*prefer, return, hold, inspection*)

   _____

   _____

**3 Enquiry to a
    forwarding agent**

Complete this fax enquiring about a forwarding agent's charges with the
correct prepositions.

Fax

York Instrumentation Ltd
157 Links Road, Derby
DE7 8PX
Tel: +44 (0)1332 491567
Fax: +44 (0)1332 491568

To: Bill Crowley, Landmark Freight Services
From: Stephen Lang
Subject: Quotation
Fax no.: 796543
Page(s): 2 (incl. this page)
Date: 10 November 20—

Dear Mr Crowley

You were recommended **1**_____ us **2**_____ Stellman Ltd, our

associates, **3**_____ whom you have operated as forwarding agents.

We are looking **4**_____ a reliable agent to handle our deliveries

5_____ Europe, taking care **6**_____ documentation and making sure

7_____ safe delivery – many **8**_____ our products are very fragile.

You will find a list representing a consignment we wish to send

9_____ Lausanne **10**_____ road. Could you let us have your quotation,

and if it is competitive, we can assure you **11**_____ further business

12_____ the future.

Yours sincerely

STEPHEN LANG

York Instrumentation Ltd

4 Forwarding agent's reply

Below is Bill Crowley's reply to Stephen Lang (see Exercise 3). Write it out, putting the phrases in the correct order and adding paragraphs, capitals, and punctuation where necessary.

Fax

Landmark Freight Services Ltd
Unit 7B, Barrow Business Park,
Derby
DE12 8ER
Tel.: +44 (0)1332 796537
Fax: +44 (0)1332 796543

To:	S. Lang, York Instrumentation
From:	Bill Crowley
Fax no.:	491568
Subject:	Quotation
Date:	11 November 20—
Page/s:	2

Dear Mr Lang

— our freight charges / of 10 November / thank you / enquiring about / for your fax

— for shipments / I enclose / which includes all transport customs and documentation charges / our tariff list

— are highly competitive / I think / that these rates / you will find

— that we have / in handling fragile consignments / in addition / extensive experience / I can confirm

— and I will be very pleased / any further questions / please contact me / to help / if you have

— to hearing / I look forward / from you

Yours sincerely

Bill Crowley

5 Words and definitions

Make words from the jumbled letters and match them with the definitions below.

a LPDOAYA   e EIRTCEP
b NDSEERO   f NOSTDINOCALOI
c LSDCAUE   g PIBKRORSHE
d ODTMLMILAU   h RECNOTNIA

1 When small consignments from different exporters are loaded into a single container.
2 Document showing that goods have been paid for.
3 Unit of transportation, e.g. a container, that can be transferred between different systems, e.g. train and ship.
4 Agent who arranges the transport of cargo by ship.
5 The part of a cargo that earns money for the shipping company.
6 Large metal box in which goods are packed for transportation.
7 Term used on a bill of lading to indicate that goods were damaged or incomplete when they came on board.
8 To transfer a cheque or bill of exchange to someone else by signing it on the back.

6 Enquiry to a container company

John Merton, Sales Manager of Glaston Potteries, emails his PA, Jill Bradley, asking her to send an email to National Containers. As Jill Bradley, draft the email. Start: *I am contacting you on behalf of John Merton concerning...*

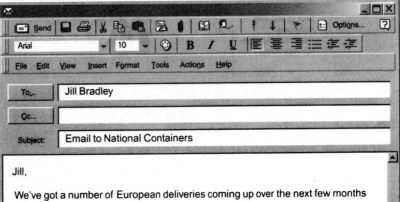

To... Jill Bradley

Cc...

Subject: Email to National Containers

Jill,

We've got a number of European deliveries coming up over the next few months which I'd like National Containers to handle. Consignments consist of fragile crockery. Average crate measures 187x172x165cm. Approx weight 35kg each. We want door-to-door delivery.

Please email them asking them for schedules and sample quotations. I'd also like information concerning documentation.

Thanks, John
John Merton
15 July 20—

PS The person to contact is Brian Close – you have his email address.

7 Container company's reply This is Brian Close's reply to Jill Bradley (see Exercise 6). He has written the email but not yet checked it through. Find and correct the mistakes – there are ten of them.

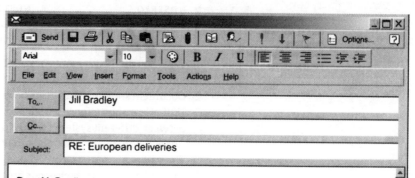

> **To...** Jill Bradley
>
> **Cc...**
>
> **Subject:** RE: European deliveries
>
> Dear Mr Bradley
>
> Thank you for your email yesterday I am sending you the shedules and sample quotations you requested. They should reach you by tommorow.
>
> With regard to your enquiry about documentation, we sugest you use our combined transport bill as the goods will then be covered by road and ferry. I am also sending you our EXPORT CARGO PACKING INSTRUCTIONS. These should be handed to our driver when he calls. Consignment will be delivered to our depot for consolidation, and you will be charged at our very competitive groupage rates (see smaple quotations).
>
> We will take the usual responsibilites for handling cargo, but suggest you take out allrisk insurance cover on a door-to-dor basis.
>
> Please let us know if there is any other details you require.
>
> Yours sincerely
> Brian Close
> Freight Manager
> National Containers Ltd
> 16 July 20--

12
Insurance

1 Terms used in insurance

Complete the missing terms used in insurance. Each blank stands for a missing letter.

1 An i __ __ __ __ __ __ __ __ company indemnifies clients against loss.

2 Underwriters at Lloyds work in groups called s __ __ __ __ __ __ __ __ __ .

3 An insurance p __ __ __ __ __ is a contract taken out to protect someone against future risks.

4 Clients are i __ __ __ __ __ __ __ __ __ __ against loss or damage when they have insurance policies.

5 A p __ __ __ __ __ __ is the amount of money paid to an insurance company for cover.

6 L __ __ __ __ __ List is a daily newspaper about shipping movements and cargo markets.

7 A p __ __ __ __ __ __ __ form is completed by a firm or person who wants insurance cover.

8 A client sends their insurance company a c __ __ __ __ form when they have suffered damage or loss.

9 Under f __ __ __ __ __ __ __ bonds, companies can insure themselves against dishonest employees.

10 The job of an average a __ __ __ __ __ __ __ is to examine damage and estimate compensation.

2 Request for comprehensive insurance

Read the following request for comprehensive insurance and choose the best words from the options in brackets.

HUMBOLDT EXPORTERS LTD

Exode House | 115 Tremona Road | Southampton SO9 4XY

Telephone: +44 (0)23 80 149783
Fax: +44 (0)23 80 149784
Email: hindp@humboldt.co.uk

15 February 20—

International Insurance plc
153 Western Road
Brighton
Sussex
BN1 4EX

Dear Sir

We are a **1**_____ (grand, large, wide) export company **2**_____ (who, which, what) ships consignments **3**_____ (in, to, towards) Europe and North America. We **4**_____ (want, would like, request) to know if you can **5**_____ (suggest, supply, present) us with a quotation for a comprehensive policy, **6**_____ (assuring, protecting, covering) our warehouse at Dock Road, Southampton.

We would like the policy to **7**_____ (consist, contain, include) fire, flood, theft, burglary, and the usual contingencies affecting this **8**_____ (form, kind, variety) of enterprise. At any one time, there may be about £800,000 in stock on the **9**_____ (premises, grounds, floors).

If you can give us a **10**_____ (competing, competition, competitive) quote, we will **11**_____ (think, imagine, consider) taking out further policies with you.

We look forward to hearing from you **12**_____ (soon, presently, immediately).

Yours faithfully

Peter Hind

Company Secretary

3 Reply to request for comprehensive insurance

Below is an email from Gerald Croft, Regional Manager of International Insurance, to Natalie Weston, his secretary, asking her to draft a reply to Peter Hind's letter (see Exercise 2). As Natalie Weston, draft the reply for Gerald Croft to sign.

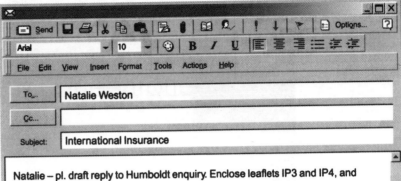

To..: Natalie Weston
Cc...:
Subject: International Insurance

Natalie – pl. draft reply to Humboldt enquiry. Enclose leaflets IP3 and IP4, and suggest that one of our agents calls on them to discuss which policy would best suit them. Ask Hind to call you if he'd like to arrange an appointment.
(NB remember our new number is 01273 547231, and you're on ext. 12!) I'll sign.
Thanks, GC

Gerald Croft
18 February 20—

4 Claim for fire damage

Humboldt Exporters insured their Southampton Warehouse with International Insurance (see Exercises 2 and 3), but unfortunately suffered a fire a few months later. Mr Hind has made some notes for an email telling International Insurance about the fire and asking them to send a claim form. Write the email.

policy no. 439178/D
regret fire broke out in S'ton warehouse early y'day. extensive damage (approx. £7,000) to textiles stored for shipment. fire service has provided evidence that electrical fault was cause. pl. send claim form asap.

5 Request for open cover

There are no capitals, punctuation, or paragraphs in this letter requesting open cover. Write out the letter correctly. Divide the body of the letter into four paragraphs.

UK engineering PLC

1 may 20—

sugden & able
insurance brokers
63 grover street
manchester m5 6ld

dear sir madam

we are a large engineering company exporting machine parts worldwide and have a contract to supply a middle eastern customer for the next two years as the parts we will be supplying are similar in nature and are going to the same destination over this period we would prefer to insure them under an open cover policy would you be willing to provide open cover for £500,000 against all risks for this period i look forward to hearing from you yours faithfully

jack turner

shipping manager

6 Reply to request for open cover

Alan Able, Director of Sugden and Able, asks his secretary, Mary Todd, to reply to Jack Turner's letter (see Exercise 5). Read their conversation and, as Mary Todd, write the email. (Alan Able's telephone number is 0161 542783.)

ALAN ABLE Oh, and Mary, could you email UK Engineering – Jack Turner I think the chap's name was – anyway, the email's on the letterhead. Thank him for his enquiry and tell him that we offer two types of cover, either of which might suit them.

MARY TODD Which ones do you mean?

ALAN ABLE The floating policy – that would cover all the shipments they plan to make up to an agreed maximum value, and can be renewed when necessary.

MARY TODD And the other one?

ALAN ABLE Open cover – that's the one he seems to know something about, but you'd better explain it anyway. It's where we provide cover for all shipments over a given period. Tell him I'd be very pleased to discuss these options if he'd like to give me a call.

13
Miscellaneous correspondence

1 Prepositions

Make eight complete sentences used in general and social correspondence by joining phrases from column A and phrases from column B with one of the prepositions. You will need to use some of the prepositions more than once, but each phrase should be used only once. The first sentence has been done for you.

Column A		Column B
I would like to congratulate you	by	Eid Al-Fittr.
Please send the tickets		your promotion.
May I offer my best wishes	for	full conference facilities.
She offers her apologies		effective website design.
I would like to speak	with	the inconvenience.
I hope to return the favour		my attention.
Please confirm these reservations	on	some future occasion.
We will need a room		return.

2 Formal and informal English

Complete the following sentences so that they have a similar meaning to the one above, but are more suitable for formal business correspondence.

1 He's sorry he can't come, but hopes he can come another time.
   He sends his _____ .

2 It's such a shame that your brother is ill. I'm really sorry.
   I was sorry _____ .

3 So you've been elected Chairman of the company! Well done!
   I would like _____ .

4 Mr Norman wants to drop in on you next week about the contract.
   Mr Norman would _____ .

5 Mr Chung can't see you on Friday for your appointment after all.
   Unfortunately, _____ .

6 Can you come to our Sales Conference on 18 March?
   We would like _____ .

7 Thanks for helping me while I was in Hamburg last week.
   I would _____ .

8 It'll be good to see you on Friday.
   I look _____ .

3 Conference facilities

Diane Taylor, Sales Director of Data Unlimited plc, has emailed her PA, Lynn Paul, with details of a sales conference she is planning for December. As Lynn Paul, draft the letter she mentions.

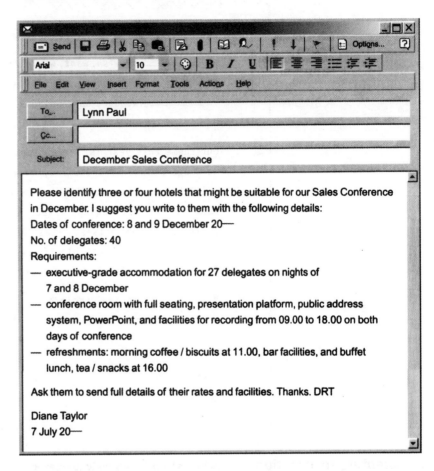

To.. Lynn Paul

Cc...

Subject: December Sales Conference

Please identify three or four hotels that might be suitable for our Sales Conference in December. I suggest you write to them with the following details:

Dates of conference: 8 and 9 December 20—

No. of delegates: 40

Requirements:

— executive-grade accommodation for 27 delegates on nights of 7 and 8 December

— conference room with full seating, presentation platform, public address system, PowerPoint, and facilities for recording from 09.00 to 18.00 on both days of conference

— refreshments: morning coffee / biscuits at 11.00, bar facilities, and buffet lunch, tea / snacks at 16.00

Ask them to send full details of their rates and facilities. Thanks. DRT

Diane Taylor
7 July 20—

4 Hotel reservation

Diane Taylor chose the Royal Hotel for Data Unlimited's sales conference (see Exercise 3). It is now only a few days before the conference and two delegates, Charles Bickford and Claire Ramal, have made a last-minute decision to stay at the hotel. As Lynn Paul, complete the fax below. Ask the hotel if they have two extra rooms available and apologize for the short notice.

Fax

Data Unlimited plc
Data House
Chertsey Road
Twickenham
TW1 1EP
Telephone: +44 (0)20 81 460259
Fax: +44 (0)20 81 985132

To: _____
From: _____
Fax: 01372 908754
Subject: _____
Date: 3 December
Page/s: 1

5 Invitation

Read this invitation from a Chamber of Commerce and choose the best words from the options in brackets.

Dear Herr Boldt

We **1**_____ (wish, want, would like) to invite
you to our annual dinner on 15 February, and
2_____ (wonder, ask, demand) if you would consider being
one of our guest **3**_____ (announcers, speakers, talkers).

Our theme this year is 'The effects of the euro', and
we would **4**_____ (admire, seek, appreciate) a
contribution from your field of manufacturing on how this is
5_____ (afflicting, affecting, altering) you and your
colleagues enterprises. Please **6**_____ (let, leave, make)
us know as soon as possible if you are able to
7_____ (talk, speak, discuss).

8_____ (Inside, Enclosed, Within) you will find a formal
invitation for yourself and a guest.

Yours sincerely

Peter House

Chairman

6 Accepting an invitation

Below is Herr Boldt's reply to Peter House (see Exercise 5). Write it out, putting the phrases in the correct order and adding paragraphs, capitals, and punctuation where necessary.

Dear Mr House

for your letter / inviting me to speak / on 15 February /
thank you / at your annual dinner

I am honoured / your kind invitation / to accept

I would like to focus / on the cost of raw materials /
in my talk / on the effects that the euro is having

and would welcome / you care to make / I will send you /
next week / any comments or suggestions / a transcript

to meeting you / very much / I look forward /
on February 15

Yours sincerely

Gunther Boldt

Chairman

14
Memos and reports

1 Formal and informal English

Match the sentences in column A with sentences in column B with similar meanings. Then put a tick by the sentences which are more suitable for a formal memo.

Column A

1 We haven't decided so far.

2 No-one will lose their job because of what we're doing.

3 Your cooperation in this matter is essential.

4 He's always off sick so he's leaving.

5 The company has expanded a lot recently.

6 Please see your manager if you have any questions.

7 Staff should close windows and take personal belongings with them.

8 The staff restaurant will be relocated in the near future.

Column B

a The last few months have seen a period of unprecedented growth.

b Have a word with your boss if you don't understand.

c No firm decision has yet been reached.

d Don't forget to take your coat and bag, and shut the windows.

e You've got to do what we say.

f We're going to move the canteen.

g There will be no redundancies as a result of this measure.

h He has decided to retire on the grounds of ill-health.

2 Memo about documentary credits

The Finance Director of your company, Interbank, has asked you to write a memo reminding staff how important it is to carefully check all details of documents associated with documentary credits. £250,000 has been lost in the past year over mistakes in effecting documentary credit transactions. Select the five most relevant points from the check list below and, as his PA, write the memo.

- Check that all trains are running on time.
- Check all transport documents, insurance certificates, invoices and customs clearance certificates.
- Check staff holidays have been arranged for this year.
- Check details of hotels in the local areas.
- Check bills of exchange and letters of credit.
- Check the spelling in the names of the parties is correct.
- Check if local events will interfere with our hotel bookings.
- Check that places of departure and destinations are correct.
- Check the right amounts for the transactions are listed and the correct currencies have been written in.
- Check salary scales for the members of the Documentary Credit Department.

3 Memo about fraud

Terry Fairman is the Chief Accountant at National Stores plc. He has just attended a Directors' meeting about fraud when customers pay by cheque, and has been asked to write a memo to sales staff about this problem. As Terry Fairman, write the memo, selecting information from the notes he made at the meeting. It should cover the following points:
- what the problem is
- what practical measures sales staff should take to reduce it

1 Sales staff should carefully match signatures on cheque cards with those on cheques.
2 The value of bad cheques presented over the past year amounts to over £50,000.
3 Sales staff should not make customers feel like criminals.
4 Most customers use a credit card or cash to pay for goods.
5 Write the cheque card number and expiry date on the back of the cheque.
6 Supervisors should be contacted if sales staff are unsure about a payment.
7 Customers' reactions should be noted for nervousness.
8 Cheques should be examined to see that they have been completed properly.
9 Banks also lose a great deal of money through cheque fraud.
10 The problem of bad cheques cannot be eliminated, but sales staff can help reduce it significantly.

4   Reports: past tenses

Complete the following extracts from reports, using either the present perfect continuous (e.g. *have been working*) or the simple past (e.g. *worked*).

EXTRACT 1

Our organization **1**_____ (*export*) precision tools to the Middle East for over forty years. We **2**_____ (*open*) our first office in Iraq in the early 1960s and it **3**_____ (*remain*) open for five years until we **4**_____ (*move*) our headquarters to Jordan. In the last few months we **5**_____ (*negotiate*) a contract with Saudi Arabia, which we hope will be signed soon.

EXTRACT 2

Since the beginning of this year, the department store **6**_____ (*lose*) over £5,000 per month due to theft, and last month this **7**_____ (*rise*) to £8,500. We believe that a gang of shoplifters **8**_____ (*operate*) in the building for the last few weeks, and that this may account for the losses that **9**_____ (*occur*) in June. Over the last few days we **10**_____ (*have*) discussions with our security consultants who will produce a report shortly.

EXTRACT 3

Trading in the market **11**_____ (*be*) slack for the first two months of the year, as investors **12**_____ (*feel*) worried by the uncertain political climate, and interest rates **13**_____ (*remain*) high. However, in the last few weeks, interest rates **14**_____ (*fall*) gradually and look as if they will continue to do so. Investors **15**_____ (*return*) to the market slowly and volumes **16**_____ (*increase*).

5 Report on introduction of flexitime

John Holland, Company Secretary of Elland Hughes Advertising, has been asked to prepare a report on the introduction of a flexitime system. Read Documents 1, 2, 3, and 4 carefully. Then, as John Holland, write the report. It should take the following form:

- Introduction: give details of the proposed flexitime system.
- Outline the advantages of the system to the company.
- Outline the advantages of the system to the staff.
- Mention the financial costs and benefits.
- Make your conclusions and recommendations.

DOCUMENT 1

Memo from the Chief Executive

Memo

To: John Holland
From: Ian Peters
Date: 12 February 20—
Subject: Flexitime

The Board have recently been considering the introduction of a flexitime system. Please prepare a report on the feasibility of introducing this system. The report should cover:

- Staff attitude towards flexitime
- Benefits to the company of flexitime
- Financial implications
- Disadvantages (if any)
- Conclusions and recommendations

We propose that the new times might be from 07.00 to 21.00. Staff would be able to choose their hours of work between these times, and could have a weekday off in lieu of Saturday if they prefer.

Please let me have the report and your findings by 18 March.

Results of staff questionnaire

1 Are you in favour of the introduction of a flexitime system?

Yes	87%
No	4%
Don't know	9%

2 Would you prefer to have a day off in the week instead of Saturday?

Yes	76%
No	11%
Don't know	13%

3 Which facilities do you find most crowded?

Photocopiers	35%
Fax machines	24%
Canteen	21%
Toilet	3%
Other	2%

4 What is your average journey time to work during the rush hour?

Less than ½ hour	12%
½ hour to 1 hour	29%
1 hour to 1½ hours	48%
More than 1½ hours	11%

5 If flexitime were introduced, which hours would you prefer?

7 a.m. to 3 p.m.	18%
8 a.m. to 4 p.m.	21%
9 a.m. to 5 p.m.	16%
10 a.m. to 6 p.m.	20%
11 a.m. to 7 p.m.	10%
midday to 8 p.m.	10%
1 p.m. to 9 p.m.	5%

6 If the office was open six days a week, which day would you choose to have free in addition to Sunday?

Monday	16%
Tuesday	7%
Wednesday	23%
Thursday	14%
Friday	19%
Saturday	21%

7 What would be the main advantage of a free day during the week for you?

Being with partner	34%
Shopping	23%
Making other appointments	17%

8 In what way would the company benefit most from a flexitime system?

Clients in different time zones would find it easier to contact us	34%
Clients could contact us on Saturday	26%
Staff would not be tired after the rush-hour	24%
Security would be improved	12%
Other	4%

9 Would you be in favour of the introduction of a clocking-in system?

Yes	26%
No	48%
Don't know	26%

10 Would you be in favour of a one-year trial period?

Yes	76%
No	14%
Don't know	10%

DOCUMENT 3

Selection of comments from '*Do you have any other comments?*' section on staff questionnaire

> 'A great idea – I'm sure we'd all work better.'
>
> 'I'd be able to spend more time with my family.'
>
> 'Would make all the difference if I didn't have to get to work in the rush hour.'
>
> 'Could take the kids to school, which would help a lot.'

DOCUMENT 4

Memo from the Accounts Department

Memo

To: John Holland
From: Irene Allen, Chief Accountant
Subject: Flexitime

You asked us to examine the financial implications of the flexitime system, and our general conclusions are as follows:

1 Overheads will increase because of the need for extra heating and lighting. Gas and electricity bills will rise by approximately 7%, but this may be offset by slightly lower insurance premiums because of the increased security of having staff on the premises longer. There may also be a reduction in photocopying costs if we do not need to use outside agencies so much.

2 Wages will not increase as long as staff who choose to work on Saturdays are not paid the overtime rate (standard wage plus 50%).

3 The clocking-in system will cost approximately £5,500 + VAT. This is a fixed cost and can be offset against tax.

A more detailed Costing Sheet Estimate is attached.

15
Personnel appointments

1 Words and definitions

Make words from the jumbled letters and match them with the definitions below.

a DLOUETCIISN
b CNYCAVA
c MRCUCIRUUL TVIEA
d EEREFRE

e EPRESNONL
f RACERE MYASURM
g NOVCRIEG TERELT

1 Another word for *appointment* or *post*.
2 Short profile of the job applicant at the beginning of a CV.
3 Person who writes a reference.
4 Document describing a job applicant's qualifications, work experience, and interests.
5 A job applicant may send this with a CV or application form.
6 Another word for *human resources*.
7 Application for a post that has not been advertised.

2 Follow-up to a job application

Robin Anakin sent an email to Glaston Potteries in response to an advertisement for an Administrator, but received no reply. Here he is following up with another email, but there are several mistakes in it relating to spelling, punctuation, paragraphing, language, and content. Rewrite the email in a more acceptable form.

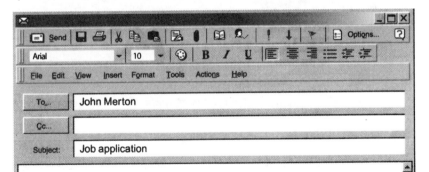

To... John Merton
Cc...
Subject: Job application

I sent an emial to you requesting an aplication from for the job of administrator witch you advertised in the Burnley Despatch at the begginning of this month – I realise you might have been too busy around new years day to answer me. however, I am still interested in the job as I like acounts and all areas of bussiness and theres good money in it. If you want to offer me an interview you can reply to this mesage or phone me I look forward to hear from you

Robin
17 January 20—

3 Job advertisement

Choose the best words from the options in brackets to complete the job advertisement below.

Personal Assistant to the Managing Director

We are looking for someone with **1**_____ (*current, fluent, spoken*) English and Italian, and preferably another language such as French or German. The **2**_____ (*secretary, interviewee, applicant*) should have at least five years' secretarial **3**_____ (*work, experience, employment*), preferably in an international environment. The work **4**_____ (*consists, contains, includes*) the usual secretarial **5**_____ (*work, duties, employment*), customer liaison, and **6**_____ (*doing, making, acting*) as an interpreter for the Managing Director, both here and elsewhere in Europe. For a(n) **7**_____ (*application form, CV, interview*), phone Paula Prentiss, the Personnel Manager, on (01223) 6814, Ext. 412, quoting **8**_____ (*number, reference, figure*) PP 391.

 International Publishing Ltd
60 Girton Street, Cambridge CB2 3EU

---

4 Covering letter

Carla Giuliani has decided to apply for the post of Personal Assistant to the Managing Director at International Publishing Ltd (see Exercise 3). She has completed the application form below. Using information from the job advertisement and the application form, write Carla's covering letter. Include the reference and the date, and remember to say:

- what job you are applying for
- why you would be suitable for the job, and why you are interested in it

---

 International Publishing Ltd
60 Girton Street, Cambridge CB2 3EU

APPLICATION FORM

Surname	*Giuliani*
Forename(s)	*Carla*
Address	*114 Ellesmere Walk, Finchley, London NW3 1DP*
Age	*28*
Date of birth	*4 January 19—*
Qualifications	*Degree in English and French (Università di Genova)*
	Secretarial Diploma (Pitman College, London)
Experience	*20— – 20— Secretary to Area Manager (N. Italy), Morgan Brice Ltd*
	20— – 20— PA to Sales Director, Morgan Brice Ltd
Languages	*Italian (mother tongue), English, French, German*
Office Skills	*Typing 60 w.p.m.*
	Shorthand 85 w.p.m.
	Familiar with Word, including spreadsheets
Hobbies and interests	*Tennis, swimming, horse riding, cinema*
Signature	*Carla Giuliani*
Date	*29 May 20—*

5 Invitation for an interview

Paula Prentiss has read Carla's application form and covering letter (see Exercise 4) and would like to interview her. As Paula Prentiss, write the letter inviting her to attend.

- Invite her to come for an interview at 14.30 on Thursday 18 June in Cambridge.
- Tell her that there will be a short Italian and French translation test before the interview.
- Send her a map with details, and tell her there are frequent trains to Cambridge from Liverpool Street.
- Ask her to phone you to confirm the date of the interview, or to arrange another one if she cannot attend on that day.

15

6 Making a job offer

Following a successful interview, Kevin Wheeler, Managing Director of International Publishing, would like the post of Personal Assistant to be offered to Carla (see Exercises 3–5) and has sent an email to Paula Prentiss. As Paula Prentiss, write the letter.

To... Paula Prentiss

Cc...

Subject: Appointment of PA

Dear Ms Prentiss

With reference to our discussion this afternoon, I'd like you to offer the post to Carla Giuliani on a starting salary of £18,000. Start 23 July if possible – get her to ring you asap if there are problems about this. Please send 2 copies of contract as usual – say we're looking forward to seeing her. Thanks. KHRW

Kevin Wheeler
18 June 20—

Answer key

Note: For reasons of space, information such as addresses and dates is not set out at the top of most model letters, faxes, or emails in this Answer key (email signature blocks are also not included). If you are unfamiliar with the layout of a formal letter, a business fax, or a business email in English, you should work through the exercises in Units 1 and 2 of this Workbook before proceeding to the other units.

Unit 1
Letters, faxes, and emails

1 Letters: true or false?

1 F Yours sincerely
2 F carbon copy
3 F Dear Mr Smith
4 F chairman
5 T
6 F 2 June 2005

7 T
8 F Public Limited Company
9 T
10 T
11 T
12 F used for someone you know well

2 Order of addresses

1 Soundsonic Ltd
   Warwick House
   57–59 Warwick Street
   London
   SE23 1JF

2 Sig. D. Fregoni
   Managing Director
   Fregoni S.p.A.
   Piazza Leonardo da Vinci 254
   I-20133 Milano

3 Herr Heinz Bente
   Chairman
   Bente Spedition GmbH
   Feldbergstr. 30
   D-6000 Frankfurt 1

4 The Sales Manager
   Sportique et Cie
   201 rue Sambin
   F–21000 Dijon

5 Mrs S. Moreno
   Chief Accountant
   Intercom
   351 Avda Luis de Morales
   E–41006 Sevilla

6 Ms Maria Nikolakaki
   Nikitara 541
   85100 Rhodes
   Greece

7 Mrs Junko Shiratori
   Excel Heights 501
   7–3–8 Nakakasai
   Edogawa-ku 139
   Tokyo
   Japan

8 The Transport Director
   VHF Vehicles Ltd
   301 Leighton Road
   Kentish Town
   London NW5 2QE

3 Letters: parts and layout

2 letterhead

1 date

7 inside address

3 salutation

8 body

5 complimentary close

4 signature block

6 enclosure

4 Faxes and emails:
true or false?

1 T
2 F fax copy not valid
3 F facsimile
4 F not if you know recipient well
5 F use in informal email
6 T
7 F at
8 T use letter or card
9 F carbon copy
10 T
11 F use same principles as in letter
12 T

5 Fax transmission form

Fax

BRITISH CRYSTAL Ltd
Glazier House, Green Lane, Derby DE1 1RT

To: *Mohamed Kassim (Director, S.A. Importers Ltd, Riyadh)*

From: *Yvonne Feltham (Export Manager)*

Fax no.: *(+966) 1 34981*   Subject: *Tableware – new lines*

Date: *17 September, 20—*   Page/s: *4*

As requested. I hope this is helpful. YF

---

6 Email: request for further information

To... | Yvonne Feltham
Cc... |
Subject: | Your fax, further info.

Dear Yvonne

Many thanks for your fax. Just a few further questions:

Will the 'York' range be available before the end of October?

Do you have approximate sales figures for the 'Cambridge' range in other main markets?

Is the 'Bristol' range available in green?
(I'm afraid I can't read the list of colours in the fax.)

Is the 'Durham' range dishwasher-proof? (Again, I can't read the fax.)

I look forward to hearing from you.

Best wishes

Mohamed

Mohamed Kassim
Director, S.A. Importers Ltd
Al Manni Way, Riyadh
SAUDI ARABIA
Tel: (+966) 1 35669
Fax: (+966) 1 34981
m.kassim@saimp.co.sa

18 Sept 20—

---

7 Email: checking

1 Change *Sir / Madam* to *Ms Bell*.
   (He knows her name from the header information.)
2 First sentence should start with a capital letter, but the rest should be in lower case. (Remember, using capitals in emails is like shouting.)
3 *facilities*
4 Full stop after *facilities*.
5 *accommodate*
6 *July*
7 Delete *full board* (repeated later on)
8 *equipped*
9 *The*
10 *tariff*
11 *coffee*
12 *mid-morning*
13 *acceptable*
14 *sincerely*

8 Words and definitions

a 3 (blocked style)
b 6 (signature block)
c 2 (reference)
d 1 (enclosure)

e 5 (private and confidential)
f 8 (job title)
g 4 (yours sincerely)
h 7 (attachment)

Unit 2
Content and style

1 Typical sentences

1 We would be grateful for a reply as soon as possible.
2 Please find enclosed a cheque for £49.50.
3 If you need any further information, please contact us. /
   Please contact us if you need any further information.
4 Thank you for your letter of 5 April. / Thank you for your letter of April 5.
5 We look forward to hearing from you.
6 I have pleasure in enclosing our spring catalogue and a price list.

2 Courtesy

```
Dear Sir

We are writing concerning the February balance of £567.00
on your account, which has been outstanding for three months.
We wrote to you on 15 March and 4 April asking you to clear this
balance, but did not receive a reply, which surprised us as you
have been a regular customer for a number of years.

We would like to remind you that credit was offered on the
understanding that balances would be cleared on the due dates;
failure to do so could create difficulties for us with our
own suppliers.

We are prepared to offer you a further ten days to clear
the balance on this account, or explain why you cannot do so,
otherwise we will, reluctantly, have to take legal action.

Yours faithfully
```

R. Lancaster (Mr)

3 Summarizing

To... Ron Lancaster

Cc...

Subject: Letter from Mr Games

Dear Ron

We've had a reply from Mr T.D. Games concerning delayed payment of his February account. He says the delay is the result of a serious fire, which destroyed the company's records. However, their insurers are about to release funds to enable them to start settling their debts, and Mr Games assures us that we will be fully repaid as soon as funds are available. Meanwhile, he apologizes profusely, and encloses a cheque for £55.00.

Pat

---

4 Basing a letter on notes

bp

Barnard Press Limited

183–7 Copwood Road
North Finchley
London N12 9PR
Telephone: +44 (0)20 8239 9653
Facsimile: +44 (0)20 8239 9754
Email: barnards@barnardpress.co.uk
www.barnardpress.co.uk

Our ref: SB/RW

1 March 20—

Sig. Claudio Bini
International Books
Via Santovetti 117/9
00045 Grottaferrata
Rome

Dear Sig. Bini,

Thank you for your enquiry of 15 February about readers for intermediate students of English.

Unfortunately, we have no readers in stock at the moment, but will be publishing a new series of intermediate-level readers, 'Storyworld', in the autumn. I have pleasure in enclosing a leaflet about the series, and our current catalogue.

We hope you will be interested in the new series, and look forward to hearing from you.

Yours sincerely
Rosalind Wood

p.p. Sarah Barnard

Sales Manager

5 Clear sequence

Dear Mr Jackson

NICOSIA COMPUTER TRAINING COURSE

Thank you for your letter of 18 May giving us the dates of your trip. I am writing with information about the arrangements we have made for your visit.

On Friday 9 June your flight to Larnaca will be met by our driver, who will take you to the Amathus Beach Hotel, where we have booked you in for the first two nights. We hope you enjoy your weekend at the hotel.

The driver will call for you at 17.00 on Sunday and drive you to the Training Centre at Nicosia. Most of the trainee operators will have had some experience of the new program by the time you arrive at the centre, but they will need a good deal of instruction on the more complex areas of the system.

The driver will pick you up from the Training Centre on Wednesday evening, at the end of the course, and take you back to the Amathus Beach Hotel, where I have booked you in for a further two nights. Unfortunately, Mr Charalambides will not be able to meet you in Larnaca on Thursday 15 June, as you requested, because he will be returning from a visit to our subsidiary in Spain. However, he will be back in the office the following day, so I have arranged for him to see you at 14.30.

Please could you confirm that you plan to return to London on the 18.30 flight on Friday 16, and also that the arrangements outlined here suit you?

I look forward to hearing from you.

Yours sincerely

Elena Theodorou

Training Manager

6 Planning

paragraph 1	Acknowledge letter
paragraph 2	Travel arrangements arrival time (Friday 9 June, Larnaca 15.30) departure time (Friday 16 June, 18.00, not 18.30)
paragraph 3	Training course No. of trainees? Photocopying facilities?
paragraph 4	Confirm time of meeting with Mr Charalambides OK
paragraph 5	Thank Ms Theodorou for her help

→

Dear Ms Theodorou

Thank you for your letter concerning the arrangements you have made for my trip to Cyprus in June. In general, I am very happy with them, but there are one or two things I would like to raise.

First, concerning the travel arrangements, please could you inform your driver that my flight on 9 June is scheduled to arrive in Larnaca at 15.30. And please note that my return flight to London on 16 June leaves Larnaca at 18.00, not 18.30.

With reference to the training course, how many trainees are there likely to be? Also, are there photocopying facilities at the Training Centre?

Finally, I can confirm that it will be convenient for me to meet Mr Charalambides at 14.30 on Friday 16 June.

Thank you for all your help.

Yours sincerely
Tom Jackson

Unit 3
Enquiries

1 Enquiry from
a building company

Fax

Clark Fitzpatrick Builders plc
Dunstable Road
Luton, Bedfordshire
LU2 3LM

To:	Ms Doreen French
From:	Terry Spalding, Household Installations Ltd
Fax no:	01582 351711
Subject:	Kitchen units
Date:	3 April 20—
Page/s:	2

Dear Ms French

Thank you for your letter and the enclosed catalogue giving details of your kitchen units.

The main item we are interested in is the unit on page 22. It appears to meet all our specifications for the apartment block I described in my letter. I am sending herewith a plan of a typical apartment which gives the exact dimensions.

Before placing a firm order we would need samples of all materials used in the manufacture of the units. Could you please confirm that you guarantee all your products for two years against normal wear and tear? I would also be grateful for details of your terms regarding payment, and of any trade and quantity discounts.

If the price and quality of your products are satisfactory, we will place further orders as we have several projects at the planning stage.

Yours sincerely
Terry Spalding
Purchasing Manager

2 Words and definitions

a 5 (catalogue)
b 6 (estimate)
c 7 (tender)
d 2 (customer)
e 9 (wholesaler)

f 4 (showroom)
g 1 (subsidiary)
h 8 (prospectus)
i 10 (sale or return)
j 3 (quantity discount)

3 Polite requests

1 It is essential that the consignment is delivered before the end of September.
2 Could you please send us your catalogue and a price list?
3 As we intend to place a substantial order, we would like to know if you allow quantity discounts?
4 Please could you email us if you are unable to deliver the goods before Friday?
5 We would appreciate it if you could send us some samples.
6 We would be grateful if you could send one of your representatives here to give us an estimate.
7 We would be interested in seeing a demonstration of both models.
8 Would you be able to let us have twenty units on approval?
9 I am writing to enquire when you will be able to let us have the cheque?
10 As a rule, our suppliers allow us to settle by monthly statement.

4 Enquiry to a college

1 at   3 in   5 in   7 to   9 of   11 in
2 of   4 in   6 for   8 by   10 for   12 with

5 An application form

Student Application Form

International College • 145–8 Regents Road • Falmer • Brighton • BN1 9QN

APPLICANT

Family Name: _Ortega_

Other Names: _Maria_

Title Mr / Mrs / Miss / Ms: _Ms_   Age: _23_

Address: _Avda. San Antonio 501,_
80260 Bellaterra

Town / City: _Barcelona_   Country: _Spain_

Do you have a job or are you a student? _I am a student._

Job title / Subject of study: _Business Studies_

Name of business / university / college: _University of Barcelona_

Course applied for: _First Certificate_

Course dates: _3 January – 26 June 20—_

Are you paying your own fees, or is your company paying for you?
I am paying my own fees.

Will you find your own accommodation or do you want this to be arranged by the College? _I would like this to be arranged by the College._

Please tick how you found out about International College.

☐ Newspaper   ☑ Friend's recommendation

☐ Through your university / college   ☐ Other source: _____

Signature: _Maria Ortega_   Date: _10 November 20—_

6 Enquiry from a retailer

```
                                             Cuisines Morreau S.A.
                                             1150 boulevard Calbert
                                             F—54015 Nancy Cedex
                                             T l: +33 3 567349
            R f: JFM/PS                      Fax: +33 3 567350


            28 June 20—

            Sales Manager
            Glaston Potteries Ltd
            Clayfield
            Burnley BB10 1RQ
            UK


            Dear Sir / Madam

            I was impressed by your latest designs for oven-to-table ware
            advertised in the May edition of International Homes, and would be
            interested in retailing a selection from your range in my two shops
            here in Nancy.

            It might be useful if I give you some idea of the terms on which
            I usually deal. I receive a 20% trade discount off ex-works prices
            from most of my suppliers, plus a 10% quantity discount if I place
            an order of over €10,000. I require delivery within two months of
            placing an order.

            I would be grateful if you could send me a catalogue and price list,
            and also let me know what method of payment you would require.

            I look forward to hearing from you soon.


            Yours faithfully,

            M. J.F. Morreau

            Director
```

Unit 4
Replies and quotations

1 Reply to an enquiry

1, 2, 3, 4, 6, 7, 9, 11

2 Question forms

1 Please can you send me details of your prices?
2 Do you offer an after-sales service?
3 How long are the goods guaranteed for?
4 How soon can the goods be delivered?
5 What are your terms of payment?
6 Where can I buy the goods?
7 What sort of quantity discounts do you offer?
8 Can you please / Please can you send me your catalogue by express mail?

3 Words and definitions

a 2 (incoterm)
b 3 (net price)
c 1 (carriage forward)
d 7 (quotation)

e 5 (under separate cover)
f 6 (gross price)
g 4 (loyalty discount)

4 Reply to a request for information (1)

Dear Mr Russell

Thank you for your phone call of Thursday 4 March enquiring about hiring our delivery vans.

My colleague Ms Angela Smith, who took the call, said you were mainly interested in 5-ton vehicles like the 'Tobor', so I am enclosing our booklet 'Small Truck Hire', giving you details of our charges. These also appear on our website at www.vanhire.co.uk. You will notice that the summer months of June, July, and August are the least expensive and that we offer a 20% discount on weekend hire, starting Saturday at 08.00 and ending Sunday at 20.00.

Our main offices in the UK are in London and Birmingham, but we also have branches in France, Germany, and Italy. If you are thinking of hiring abroad you will find details on our website.

Please let me know if I can be of further help.

Yours sincerely

Michael Craddock

Transport Manager
Van Hire Unlimited

5 Incoterms

1	DDU	(delivery duty unpaid)	c	The seller pays all delivery costs, except for import duty, to a named destination.
2	CFR	(cost and freight)	d	The seller pays all delivery costs to a named destination, except for insurance.
3	CIF	(cost, insurance, and freight)	f	The seller pays all delivery costs to a named destination.
4	EXW	(ex-works)	a	The buyer pays all delivery costs once the goods have left the seller's factory or warehouse.
5	FAS	(free alongside ship)	b	The seller pays all delivery costs to the port.
6	FOB	(free on board)	e	The seller pays all delivery costs to when the goods are on board ship.

6 Reply to a request for information (2)

Dear Ms Croft

Thank you for your enquiry of 14 May about our fitness equipment.

I can confirm that only the highest-quality materials are used in all our equipment, and this is reflected in our 5-year guarantee.

Our prices are highly competitive, due to small profit margins, so I regret that we cannot offer credit terms. However, we do offer a 5% quantity discount on orders over €5,000.

I have pleasure in enclosing our catalogue and a price list. Please note that all prices are quoted CIF London.

If there is any further information you need, please contact us. Once again, thank you for your letter.

Yours sincerely

Birgit Lange

p.p. Gerd Busch

7 An estimate

Dear Mr Frost

Thank you for your telephone enquiry about upgrading the central heating system in your offices. I have pleasure in enclosing our estimate.

Draw down system	£40.00
Fit 7 thermostatic valves @ £20.00 per valve	£140.00
Fit 1 lockshield valve	£20.00
Fill and balance system	£50.00
Subtotal	£250.00
plus VAT @ 17.5%	£43.75
TOTAL	£293.75

Prices quoted include materials and labour with VAT added as shown.

We confirm that we can complete the work before the end of September. If the work is to be carried out on a Saturday, you would need to add a total of £80.00 to this bill for overtime.

If you have any further questions, please contact me. I look forward to hearing from you.

Yours sincerely,

Steve Smart

MG Heating Engineers

Unit 5
Orders

1 Verbs used with *order*

1 We would like to *place* an order with you for 5,000 units.
2 As we are unable to supply the quantity you asked for, we shall have no objection if you prefer to *cancel* your order.
3 I am writing to *acknowledge* your order, which we received this morning, for 20 'Omega Engines'.
4 We are pleased to inform you that your order K451 has already been *despatched* from our depot.
5 Please *confirm* your order in writing, so we can inform our distribution depot.
6 Your order was *shipped* yesterday on the MV *Oxford*.
7 Unfortunately, we shall have to *refuse* your order unless payment is settled in cash.
8 I would like to reassure you that your order will be *made up* in our depot by staff who have experience in handling these delicate materials.

2 Placing an order: accompanying email

Send | Options...

Arial | 10 | **B** *I* U

File Edit View Insert Format Tools Actions Help

To... | Daniele Causio

Cc... |

Subject: | Order No. 49301/231

(5) Dear Sig. Causio

(6) I attach our order No. 49301/231 for the selection of shirts, trousers, and jackets which we discussed on the phone yesterday.

(4) I can confirm that the 10% quantity discount off net prices that you offered is acceptable.

(3) When you send the order, please make sure all cartons are clearly labelled with our logo and numbered. (2) If some of the items are out of stock, please do not send substitutes.

(8) As agreed, we will pay by letter of credit – I have already arranged this with the bank. (10) As soon as the bank hands over the shipping documents, the credit will be released.

(9) Please note the order must be here by 10 April, in time for the new season.

(1) Best wishes
(7) Kosaburo Takahashi

3 Order form

Satex S.p.A.
ORDER FORM

Via di Pietra Papa, 00146 Roma

Date: _____

Name of company: Reiner GmbH

Order No: W6164

Telephone: +49 541 798252

Fax: +49 541 798253

Email: faustd@reiner.co.de

Address for delivery:

Wessumerstrasse 215–18,

D–4500 Osnabrück

_____

Authorized: (D. Faust)

Item description	Cat. no.	Price € per item	Quantity	Total €
Shirts, plain white	S288	30	50	1,500
Shirts, plain blue	S289	30	50	1,500
Sweaters (V-neck), plain red	P112	40	20	800
Sweaters (V-neck), plain blue	P113	40	20	800

Amount due: € 4,600

Terms of payment: Banker s draft

Requested delivery date: Before 28 August 20—

4 Placing an order: covering letter

Sig. Daniele Causio
Sales Director
Satex S.p.A.
Via di Pietra Papa
00146 Roma

Dear Sig. Causio

Order No. W6164

Thank you for your letter of 1 July, and the catalogue and price list.

Please find enclosed the above order. We would like to remind you that we expect delivery before 28 August, i.e. within six weeks. We will pay by banker's draft as soon as we receive the shipping documents.

If any of the items we have ordered are not available, please do not send substitutes. And please could you email Herr Faust if there are any problems with delivery?

We look forward to receiving acknowledgement of this order.

Yours sincerely

Beatrice Mey

pp. Dieter Faust

Buying Manager

5 Acknowledging an order

To... George Delmas

Cc...

Subject: Your order No. R497

Dear M. Delmas

Thank you for your order (No. R497) which we are at present making up. The instruments will be packed individually in 8 crates numbered and marked with our logo. They will be sent airfreight CIF Marseille to reach you no later than 18 May.

Our invoice showing the 12% trade and 3% quantity discounts, the insurance certificate,* and the air waybill will be sent to the Bank of Marseille as requested.

Harald Kjaer

Sales Manager
Dansk Industries, Kongens Nytorv 1, DK–1050 København K
Tel: +45 367521
Fax: +45 367522
Email: hkjaer@dansk.co.de
7 May 20—

---

*The comma between *certificate* and *and* is optional.

6 Delay in delivery

1 concerning
2 placed
3 apologize
4 shortage
5 taken on
6 reach
7 care
8 consignment
9 according
10 prevent

7 Refusing an order

1 d ✓   2 e ✓   3 ✓ b   4 a ✓   5 ✓ c

8 Words and definitions

a 6 (compliments slip)
b 3 (invoice)
c 1 (forwarding agent)
d 5 (settlement)
e 8 (air waybill)
f 7 (ship)
g 2 (covering letter)
h 4 (advice note)

Unit 6
Payment

1 Invoice

GLASTON POTTERIES LTD

Clayfield | Burnley | BB10 1RQ

Telephone + 44 (0)1282 46125
Facsimile + 44 (0)1282 63182
Email accounts@glaston.co.uk
www.glaston.com

J. F. Morreau
1150 boulevard Calbert
F–54015 Nancy Cedex

9 May 20—

Your order No. 3716

Quantity	Description	Cat. No.	£ each	£
10	Lotus	L305	35	350
20	Wedgwood	W218	43	860

CIF _15%_   181.50

Less _____   discount off net price   1,028.50

Total _____

Payment due within 28 days of date of invoice.

E&OE

Registered No. 716481
VAT Reg. No. 133 53431 08

2 Statement of account

HOMEMAKERS

54–59 Riverside, Cardiff CF1 1JW
Telephone: +44 (0)29 20 49721
Fax: +44 (0)29 20 49937

statement

To: R. Hughes & Son Ltd, 21 Mead Road, Swansea, West Glamorgan, 3ST 1DR

Date	Item	Debit	Credit	Balance
1 May	Account Rendered			461.00
5 May	Inv. 771/2	781.00		1,242.00
7 May	Cheque		300.00	942.00
12 May	C/N 216		285.00	657.00
16 May	Inv. 824/2	302.00		959.00
18 May	Cheque		200.00	759.00
23 May	D/N 306	100.00		859.00

Terms:
Cash discount 3% if paid within 10 days

3 Request for more time to settle an account

Dear Mr Merton

I am sorry that at present I am unable to settle your invoice dated 9 May for my order No. 3716. The reason for this is that my stockroom was flooded after recent heavy rain, and much of the stock damaged or destroyed.

Unfortunately, I am unable to pay any of my suppliers until I receive compensation from my insurers. They have promised me this within the next four weeks. As soon as I receive payment, I will settle the invoice in full.

I hope that you will understand the situation.

Yours sincerely

Jean Morreau (M.)

4 Crossword

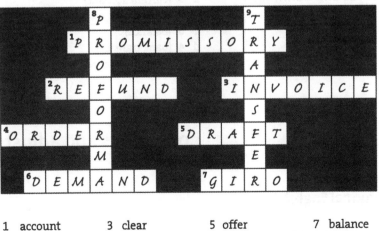

5 Request for payment

1 account	3 clear	5 offer	7 balance
2 for	4 on	6 with	8 within

6 Reply to request for payment

3 May 20—
Ms Helen Stuart
Chief Accountant
UK Cycles Ltd
Borough House
Borough Road
Cleveland
TS1 3BA
UK

Dear Ms Stuart

Account No. VS 301632

Thank you for your letters of 25 March and 28 April regarding the delay in settling our account with you.

Unfortunately, a recent fire at our Head Office has destroyed a great deal of our computer data, with the result that all correspondence with both suppliers and customers has been disrupted. I am afraid that we will need time to return to our normal routine.

Would it be possible for you to allow us a further 30 days to settle? By that time, our insurance company will have released compensation, and we can pay the outstanding amount in full.

I would be most grateful if you could allow us this extra time.

Yours sincerely,

Karl Janssen

Managing Director

7 Formal and informal English

1 (F) and a (I)	3 (F) and b (I)	5 (F) and c (I)
2 (I) and d (F)	4 (F) and e (I)	

8 Words and definitions

a 3 (current account)	f 2 (due date)
b 9 (sight draft)	g 1 (protest)
c 6 (balance)	h 5 (remittance)
d 4 (bank transfer)	i 7 (statement of account)
e 10 (documentary credit)	j 8 (debit note)

Unit 7
Complaints and adjustments

1 Formal and informal English

1 b ✓   2 ✓ h   3 ✓ g   4 ✓ a   5 c ✓   6 d ✓   7 e ✓   8 ✓ f

2 Complaint about damage

1 complain	4 handled	7 wear	10 insurers
2 invoice	5 rusty	8 consignment	11 carriage forward
3 crates	6 torn	9 inspecting	12 refund

3 Complaint about late delivery

ISTITUTO DI MEDICINA

Viale Bracci
1–61001 Siena
Telefono: +39 0586 43-74-25
Fax: +39 0586 43-74-26
Email: clotti@imed.ac.it

15 June 20—

Mr H. Toda
Sales Manager
Nihon Instruments
12–18 Wakakusa-cho
Hagashi-Osaka-Shi
Osaka-fu
Japan

Dear Mr Toda

AWB 4156/82

We are writing to point out that the above delivery, which arrived
yesterday, was a week late. This is the second time we have had to
write to you on this subject, and we cannot allow the situation to
continue. We have already explained that it is essential for medical
equipment to arrive on due dates as late delivery could create a very
serious problem.

Unless we have your firm guarantee on the promptness of all future
deliveries, we will have to look for another supplier. Please could you
confirm this before we place our next order?

Yours sincerely

Carlo Lotti (Sig.)

Head of Administration

4 Reply to complaint about damage

Dear Sr Méndez

Thank you for your letter of 15 October concerning the damage
to a consignment of garden furniture against invoice No. G3190/1.
I can confirm that the goods were checked before they left our
warehouse, so it appears that the damage occurred during shipment.

Please could you return the goods to us, carriage forward?
We will send a refund by banker s draft as soon as we receive them.

In your letter you mention two further crates.
Could you let me know whether you have received these safely?

Please accept my apologies for the inconvenience caused.

Yours sincerely

Brian Harrison

5 Reply to complaint about late delivery

(9) Dear Mr Lotti

(1) **Consignment no. AWB 4156/82**

(6) Thank you for your letter of 15 June concerning late delivery of the above consignment.

(8) We understand how important prompt deliveries are to our customers. (3) However, the two orders you mentioned were sent to our factory rather than our administrative offices at the above address.

(4) We would like to take this opportunity of reminding you that to avoid delay in future all orders should be sent to our office address.

(2) I trust that this will clarify the situation, and look forward to continued good trading with you.

(10) Yours sincerely

(7) Hirio Toda (Mr)

(5) Sales Manager

6 Complaint about accounting errors

Mrs B. Grevon
Accounts Department
Excel Stationers Ltd
28 Langley Estate
Templetown
London WC3 7AL

22 November 20—

Dear Mrs Grevon

Invoice no. 3910

We have received the above invoice, but notice it contains a number of errors.

1. 12 writing pads @ 2.80 each total £33.60, not £35.30
2. 3 boxes pens @ 1.50 each total £4.50, not £3.50
3. 8 reams multi-purpose paper @ 3.90 each total £31.20, not £33.20

The correct final total is therefore £86.90, not £89.60.

We will settle the account as soon as we receive a corrected invoice.

As we have been sent incorrect invoices several times in the past, I regret to tell you that it will be necessary for us to change our suppliers if this happens again.

Yours sincerely

Unit 8
Credit

1 Formal and informal English

1 Thank you for forwarding the documents so *promptly*.
2 We feel that *sufficient* time has *elapsed* for you to *settle*.
3 I am writing to *request* open account facilities.
4 We would like to remind you that this information is highly *confidential*.
5 Your quarterly settlement is three weeks *overdue*.
6 We are pleased to *inform* you that the credit facilities you asked for are *acceptable*.
7 Our prices are very *competitive*.

2 Agreeing to credit

Subject: RE: Terms of payment

Tom

Thanks for your email asking for a change in your terms of payment to settlement by 60-day bill of exchange, D/A.

While we would be happy for you to settle by bill of exchange, according to my records the period suggested for settlement was 30 days, not 60. My apologies if there was any misunderstanding.

Please can you let me know whether these terms are acceptable? If they are, it will not be necessary for you to provide references.

Alex Rempel
Sales Manager, Rempel GmbH
13 May 20—

3 Request for a reference

1 to	3 of	5 of	7 on/by	9 for
2 on	4 at	6 for	8 to	10 at

4 Reply to request for a reference

Dear Sra. Gómez

I am replying to your enquiry of 18 May concerning D.L. Cromer Ltd.

The company has an excellent reputation in the UK and has been a customer of ours for a number of years. Their credit limit with us is slightly lower than the level you mentioned, but we have always found that they settle on, or before, due dates.

We would be grateful if you could treat this information in the strictest confidence.

Yours sincerely

Gerald MacFee

Credit Controller

5 Unfavourable reply

Dear Ms Allard

I am replying to your enquiry of 19 September about *one of our mutual business associates.*

We have allowed *that company* credit in the past, but *nowhere near the amount* you mentioned. We have also found that they need *several* reminders before clearing their account.

Please treat this information in the strictest confidence.

Yours sincerely

P.M. Lord

Accountant

6 Words and definitions

a 2 (bad debt)   c 3 (bill of exchange)   e 6 (reference)
b 4 (credit rating) d 5 (default)   f 1 (credit facilities)

Unit 9
Banking

1 Reporting verbs

1 thank   3 refuse   5 promise   7 explain
2 suggest   4 advise   6 admit   8 apologize

2 Word forms

1 endanger   4 insurance   7 confirmation   9 expansion
2 completing   5 overdraft   8 signature   10 reference
3 payable   6 arrangement

3 Bill of exchange

At **1** *60 days after date*_____ pay this **2** *sola*_____ Bill of Exchange

2_____ to the order of Number 40031 3021

Exchange for **3**_____ *$28,000*_____ **4** *28 February 20—*

5 *Hartley-Mason Inc.*

6 *US dollars twenty-eight thousand*

Value Received **7** *payable at the current rate of exchange for bankers' drafts in London*_____ placed to account

To   For and on behalf of
8 *Glough and Book Motorcyles Ltd*   **9** *Hartley-Mason Inc.*
31–37 Trades Street   *618 West and Vine Street*
Nottingham   *Chicago*
NG13AA   *Illinois*

Signed
9 *J.R. Mason*
President

4 Request for a loan

To: The Board of Directors
From: John Steele
Subject: Bridging loan, RG Logistics Ltd
Date: 19 September 20—

STRICTLY CONFIDENTIAL

I had a meeting with Mr Richard Grey, of RG Logistics Ltd, on 17 September. He admitted that his company has had difficulties recently, but he would like to expand his fleet by buying a further two second-hand trucks, and requested an extension on his loan to cover the investment.

I informed him that we would have to refuse an extension on his existing loan, but explained that we may be able to offer a bridging loan. He suggested that he would need around £50,000, but he is confident that the revenue generated by the extra trucks would enable him to repay the loan within a year. He is able only to offer the trucks themselves as security.

I promised him that I would consult you this week.

5 Refusing a loan

Dear Mr Grey

Further to our meeting on 17th September, I regret that we will not be able to offer you a bridging loan. The Board of Directors have asked me to inform you that it is the bank's policy only to offer substantial loans against negotiable securities such as shares or bonds.

You may be able to raise the capital you need from another source, for example a finance corporation. However, I should warn you that their interest rates are likely to be significantly higher than ours.

Once again, I regret that we have to disappoint you in this matter, but hope that we may be of more help in the future.

Yours sincerely

John Steele

Manager

6 Words and definitions

a 1 (endorse)
b 5 (documentary credit)
c 3 (certificate of origin)
d 4 (clean bill)
e 6 (days after sight)
f 2 (merchant bank)
g 7 (overhead)
h 8 (sight draft)

7 Abbreviations

1 bill of exchange
2 documents against payment
3 letter of credit
4 documents against acceptance
5 errors and omissions excepted
6 documentary credit
7 carriage paid
8 days after sight
9 international money order
10 carriage forward

8 Documentary credit 1

Letter from the confirming bank to the exporters

1 acting
2 inform
3 opened
4 valid
5 charges
6 documents
7 draw
8 settle

9 Documentary credit 2

Letter from the exporters to the confirming bank

Dear M. Diderot

L/C No. 340895/AGL

Thank you for your advice of 8 July. We have now effected shipment to BestValue and enclose the shipping documents you requested and our draft for €5,300.

Please will you accept the draft and remit the proceeds to our account at the Banque de Commerce, 28 rue Gaspart-André, 69002, Lyon.

Yours sincerely

James Freeland

Château Wines

Enc. Air waybill
     Invoice CIF London
     Insurance certificate

Unit 10
Agents and agencies

1 Find the keyword

1 STOCK EXCHANGE	7 NET
2 CONFIRMING	8 COMMODITY
3 SOLE AGENT	9 DEL CREDERE
4 COMMISSION	10 BUYING HOUSE
5 PRINCIPAL	11 MARKET
6 FACTORING	12 keyword = CONSIGNMENT

2 Phrasal verbs

1 work out	3 draw up	5 turn down	7 fill in
2 take on	4 back up	6 make out	8 take up

3 Offer of an agency

1 said	4 settle	7 offer	9 researchers
2 approval	5 trial	8 cost	10 current
3 sole	6 extend		

4 Reply to an offer of an agency

1 c   2 a   3 c   4 c   5 a   6 b

```
Sig. Pietro Grazioli
Chairman
Grazioli S.p.A.
Via Gradenigo 134
50133 Firenze
Italy

31 October 20—

Dear Sig. Grazioli

Thank you for your letter of 23 October.

I can confirm that we would be interested in representing you, but
not on a sole agency basis, as this would restrict our sales. Also,
our usual terms are a 10% commission on ex-works prices and 75% of
the advertising costs.

However, we were very impressed by the high quality of the products
in your catalogue. If you are able to revise your terms, we would be
interested in receiving a draft contract.

I look forward to hearing from you.

Yours sincerely

Otto Grassmann

Grassmann AG
```

5 Request for an agency

1 recommendation	4 principals	7 rates	10 del credere
2 manufacturers	5 freight	8 documentation	11 offer
3 terms	6 factory	9 commission	12 brochure

6 Reply to a request for an agency

To... Manfred Kobelt

Cc...

Subject: Your letter, 24 June

Dear Herr Kobelt

Thank you for your letter of 24 June in which you expressed an interest in acting as a buying agent for us in Germany.

We are interested in your proposals as there is an increasing demand for precision tools here in Portugal. In principle, we could accept either a 3% commission on CIF values, or the del credere commission of 2.5% that you mention. Can you act as a clearing and forwarding agent, offering a door-to-door facility?

Would you be willing to send us contact details of two other companies you act for who can offer references? If you are able to do this, we would be interested in discussing a contract.

I look forward to hearing from you.

Yours sincerely
Cristina Neves
Buying Manager
Portuguese Industrial Importers

Unit 11
Transportation and shipping

1 Two-word terms

1 forwarding agent
2 bulk carrier
3 charter party
4 delivery note

5 air waybill
6 all risks
7 shipping note
8 shipping mark

2 Formal and informal English

1 Please fill in the despatch form and send it to us with the consignment.
2 If you have any queries, please do not hesitate to contact me.
3 I have checked with our Despatch Department and their records show that the crockery left here in perfect condition.
4 Please quote for collection of a consignment of ten armchairs from the above address and delivery to R. Hughes & Son Ltd, Swansea.
5 We estimate the loss on invoice value to be £300.00 and we are claiming compensation for that amount.
6 Would you prefer us to return the goods to you, or to hold them for inspection?

3 Enquiry to a forwarding agent

1 to   3 for   5 in   7 of   9 to   11 of
2 by   4 for   6 of   8 of   10 by   12 in

4 Forwarding agent's reply

Dear Mr Lang

Thank you for your fax of 10 November enquiring about our freight charges.

I enclose our tariff list for shipments which includes all transport, customs, and documentation charges. I think you will find that these rates are highly competitive. In addition, I can confirm that we have extensive experience in handling fragile consignments.

If you have any further questions, please contact me and I will be very pleased to help.

I look forward to hearing from you.

Yours sincerely

Bill Crowley

5 Words and definitions

a 5 (payload) d 3 (multimodal) g 4 (shipbroker)
b 8 (endorse) e 2 (receipt) h 6 (container)
c 7 (claused) f 1 (consolidation)

6 Enquiry to a container company

```
[Email window]
To...    Brian Close
Cc...
Subject: European deliveries

Dear Mr Close

I am contacting you on behalf of John Merton concerning a number of European
deliveries which we would like you to handle. These are scheduled for the next few
months. The consignments will consist of fragile crockery. An average crate
measures 187x172x165cm, with an approximate weight of 35kg each.

Please could you let us have details of your schedules and sample quotations for
major European cities? We would need door-to-door delivery.

I would also be grateful for information concerning the necessary documentation.

Yours sincerely
Jill Bradley
PA to John Merton
Glaston Potteries
15 July 20—
```

7 Container company's reply

1 full stop after *yesterday*
2 *schedules*, not *shedules*
3 *tomorrow*, not *tommorow*
4 *suggest*, not *sugest*
5 *export cargo packing instructions* in lower-case, not capitals
6 *Consignments*, not *Consignment*
7 *sample*, not *smaple*
8 *responsibilities*, not *responsibilites*
9 *all risk* or *all-risk*, not *allrisk*
10 *are any other details*, not *is any other details*

Unit 12
Insurance

1 Terms used in insurance

1 insurance 4 indemnified 7 proposal 9 fidelity
2 syndicates 5 premium 8 claim 10 adjuster
3 policy 6 Lloyd's

2 Request for comprehensive insurance

1 large 4 would like 7 include 10 competitive
2 which 5 supply 8 kind 11 consider
3 to 6 covering 9 premises 12 soon

3 Reply to request for comprehensive insurance

18 February 20—

Peter Hind
Company Secretary
Humboldt Exporters Ltd
Exode House
115 Tremona Road
Southampton S09 4XY

Dear Mr Hind

Thank you for your letter of 15 February enquiring about comprehensive cover for your warehouse at Dock Road, Southampton.

I enclose details of two fully comprehensive industrial policies which offer the sort of cover you describe in your letter. It would probably be best if one of our agents called on you to discuss which of these policies would best suit your requirements.

If you would like to arrange an appointment, please call my secretary, Natalie Weston, on 01273 547231, extension 12.

We hope to hear from you in the near future.

Yours sincerely

Gerald Croft

Regional Manager

Encl. Leaflets IP3, IP4

4 Claim for fire damage

From: Peter Hind
To: Gerald Croft
Subject: Warehouse fire
Date: 7 October 20—

Policy No. 439178/D

I regret to inform you that fire broke out in our Southampton warehouse early yesterday morning. This resulted in extensive damage, to the value of approximately £7,000, to textiles stored for shipment.

The Fire Service has provided evidence that the fire was caused by an electrical fault.

Please could you send me the necessary claim forms as soon as possible?

Peter Hind

5 Request for open cover

```
1 May 20—

Sugden & Able
Insurance Brokers
63 Grover Street
Manchester M5 6LD

Dear Sir / Madam

We are a large engineering company exporting machine parts
worldwide, and have a contract to supply a Middle Eastern customer
for the next two years.

As the parts we will be supplying are similar in nature and are
going to the same destination over this period, we would prefer to
insure them under an open cover policy.

Would you be willing to provide open cover for £500,000 against
all risks for this period?

I look forward to hearing from you.

Yours faithfully
```

Jack Turner

```
Shipping Manager
```

6 Reply to request
for open cover

To...	Jack Turner
Cc...	
Subject:	Your letter, 1 May

Dear Mr Turner

Thank you for your enquiry of 1 May concerning all risks cover for shipments of machine parts to the Middle East.

We offer two types of cover, either of which might suit your requirements:
— Floating cover. We provide cover for all the shipments you plan to make up to an agreed maximum value. It can be renewed when necessary.
— Open cover. We provide cover for all shipments over a given period.

Mr Able would be very pleased to discuss these options if you would like to give him a call on 0161 542783.

Mary Todd
Secretary to Alan Able
3 May 20—

Unit 13
Miscellaneous correspondence

1 Prepositions

Please send the tickets for my attention / by return.
May I offer you my best wishes for Eid Al-Fittr.
She offers her apologies for the inconvenience.
I would like to speak on effective website design.
I hope to return the favour on some future occasion.
Please confirm these reservations by return / for my attention.
We will need a room with full conference facilities.

2 Formal and informal English

1 He sends his apologies, and hopes to be able to attend on another occasion.
2 I was sorry to hear that your brother is ill.
3 I would like to congratulate you on being elected Chairman of the company.
4 Mr Norman would like to make an appointment to see you next week about the contract.
5 Unfortunately, Mr Chung will not be able to keep his appointment with you on Friday.
6 We would like to invite you to our Sales Conference on 18 March.
7 I would like to thank you for assisting me while I was in Hamburg last week.
8 I look forward to seeing you on Friday.

3 Conference facilities

Dear Sir / Madam

We are planning a Sales Conference on 8 and 9 December this year and are looking for a hotel which can offer us accommodation and conference facilities for forty delegates.

We require executive-grade accommodation for twenty-seven delegates on the nights of 7 and 8 December, and a conference room with full seating, presentation platform, public address system, PowerPoint, and facilities for recording from 09.00 to 18.00 on both days of the conference. We would also like morning coffee and biscuits at 11.00, bar facilities, a buffet lunch, and tea with snacks at 16.00.

If you can meet these requirements, I would be grateful if you could send me full details of your rates and facilities.

Yours faithfully

Lynn Paul

PA to Diane Taylor

4 Hotel reservation

Fax

Data Unlimited plc
Data House
Chertsey Road
Twickenham
TW1 1EP
Tel: +44 (0)20 81 460259
Fax: +44 (0)20 81 985132

To: The Manager, Royal Hotel
From: Lynn Paul
Fax: 01372 908754
Subject: Additional reservations
Date: 3 December
Page/s: 1

Dear Sir / Madam

I would like, if possible, to make reservations for the nights of 7 and 8 December for two more delegates attending our Sales Conference. Their names are Charles Bickford and Claire Ramal. Preferably, the reservations should be for executive-grade rooms.

I would be grateful if you could let me know by return if you can accommodate them.

My apologies for the short notice.

Lynn Paul

PA to Diane Taylor

5 Invitation

1	would like	5	affecting
2	wonder	6	let
3	speakers	7	speak
4	appreciate	8	Enclosed

6 Accepting an invitation

Dear Mr House

Thank you for your letter inviting me to speak at your annual dinner on 15 February.

I would like to accept your kind invitation. In my talk, I would like to focus on the effects that the euro is having on the cost of raw materials. I will send you a transcript next week and would welcome any comments or suggestions you would like to make.

I look forward very much to meeting you on 15 February.

Yours sincerely

Gunther Boldt

Chairman

Unit 14
Memos and reports

1 Formal and informal English

1 c ✓   2 g ✓   3 ✓ e   4 h ✓   5 a ✓   6 ✓ b   7 ✓ d   8 ✓ f

2 Memo about documentry credits

Memo

To: All Documentary Credit Department Staff
From: Finance Director
Date: 20 March 20—
Subject: Verification of Documentary Credits

Would all staff be extremely careful in checking documentary credits in future. Over the past year £250,000 has been lost in paying clients compensation for mistakes in documentary credits.

Pay particular attention to the following points:

- Check all transport documents, insurance certificates, invoices and customs clearance certificates.
- Check bills of exchange and letters of credit.
- Check the spelling in the names of the parties is correct.
- Check that places of departure and destinations are correct.
- Check the right amounts for the transactions are listed and the correct currencies have been written in.

3 Memo about fraud

Memo

National Stores plc
528 Marylebone Road
London W1B 3MC

To: Sales staff
From: Fred Hanbury, Chief Accountant
Date: 18th November 20—
Subject: Payments by cheque

The value of bad cheques presented in this store over the past year amounts to over £50,000. This problem cannot be eliminated, but you can help reduce it significantly by taking the following measures:

1 Examine cheques to see that they have been completed properly.
2 Carefully match signatures on cheque cards with those on cheques.
3 Write the cheque card number and expiry date on the back of the cheque.
4 If you are unsure about a cheque, contact a supervisor immediately.

Terry Fairman

Chief Accountant

4 Reports: past tenses

EXTRACT 1

1 has been exporting
2 opened
3 remained
4 moved
5 have been negotiating

EXTRACT 2

6   has been losing
7   rose
8   has been operating
9   occurred
10   have been having

EXTRACT 3

11   was
12   felt
13   remained
14   have been falling
15   have been returning
16   have been increasing

5   Report on introduction of flexitime

To: The Board of Directors
From: John Holland, Company Secretary
Date   16 March 20—
Subject: Proposed flexitime system

Management proposes to introduce a flexitime system for all staff. Under this system, staff would be able to choose their hours of work between 07.00 and 21.00, and have a weekday off in lieu of Saturday if they prefer.

Advantages to the company

There are several advantages to the company. For example, increased working hours would mean that overseas clients in different time zones would find it easier to contact us, and clients could contact us on Saturdays. Pressure on office equipment such as photocopiers would be relieved and therefore efficiency would be improved.

Advantages to staff

The two most significant advantages to staff are that they would be able to avoid rush hour travel, and they would also be able to spend more time with their families. This is likely to lead to a significant improvement in morale and productivity.

Financial costs and benefits

The financial cost of such a scheme is considerable. The initial cost of installing a clocking-in system would be approximately £5,500 + VAT. (However, this is a fixed cost and can be offset against tax.) The estimated increase in overheads would be 7%, but this can be offset against benefits such as lower insurance premiums and photocopying costs. There is also, as noted above, likely to be a substantial increase in productivity.

Conclusion

The idea is very popular among the staff: an overwhelming majority of 87% are in favour of it, although it should be noted that a significant number (48%) are not in favour of a clocking-in system, so this would need to be introduced carefully.

After careful analysis of the information provided, I conclude that the introduction of a flexitime system would be viable financially. I therefore recommend its introduction within the next six months.

Unit 15
Personnel appointments

1 Words and definitions

a 7 (unsolicited)
b 1 (vacancy)
c 4 (curriculum vitae)
d 3 (referee)

e 6 (personnel)
f 2 (career summary)
g 5 (covering letter)

2 Follow-up to a job application

Send | Options...

Arial | 10 | B I U

File Edit View Insert Format Tools Actions Help

To... | John Merton

Cc... |

Subject: | Vacancy for Administrator

Dear Mr Merton

With reference to my email of 5 January, requesting an application form for the post of Administrator which you advertised in the Burnley Despatch of 4 January, so far I have received no reply. (This may be the result of problems I was experiencing with my email last week.)

I am writing to you again to say that I am still interested in this post and have considerable experience in the areas described in your advertisement.

I would be most grateful if you could send me an application form, and look forward to hearing from you.

Robin Anakin
17 January 20—

3 Job advertisement

1 fluent
2 applicant
3 experience
4 includes

5 duties
6 acting
7 application form
8 reference

4 Covering letter

Your ref. PP391

29 May 20—

Dear Ms Prentiss

I would like to apply for the vacancy of PA to the Managing Director.

As you will see from my application form, Italian is my mother tongue and I studied English and French at university. I also speak good German. In my current job as PA to the Sales Director of Morgan Brice Ltd, I accompany her on trips to our offices in Italy and France, where I am often required to translate and interpret.

I am very interested in this post as I would like to develop my career in an international environment. On a more personal level, I would also like, if possible, to move away from London.

I look forward to hearing from you.

Yours sincerely

Carla Giuliani (Ms)

Enc. Application form

5 Invitation for an interview

Dear Ms Giuliani

Thank you for your application of 29 May for the post of PA to the Managing Director.

We would like you to come for interview in Cambridge on Thursday 18 June at 14.30. There will be a short Italian and French translation test before the interview. I enclose a map with details of how to reach us by car. Alternatively, there are frequent trains to Cambridge from Liverpool Street.

I would be grateful if you could phone me on 01223 6814, Ext. 412 to confirm that you will be able to attend, or to arrange an alternative date if you cannot attend on that day.

I look forward to hearing from you.

Yours sincerely

Paula Prentiss (Ms)

Personnel Manager

6 Making a job offer

Dear Ms Giuliani

I have much pleasure in offering you the post of Personal Assistant to Kevin Wheeler.

I can confirm that your starting salary will be £18,000. We would like, if possible, for your employment to commence on 23 July. Can you please ring me as soon as possible if you are unable to start on this date?

Please sign both copies of the enclosed Contract of Employment and return one to me, keeping the other for your records.

We look forward to welcoming you to the company.

Yours sincerely

Paula Prentiss

Personnel Manager

Enc. Contract of Employment (x2)